Lecture Notes in Computer Science 16447

Founding Editors

Gerhard Goos
Juris Hartmanis

The series Lecture Notes in Computer Science (LNCS), including its subseries Lecture Notes in Artificial Intelligence (LNAI) and Lecture Notes in Bioinformatics (LNBI), has established itself as a medium for the publication of new developments in computer science and information technology research, teaching, and education.

LNCS enjoys close cooperation with the computer science R & D community, the series counts many renowned academics among its volume editors and paper authors, and collaborates with prestigious societies. Its mission is to serve this international community by providing an invaluable service, mainly focused on the publication of conference and workshop proceedings and postproceedings. LNCS commenced publication in 1973.

Jun Ma · Sumin Kim · Yuyin Zhou · Bo Wang
Editors

Foundation Models for 3D Biomedical Image Segmentation

CVPR 2025 Challenge, MedSegFM 2025
Held in Conjunction with CVPR 2025
Nashville, TN, USA, June 11–15, 2025
Proceedings

Editors
Jun Ma
University Health Network
Toronto, ON, Canada

Sumin Kim
University of Toronto
Toronto, ON, Canada

Yuyin Zhou
University of California
Santa Cruz, CA, USA

Bo Wang
University Health Network
Toronto, ON, Canada

ISSN 0302-9743 ISSN 1611-3349 (electronic)
Lecture Notes in Computer Science
ISBN 978-3-032-23495-7 ISBN 978-3-032-23496-4 (eBook)
https://doi.org/10.1007/978-3-032-23496-4

This Springer imprint is published by the registered company Springer Nature Switzerland AG
The registered company address is: Gewerbestrasse 11, 6330 Cham, Switzerland

Preface

This volume contains the proceedings of the International Challenge on Foundation Models for Interactive and Text-guided 3D Biomedical Image Segmentation, held in conjunction with the IEEE/CVF Conference on Computer Vision and Pattern Recognition (CVPR) in 2025. By "proceedings", we refer to the collection of papers authored by participants, detailing their solutions for general medical image segmentation models using the official training dataset curated for this challenge.

The rapid development of biomedical imaging technologies has led to ever-increasing volumes of complex 3D datasets. Accurate and efficient segmentation of structures within these images is essential for biology and clinical research. However, current segmentation algorithms often struggle with the diversity of imaging modalities and variabilities. This competition sought universal 3D biomedical image segmentation models that can not only adapt to various anatomical structures and imaging conditions but also iteratively improve the segmentation quality based on user interactions. In particular, this competition was the first competition for interactive and text-guided 3D biomedical image segmentation foundation models. We provided large-scale well-organized 3D biomedical datasets with more than 200,000 3D image-mask pairs. The evaluation metrics included both segmentation accuracy and efficiency, including Dice Similarity Coefficient (DSC) and Normalized Surface Dice (NSD), and the inference speed (runtime).

The competition was hosted on the CodaBench platform, including Interactive 3D Biomedical Image Segmentation (https://www.codabench.org/competitions/5263/) and Text-guided 3D Biomedical Image Segmentation (https://www.codabench.org/competitions/5651/).

More than 400 participants registered for the competition, and we ultimately invited the top 20 teams to submit their algorithm Docker containers during the testing phase. Participants also submitted methodology papers through the OpenReview platform, each of which received three to five review comments under single-blind review. Based on the initial reviews and subsequent author revisions, 13 papers were accepted. This proceedings volume presents state-of-the-art algorithms for biomedical image segmentation foundation models. We thank all participants, reviewers, and program committee members whose outstanding contributions made this possible.

January 2026

Jun Ma
Sumin Kim
Yuyin Zhou
Bo Wang

Organization

Organizing Committee

Jun Ma	University Health Network, Canada
Sumin Kim	University of Toronto; University Health Network; Vector Institute, Canada
Yuyin Zhou	University of California, Santa Cruz, USA
Bo Wang	University of Toronto; University Health Network; Vector Institute, Canada

Program Committee

Challenge Coordinators

Zdravko Marinov	Karlsruhe Institute of Technology, Germany
Beatrice Chen	University of Toronto, Canada
Feifei Li	National University of Singapore, Singapore
Cheng Xing	University of Toronto, Canada

Data Contributors

Minghui Zhang	Shanghai Key Laboratory of Flexible Medical Robotics, China
Hanxiao Zhang	Shanghai Key Laboratory of Flexible Medical Robotics, China
Guang-Zhong Yang	Shanghai Key Laboratory of Flexible Medical Robotics, China
Yun Gu	Shanghai Key Laboratory of Flexible Medical Robotics, China
Luca Lumetti	University of Modena and Reggio Emilia, Italy
Federico Bolelli	University of Modena and Reggio Emilia, Italy
Costantino Grana	University of Modena and Reggio Emilia, Italy
Ying Chen	Institute for Stroke and Dementia Research, Germany
Ali Erturk	Institute for Intelligent Biotechnologies, Germany
Thomas Küstner	University Hospital Tübingen, Germany

Sean Deoni	Gates Foundation, USA
Xin Yang	Shenzhen University, China
Qing Zhou	Renmin Hospital of Wuhan University, China
Rusi Chen	Shenzhen University, China
Zhaodong Wu	Xi'an Jiaotong-Liverpool University, China
Jionglong Su	Xi'an Jiaotong-Liverpool University, China
Feilong Tang	Monash University, Australia
Haochen Xue	Xi'an Jiaotong-Liverpool University, China
Ting Lei	Peking University, China

Baseline Contributors: Interactive Segmentation

Yufan He	NVIDIA, USA
Wenqi Li	NVIDIA, USA
Fabian Isensee	German Cancer Research Center, Helmholtz Imaging, Heidelberg University, Germany
Maximilian Rokuss	German Cancer Research Center, Heidelberg University, Germany
Lars Krämer	German Cancer Research Center, Helmholtz Imaging, Germany
Klaus Maier-Hein	German Cancer Research Center, Helmholtz Imaging, Heidelberg University, HIDSS4Health, Heidelberg University Hospital, Germany
Yuxin Du	Shanghai Jiao Tong University, BAAI, China
Bo Zhao	Shanghai Jiao Tong University, BAAI, China
Haoyu Wang	Shanghai Jiao Tong University, Shanghai Artificial Intelligence Laboratory, China
Junjun He	Shanghai Jiao Tong University, China
Yu Qiao	Shanghai Jiao Tong University, China
Yiqing Shen	Johns Hopkins University, USA
Chong Wang	Xinxiang Medical University, China
Mathias Unberath	Johns Hopkins University, USA

Baseline Contributors: Text-guided Segmentation

Theodore Zhao	Microsoft Research, USA
Mu Wei	Microsoft Research, USA
Zhongzhen Huang	Qing Yuan Research Institute, Shanghai Jiao Tong University; Shanghai AI Laboratory, China

Shaoting Zhang — Qing Yuan Research Institute, Shanghai Jiao Tong University; Shanghai AI Laboratory, China

Xiaofan Zhang — Qing Yuan Research Institute, Shanghai Jiao Tong University; Shanghai AI Laboratory, China

Ziheng Zhao — Shanghai Jiao Tong University; Shanghai AI Laboratory, China

Yanfeng Wang — Shanghai Jiao Tong University; Shanghai AI Laboratory, China

Weidi Xie — Shanghai Jiao Tong University; Shanghai AI Laboratory, China

Contents

Exploring Foundation Model Adaptations for 3D Medical Imaging: Prompt-Based Segmentation with xLSTM Network

Abdul Qayyum[1(✉)], Moona Mazher[2], and Steven A Niederer[1]

[1] National Heart and Lung Institute, Imperial College, London, UK
a.qayyum@imperial.ac.uk

[2] Hawkes Institute, Department of Computer Science, University College London, London, UK

Abstract. Accurate segmentation of anatomical and pathological structures in 3D medical imaging is critical for effective diagnosis, treatment planning, and disease monitoring. Despite recent advances in deep learning, automated 3D medical image segmentation remains challenging due to anatomical variability, imaging artifacts, and the limited availability of annotated data. To address these issues, we present an interactive segmentation framework in the SAM-Med3D architecture with an xLSTM-UNet image encoder. Our encoder is specifically designed to capture long-range dependencies and hierarchical spatial features in volumetric medical data, improving contextual awareness while maintaining computational efficiency. We validate our approach using the CoreSet from the CVPR 2025 Foundation Models for 3D Biomedical Image Segmentation Challenge. Initial results demonstrate that our model achieves competitive performance in limited-scale testing, with DSC Final scores of 0.4855 (CT), 0.3071 (MRI), 0.4070 (PET), and 0.4458 (Ultrasound. NSD Final scores follow a similar trend, reaching 0.4992 (Ultrasound) and 0.4545 (CT). These early findings suggest strong potential for our architecture, particularly with further training on the full dataset. The proposed model supports multimodal prompts, including points and bounding boxes, allowing for flexible and intuitive user interaction a key requirement in clinical workflows. Our contributions include the development of a 3D-optimized interactive segmentation encoder, its integration into an existing foundation model framework, and an empirical evaluation that highlights the feasibility of our design. Future work will focus on full-scale training and refinement to bridge the performance gap with state-of-the-art methods.

Keywords: 3D medical image segmentation · Interactive segmentation · Vision transformers · xLSTM-UNet · SAM-Med3D · Foundation Models · User-Guided Refinement · Volumetric Data · Prompt-Based Segmentation

J. Ma et al. (Eds.): MedSegFM 2025, LNCS 16447, pp. 1–13, 2026.
https://doi.org/10.1007/978-3-032-23496-4_1

1 Introduction

Medical image segmentation plays a critical role in various clinical tasks, including diagnosis, treatment planning, and disease monitoring. Accurate delineation of anatomical structures or pathological regions in 3D medical scans is essential for reliable clinical decision-making. However, automated segmentation remains a challenging problem due to the high variability in anatomical shapes, ambiguous boundaries, imaging artifacts, and the scarcity of annotated data. Furthermore, medical data is often acquired in 3D volumes, which makes the segmentation process more computationally intensive and complex compared to natural 2D images.

Recent advances in deep learning, especially vision transformers and convolutional neural networks (CNNs), have significantly improved segmentation accuracy. Yet, these models typically require large-scale annotated datasets, which are expensive and time-consuming to obtain in the medical domain. Additionally, these models lack flexibility in adapting to new tasks without retraining, highlighting the need for interactive and generalizable segmentation frameworks. In the domain of natural image segmentation, foundation models such as the Segment Anything Model (SAM) [6] and its improved variant SAM2 [16] have demonstrated impressive zero-shot and few-shot capabilities. These models leverage powerful vision-language pretraining to generalize across image domains and tasks. However, directly applying these models to medical images has limitations due to domain differences and the lack of medical-specific priorities.

To address this, adaptations like MedSAM [8] and MedSAM2 [14] were proposed to better fit the medical image domain. These models incorporated domain-specific fine-tuning and data augmentations. Despite improvements, they still suffer from limited interactive refinement ability and lack support for multimodal prompts, such as textual descriptions or radiological terms, which are common in medical diagnostics. To further enhance interaction, methods such as SegVol [1], SAM-Med3D [16], VISTA3D [2], and nnInteractive [4], have introduced mechanisms for user-guided refinement, such as point-based corrections or region proposals.

Despite recent progress, a significant gap remains in developing interactive medical image segmentation frameworks that are both robust and efficient for 3D volumetric data. Our work is motivated by the need to enhance interactive segmentation while addressing domain-specific challenges in medical imaging. We build upon the SAM-Med3D framework, known for its prompt-based interaction capabilities, and propose architectural enhancement through a proposed encoder design.

Specifically, we introduce a customized encoder based on xLSTM-UNet, a hybrid architecture aimed at capturing long-range dependencies and hierarchical features within 3D medical volumes. This encoder is integrated into the SAM-Med3D pipeline, where we retain the original prompt decoder to support user-driven segmentation via points and bounding boxes. The design aims to balance contextual awareness with computational efficiency, tailored for medical scenarios.

Our main contributions are as follows:

1. We propose a xLSTM-UNet encoder, optimized for 3D medical imaging tasks, and integrate it within the interactive SAM-Med3D framework. Our model supports a variety of prompt types, enhancing usability in clinical settings through flexible user interaction.
2. We conduct initial experiments using the CVPR 2025: Foundation Models for 3D Biomedical Image Segmentation Challenge CoreSet dataset, training our encoder from scratch to evaluate its design independently.
3. While our proposed encoder does not yet outperform strong baselines like VISTA3D or nnInteractive, it demonstrates promising results in limited-scale testing.

Due to hardware and time constraints, we were unable to train our proposed model on the full challenge dataset. As a result, the performance reported here reflects partial training on the CoreSet. We plan to extend our evaluation to the full dataset in future work to better assess the potential of our approach and its capacity to close the performance gap with state-of-the-art methods.

2 Method

Our proposed model is shown in Fig. 1. The detail of each component is described in the following sections.

2.1 Proposed xLSTM Encoder

There are various UNet based models that are proposed in medical image segmentation [3,7,10,11,15]. The xLSTM block is a hybrid architectural component designed to integrate convolutional feature extraction with sequential modeling capabilities provided by a modified Long Short-Term Memory (mLSTM) unit. This integration is especially beneficial for medical image analysis, where both local spatial patterns and long-range dependencies across slices are crucial. The xLSTM begins with a convolutional layer that extracts spatial features from the input slice. This is followed by instance normalization (IN) to stabilize training and Leaky ReLU activation to introduce non-linearity, which together enhance the learning of meaningful spatial representations.

After this initial processing, the feature map is flattened and normalized before being divided into two distinct processing pathways. In the first pathway, the features undergo a linear transformation followed by the SiLU activation function, allowing for complex nonlinear interactions within local regions. The second pathway introduces a flip mechanism, which reverses the input along the slice axis to enable bidirectional processing. This flipped sequence is passed through the mLSTM, which captures long-range dependencies by modeling relationships between distant slices. The outputs of both pathways are then merged to form a unified representation.

To ensure effective information flow and model stability, the merged features are further refined through a final linear transformation and combined with the original input via a residual connection. This residual link preserves input information and supports efficient gradient propagation during training. The inclusion of the flip operation is key to capturing both past and future contextual information, providing a bidirectional perspective that is vital for tasks such as segmentation where anatomical continuity across slices is important.

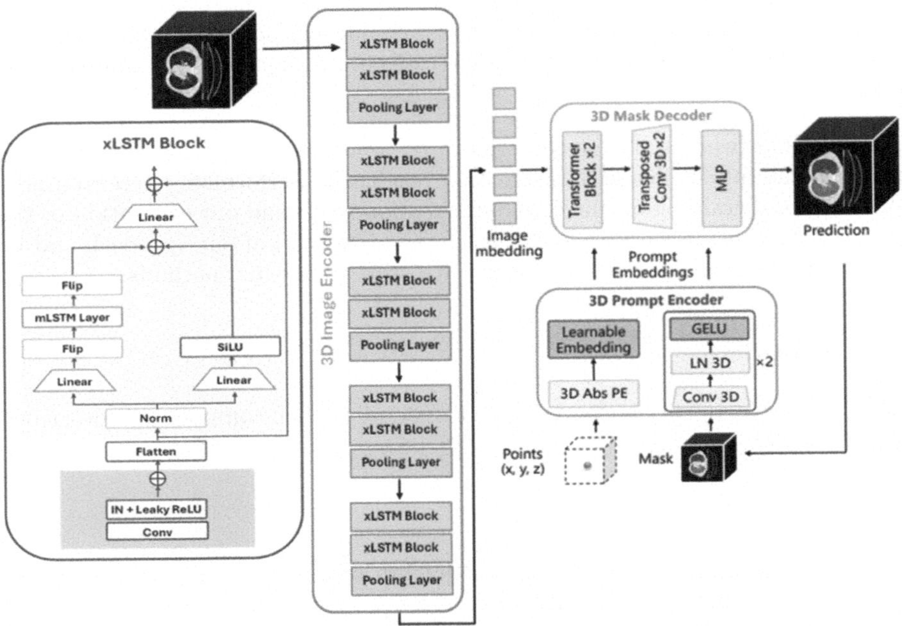

Fig. 1. Overview of the proposed interactive segmentation framework. The architecture integrates a customized image encoder based on xLSTM-UNet, a prompt encoder for handling interactive inputs such as points and bounding boxes, and a mask decoder that generates the final segmentation output. This modular design enables effective processing of 3D medical volumes while supporting flexible user interaction for refined and accurate segmentation.

In our proposed encoder module, the xLSTM [12,13] is employed across five encoder layers, each also incorporating convolutional and pooling operations. This multi-layer design allows the model to hierarchically extract features while modeling slice-to-slice relationships in 3D medical images. Unlike Vision Transformers (ViTs), which rely on self-attention mechanisms, our xLSTM-based approach offers a more efficient and tailored method for volumetric medical data. By combining convolutional and recurrent components, the xLSTM ensures both local detail preservation and global contextual awareness, which are essential for accurate and coherent segmentation outcomes.

2.2 3D Prompt Encoder

The 3D prompt encoder in our architecture is responsible for embedding user-provided interaction cuessuch as point coordinates, bounding boxes, or coarse masksinto a latent representation that guides the mask generation process. This module begins by converting raw prompt inputs into dense learnable embeddings. Each interaction type (e.g., positive point, negative point, or mask) is assigned a unique token that is further enriched through positional encoding. Specifically, we use 3D absolute positional encoding (3D Abs PE) to ensure that the spatial location of the prompts within the volumetric space is preserved. These embeddings are passed through a series of lightweight but expressive 3D convolutional layers to model local spatial interactions, followed by non-linear activation (GELU) and layer normalization (LayerNorm) to ensure stable feature transformation. By encoding spatial and semantic context from the user prompts, the 3D prompt encoder effectively translates interactive inputs into a form that the mask decoder can leverage to produce anatomically meaningful segmentation results. Importantly, this module remains unchanged from the SAM-Med3D pipeline to preserve its proven interactive refinement capabilities.

2.3 3D Mask Decoder

The 3D mask decoder is a critical component of the segmentation pipeline, tasked with synthesizing both the image features (from the encoder) and the prompt embeddings (from the prompt encoder) into a coherent segmentation output. This component operates on the fused feature space and is composed of a stack of Transformer blocks adapted for 3D inputs. These blocks allow for both self-attention (within image features) and cross-attention (between image and prompt features), enabling the model to contextualize anatomical structures relative to the spatial hints provided by the user. After attention-based fusion, the decoder incorporates several 3D convolutional layers that refine the transformer outputs by capturing fine-grained spatial patterns. These layers are followed by normalization and activation functions to improve gradient flow and feature discriminability. Finally, the decoder ends with a multi-layer perceptron (MLP) head that maps the refined features to voxel-level predictions. The output is a 3D binary or multi-class mask, depending on the target task. By maintaining the original design of the 3D mask decoder from SAM-Med3D, we ensure strong support for interactive segmentation while integrating our custom encoder module seamlessly. In our experiments, the prompt encoder and 3D mask decoder were frozen, while the xLSTM-UNet encoder was fine-tuned on the training dataset.

3 3 Experiments

3.1 Dataset and Evaluation Metrics

The development set is an expanded version of the dataset introduced in the CVPR 2024 MedSAM on Laptop Challenge [9], including more 3D cases from public datasets (A complete list is available at https://medsam-datasetlist.github.io/) and covering commonly used 3D modalities, such as Computed Tomography (CT), Magnetic Resonance Imaging (MRI), Positron Emission Tomography (PET), Ultrasound, and Microscopy images. The hidden testing set is created by a community effort where all the cases are unpublished. The annotations are either provided by the data contributors or annotated by the challenge organizer with 3D Slicer [5] and MedSAM2 [14]. In addition to using all training cases, the challenge contains a coreset track, where participants can select 10% of the total training cases for model development. For each iterative segmentation, the evaluation metrics include Dice Similarity Coefficient (DSC) and Normalized Surface Distance (NSD) to evaluate the segmentation region overlap and boundary distance, respectively. The final ranking metrics are defined as follows:

1. **DSC_AUC and NSD_AUC:** Area Under the Curve (AUC) scores for DSC and NSD, representing cumulative segmentation improvement over five iterative user interactions. The AUC is computed only for click-based predictions, excluding the optional initial bounding box.
2. **Final DSC and NSD:** Scores measured after all refinement steps, reflecting the final segmentation accuracy.
3. Algorithm runtime is restricted to 90 s per class; exceeding this limit results in all DSC and NSD metrics for that case being set to zero.

3.2 Implementation Details

Preprocessing. Following the practice in MedSAM [8], all images were processed to npz format with an intensity range of [0, 255]. Specifically, for CT images, we initially normalized the Hounsfield units using typical window width and level values: soft tissues (W:400, L:40), lung (W:1500, L:-160), brain (W:80, L:40), and bone (W:1800, L:400). Subsequently, the intensity values were rescaled to the range of [0, 255]. For other images, we clipped the intensity values to the range between the 0.5th and 99.5th percentiles before rescaling them to the range of [0, 255]. If the original intensity range is already in [0, 255], no preprocessing was applied. We have cropped a 3D volume in spatial size 128×128x128 and resampled the whole dataset for training the model.

Environment Settings. The development of environments and requirements are presented in Table 1. The training protocol used in our proposed model is shown in Table 2.

Table 1. Development environments and requirements.

System	Ubuntu 20.04.6 LTS
CPU	AMD Ryzen Threadripper PRO 5955WX (16 cores / 32 threads)
RAM	128 GB (16 8 GB), 2.67 MT/s
GPU	NVIDIA RTX A6000 48 GB
CUDA version	12.2
Programming language	Python 3.8.3
Deep learning framework	PyTorch 2.0.1+cu118, Torchvision 0.15.2+cu118

Training Protocols. In our experiments, we adopted the same training protocols described in SAM2 [16] to ensure consistency and fair comparison. The following outlines the key components of the training procedure:

1. **Data Augmentation:** To improve generalization across diverse medical imaging modalities and reduce overfitting, extensive 3D data augmentation strategies were applied. These include random cropping, flipping, rotation, intensity scaling, and Gaussian noise injection. Such augmentations help the model learn robust representations under varying anatomical and imaging conditions.
2. **Data Sampling Strategy:** We employed a patch-based sampling strategy, where volumetric image patches were sampled around annotated structures or user-provided prompts. This focused sampling allows the model to better learn localized anatomical features and improves efficiency during training, especially for high-resolution 3D volumes.

Table 2. Training protocol.

Configuration	Details
Pre-trained Model	None
Batch Size	12
Patch Size	$128 \times 128 \times 128$
Total Epochs	200
Optimizer	Adam
Initial Learning Rate (lr)	8×10^{-4}
LR Decay Schedule	MultiStepLR (milestones: [120, 180], gamma = 0.1)
Gradient Accumulation Steps	20
Weight Decay	0.1
Loss Function	DiceCELoss
Number of Model Parameters	24,867,472
Training Time	6 days
Image Size	128

3. **Model Selection Criteria:** The optimal model was selected based on validation performance, using the average Dice Similarity Coefficient (DSC) and Normalized Surface Dice (NSD) scores as the primary metrics. The model achieving the highest average DSC on the CoreSet validation split was selected for evaluation and comparison.

4 Results and Discussion

4.1 Quantitative Results on Validation Set

Table 3 shows the performance evaluation of our proposed xLSTM encoder within the SAM-Med3D framework was conducted across five imaging modalities CT, MRI, microscopy, PET, and ultrasoundusing standard metrics: DSC AUC, NSD AUC, DSC Final, and NSD Final. Overall, our model demonstrated promising trends in terms of foundational performance, but it underperformed compared to state-of-the-art models such as VISTA3D and nnInteractive. For CT images, the proposed model achieved a DSC Final of 0.4855, which, while lower than VISTA3D (0.8041) and nnInteractive (0.8764), is competitive given that our model was trained on a limited dataset and from scratch. In MRI, a similar trend was observed, with our model achieving 0.3071 DSC Final versus 0.7302 for nnInteractive, highlighting room for improvement in capturing complex anatomical structures. For microscopy, the model did not achieve any segmentation accuracy (DSC = 0), likely due to modality-specific domain shifts and insufficient adaptation, suggesting the need for modality-specific fine-tuning.

In PET imaging, the model achieved a moderate DSC Final of 0.4070, outperforming the baseline SAM-Med3D (0.5344) in terms of NSD AUC in some settings, though trailing behind more mature methods. Lastly, for ultrasound, the model yielded a DSC Final of 0.4458, which is an improvement over SegVol (0.3109), but still below nnInteractive (0.8547). These results reflect the current limitations of our partially trained model but also demonstrate its potential as a generalizable encoder. With full training and further optimization, particularly through integration into mature frameworks like VISTA3D or 3DSegVol, we expect significant performance gains across all modalities.

Our model was evaluated on an independent test set spanning multiple imaging modalities as shown in Table 4. Performance was assessed using the area under the curve (AUC) and final values of the Dice Similarity Coefficient (DSC) and Normalized Surface Dice (NSD). The results demonstrate strong cross-modality generalization, with good performance for CT and MR, followed by moderate performance for PET. As expected, performance degrades for ultrasound and microscopy due to limited anatomical contrast and scale mismatch. Zero NSD values for microscopy reflect insufficient surface correspondence at the evaluated resolution.

Table 3. Quantitative evaluation results of the validation set on the coreset track.

Modality	Methods	DSC AUC	NSD AUC	DSC Final	NSD Final
CT	SAM-Med3D	2.2408	2.2213	0.5590	0.5558
	VISTA3D	3.1689	3.2652	0.8041	0.8344
	SegVol	2.9809	3.1235	0.7452	0.7809
	nnInteractive	3.4337	3.5743	0.8764	0.9165
	Proposed model	**1.9326**	**1.8080**	**0.4855**	**0.4545**
MRI	SAM-Med3D	1.5222	1.5226	0.3903	0.3964
	VISTA3D	2.5895	2.9683	0.6545	0.7493
	SegVol	2.6719	3.1535	0.6680	0.7884
	nnInteractive	2.6975	3.0292	0.7302	0.8227
	Proposed model	**1.1861**	**1.1291**	**0.3071**	**0.3115**
Microscopy	SAM-Med3D	0.1163	0	0.0291	0
	VISTA3D	2.1196	3.2259	0.5478	0.8243
	SegVol	1.6846	2.9716	0.4211	0.7429
	nnInteractive	2.3311	3.1109	0.5943	0.7890
	Proposed model	**0**	**0**	**0**	**0**
PET	SAM-Med3D	2.1304	1.7250	0.5344	0.4560
	VISTA3D	2.6398	2.3998	0.6779	0.6227
	SegVol	2.9683	2.8563	0.7421	0.7141
	nnInteractive	3.1877	3.0722	0.8156	0.7915
	Proposed model	**1.6267**	**0.9885**	**0.4070**	**0.2473**
Ultrasound	SAM-Med3D	1.4347	1.9176	0.4102	0.5435
	VISTA3D	2.8655	2.8441	0.8105	0.8079
	SegVol	1.2438	1.8045	0.3109	0.4511
	nnInteractive	3.3481	3.3236	0.8547	0.8494
	Proposed model	**1.6074**	**1.8157**	**0.4458**	**0.4992**

Table 4. Test results of the proposed model on different imaging modalities.

Modality	DSC_AUC	NSD_AUC	DSC_Final	NSD_Final
CT	1.99	1.61	0.51	0.41
MRI	1.81	1.69	0.46	0.42
Microscopy	0.20	0.00	0.05	0.00
PET	1.41	0.90	0.35	0.23
Ultrasound	0.41	0.26	0.10	0.06

4.2 Qualitative Results on Validation Set

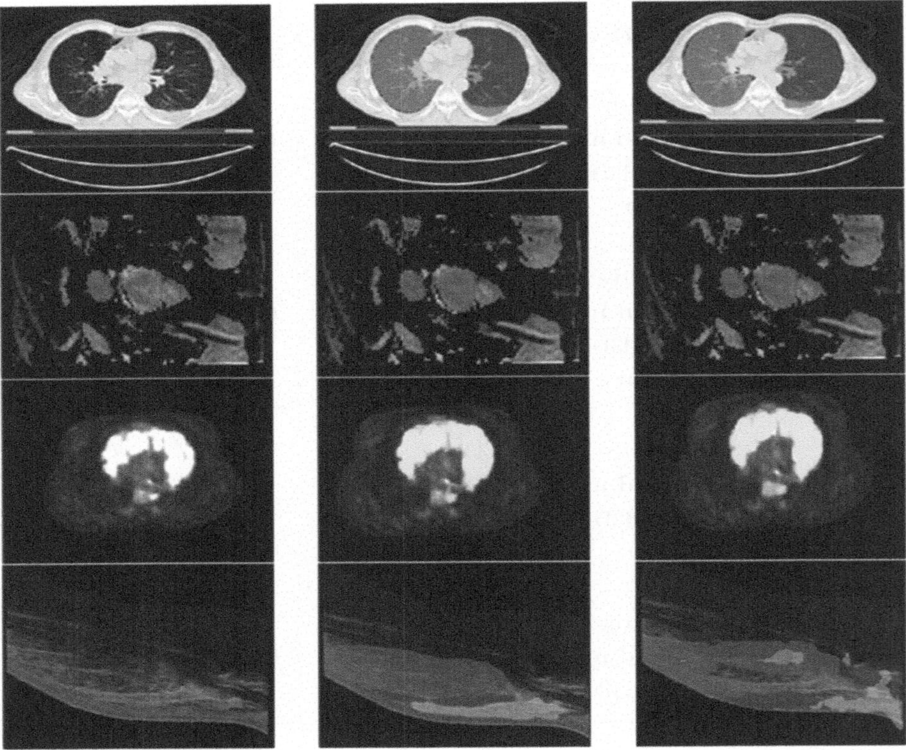

Fig. 2. Representative examples of the best segmentation performance achieved by the proposed model across all evaluated modalities. The first column displays the original input images, the second column overlays the ground truth annotations on the input, and the third column overlays the models predicted segmentations. These cases demonstrate the models ability to accurately capture anatomical and pathological structures, showing high spatial agreement with the ground truth even in complex 3D medical imaging scenarios.

We have validated our proposed model using representative examples of both good and poor segmentation performance across different modalities, as illustrated in Fig. 2 and Fig. 3. Figure 2 presents successful segmentation results for CT, MR, PET, and ultrasound (US) images, where the proposed model accurately delineates anatomical structures with high overlap compared to ground truth, as shown in Column 3. These examples highlight the models ability to capture relevant features and boundaries effectively in varied imaging contexts. In contrast, Fig. 3 showcases failure cases where the model struggles to produce accurate segmentations, particularly in regions with ambiguous boundaries, low contrast, or structural variability. These visualizations underscore the strengths of our model in common clinical scenarios while also revealing limitations that motivate further refinement.

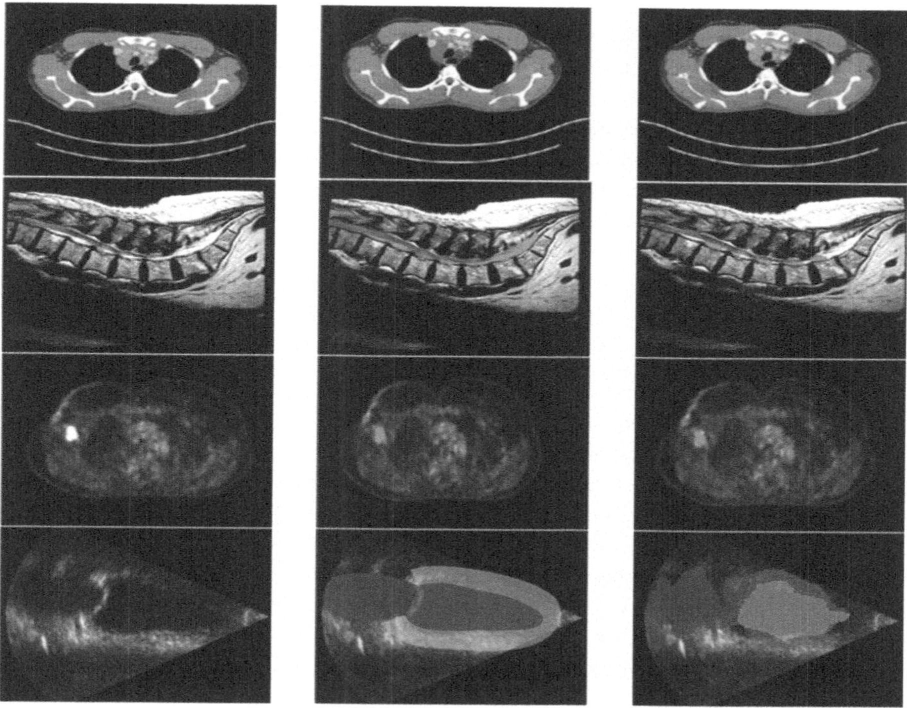

Fig. 3. Poor segmentation examples across all evaluated modalities using the proposed model. The first column displays the input images, the second column shows the ground truth annotations overlaid on the input, and the third column presents the model's predicted segmentations overlaid on the same input images. These examples illustrate the models limitations in challenging scenarios such as low-contrast regions, irregular anatomical structures, or noisy inputs, where segmentation quality significantly degrades.

4.3 Limitations and Future Work

While our proposed xLSTM-UNet encoder integrated into the SAM-Med3D framework shows promising early results, several limitations remain. Due to hardware and time constraints, our current experiments were limited to partial training on the CVPR 2025 Foundation Models for 3D Biomedical Image Segmentation Challenge CoreSet. As a result, the performance does not yet fully reflect the models capacity. Furthermore, although the xLSTM-UNet design is intended to capture long-range spatial dependencies in 3D volumes, it currently underperforms compared to leading interactive methods, likely due to limited training scale and lack of comprehensive hyperparameter tuning. The framework presently supports only basic prompts (points and bounding boxes), lacking richer or multimodal guidance (e.g., textual or anatomical region descriptors) that could improve usability in clinical settings.

Additionally, the xLSTM layers introduce moderate computational overhead, which may affect scalability for real-time or low-resource environments. In future work, we plan to train our model on the full challenge dataset, explore optimizations for inference efficiency, and extend support for multimodal and domain-aware prompting. Importantly, we also intend to evaluate the generalizability of our xLSTM-UNet encoder by integrating it into other advanced foundation model frameworks such as VISTA3D and 3DSegVol, enabling a broader and more rigorous assessment of its effectiveness across segmentation paradigms.

5 Conclusion

In this work, we proposed an xLSTM-UNet encoder designed to enhance interactive 3D medical image segmentation within the SAM-Med3D framework. Our motivation stemmed from the limitations of existing foundation models in handling the unique challenges of 3D biomedical data, such as long-range spatial dependencies, ambiguous anatomical boundaries, and limited annotated datasets. By integrating the xLSTM-UNet architecture, combining convolutional hierarchies with LSTM-style sequence modeling into the SAM-Med3D pipeline, we aimed to improve both contextual representation and user-guided segmentation performance. Experiments were conducted using a subset of the CVPR 2025 Challenge dataset. Despite the limited training scale, our model demonstrated promising segmentation accuracy and effective prompt-based interaction capabilities. While the xLSTM-UNet did not yet surpass state-of-the-art methods like VISTA3D or nnInteractive in quantitative performance, it showed competitive results and practical feasibility, especially in scenarios with minimal supervision.

Our findings suggest that incorporating long-range sequence modeling into 3D encoders is a viable direction for enhancing foundation model frameworks in medical imaging. Future work will involve training on the full challenge dataset, supporting multimodal prompts, and testing the encoders adaptability in other interactive frameworks such as VISTA3D and 3DSegVol. Ultimately, this research contributes toward building more flexible, interactive, and generalizable foundation models for 3D biomedical image segmentation.

Disclosure of Interests. The authors have no competing interests to declare that are relevant to the content of this article.

Acknowledgements. We thank all the data owners for making the medical images publicly available and CodaLab [17] for hosting the challenge platform.

References

1. Du, Y., Bai, F., Huang, T., Zhao, B.: Segvol: universal and interactive volumetric medical image segmentation. Adv. Neural. Inf. Process. Syst. **37**, 110746–110783 (2024)
2. He, Y., et al.: Vista3d: a unified segmentation foundation model for 3D medical imaging. In: Proceedings of the Computer Vision and Pattern Recognition Conference, pp. 20863–20873 (2025)
3. Imran, M., et al.: Multi-class segmentation of aortic branches and zones in computed tomography angiography: The aortaseg24 challenge. arXiv preprint arXiv:2502.05330 (2025)
4. Isensee, F., et al.: nninteractive: Redefining 3d promptable segmentation. arXiv preprint arXiv:2503.08373 (2025)
5. Kikinis, R., Pieper, S., Vosburgh, K.: 3D slicer: A platform for subject-specific image analysis. Visualization, and Clinical Support, pp. 277–289 (2013)
6. Kirillov, A., et al.: Segment anything. In: Proceedings of the International Conference on Computer Vision, pp. 4015–4026 (2023)
7. Luo, G., et al.: Tumor detection, segmentation and classification challenge on automated 3D breast ultrasound: The tdsc-abus challenge. arXiv preprint arXiv:2501.15588 (2025)
8. Ma, J., et al.: Efficient medsams: Segment anything in medical images on laptop. arXiv preprint arXiv:2412.16085 (2024)
9. Ma, J., et al.: Medsam2: Segment anything in 3d medical images and videos. arXiv preprint arXiv:2504.03600 (2025)
10. Nan, Y., et al.: Hunting imaging biomarkers in pulmonary fibrosis: benchmarks of the aiib23 challenge. Med. Image Anal. **97**, 103253 (2024)
11. Payette, K., et al.: Multi-center fetal brain tissue annotation (feta) challenge 2022 results. IEEE transactions on medical imaging (2024)
12. Qayyum, A., Mazher, M., Ugurlu, D., Lemus, J.A.S., Rodero, C., Niederer, S.A.: Foundation model for whole-heart segmentation: Leveraging student-teacher learning in multi-modal medical imaging. arXiv preprint arXiv:2503.19005 (2025)
13. Qayyum, A., et al.: Transforming heart chamber imaging: self-supervised learning for whole heart reconstruction and segmentation. arXiv preprint arXiv:2406.06643 (2024)
14. Ravi, N., et al.: Sam 2: Segment anything in images and videos. arXiv preprint arXiv:2408.00714 (2024)
15. de la Rosa, E., et al.: Deepisles: a clinically validated ischemic stroke segmentation model from the isles'22 challenge. Nat. Commun. **16**(1), 7357 (2025)
16. Wang, H., et al.: Sam-med3d: A vision foundation model for general-purpose segmentation on volumetric medical images. IEEE Transactions on Neural Networks and Learning Systems (2025)
17. Xu, Z., et al.: Codabench: Flexible, easy-to-use, and reproducible meta-benchmark platform. Patterns **3**(7), 100543 (2022)

ENSAM: An Efficient Foundation Model for Interactive Segmentation of 3D Medical Images

Elias Stenhede[1,2], Agnar Martin Bjørnstad[1,2], and Arian Ranjbar[1(✉)]

[1] Medical Technology and E-health, Akershus University Hospital, Lørenskog, Norway
arian.ranjbar@medisin.uio.no

[2] Faculty of Medicine, University of Oslo, Oslo, Norway

Abstract. We present ENSAM (Equivariant, Normalized, Segment Anything Model), a lightweight and promptable model for universal 3D medical image segmentation. ENSAM combines a SegResNet-based encoder with a prompt encoder and mask decoder in a U-Net-style architecture, using latent cross-attention, relative positional encoding, normalized attention, and the Muon optimizer for training. ENSAM is designed to achieve good performance under limited data and computational budgets, and is trained from scratch on under 5,000 volumes from multiple modalities (CT, MRI, PET, ultrasound, microscopy) on a single 32 GB GPU in 6 h. As part of the CVPR 2025 Foundation Models for Interactive 3D Biomedical Image Segmentation Challenge, ENSAM was evaluated on the hidden test set with multimodal 3D medical images, obtaining a DSC AUC of 2.404, NSD AUC of 2.266, final DSC of 0.627, and final NSD of 0.597, outperforming two previously published baseline models (VISTA3D, SAM-Med3D) and matching the third (SegVol), surpassing its performance in final DSC but trailing behind in the other three metrics. In the coreset track of the challenge, ENSAM ranks 5th of 10 overall and best among the approaches not utilizing pretrained weights. Ablation studies confirm that our use of relative positional encodings and the Muon optimizer each substantially speed up convergence and improve segmentation quality.

Keywords: Medical Imaging · Multimodal · Interactive Segmentation

1 Introduction

Accurate segmentation of three-dimensional (3D) or two-dimensional plus time (2D+t) medical images has become fundamental for numerous clinical tasks, including diagnosis, treatment planning, and disease monitoring. While 3D images provide much richer spatial context compared to 2D images, technical challenges arise in processing and storing large amounts of high-resolution 3D data. In the last decade, specialized deep learning models have shown success

J. Ma et al. (Eds.): MedSegFM 2025, LNCS 16447, pp. 14–35, 2026.
https://doi.org/10.1007/978-3-032-23496-4_2

in automating segmentation tasks when trained using high-quality pixel-level labels [22]. More recently, the advent of large pretrained foundation models in natural language processing has demonstrated that models trained on massive and diverse datasets can generalize effectively to downstream tasks [6,7,36,39], surpassing the performance of specialized models.

Motivated by this, foundation models for natural image segmentation have been developed, most notably SAM [20] for 2D and subsequently SAM2 [37] for 2D+t. While providing impressive segmentations for natural images, they do not immediately provide useful segmentations when applied to medical images. To address this performance gap, the 2025 CVPR Workshop on Foundation Models for Medical Vision was established, including a challenge aimed at improving segmentation accuracy on medical modalities. In this paper, we present our contribution to that effort: an efficient SAM model for medical 3D imaging.

1.1 Related Work

Several previous attempts at building a SAM for medical imaging exist. MedSAM [26] adapts SAM to the medical domain by fine-tuning on medical segmentation datasets, achieving improved performance across several imaging modalities, but is limited by only supporting an initial bounding box and no subsequent clicks. It further only supports 2D slices and lacks volumetric consistency. MedSAM2 [28] adapts SAM2 for and supports segmentation of 2D+t and 3D medical images, but also lacks support for iterative segmentation refinement.

Models inspired by but not directly utilizing weights from SAM or SAM2 have also been proposed. SAM-Med3D [40] demonstrates the feasibility of training using medical data only and supports iterative refinement, but fails to generalize well to unseen classes and requires many interactions to match the performance of task-specific baselines such as nnU-Net [13]. SegVol [8] introduces more prompt types, including text, boxes, and clicks, and is trained on Computed Tomography (CT) images only.

Other models build on established segmentation architectures to enhance performance in medical imaging tasks. SegResNet [29], a U-Net-based architecture augmented with a variational decoder head for regularization, has proven highly effective, winning multiple 3D medical image segmentation challenges [30–32]. It serves as the backbone in VISTA3D [11], a model trained on both CT and MRI data, which leverages supervoxels generated by SAM during training in addition to conventional segmentation masks.

The model nnInteractive [9] advances the state-of-the-art further by supporting bounding box, click, lasso, and scribble prompts, with the latter two providing stronger guidance. It is trained on a multimodal set of 3D medical datasets using both traditional segmentation masks and supervoxels from SAM and SAM2. Unlike the other models that rely on cross-attention, nnInteractive integrates user input through dense feature maps.

1.2 Objective and Contribution

As the field of interactive 3D medical image segmentation rapidly evolves, each new model often demonstrates improvements over selected baselines. However, a unified and independent comparison of these models on a common benchmark has not yet been established. This challenge addresses that gap by evaluating participants on a standardized hidden test set comprising multiple imaging modalities, enabling a fair and unbiased comparison of methods based solely on their generalization and segmentation performance.

ENSAM (Equivariant, Normalized, SAM in 3D) is designed to improve both training efficiency and segmentation accuracy, addressing the often prohibitive computational cost of training foundation models. Our objective is to achieve performance comparable to, or surpassing, current state-of-the-art models, while training on a single GPU. The name ENSAM also subtly reflects this goal, as ensam (Swedish spelling) means sole/lonely in Germanic languages.

Our proposed model is inspired by SAM and the SegResNet architecture, and introduces several improvements, such as relative position encodings in 3D together with a normalized attention mechanism for the encoded user input, trained by a Muon optimizer in place of Adam. All modifications are aimed at accelerating training and enhancing data efficiency, while being scalable to larger setups. Furthermore, our solution targets the coreset challenge, a sub-track of the challenge, limiting the training dataset to 10% of the full set.

2 Method

The goal of the challenge is to develop a foundation model for universal medical image segmentation; that is, given a medical image, the model should segment any anatomical or pathological structure indicated by a user prompt (specifically, a bounding box or point-based clicks). Evaluation is conducted through a simulated interactive setting, in which the model receives an image during inference, with or without an initial bounding box, followed by five simulated clicks representing iterative corrections made by a clinician.

To address this task, we propose a model based on three components: an image encoder, a prompt encoder, and a mask decoder, configured into a U-Net architecture. User prompts are integrated into the model via cross-attention mechanisms applied at the bottleneck layer. With the chosen structure, we are capable of simultaneously training all components, end-to-end. The following subsections detail the proposed method, and an overview of the architecture is provided in Fig. 1.

2.1 Image Encoder

With the advent of vision transformers, several efforts have been made to adapt transformer-based backbones for use as image encoders in segmentation models. However, most benchmarks continue to show that CNN-based encoders outperform their transformer-based counterparts [3]. We adopt an architecture based

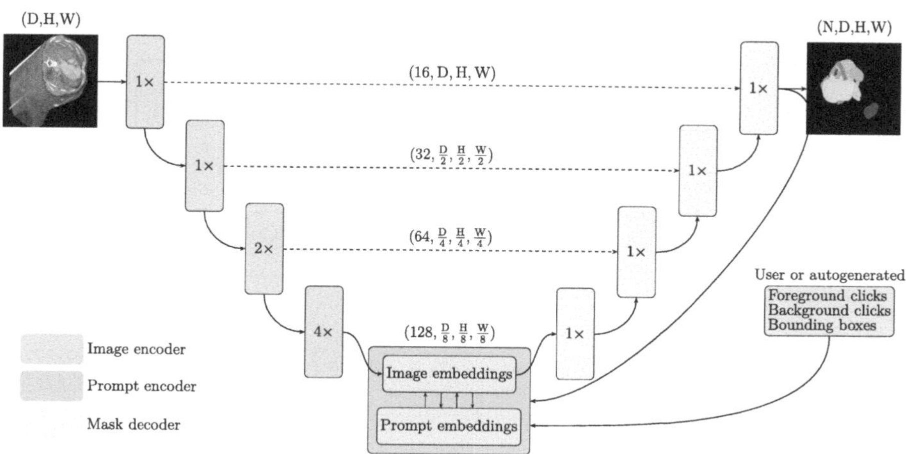

Fig. 1. Network architecture of the proposed interactive segmentation model, consisting of three main components: image encoder, prompt encoder, and mask decoder. During an interactive segmentation session on a single sample, the image encoder runs once, while the decoder updates the segmentation with each new user input.

on the SegResNet model, [29], which comprises a cascade of residual blocks interleaved with downsampling layers. An overview of the image encoder is illustrated in Fig. 2.

2.2 Prompt Encoder

The prompt encoder is responsible for taking input from the user and encoding it in a format compatible with the rest of the model. The prompt encoder currently supports 3D bounding boxes as well as foreground and background clicks. All user interactions are represented as unit vectors with the same dimension d as the image embeddings at the bottom latent space of the U-Net. In its current implementation, boxes are represented by a pair of unit vectors and clicks by a single vector, one for foreground and another for background clicks.

Each prompt and image embedding is associated with a 3D coordinate. This coordinate information is essential for the mask decoder to reason about spatial relations between prompts and image content. Traditionally, absolute positional information has been added element-wise to embedding vectors [20, 26]. However, absolute encoding breaks equivariance. Using methods that instead encode relative positional information has been shown to improve training efficiency and final model performance both in 1D [38] as well as 2D and 3D tasks [34].

Lie Rotational Positional Encoding. To include relative positional information when computing attention between embedding vectors, the attention blocks are given pairs of embedding vectors and coordinates. Technically, positional information is encoded by applying position-dependent rotation matrices

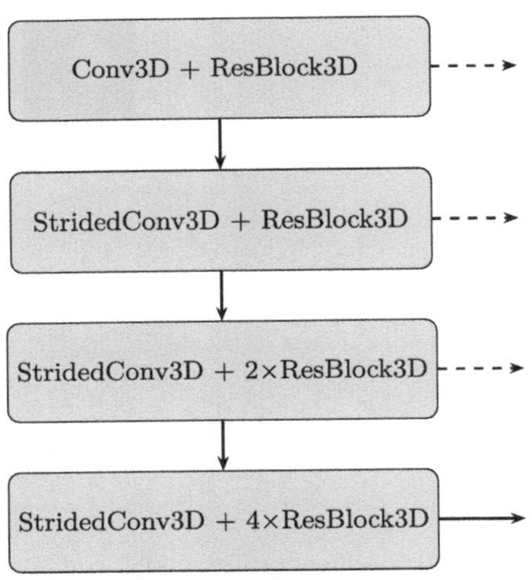

(a) The image encoder consists of four blocks. The initial Conv3D layer transforms the image from single-channel to 16 channels. The StridedConv3D layers reduce the spatial dimensions by a factor of 2 and double the number of channels.

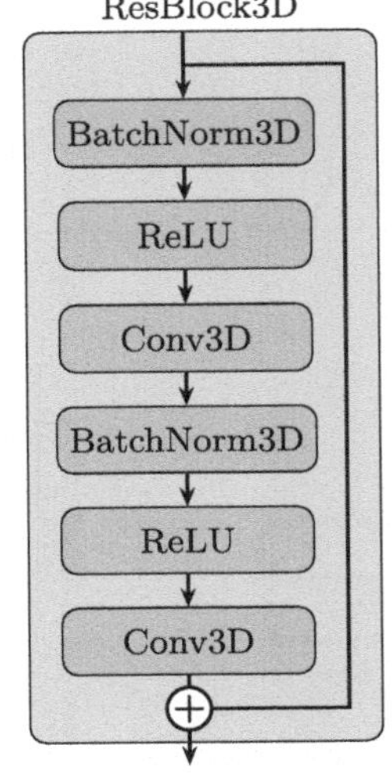

(b) Each residual block contains convolutional layers with skip connections. Through all layers, the channel dimension is kept constant, allowing for element-wise addition of the residual activations.

Fig. 2. Architecture overview: (a) image encoder; (b) residual block used within the encoder.

to key and query vectors. As previously noted in [34], Lie algebras provide a suitable framework in this setting, as the group of rotations SO(n) can be generated from the Lie algebra $\mathfrak{so}(n)$. In other words, for an embedding vector e_i with coordinate $p_i = (x_i, y_i, z_i)$, the corresponding rotation matrix can be written as

$$R(p_i) = \exp\left(A_x x_i + A_y y_i + A_z z_i\right), \tag{1}$$

where A_x, A_y, A_z are learnable, skew-symmetric matrices of size $d \times d$, where d is the embedding dimension. Each matrix is parameterized by $d(d-1)/2$ values due to the skew-symmetry ($A^\top = -A$).

Letting q_i and k_j be key and query vectors with positions $p_i = (x_i, y_i, z_i)$ and $p_j = (x_j, y_j, z_j)$ respectively. The attention scores between q_i and k_j are then calculated as

$$
\begin{aligned}
\text{AttnScore}(q_i, k_j) &= (R(p_i)q_i)^\top (R(p_j)k_j) \\
&= q_i^\top R(p_i)^\top R(p_j)k_j \\
&= q_i^\top \exp\left(A_x x_i + A_y y_i + A_z z_i\right)^\top \exp\left(A_x x_j + A_y y_j + A_z z_j\right) k_j \\
&= q_i^\top \exp\left(-A_x x_i - A_y y_i - A_z z_i\right) \exp\left(A_x x_j + A_y y_j + A_z z_j\right) k_j \\
&= q_i^\top \exp\left(A_x(x_j - x_i) + A_y(y_j - y_i) + A_z(z_j - z_i)\right) k_j \\
&= q_i^\top R(p_j - p_i)k_j,
\end{aligned}
$$

which shows that the attention scores depend only on the relative position $p_j - p_i$ and coincides with the standard attention calculation when $p_j = p_i$, as $\exp(0) = I$.

Normalized Attention. Recent work by Loshchilov et al. [24] introduces a normalized transformer architecture, which can converge in 4–20 times fewer training steps compared to the standard transformer, primarily demonstrated on 1D natural language tasks. In ENSAM, we extend this approach to the 3D medical image domain, combining it with LieRE. We hypothesize that their benefits, namely faster convergence and improved numerical stability, can generalize to volumetric data.

The normalized transformer replaces traditional layer normalization (e.g., RMSNorm [42] or LayerNorm [2]) and weight decay with ℓ_2 normalization applied to all weight matrices after each optimization step. An additional ℓ_2 normalization of activations is also performed. As a result, attention and MLP outputs are constrained to lie on a unit hypersphere, which requires a modified residual update strategy. Specifically, the standard residual addition:

$$x \leftarrow x + \text{Block}(x) \tag{2}$$

is replaced by

$$x \leftarrow \text{Norm}\left(\text{Norm}(x) + \lambda(\text{Norm}(\text{nBlock}(x)) - \text{Norm}(x))\right). \tag{3}$$

In Fig. 3, Norm denotes ℓ_2 normalization and $\lambda \in \mathbb{R}_+^d$ is an eigen learning rate that is learned for each block in the model. Block and nBlock denote the blocks in a transformer architecture and a normalized transformer architecture, respectively. Steps performed by cross-attention and MLP layers are performed using the same logic. This update rule can be interpreted as a constrained optimization step on the unit hypersphere, which empirically stabilizes training and accelerates convergence.

For initialization of e.g. λ, we used the values recommended by the original authors. For such implementation, specific details and theoretical justifications, we refer readers to the original study [24].

Image-Prompt Interaction. The interaction between user prompts and image embeddings builds on the original SAM model, with modifications to the attention mechanism, positional encoding, and postprocessing. Besides the image embeddings, the prompt encoder processes user inputs and, when available, segmentation logits from the previous step. These segmentation logits are downsampled using strided convolutions to align with the image embeddings and are added element-wise. The interaction between user input and the modified image embeddings follows a four-step process, using normalized attention and relative positional encoding as core components.

1. Normalized self-attention is applied to the prompt embeddings.
2. The prompt embeddings attend to the image embeddings.
3. The updated prompt embeddings are passed through a multi-layer perceptron (MLP) with ReLU activation and a hidden dimension of $2d$.
4. The image embeddings attend to the updated prompt embeddings.

All four steps incorporate residual connections on the hypersphere using Fig. 3. This four-step process is repeated twice and is illustrated in Fig. 3.

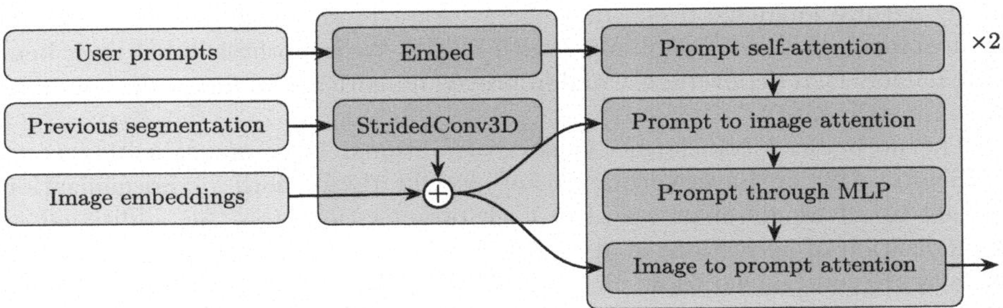

Fig. 3. The prompt encoder module encodes user input and modifies the image embeddings before it is passed to the mask decoder. If a previous segmentation exists, it is incorporated into the image embeddings via strided convolutions, allowing for iterative refinement.

2.3 Mask Decoder

The mask decoder mirrors the image encoder, except for single residual blocks per upsampling layer. The activations from skip-connections are concatenated along the channel dimension and processed by a single ResBlock3D, followed by trilinear upsampling. The final layer outputs logits with the same shape as the input, containing the segmentation mask.

2.4 Model Training and Interaction Simulation

During training, user interactions are simulated. If provided, initial prompts are given as bounding boxes, calculated using the ground truth labels with an added random offset, to mimic human generation. An iterative refinement click is then placed in the middle of the largest error region. In case the largest error region is an undersegmentation, a foreground click is placed; otherwise, a background click is used. In total, a bounding box and five clicks are provided per training step.

To provide supervision for the model, we use the sum of generalized dice loss and cross-entropy, as compound loss functions have been proven to be robust in various medical image segmentation tasks [25]. Specifically, the cross-entropy carries double the weight,

$$\mathcal{L} = \mathcal{L}_{\text{Dice}} + 2 \cdot \mathcal{L}_{\text{CE}} = 1 - \frac{2\sum_i p_i g_i}{\sum_i p_i^2 + \sum_i g_i^2} - \frac{2}{N}\sum_i g_i \log p_i, \tag{4}$$

where N is the number of voxels, p denotes the prediction and g the ground-truth. The loss is averaged across all iterative steps.

To train the model in as high a resolution as possible without exceeding the GPU memory constraints, gradient accumulation and a batch size of one are used. The usage of a batch size of one is also partly motivated by the varying data shapes. A standard torch dataset/dataloader setup was used with 32 worker threads for parallel data loading. Data preprocessing and augmentation were performed on the fly within the dataset, as it did not serve as a bottleneck for the training pipeline.

Muon Optimizer. Following its recent success in speedrunning training of image classification and language models, [17,23], we investigate if the Muon optimizer [18] is effective for segmentation models. The Muon optimizer has, to the best of our knowledge, not been benchmarked for segmentation tasks at the time of writing. Unlike traditional optimizers like Adam or SGD, Muon operates on 2-dimensional weight matrices. To apply Muon to ENSAM, all weights with dimension ≥ 2 are flattened beyond the first dimension. For example, 3D convolutional kernels are 5-dimensional and need flattening. For parameters with dimension 1, Adam is used as per usual.

Muon replaces the conventional gradient descent update with a step along $UV^\top$, where $U\Sigma V^\top$ is the singular value decomposition (SVD) of the gradient matrix. Rather than computing the full SVD, Muon employs an efficient approximation [4,5], which has been shown to achieve similar performance [23] while significantly reducing computational cost.

2.5 Coreset Selection Strategy

The coreset track in the challenge required the use of no more than 10% of the total training data, corresponding to a maximum of 4,471 samples. To ensure diverse representation under this constraint, we aimed to select an approximately equal number of samples from each dataset. In cases where a dataset contained fewer than $4471/N$ samples (where N is the number of eligible datasets), all available samples from that dataset were included.

Some datasets were excluded from the coreset selection process. The CT Aorta dataset was omitted due to apparent issues with image normalization. In addition, the microscopy datasets were excluded as many of them had issues in the provided format. Since the ground truth annotations were stored using the `uint8` format, this led to instance merging due to label value overflow.

2.6 Post-processing

Although the model is trained to segment one instance at a time, multiple instance prompts are typically provided during inference. To handle this, only one encoder pass is needed for the input, while the prompt encoder and decoder can be run in parallel for each instance. The final segmentation assigns each voxel to the instance with the highest output logit, or to the background if no logit exceeds a predefined threshold, such as 0.

To ensure that each instance is assigned at least one voxel, the logits are adjusted by adding a constant inside the bounding box of any instance that initially has no assigned voxels. If every instance already has at least one voxel assigned, no changes are made to the logits.

3 Experiments

3.1 Dataset and Evaluation Metrics

The development set is compiled by the organizers of the CVPR 2025 Foundation Models for Interactive 3D Biomedical Image Segmentation Challenge. This includes data normalization. The development set is an extension of the CVPR 2024 MedSAM on Laptop Challenge [27], including more 3D cases from public datasets[1] and covering commonly used 3D modalities including CT, MRI, Positron Emission Tomography (PET), Ultrasound (US), and microscopy images. The hidden test set is created by a community effort where all the cases are unpublished. The annotations are either provided by the data contributors or annotated by the challenge organizer with 3D Slicer [19] and MedSAM2 [28]. In addition to using all training cases, the challenge contains a coreset track, where participants can select 10% of the total training cases for model development. The solution proposed in this paper specifically targets the latter coreset track.

Each interactive segmentation is evaluated using the Dice Similarity Coefficient (DSC) and Normalized Surface Distance (NSD), which measure the overlap of segmentation regions and the accuracy of boundaries, respectively.

Ranking of participants is performed using four metrics: Area Under the Curve (AUC) for DSC and NSD, as well as final AUC and NSD. Denoting AUC_i as the DSC after the i-th user interaction, the AUC is calculated as

$$\text{AUC\_DSC} = \frac{1}{2}\left(\text{DSC}_1 + 2 \cdot \text{DSC}_2 + 2 \cdot \text{DSC}_3 + 2 \cdot \text{DSC}_4 + \text{DSC}_5\right). \quad (5)$$

[1] A complete list is available at https://medsam-datasetlist.github.io/.

The initial bounding box prediction is excluded from this calculation, as it is optional. The same formula is used for computing AUC_NSD, mutatis mutandis. The four metrics intend to capture both the iterative refinement and final predictions.

Finally, to ensure practical applicability, inference time is capped at 90 s per class. Any submission exceeding this limit receives a score of zero for both DSC and NSD on the corresponding test case.

3.2 Implementation Details

Preprocessing. Following the practice in MedSAM [26], all images were preprocessed by the challenge organizers into `.npz` format with an intensity range normalized to $[0, 255]$. For CT images, the Hounsfield units were normalized using standard window width and level settings: soft tissue (W:400, L:40), lung (W:1500, L:-160), brain (W:80, L:40), and bone (W:1800, L:400). Subsequently, the intensity values were rescaled to the range of $[0, 255]$. For other images, the intensity values were clipped to the range between the 0.5th and 99.5th percentiles before rescaling them to the range of $[0, 255]$. If the original intensity range is already in $[0, 255]$, no preprocessing was applied.

Environment Settings. The development environments and requirements are presented in Table 1.

Table 1. Development environments and hardware.

Component	Specification
System	Debian 12
CPU	Intel(R) Core(TM) i9-14900KF
RAM	2×48 GB; 4800 MT/s
GPU	NVIDIA GeForce RTX 5090 32 GB
CUDA version	12.8
Programming language	Python 3.12
Deep learning framework	PyTorch 2.7.0, Torchvision 0.22.0

Training Protocols. Training was performed after coreset selection, which involved nearly uniform sampling across datasets. Therefore, oversampling was not employed. Each training epoch consisted of sampling every data instance once in randomized order and generating boxes or clicks for one randomly selected labelled instance from the label data.

Part of the datasets used during training included irrelevant regions surrounding the areas of interest. To focus computational resources on relevant structures, training volumes were randomly cropped around the labelled regions with a variable margin of 1 to 64 voxels in each spatial dimension. After cropping, volumes that exceeded a predefined size threshold were downscaled via max pooling to fit within GPU memory constraints. The shapes of training volumes varied across samples. However, to ensure compatibility with the network architecture, all spatial dimensions were adjusted to be divisible by 8 by zero padding.

Following the spatial augmentations, the volumes were converted from `uint8` format to a range between $[0, 1]$, and an intensity augmentation was applied with a probability of 0.5. Specifically, one of the following was randomly applied: bias field distortion, Gaussian smoothing, or histogram shift (Table 2).

Table 2. Parameters used during model training. FLOPs were calculated for one forward pass with the maximum patch volume and only one user interaction.

Parameter	Value
Batch size	1
Gradient accumulation steps	4
Patch size	Variable
Maximum patch volume	$4{,}194{,}304 \approx 161^3$
Simulated clicks per step	5
Total epochs	15
Optimizer	Muon and AdamW
Muon momentum	0.95
Initial learning rate	10^{-3}
Learning rate scheduler	Halved at epochs 2, 5, 10
Training time	6 h
Loss function	Soft Dice + 2·BCE
Number of model parameters	5.5 M
Number of FLOPs	368 G

3.3 Ablations

To evaluate the contributions of LieRE and Muon, we conducted an ablation study. First, ENSAM was trained using absolute position encoding with the Adam optimizer. Next, we replaced absolute encoding with LieRE while retaining the Adam optimizer. Finally, ENSAM was trained using both LieRE and the Muon optimizer. The results can be found in Fig. 4, and we note that relative position encoding and switching optimizer improve training speed, making the model fit faster to the training data.

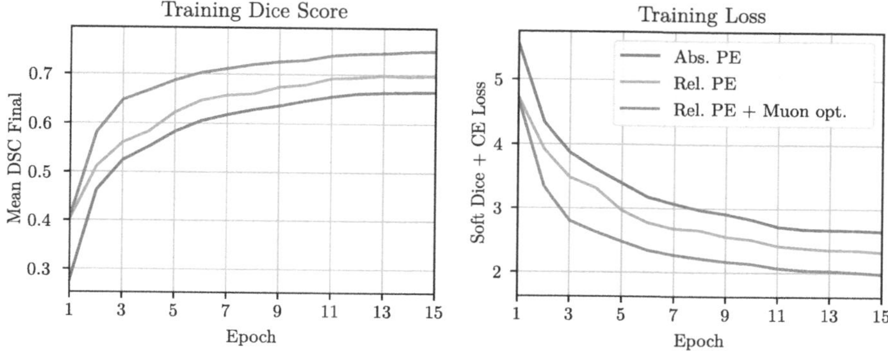

Fig. 4. Three variants of ENSAM trained on the same coreset using the same seed. Relative position encodings improve training efficiency over absolute position encodings. The Muon optimizer further improves upon the relative position encodings. Besides speeding up training, the model trained with Muon also ends up at a better final loss.

4 Results and Discussion

4.1 Quantitative Results on Validation Set

Our proposed model is benchmarked against four previously published interactive segmentation models across all five modalities, and the results are shown in Fig. 3. On all five modalities, either VISTA3D or SegVol obtains the highest score. Among the five modalities, ENSAM is second in ultrasound, third in MRI and microscopy, and fourth in CT.

4.2 Fair Comparison and Reporting Standards

Common pitfalls in evaluating segmentation models include confounding performance boosters, lack of well-configured baselines, insufficient testing data, and inconsistent use of evaluation metrics [14]. In this work, the same evaluation data and metrics are used across all methods, providing a transparent and accurate depiction of each model's performance. That being said, our approach is trained from scratch, only using 10% of the full challenge dataset, without relying on pretrained model weights. Further, our method is trained on a single GPU with 32 GB of VRAM for 6 h as opposed to the baseline methods that were originally trained using 100–1000 times more computational resources. Lastly, we do not ensemble predictions or perform augmentations during evaluation, to ensure performance is not artificially inflated in comparison to the other methods. Thus, any observed performance gains should stem from methodological advancements, and not increased compute budget, training data, or test-time tricks.

Table 3. Quantitative evaluation results on the validation set for the coreset track. The maximum value for DSC AUC and NSD AUC is 4, while the maximum value for DSC Final and NSD Final is 1.

Modality	Method	DSC AUC	NSD AUC	DSC Final	NSD Final
CT	SegVol	2.98	3.12	0.75	0.78
	ENSAM (ours)	2.03	1.90	0.50	0.47
	VISTA3D	2.81	2.84	0.72	0.73
	SAM-Med3D	2.28	2.27	0.57	0.57
MRI	SegVol	2.67	3.15	0.67	0.79
	ENSAM (ours)	1.84	2.07	0.45	0.51
	VISTA3D	2.53	2.82	0.65	0.73
	SAM-Med3D	1.76	1.81	0.45	0.46
Microscopy	SegVol	2.04	3.47	0.51	0.87
	ENSAM (ours)	1.27	1.74	0.34	0.45
	VISTA3D	1.72	2.71	0.45	0.69
	SAM-Med3D	0.30	0.02	0.08	0.00
PET	SegVol	2.97	2.86	0.74	0.71
	ENSAM (ours)	2.16	1.94	0.51	0.45
	VISTA3D	2.39	2.10	0.61	0.54
	SAM-Med3D	2.13	1.82	0.53	0.46
Ultrasound	SegVol	1.24	1.80	0.31	0.45
	ENSAM (ours)	2.10	2.41	0.55	0.62
	VISTA3D	2.60	2.61	0.71	0.72
	SAM-Med3D	1.36	1.81	0.39	0.51

4.3 Qualitative Results on Validation Set

In this section, we provide examples of relatively successful segmentations, as well as interesting failure cases for images in each of the five modalities. For each modality, we compare ENSAMs outputs against the all-data submissions from SAM-Med3D, VISTA3D, and SegVol. Each of which was trained on roughly ten times more annotated volumes than ENSAM.

Figure 5 presents two AbdomenAtlas CT examples: In the first, ENSAM accurately delineates the liver, spleen, and kidneys. In the second, ENSAM over-segments some parts in the left and middle parts of the slice.

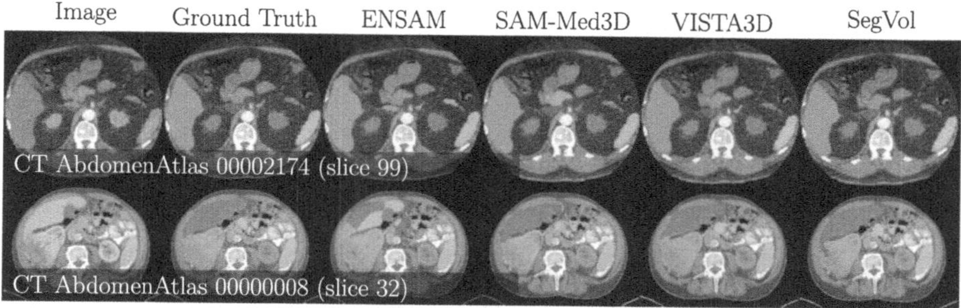

Fig. 5. Top row: Shows an example from the AbdomenAtlas dataset where ENSAM successfully segments the liver, spleen, and kidneys. **Bottom row:** Shows an example from the same dataset where ENSAM oversegments some parts.

Figure 6 presents two MRI slices: a slice from the Spider dataset where ENSAM captures the central vertebral bodies but fails at posterior elements; a slice from the TotalSeg dataset illustrating correct localization of large structures but failure on smaller structures.

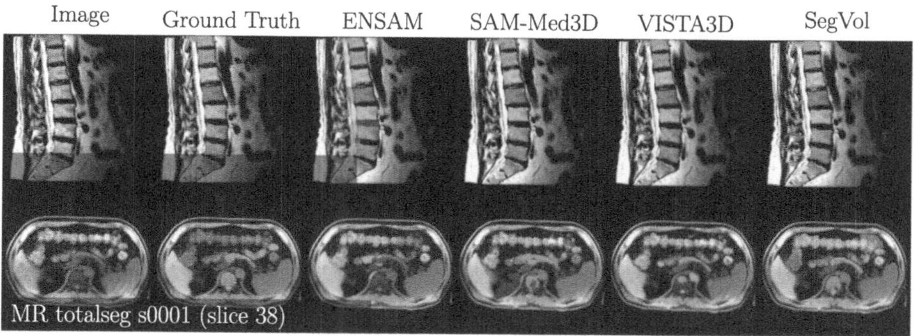

Fig. 6. Top row: Shows an example from the MR Spider dataset, where ENSAM successfully segments the body of the vertebra but then fails to segment the posterior. **Bottom row:** shows an example where ENSAM is relatively successful in segmenting the bottom part, whereas all models fail in segmenting the top part of the slice.

Figure 7 illustrates PET segmentation: both ENSAM and the baseline models provide similar outputs but are often over- or undersegmented, likely due to intensity clipping during preprocessing.

Figure 8 highlights microscopy challenges: first, a slice from a microscopy volume, dense, small regions where some baseline models oversegment the image. Second, a slice with vessels where all models fail to detect thin vasculature. This might reflect the absence of microscopy data in the coreset when training ENSAM (see Sect. 2.5), but also the general ambiguity in segmenting vessels using sparse prompts like single points.

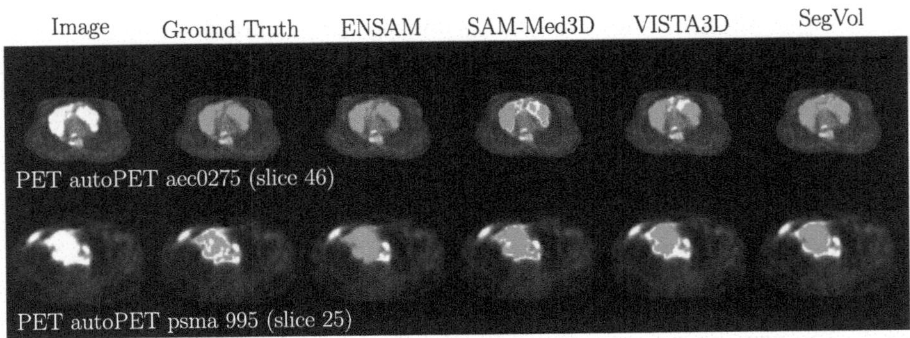

Fig. 7. Top row: Shows a PET image where ENSAM successfully segments high-uptake regions. **Bottom row:** Shows a PET image where ENSAM oversegments a high-uptake region. Due to the preprocessing of the PET images, all values in their neighbourhood are maximally bright, possibly making it difficult for ENSAM to distinguish the borders.

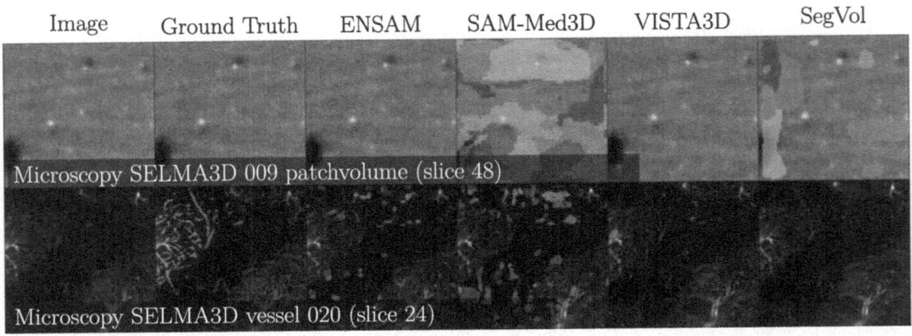

Fig. 8. Top row: Shows an example of a microscopy image where all labelled areas are very small, making it easy to obtain high scores for surface-distance-based metrics. It is hard to visually determine how well the model performs on this slice. In this case, SAM-Med3D and SegVol oversegment the volume. **Bottom row:** Shows an example where all models fail to segment the vessels.

Figure 9 presents two ultrasound frames: The first is a frame from a cardiac 2D+t video where ENSAM outlines the left ventricle and atrium with jagged edges from motion and speckle noise; The second shows a freehand-leg reconstruction slice segmenting three lower-leg muscles with minor boundary artifacts. For this case, SAM-Med3Ds inference code crashed, and the other baseline models severely undersegmented all three muscles.

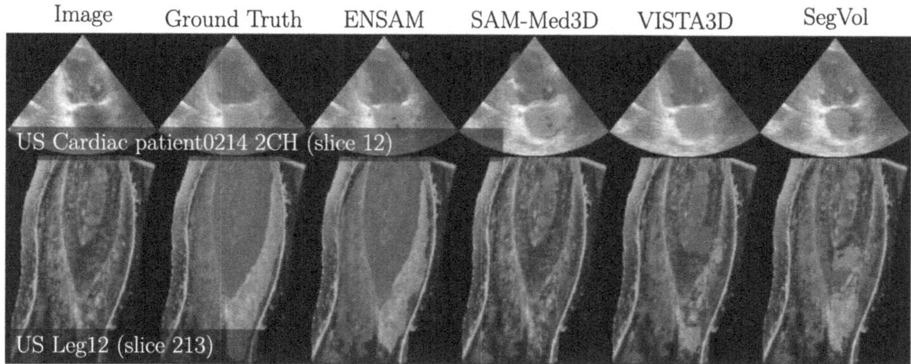

Fig. 9. Top row: Shows a frame in a cardiac ultrasound video, where the left atrial walls, blood volume, and left atrium are annotated. The surface of ENSAM's predictions is not as smooth as the annotations. **Bottom row:** Shows a slice from a 3D volume reconstructed from 2D handheld ultrasound. Three muscles in the lower leg are annotated and segmented relatively successfully by ENSAM. For this case, the inference code provided for SAM-Med3D crashed.

4.4 Results on Final Testing Set

Results for the hidden test set were calculated by challenge participants and baseline contributors submitting Docker containers to the challenge organizers, ensuring fair comparison.

Comparison Against Baseline Models. Qualitative results when compared to previously published baselines are summarized in Table 4. ENSAM outperforms VISTA3D and SAM-MED3D. Across all modalities and metrics, either ENSAM or SegVol performs the best except for CT, where VISTA3D achieves 2.95 NSD AUC. Notably, ENSAM performs better on the hidden test set as compared to the validation set. This likely reflects the uniform sampling strategy used during training: its broad coverage supports generalization to the diverse hidden test set but is less optimal for the unbalanced validation set.

4.5 Unified Analysis of Validation Results

When jointly considering the quantitative and qualitative validation results, several trends emerge. First, the baseline models generally perform strongly on CT and MR, where SegVol and VISTA3D consistently outperform ENSAM in both AUC-based metrics and final DSC/NSD scores (Fig. 3). This reflects the relative advantage of methods trained on larger or more modality-specific datasets; some of the baselines also include the validation set for pretraining.

Second, it is worth noting that the AUC metrics reported in Fig. 3 are not directly visible in the qualitative plots, which only illustrate the final segmentation after the last user interaction. In this final step, ENSAM often produces

Table 4. Quantitative evaluation results on the test set for the coreset track. The maximum value for DSC AUC and NSD AUC is 4, while the maximum value for DSC Final and NSD Final is 1.

Modality	Method	DSC AUC	NSD AUC	DSC Final	NSD Final
CT	SegVol	**2.38**	2.35	0.60	**0.59**
	ENSAM (ours)	2.35	2.05	**0.62**	0.55
	VISTA3D	2.16	**2.95**	0.57	0.52
	SAM-Med3D	2.08	1.71	0.53	0.44
MRI	SegVol	**2.74**	**3.03**	**0.68**	**0.76**
	ENSAM (ours)	2.45	2.52	0.63	0.65
	VISTA3D	2.41	2.51	0.63	0.67
	SAM-Med3D	2.12	2.12	0.54	0.54
Microscopy	SegVol	**2.74**	**3.88**	**0.68**	**0.97**
	ENSAM (ours)	2.57	3.76	0.67	0.94
	VISTA3D	1.84	2.50	0.47	0.63
	SAM-Med3D	0.31	0.03	0.08	0.01
PET	SegVol	**2.78**	**2.30**	**0.70**	**0.57**
	ENSAM (ours)	2.28	1.84	0.56	0.46
	VISTA3D	1.76	1.28	0.45	0.33
	SAM-Med3D	2.31	1.76	0.58	0.45
Ultrasound	SegVol	0.79	1.29	0.20	0.32
	ENSAM (ours)	**1.79**	**2.04**	**0.47**	**0.55**
	VISTA3D	0.76	0.82	0.24	0.31
	SAM-Med3D	0.60	0.40	0.15	0.10

competitive or visually appealing results, particularly in some ultrasound and microscopy cases.

Third, the hidden test set provides additional evidence: ENSAM slightly surpasses all baselines in the final DSC metric after five refinement iterations Table 4. This suggests that ENSAM, although initially trailing, converges to a performance level comparable to state-of-the-art baselines after sufficient user interaction.

Finally, it should be emphasized that the validation set was imbalanced in terms of dataset composition, with many samples drawn from only a few datasets. This imbalance may have biased performance estimates for certain modalities, especially microscopy, and limits the reliability of conclusions drawn solely from validation results.

Comparison Against Other Challenge Participants. Table 5 summarizes the performance of the coreset track participants. Our submission ranked 5th out of 10 teams, placing highest among the participants not leveraging any external pretrained weights.

Table 5. Quantitative evaluation results on the test set for the coreset track. The team names correspond to the names on the official leaderboard. DSC AUC and NSD AUC range from 0 to 4; higher is better.

Team	Initialization	DSC AUC	NSD AUC	DSC Final	NSD Final
aim [10]	EfficientTAM	3.10	3.23	0.80	0.89
norateam [33]	nnInteractive	2.91	2.97	0.75	0.78
yiooo [43]	VISTA3D & SAM-Med3D	2.90	2.90	0.75	0.75
lexor [1]	SegVol	2.50	2.57	0.63	0.64
ahus (ours)	-	2.40	2.27	0.63	0.60
hanglok [15]	VISTA3D	2.12	2.01	0.55	0.53
cemrg [35]	-	1.89	1.62	0.48	0.41
sail [16]	SAM-Med2D	1.65	1.59	0.41	0.40
dtftech [12]	SegVol	1.59	1.08	0.42	0.28
owwwen [21]	SAM-Med3D	0.96	0.50	0.24	0.12

4.6 Limitation and Future Work

Limitations to ENSAM. There are several limitations to our work, both in the training and inference setup, as well as the model architecture.

First, our model was trained under constrained data and computational budgets. Leveraging the full dataset alongside increased computational resources would likely yield improved performance.

Second, while we conducted targeted ablation studies demonstrating that the Muon optimizer outperforms AdamW and that relative positional encoding is preferable to absolute positional encoding, we did not evaluate the impact of normalized attention compared to the standard attention mechanism. Additionally, due to computational constraints, we did not explore variations in model size. It is therefore unlikely that the current architecture is optimal; for instance, increasing the depth of the U-Net may lead to better results.

Third, as noted by Isensee et al. [9], 2D bounding boxes can be preferable to 3D ones even for 3D segmentation tasks, and click-based prompts may convey less information compared to other prompt types. However, as the evaluation protocol for this challenge relies on 3D boxes and clicks, the current version of ENSAM supports only these prompt types.

Fourth, we have not conducted latency evaluations or user studies. To robustly assess the practical utility of interactive segmentation models, simulated user interactions alone are insufficient; real user studies are essential.

Limitations in Evaluation Pipeline. While the test set contains unpublished medical images and annotations providing a fair comparison between models, the validation set includes mostly CT and MR images. In the PET modality, a single dataset is included, and for US, two datasets are used. One of the US datasets comprises 2D+t echocardiographic videos. The microscopy modality includes just eight volumes, several of which contain only a small fraction of labelled voxels. As a result, quantitative conclusions regarding model performance on US, PET, and Microscopy should be interpreted with caution due to limited sample diversity and volume.

In addition, the CT and MR subsets of the validation set are imbalanced in terms of the number of samples taken from each dataset. This imbalance may bias the evaluation and obscure insights into how well the model generalizes across datasets within a modality. A more robust assessment, especially for modalities like CT, could be achieved through a more uniform sampling strategy that considers factors such as the number of labeled instances per dataset.

Lastly, the simulation of user input could be improved, aligning better with the use case of the model. Currently, N interactions are provided between each refinement step, with N being equal to the number of objects of interest in the image. In reality, the user would probably want an updated segmentation after each interaction.

Future Directions. The field is rapidly evolving, and future work should focus on improving multiple areas. Below, we outline promising directions.

5 Conclusion

In this paper, we presented ENSAM, an efficient, promptable model for universal medical image segmentation. With compute restraint and training on a coreset of the challenge data, we achieved a DSC AUC of 2.404, NSD AUC of 2.266, final DSC of 0.627, and final NSD of 0.597. Our results demonstrate that the combination of relative positional encoding and the Muon optimizer significantly improves both model performance and training efficiency. Furthermore, enabling the model to handle variable-shape inputs is critical for reducing computational overhead, particularly VRAM usage, and facilitates inference at resolutions closer to the native input scale.

Disclosure of Interests. The authors have no competing interests to declare that are relevant to the content of this article.

Acknowledgement. We thank all the data owners for making the medical images publicly available and CodaLab [41] for hosting the challenge platform. We also thank Akershus University Hospital for the funding that made this study possible.

References

1. Aher, V., Villa, E.S., Mosquera, L.V.G., Torres, L.F.T., Verma, V.K., Ordóñez, S.A.C.: MobileSeg3D: A Lightweight Framework for Multi-Modality 3D Medical Image Segmentation (Jun 2025). https://openreview.net/forum?id=eqVsBeWMbG
2. Ba, J.L., Kiros, J.R., Hinton, G.E.: Layer normalization (2016). https://arxiv.org/abs/1607.06450
3. Bassi, P.R., et al.: Touchstone benchmark: are we on the right way for evaluating ai algorithms for medical segmentation? Adv. Neural. Inf. Process. Syst. **37**, 15184–15201 (2024)
4. Bernstein, J., Newhouse, L.: Modular duality in deep learning. arXiv preprint arXiv:2410.21265 (2024)
5. Björck, Å., Bowie, C.: An iterative algorithm for computing the best estimate of an orthogonal matrix. SIAM J. Numer. Anal. **8**(2), 358–364 (1971)
6. Brown, T.B., et al.: Language models are few-shot learners. Adv. Neural. Inf. Process. Syst. **33**, 1877–1901 (2020)
7. Devlin, J., Chang, M.W., Lee, K., Toutanova, K.: Bert: Pre-training of deep bidirectional transformers for language understanding. arXiv preprint arXiv:1810.04805 (2018)
8. Du, Y., Bai, F., Huang, T., Zhao, B.: Segvol: Universal and interactive volumetric medical image segmentation. In: Advances in Neural Information Processing Systems, vol. 37, pp. 110746–110783 (2024)
9. Fabian, I., et al.: nninteractive: Redefining 3D promptable segmentation. arXiv preprint arXiv:2503.08373 (2025)
10. Friedetzki, T., Haberzettl, L., Buttman, R., Puppe, F., Krenzer, A.: iMedSTAM: Interactive Segmentation and Tracking Anything in 3D Medical Images and Videos (Jun 2025). https://openreview.net/forum?id=1tsCloFWFT
11. He, Y., et al.: VISTA3D: a unified segmentation foundation model for 3D medical imaging. In: Proceedings of the IEEE/CVF International Conference on Computer Vision and Pattern Recognition (2024)
12. Huang, C., Huang, J., Wang, L.: From Single-Round to Sequential: Building Stateful Interactive Segmentation with SegVol and GRU Corrector (Jun 2025). https://openreview.net/forum?id=45TSSNV3sJ
13. Isensee, F., Jaeger, P.F., Kohl, S.A.A., Petersen, J., Maier-Hein, K.H.: nnU-Net: a self-configuring method for deep learning-based biomedical image segmentation. Nat. Methods **18**(2), 203–211 (2021). https://doi.org/10.1038/s41592-020-01008-z
14. Isensee, F., Wald, T., Ulrich, C., Baumgartner, M., Roy, S., Maier-Hein, K., Jäger, P.F.: nnU-Net Revisited: A Call for Rigorous Validation in 3D Medical Image Segmentation (2024)
15. Ji, J., Lin, T., Xiong, J., Han, T.: Enhancing a 3D Foundation Model with Gaussian Sampling for Interactive Biomedical Image Segmentation (Jun 2025). https://openreview.net/forum?id=CLk0KhDXgm
16. Jo, S., Choi, A., Hong, J.H.: GAMT: A Geometry-Aware, Multi-view, Training-free Segmentation Framework for Foundation Models in Medical Imaging (Jun 2025). https://openreview.net/forum?id=DeeoLKgCVU
17. Jordan, K.: 94 % on cifar-10 in 3.29 seconds on a single gpu. arXiv preprint arXiv:2404.00498 (2024)

18. Jordan, K., Jin, Y., Boza, V., You, J., Cesista, F., Newhouse, L., Bernstein, J.: Muon: an optimizer for hidden layers in neural networks (2024). https://kellerjordan.github.io/posts/muon/
19. Kikinis, R., Pieper, S.D., Vosburgh, K.G.: 3D Slicer: a platform for subject-specific image analysis, visualization, and clinical support, pp. 277–289. Springer (2013)
20. Kirillov, A., et al.: Segment anything. In: Proceedings of the International Conference on Computer Vision, pp. 4015–4026 (2023)
21. Lin, J., zhengdong, Ma, Z., Xiao, Y., Fu, H., Pan, Y.: Enhanced SAM-Med3D: A Robust Solution for 3D Medical Image Segmentation with Advanced Post-processing (Jun 2025). https://openreview.net/forum?id=Y3zTAf99Vr
22. Litjens, G., et al.: A survey on deep learning in medical image analysis. Med. Image Anal. **42**, 60–88 (2017). https://doi.org/10.1016/j.media.2017.07.005
23. Liu, J., et al.: Muon is scalable for LLM training (2025)
24. Loshchilov, I., Hsieh, C.P., Sun, S., Ginsburg, B.: NGPT: Normalized transformer with representation learning on the hypersphere. In: Proceedings of the International Conference on Learning Representations (ICLR) (2025). arXiv:2410.01131 [cs.LG]
25. Ma, J., et al.: Loss odyssey in medical image segmentation. Med. Image Anal. **71**, 102035 (2021)
26. Ma, J., He, Y., Li, F., Han, L., You, C., Wang, B.: Segment anything in medical images. Nat. Commun. **15**, 654 (2024)
27. Ma, J., et al.: Efficient medsams: Segment anything in medical images on laptop. arXiv:2412.16085 (2024)
28. Ma, J., et al.: Medsam2: Segment anything in 3d medical images and videos. arXiv preprint arXiv:2504.03600 (2025)
29. Myronenko, A.: 3D MRI brain tumor segmentation using autoencoder regularization. In: International MICCAI Brainlesion Workshop, pp. 311–320. Springer (2018)
30. Myronenko, A., Siddiquee, M.M.R., Yang, D., He, Y., Xu, D.: Automated head and neck tumor segmentation from 3D pet/ct hecktor 2022 challenge report. In: 3D Head and Neck Tumor Segmentation in PET/CT Challenge, pp. 31–37. Springer (2022)
31. Myronenko, A., Yang, D., He, Y., Xu, D.: Aorta segmentation from 3D CT in MICCAI seg. a. 2023 challenge. In: MICCAI Challenge on Segmentation of the Aorta, pp. 13–18. Springer (2023)
32. Myronenko, A., Yang, D., He, Y., Xu, D.: Automated 3D segmentation of kidneys and tumors in MICCAI kits 2023 challenge. In: International Challenge on Kidney and Kidney Tumor Segmentation, pp. 1–7. Springer (2023)
33. Ndir, T.C., Pfefferle, A., Schirrmeister, R.T.: Dynamic Prompt Generation for Interactive 3D Medical Image Segmentation (Jun 2025). https://openreview.net/forum?id=EnSf2D1blH
34. Ostmeier, S., Axelrod, B., Moseley, M.E., Chaudhari, A., Langlotz, C.: LieRE: Generalizing Rotary Position Encodings (2025). arXiv:2406.10322
35. Qayyum, A., Mazher, M., Niederer, S.: Exploring Foundation Model Adaptations for 3D Medical Imaging: Prompt-Based Segmentation with xLSTM network (Jun 2025). https://openreview.net/forum?id=eMskbK0uSY
36. Radford, A., Wu, J., Child, R., Luan, D., Amodei, D., Sutskever, I.: Language models are unsupervised multitask learners. OpenAI Blog **1**(8) (2019)
37. Ravi, N., et al.: Sam 2: Segment anything in images and videos. In: International Conference on Learning Representations (2025)

38. Su, J., Lu, Y., Pan, S., Murtadha, A., Wen, B., Liu, Y.: RoFormer: Enhanced Transformer with Rotary Position Embedding (2023). arXiv:2104.09864.
39. Touvron, H., et al.: Llama: Open and efficient foundation language models. arXiv preprint arXiv:2302.13971 (2023)
40. Wang, H., et al.: Sam-med3d: Towards general-purpose segmentation models for volumetric medical images. arXiv preprint arXiv:2310.15161 (2024)
41. Xu, Z., et al.: Codabench: Flexible, easy-to-use, and reproducible meta-benchmark platform. Patterns **3**(7), 100543 (2022)
42. Zhang, B., Sennrich, R.: Root mean square layer normalization (2019). https://arxiv.org/abs/1910.07467
43. Zhang, Z., Yu, Y., Xue, Y.: Rethinking RoI Strategy in Interactive 3D Segmentation for Medical Images (Jun 2025). https://openreview.net/forum?id=jospESnUL9

GAMT: A Geometry-Aware, Multi-view, Training-Free Segmentation Framework for Foundation Models in Medical Imaging

Sun Jo[1(✉)], Ahjin Choi[2], and Je Hyeong Hong[1,2]

[1] Department of Artificial Intelligence, Hanyang University, Seoul, Republic of Korea
{choyw5,jhh37}@hanyang.ac.kr

[2] Department of Electronic Engineering, Hanyang University, Seoul, Republic of Korea
caj0328@hanyang.ac.kr

Abstract. Medical image segmentation is a critical task in clinical diagnostics and biomedical research. While deep learning has significantly advanced the field, most existing methods rely on task-specific models that require extensive manual annotations for training or adaptation. Vision foundation models, such as the Segment Anything Model (SAM), offer a promising alternative with their universal segmentation capabilities. However, their application to 3D medical imaging remains limited, especially in zero-shot scenarios involving previously unseen anatomical structures. In this work, we introduce GAMT, a zero-shot, training-free framework that repurposes powerful 2D foundation segmentation models (e.g., SAM, SAM-Med2D) for universal 3D biomedical image segmentation. To bridge the dimensionality gap, GAMT performs slice-wise inference along three orthogonal anatomical planes (axial, coronal, and sagittal) and subsequently fuses the predictions to construct a coherent 3D segmentation mask. Crucially, without any model training or fine-tuning, this framework achieves average Dice Similarity Coefficient (DSC) and Normalized Surface Dice (NSD) scores of 0.487 and 0.477, respectively-without requiring model training or fine-tuning. Our code and results are publicly available at https://github.com/SpatialAILab/GAMT.

Keywords: Medical image segmentation · foundation-model · training-free

1 Introduction

Medical image segmentation is a fundamental task in clinical workflows, supporting critical applications such as anatomical structure identification, pathology localization, treatment planning, and longitudinal disease monitoring. Accurate segmentation enables clinicians to extract quantitative biomarkers and visualize

J. Ma et al. (Eds.): MedSegFM 2025, LNCS 16447, pp. 36–50, 2026.
https://doi.org/10.1007/978-3-032-23496-4_3

target regions with high precision. Traditionally, models such as nnUNet [4] have been widely adopted for 3D medical image segmentation due to their strong performance across various datasets. However, these specialist segmentation models are usually heavily task-specific, often rely on supervised learning with large, annotated datasets, which are difficult to acquire in the medical domain and they can only segment the data from the same domain as the training set. Recently, the emergence of vision foundation models (VFMs), such as the Segment Anything Model (SAM [7]), has introduced a new paradigm of universal, prompt-driven segmentation. Leveraging such models for medical imaging offers an opportunity to reduce annotation costs and eliminate task-specific training. However, it still encounters some challenges in practical applications direct application to medical images, particularly volumetric (3D) data, remains challenging. Most VFMs are designed for 2D images, lack geometric understanding of 3D anatomy, and require significant adaptation efforts to perform reliably in the medical domain.

Initial efforts to bridge this gap, such as MedSAM [8] and MedSAM2 [10], have adapted VFMs to the medical domain by fine-tuning them on curated 2D and 3D medical datasets respectively. While improving performance on specific tasks, these methods sacrifice the zero-shot generalization ability of the original models by re-introducing training requirements. More recent works have focused on interactive 3D segmentation; for instance, SAM-Med3D [11] and SegVol [2] employ prompt propagation strategies to extend 2D inference across volumetric slices. s. Similarly, VISTA3D [5] and nnInteractive [3] explore multi-view consistency and 3D-aware attention mechanisms to improve segmentation robustness without requiring full supervision. Despite these innovations, they often still depend on partial training, exhibit limited 3D consistency, or incur substantial computational overhead, restricting their utility in truly zero-shot, training-free clinical scenarios where models must robustly segment novel structures unseen during development.

In this context, the "CVPR 2025 Foundation Models for Interactive 3D Biomedical Image Segmentation Challenge" presents the first large-scale benchmark for evaluating foundation models in interactive 3D medical image segmentation. The competition provides over 200,000 3D imagemask pairs across diverse anatomical structures and imaging modalities. Participants are required to develop interaction-efficient segmentation frameworks that can iteratively refine predictions based on user prompts (points).

This challenge emphasizes three core aspects: (1) enabling interactivity in 3D segmentation using foundation models, (2) handling diverse biomedical image types (CT, MRI, PET, Microscopy and Ultrasound) with high-quality annotations, and (3) jointly optimizing segmentation accuracy and computational efficiency. The top-performing algorithms will also be considered for integration into 3D Slicer to promote clinical usability and annotation efficiency in real-world scenarios.

Despite recent advances, foundation models for medical segmentation still face two critical hurdles for practical deployment: the reliance on costly training or fine-tuning, and the geometric inconsistencies arising from single-view (e.g., axial) inference on inherently 3D data. These challenges hinder their application in zero-shot clinical settings where adaptability and accuracy are paramount.

To overcome these limitations, we introduce **GAMT**—a **G**eometry-**A**ware, **M**ulti-view, **T**raining-free segmentation framework designed for 3D biomedical image segmentation using 2D foundation models. Our key motivation is to fully exploit the generalization ability of pre-trained models like SAM [7] and SAM-Med2D [1] without requiring any model updates, while enhancing 3D spatial consistency through geometry-aware propagation and fusion.

GAMT is composed of the following core components:

- **Three-view Prompt Inference:** We perform slice-wise inference using point and box prompts along the *axial*, *coronal*, and *sagittal* directions. Each view provides complementary spatial information that helps overcome the limitations of single-plane inference.
- **Prompt Propagation Strategy:** To ensure intra-view consistency, we implement a sequential prompt refinement mechanism that propagates segmentation guidance from one slice to the next using distance-based keypoint selection and clustering strategies.
- **Geometry-aware 3D Fusion:** After multi-view inference, the resulting masks are aggregated via a voting-based fusion strategy followed by lightweight 3D post-processing (connected component filtering and smoothing) to generate a clean and anatomically consistent 3D prediction.
- **Training-free and Model-agnostic Design:** Our method is entirely training-free and agnostic to the foundation model backbone, making it universally applicable to any SAM-compatible model.

We evaluate GAMT on the "CVPR 2025 Foundation Models for Interactive 3D Biomedical Image Segmentation Challenge" dataset, achieving competitive Dice Similarity Coefficient (DSC) and Normalized Surface Dice (NSD) across multiple anatomical structures **without any model retraining or fine-tuning**.

Our main contributions can be summarized as follows:

- We propose **GAMT**, a universal training-free framework for 3D medical image segmentation using 2D foundation models.
- We design a multi-view prompting and fusion strategy that improves geometric consistency and volumetric coverage.
- We demonstrate the effectiveness of GAMT across diverse anatomical targets, achieving competitive accuracy with minimal computational cost.

2 Method

2.1 Preprocessing

We follow a preprocessing strategy similar to SAM-Med3D [11], tailored for training-free inference with 2D foundation models on 3D volumes. Our preprocessing pipeline commences by normalizing voxel intensities via percentile-based range adjustment over the non-background foreground region. The voxel grid is then reconstructed to reflect its true physical scale by applying the provided spacing keys. This process ensures that each axis is metrically accurate and represents the original anatomical dimensions. A key step for efficiency is foreground-centered cropping, where we extract a region of interest around the target anatomy (default: 256 256 256) to significantly reduce the computational domain. From this processed 3D volume, we generate 2D slices along three orthogonal views (axial, coronal, and sagittal) to capture complementary spatial features. Finally, all geometric transformations, such as cropping coordinates and spacing, are meticulously tracked to enable accurate mapping of the 2D predictions back to the original 3D space.

This preprocessing pipeline enables efficient and anatomically faithful slice-wise segmentation using 2D SAM-based foundation models, while preserving geometric consistency and reducing computational burden.

2.2 Proposed Method

We propose **GAMT**—a **G**eometry-**A**ware, **M**ulti-view, **T**raining-free segmentation framework for 3D medical image segmentation. Our method utilizes 2D foundation models in a prompt-guided, slice-wise fashion across three anatomical planes: axial, coronal, and sagittal. The GAMT architecture is illustrated in Fig. 1 and the inference pipeline is summarized in Fig. 2.

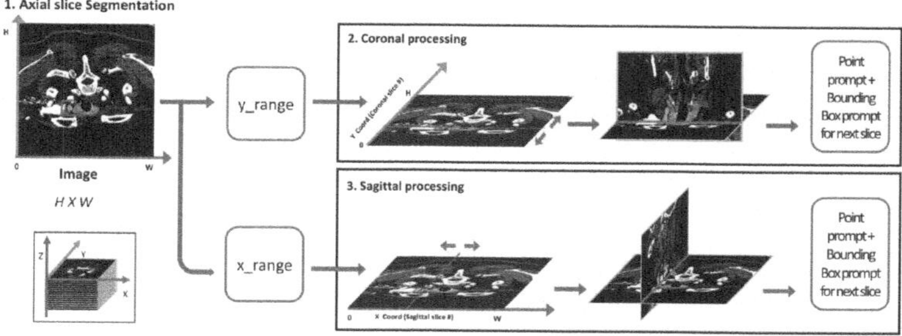

Fig. 1. Overview of the GAMT Multi-View Inference and Propagation Strategy.

GAMT: Multi-view Inference and Propagation Strategy. Our core mechanism for achieving robust 3D segmentation is a multi-view inference and propagation strategy, which is depicted in Fig. 1. This strategy ensures 3D consistency by dynamically generating and refining prompts while propagating information across and within three orthogonal planes.

1. Primary Axis (Axial) Segmentation and Range Determination. The process is initiated on a primary axial slice using an initial bounding box. Once the segmentation mask for this slice is generated, it serves as a spatial reference for the other views. To determine the relevant processing scope, we analyze the mask's projection onto the Y and X axes. Specifically, we compute the sum of segmented pixels along each axis and identify a threshold corresponding to a high percentile (e.g., the 90th percentile) of these sums. The ranges of coordinates that exceed this threshold are then designated as the regions of interest for processing in the coronal and sagittal views, respectively. This data-driven approach ensures that subsequent processing is focused only on slices containing significant portions of the target anatomy.

2. Orthogonal View Processing and Intra-view Propagation. Next, the framework performs segmentation on the two orthogonal views, guided by the ranges determined in the previous step. A key to our method is the intra-view prompt propagation mechanism employed within both the coronal and sagittal passes.
Coronal and Sagittal Processing: The y_range guides the selection of coronal slices for processing. For each selected slice, the framework performs segmentation. The novelty lies in how the output of one slice informs the next.
Automatic Prompt Refinement: For each segmented 2D slice within a given view (e.g., coronal), we generate a new set of refined prompts to guide the segmentation of the subsequent slice. This involves two steps:

- **Bounding Box Update:** A new, tight-fitting bounding box is extracted directly from the current slice's segmentation mask. This allows the prompt to adapt to the changing cross-section of the anatomy.
- **Internal Point Prompt Generation:** To enhance robustness, a new positive point prompt is automatically determined. We first apply a distance transform to the mask to identify pixels farthest from the boundary, which typically correspond to the object's core. We then analyze the intensity distribution of the original image within this core region. Finally, a point with both a high distance transform value and a representative intensity is selected as the new point prompt. This dual-criteria approach ensures the point remains stable and centered within the target structure.

An analogous process, guided by the x_range, is performed independently in the sagittal view. By continuously refining and propagating prompts within each view, our method robustly tracks the anatomical structure slice-by-slice.

3. Volumetric Consistency Across Views. This entire multi-view propagation strategy allows GAMT to leverage complementary geometric information, correct errors from a single-view perspective, and maintain volumetric coherence throughout the segmentation process.

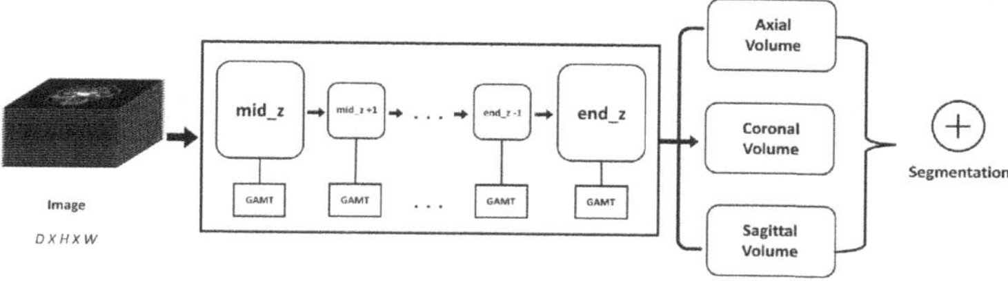

Fig. 2. The End-to-End Inference Pipeline of GAMT

The End-to-End Inference Pipeline of the GAMT Framework. Figure 2 provides a high-level schematic of our entire inference process. Given a 3D input volume (DHW) as input, our framework processes it sequentially along a primary axis. (Slice-wise Propagation) Starting from a central anchor slice (mid_z), the core GAMT module is applied iteratively to each subsequent slice until the end of the target region (end_z). As detailed in Fig. 1, this GAMT module performs its own internal multi-view analysis at each step. This iterative process results in the generation of three distinct volumetric masks, one for each orthogonal plane (Axial, Coronal, and Sagittal). Finally, these three volumes are aggregated and fused to produce the single, coherent final segmentation.

2.3 Post-processing

After multi-view segmentation is completed and fused, we perform a series of post-processing steps to restore the segmentation mask to its original coordinate space and improve anatomical consistency. This includes uncropping, resampling, and 3D volume refinement.

Uncropping. As the inference is performed on cropped regions-of-interest (ROIs), the predicted mask is first uncropped back to the original image size. The offset and crop dimensions used during preprocessing are stored in data keys and used to accurately reposition the predicted region within the full 3D volume.

Resampling to Original Spacing. To align the output with the original input file, the processed segmentation mask is resized back to the original image's raw array dimensions. This inverse-resampling step is performed using nearest-neighbor interpolation, ensuring a direct voxel-to-voxel correspondence between the final mask and the initial, unprocessed data grid.

Smoothing and Connected Component Filtering. To remove noise and non-anatomical artifacts, we apply connected component analysis in 3D. Only the largest component is preserved per structure. Optionally, morphological operations such as binary opening or closing are used to smooth rough mask boundaries and reduce voxel-level artifacts introduced during fusion.

This lightweight post-processing pipeline ensures that the final segmentation results are anatomically clean, spatially accurate, and suitable for downstream medical analysis or evaluation.

3 Experiments

3.1 Dataset and Evaluation Metrics

The development set is an extension of the CVPR 2024 MedSAM on Laptop Challenge [9], including more 3D cases from public datasets[1] and covering commonly used 3D modalities, such as Computed Tomography (CT), Magnetic Resonance Imaging (MRI), Positron Emission Tomography (PET), Ultrasound, and Microscopy images. The hidden testing set is created by a community effort where all the cases are unpublished. The annotations are either provided by the data contributors or annotated by the challenge organizer with 3D Slicer [6] and MedSAM2 [10]. In addition to using all training cases, the challenge contains a coreset track, where participants can select 10% of the total training cases for model development.

For each iterative segmentation, the evaluation metrics include Dice Similarity Coefficient (DSC) and Normalized Surface Distance (NSD) to evaluate the segmentation region overlap and boundary distance, respectively. The final metrics used for the ranking are:

- DSC_AUC and NSD_AUC Scores: AUC (Area Under the Curve) for DSC and NSD is used to measure cumulative improvement with interactions. The AUC quantifies the cumulative performance improvement over the five click predictions, providing a holistic view of the segmentation refinement process. It is computed only over the click predictions without considering the initial bounding box prediction as it is optional.
- Final DSC and NSD Scores after all refinements, indicating the model's final segmentation performance.

In addition, the algorithm runtime will be limited to 90 s per class. Exceeding this limit will lead to all DSC and NSD metrics being set to 0 for that test case.

3.2 Implementation Details

Environment Settings. The development environments and requirements are presented in Table 1.

[1] A complete list is available at https://medsam-datasetlist.github.io/.

Table 1. Development environments and requirements.

System	Ubuntu 20.04.6 LTS
CPU	AMD Ryzen 9 5900X 12-Core Processor
RAM	332GB; 3.2MT/s (DDR4-3200)
GPU (number and type)	One NVIDIA GeForce RTX 3090 Ti 16G
CUDA version	10.1
Programming language	Python 3.10.8
Deep learning framework	e.g., torch 1.13.1, torchvision 0.14.1

Inference Configuration. The challenge is structured into two distinct tracks: one utilizing the complete training set and another using a 10% coreset. As our proposed framework, GAMT, is entirely training-free, this distinction did not pertain to model training. Instead, we adapted our inference strategy and choice of foundation model for each track to adhere to the competition's computational time limits.

For the complete training set track, which involves processing a larger number of test cases, we employed a streamlined, single-view inference strategy using only the primary axial view. The foundation model backbone for this track was the pre-trained SAM with a ViT-L encoder. For the 10% coreset track, we performed inference on both the axial and coronal planes and fused the results, utilizing the pre-trained SAM-Med2D model with a ViT-B encoder. Furthermore, to ensure compliance with the challenge's computational time limit of 90 s per class, we limited the interactive refinement process to a single iteration for all cases in both tracks.

4 Results and Discussion

4.1 Quantitative Results on Validation Set

We present the quantitative evaluation of our GAMT framework on the validation set, with results analyzed separately for the all-data and coreset tracks as shown in Table 3 and Table 2, respectively. Our approach establishes a strong performance baseline for fully training-free, zero-shot 3D segmentation.

On the all-data track, where GAMT employed a streamlined single-view (axial-only) strategy with a SAM ViT-L backbone, the framework demonstrated its capability as a robust generalist model. As shown in Table 3, GAMT achieved its most competitive results in the Microscopy modality, recording a Final NSD of 0.5223. In other modalities like CT and MRI, it provided foundational performance with Final NSD scores of 0.4267 and 0.5223, respectively. However, the single-view approach showed clear limitations on Ultrasound data (Final NSD 0.3000), indicating that this modality may require more complex spatial information for accurate segmentation.

Table 2. Quantitative evaluation results of the validation set on the **coreset track**.

Modality	Methods	DSC AUC	NSD AUC	DSC Final	NSD Final
CT	SAM-Med3D	2.08012	1.7132	0.5311	0.4385
	VISTA3D	2.1644	1.9529	0.5682	0.5181
	SegVol	2.3843	2.3523	0.5961	0.5881
	dtftech	1.5793	0.8804	0.4213	0.2379
	norateam	2.8719	2.7858	0.7462	0.7290
	lexor	2.3141	2.1750	0.5785	0.5437
	owwwen	1.0046	0.4686	0.2510	0.1170
	ahus	2.3488	2.0517	0.6215	0.5518
	hanglok	2.1366	1.8805	0.5593	0.4985
	cemrg	1.9913	1.6055	0.5055	0.4082
	aim	3.0628	3.0652	0.7907	0.7966
	yiooo	2.8254	2.6523	0.7267	0.6851
	GAMT	1.3339	1.0638	0.3337	0.2665
MRI	SAM-Med3D	2.1169	2.1185	0.5355	0.5371
	VISTA3D	2.4102	2.5065	0.6327	0.6690
	SegVol	2.7383	3.0322	0.6846	0.7581
	dtftech	1.5338	1.2202	0.39342	0.3138
	norateam	3.0921	3.3433	0.7938	0.8608
	lexor	2.7082	2.9463	0.6771	0.7366
	owwwen	0.9580	0.5467	0.2389	0.1361
	ahus	2.4503	2.5190	0.6257	0.6462
	hanglok	2.2583	2.3197	0.5802	0.6048
	cemrg	1.8145	1.6895	0.4551	0.4238
	aim	3.2233	3.5378	0.8292	0.9101
	yiooo	3.0569	3.3125	0.7819	0.8487
	GAMT	1.9798	2.1028	0.4948	0.5256
Microscopy	SAM-Med3D	0.3123	0.0311	0.0781	0.0078
	VISTA3D	1.8416	2.5043	0.4701	0.6285
	SegVol	2.7359	2.9716	0.4211	0.7429
	dtftech	0.1596	0	0.0399	0
	norateam	3.3361	3.9719	0.8477	0.9952
	lexor	2.7166	3.9274	0.6792	0.9818
	owwwen	0.0391	0	0.0095	0
	ahus	2.5669	3.7553	0.6716	0.9410
	hanglok	2.0295	2.9441	0.5162	0.7463
	cemrg	0.2024	0	0.0506	0
	aim	2.9608	3.9324	0.7884	0.9885
	yiooo	3.1926	3.9722	0.8092	0.9943
	GAMT	2.3888	3.6765	0.5972	0.9191
PET	SAM-Med3D	2.3133	1.7599	0.5826	0.4465
	VISTA3D	1.7576	1.2811	0.4539	0.3332
	SegVol	2.7847	2.2974	0.6962	0.5744
	dtftech	1.2418	0.5863	0.3115	0.1478
	norateam	3.2011	2.8788	0.8051	0.7265
	lexor	2.5867	2.1837	0.6467	0.5459
	owwwen	0.2141	0.0169	0.0534	0.0042
	ahus	2.2783	1.8356	0.5614	0.4565
	hanglok	1.7187	1.3204	0.4280	0.3262
	cemrg	1.4056	0.9028	0.3545	0.2272
	aim	2.8622	2.4589	0.7665	0.6758
	yiooo	3.0282	2.6575	0.7730	0.6907
	GAMT	2.0661	1.6516	0.5165	0.4129
Ultrasound	SAM-Med3D	0.6009	0.4005	0.1502	0.1001
	VISTA3D	0.7571	0.8212	0.2378	0.3116
	SegVol	0.7931	1.2851	0.1983	0.3213
	dtftech	0.8601	0.8974	0.2150	0.2243
	norateam	1.8486	2.4444	0.5294	0.7211
	lexor	0.9981	1.4705	0.2495	0.3676
	owwwen	0.1718	0.0676	0.0425	0.0152
	ahus	1.7853	2.0378	0.4744	0.5462
	hanglok	0.6887	0.6216	0.2015	0.2214
	cemrg	0.4107	0.2575	0.1027	0.0644
	aim	1.8219	2.5373	0.5100	0.7335
	yiooo	1.5276	1.9049	0.4500	0.5894
	GAMT	0.7624	1.1207	0.1879	0.2717

Table 3. Quantitative evaluation results of the validation set on the **all-data track**.

Modality	Methods	DSC AUC	NSD AUC	DSC Final	NSD Final
CT	SAM-Med3D	2.1944	1.7887	0.5711	0.4681
	VISTA3D	2.3141	2.1127	0.6090	0.5595
	SegVol	2.5460	2.5083	0.6365	0.6271
	nnInteractive	3.2866	3.3022	0.8544	0.8715
	sjtu-426lab	2.4208	2.3965	0.6075	0.6010
	medibot	0.3860	0.4950	0.0965	0.1238
	yiooo	2.9036	2.7596	0.7467	0.7163
	hanglok	2.3997	2.1338	0.6402	0.5769
	aim	3.0839	3.0893	0.7923	0.798
	norateam-post	2.9293	2.8275	0.7611	0.7442
	GAMT	1.9837	1.7068	0.4959	0.4267
MRI	SAM-Med3D	2.1064	2.0427	0.5317	0.5169
	VISTA3D	2.4891	2.5825	0.6516	0.6859
	SegVol	2.8377	3.1261	0.7094	0.7815
	nnInteractive	3.3866	3.6611	0.868	0.9416
	sjtu-426lab	2.7898	3.0283	0.6984	0.7576
	medibot	0.1855	0.2108	0.0464	0.0527
	yiooo	3.1327	3.4052	0.8022	0.8730
	hanglok	2.5103	2.6376	0.6577	0.7028
	aim	3.2461	3.5557	0.8330	0.9122
	norateam-post	3.1851	3.4206	0.8185	0.8840
	GAMT	1.9325	2.0894	0.4831	0.5223
Microscopy	SAM-Med3D	0.3115	0.1726	0.0778	0.0431
	VISTA3D	2.4526	3.4035	0.6231	0.8528
	SegVol	2.9603	3.9472	0.7401	0.9868
	nnInteractive	3.4580	3.9895	0.8743	0.9980
	sjtu-426lab	3.0123	3.9737	0.7551	0.9942
	medibot	0	0	0	0
	yiooo	3.3095	3.9834	0.8358	0.9963
	hanglok	2.5402	3.5510	0.6394	0.8885
	aim	2.9065	3.9004	0.7728	0.9827
	norateam-post	3.2576	3.9844	0.8245	0.9970
	GAMT	2.4533	3.65	0.6133	0.9125
PET	SAM-Med3D	1.3004	0.7297	0.3285	0.1844
	VISTA3D	1.8687	1.3919	0.4688	0.3523
	SegVol	2.9844	2.5108	0.7461	0.6277
	nnInteractive	3.2230	3.0753	0.8170	0.7854
	sjtu-426lab	2.9323	2.4794	0.7329	0.6202
	medibot	0.3348	0.2756	0.0837	0.0689
	yiooo	3.1477	2.8841	0.7989	0.7459
	hanglok	2.1940	1.6764	0.5435	0.4144
	aim	2.9534	2.5813	0.7833	0.6976
	norateam-post	3.2047	2.8555	0.8044	0.7193
	GAMT	1.6334	1.618	0.4083	0.4045
Ultrasound	SAM-Med3D	0.8313	0.7004	0.2078	0.1751
	VISTA3D	0.9072	1.2257	0.2953	0.4789
	SegVol	0.9429	1.4435	0.2357	0.3609
	nnInteractive	2.4088	3.0407	0.7073	0.8886
	sjtu-426lab	0.9949	1.5788	0.2652	0.4112
	medibot	0	0	0	0
	yiooo	1.7710	2.2812	0.5144	0.6767
	hanglok	0.9547	1.2725	0.3159	0.4828
	aim	1.7900	2.4898	0.5102	0.7182
	norateam-post	1.9695	2.5812	0.5711	0.7809
	GAMT	0.8886	1.1999	0.2221	0.3000

For the coreset track, we utilized a more computationally intensive dual-view (axial and coronal) approach with the domain-adapted SAM-Med2D backbone. The quantitative results in Table 2 provide a valuable benchmark for this zero-shot, multi-view strategy. In this setting, GAMT achieved Final NSD scores of 0.2665 on CT, 0.5256 on MRI, and 0.2717 on Ultrasound data. While these results did not consistently surpass those of specialized or training-based methods like nnInteractive, they underscore the performance that can be achieved without any training or fine-tuning on the target dataset. This highlights both the potential and the current limitations of a purely off-the-shelf, multi-view fusion approach.

4.2 Qualitative Results on Validation Set

Figure 3 contains examples of good segmentation results on CT LungMask, MR Chaos, PET autoPET and MR_ISLES2022 data. The corresponding DSC and NSD scores were 97.13% and 86.42% for CT LungMask, 84.56% and 82.33% for MR Chaos, 83.44% and 56.18% for PET autoPET, and 84.56% and 100% for MR_ISLES2022. Figure 4 depicts examples with bad segmentation results. The observed failure cases in segmentation can be primarily attributed to the method's fundamental limitationits high dependency on the type and quality of the initial prompt. We provide a comprehensive analysis of this limitation in Sect. 4.4.

4.3 Results on Final Testing Set

In the challenge, the **sail** team submitted models for both the **all-data** and **coreset** tracks. The detailed rankings and evaluation metrics for each track are summarized in Table 4 for the all-data track and Table 5 for the coreset track. In the **all-data** track, the model achieved a DSC_AUC of 1.950, NSD_AUC of 1.907, DSC_Final of 0.487, and NSD_Final of 0.477, ranking **5**th overall. In the more data-constrained **coreset** track, the performance dropped as expected, with a DSC_AUC of 1.654, NSD_AUC of 1.593, DSC_Final of 0.413, and NSD_Final of 0.398, placing the team at **8**th.

Table 4. Testing results on **all-data track**

Rank	Team	DSC_AUC	NSD_AUC	DSC_Final	NSD_Final
1	aim_alldata	3.129	3.258	0.805	0.842
2	yiooo_alldata	2.981	3.009	0.767	0.779
3	sjtu-426lab_alldata	2.552	2.645	0.640	0.664
4	hanglok_alldata	2.372	2.296	0.632	0.624
5	sail_alldata (Ours)	1.950	1.907	0.487	0.477
6	medibot_alldata	0.098	0.109	0.025	0.027

4.4 Limitation and Future Work

Limitations. The primary limitation of GAMT is its high dependency on the type and quality of the initial prompt. Our method's propagation architecture is fundamentally designed to commence from a well-defined spatial region provided by an initial bounding box on a central anchor slice (mid_ z). Consequently, the

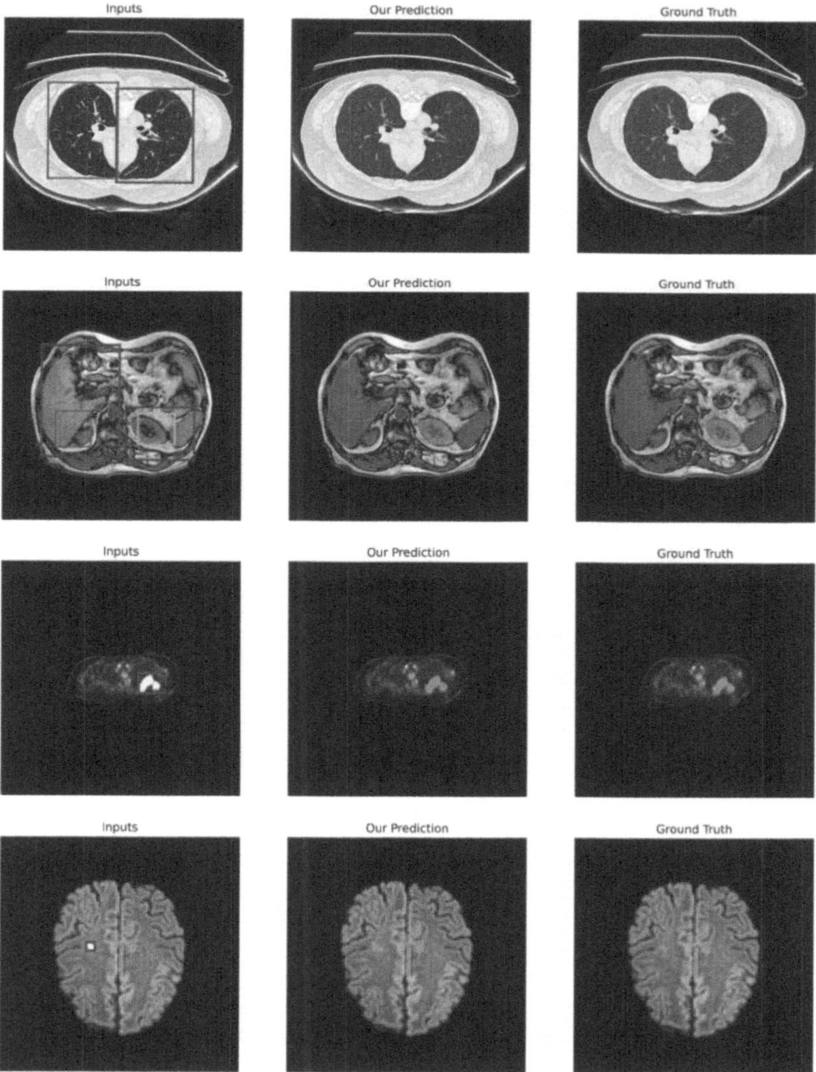

Fig. 3. Examples of Good Segmentation Results: The first row contains a CT Lung-Mask data, the second row is a MR Chaos data, the third row is PET autoPET data and the last row is a MR_ISLES2022 data.

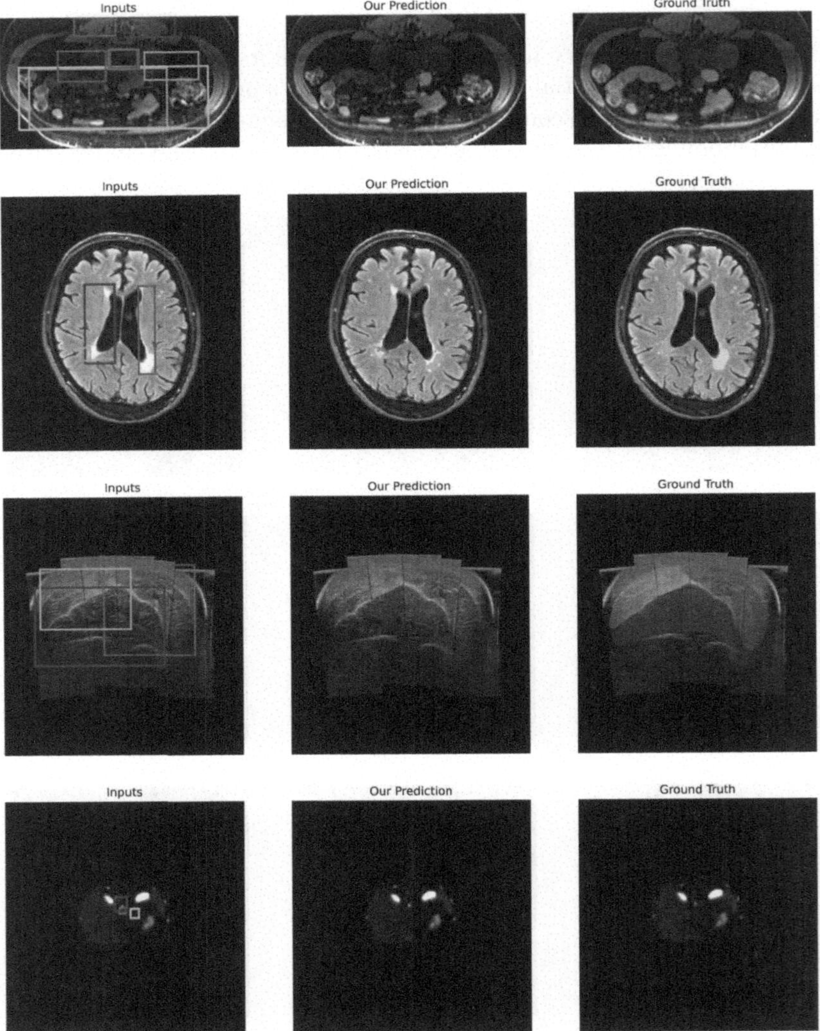

Fig. 4. Examples of Bad Segmentation Results: The first row contains a MR_totalseg data, the second row is an MR_WMH_FLAIR_Singapore data, the third row is US_Low-limb-Leg35 data and the last row is a PET_autoPET data.

quality of the entire 3D segmentation is highly contingent on this initial box prompt. If the initial box fails to capture the target structure accurately, these errors can propagate throughout the volume, leading to a suboptimal segmentation. This design choice leads to a significant performance degradation in scenarios where the initial prompt is not a bounding box. For instance, in cases such as vessel segmentation where only point prompt is provided initially, our frame-

Table 5. Testing results on **coreset-data track**

Rank	Team	DSC_AUC	NSD_AUC	DSC_Final	NSD_Final
1	aim_coreset	3.104	3.232	0.801	0.838
2	norateam_coreset	2.911	2.970	0.754	0.775
3	yiooo_coreset	2.896	2.898	0.745	0.749
4	lexor_coreset	2.501	2.572	0.625	0.643
5	ahus_coreset	2.404	2.266	0.627	0.597
6	hanglok_coreset	2.120	2.012	0.553	0.533
7	cemrg_coreset	1.885	1.624	0.476	0.410
8	sail_coreset (Ours)	1.654	1.593	0.413	0.398
9	dtftech_coreset	1.591	1.079	0.417	0.284
10	owwwen_coreset	0.956	0.496	0.239	0.124

work struggles to establish a stable starting region for propagation. The current implementation lacks a robust mechanism to translate a sparse point prompt into a reliable initial segmentation mask, making it ill-suited for such use cases without modification. Furthermore, the performance can degrade in scenarios with low contrast, where the intensity distribution of the target anatomy is not clearly distinguishable from the surrounding background tissue. This is because our internal point prompt generation mechanism for slice-to-slice propagation relies on intensity profiles to identify the core of the structure.

Future Work. Building on the strengths of our training-free, generalist approach, our future work will focus on extending GAMT's application to anatomies that are notoriously difficult for traditional supervised models. A primary area of investigation will be the segmentation of highly complex and variable structures, such as vasculature (vessels). These structures often suffer from a lack of large, annotated training datasets and exhibit significant morphological variations between patients, making them ideal candidates for a zero-shot framework like GAMT. We plan to leverage our method's ability to operate without prior training to provide robust segmentation for these novel structures, thereby addressing a significant challenge in medical imaging analysis.

5 Conclusion

In this work, we present GAMT, a novel, training-free framework designed to adapt powerful, pre-trained 2D foundation models for 3D biomedical image segmentation. Our method introduces a multi-view propagation strategy, performing slice-by-slice inference along orthogonal axial and coronal planes. The core of our approach is an automatic prompt refinement mechanism that ensures spatial consistency by dynamically updating bounding box and point prompts between adjacent slices. By fusing the segmentation results from these complementary views, GAMT achieves competitive segmentation accuracy on a diverse range of anatomical structures. Most notably, these results are obtained without any task-specific training or fine-tuning, demonstrating a practical and efficient path toward leveraging foundation models in zero-shot clinical settings. We have made our code and results publicly available on GitHub to encourage further research and collaboration within the community.

Disclosure of Interests. The authors have no competing interests to declare that are relevant to the content of this article.

Acknowledgement. We thank all the data owners for making the medical images publicly available and CodaLab [12] for hosting the challenge platform. This study was funded by X (grant number X).

References

1. Cheng, J., et al.: Sam-med2d. arXiv preprint arXiv:2308.16184 (2023)
2. Du, Y., Bai, F., Huang, T., Zhao, B.: Segvol: Universal and interactive volumetric medical image segmentation. In: Advances in Neural Information Processing Systems, vol. 37, pp. 110746–110783 (2024)
3. Fabian, I., et al.: nninteractive: Redefining 3D promptable segmentation. arXiv preprint arXiv:2503.08373 (2025)
4. Fabian, I., Paul, J., Simon, K., Jens, P., Klaus, M.H.: nnu-net: a self-configuring method for deep learning-based biomedical image segmentation. Nat. Methods **18**, 203–211 (2021)
5. He, Y., et al.: VISTA3D: A unified segmentation foundation model for 3D medical imaging. In: Proceedings of the IEEE/CVF International Conference on Computer Vision and Pattern Recognition (2024)
6. Kikinis, R., Pieper, S.D., Vosburgh, K.G.: 3D Slicer: a platform for subject-specific image analysis, visualization, and clinical support, pp. 277–289. Springer (2013)
7. Kirillov, A., et al.: Segment anything. In: Proceedings of the International Conference on Computer Vision, pp. 4015–4026 (2023)
8. Ma, J., et al.: Segment anything in medical images. Nat. Commun. **15**, 654 (2024)
9. Ma, J., et al.: Efficient medsams: Segment anything in medical images on laptop. arXiv:2412.16085 (2024)
10. Ma, J., et al.: Medsam2: Segment anything in 3d medical images and videos. arXiv preprint arXiv:2504.03600 (2025)
11. Wang, H., et al.: Sam-med3d: Towards general-purpose segmentation models for volumetric medical images. arXiv preprint arXiv:2310.15161 (2024)
12. Xu, Z., et al.: Codabench: Flexible, easy-to-use, and reproducible meta-benchmark platform. Patterns **3**(7), 100543 (2022)

Five Models for Five Modalities: Open-Vocabulary Segmentation in Medical Imaging

Lavsen Dahal(✉), Yubraj Bhandari, W. Paul Segars, and Joseph Y. Lo

Center for Virtual Imaging Trials, Department of Radiology, Duke University, Durham, NC, USA
lavsen.dahal@duke.edu

Abstract. We present a multimodal approach to open-vocabulary segmentation in medical imaging by training five modality-specific models using a unified architecture based on the SAT model. Each model is tailored to a specific imaging modality—CT, MRI, Ultrasound, Microscopy, and PET, while maintaining architectural consistency to ensure comparability and generalizability. To address the challenge of limited data availability, particularly in modalities like Ultrasound and Microscopy, we implement distinct sampling strategies designed to maximize anatomical and pathological diversity across training cases. We aim to evaluate the effectiveness of open-vocabulary segmentation across diverse medical imaging modalities using consistent text prompts and unified label representations. For CT, MRI, and Ultrasound, performance is reported using Dice Similarity Coefficient (DSC) and Normalized Surface Dice (NSD), while for Microscopy and PET, we follow challenge-specific guidelines and report F1 scores. On the official test set, the models achieved: CT (DSC: 0.2884, NSD: 0.2114), MRI (DSC: 0.1644, NSD: 0.1474), Microscopy (F1: 0.4502), and PET (F1: 0.0728). These results demonstrate the viability of modality-specific training within an open-vocabulary framework and provide a foundation for further improvements.

Keywords: open vocabulary segmentation · CT · MRI

1 Introduction

Supervised medical image segmentation has traditionally relied on fixed-class models trained with dense annotations. Large-scale efforts such as TotalSegmentator [16] and DukeSeg [1] exemplify this approach by enabling high-accuracy segmentation across 100+ predefined anatomical structures in Computed Tomography (CT) scans. While these models are robust within their respective label sets, they inherently lack the flexibility to handle unseen categories or user-defined prompts. This limitation has driven increasing interest in open-vocabulary segmentation, which enables segmentation tasks via

J. Ma et al. (Eds.): MedSegFM 2025, LNCS 16447, pp. 51–63, 2026.
https://doi.org/10.1007/978-3-032-23496-4_4

free-text descriptions [22]. Foundation models such as Segment Anything Model (SAM) [8] and SAM2 [14] have demonstrated impressive segmentation capabilities through user-interactive prompts in natural image domains. However, these interactive foundation models inherently lack support for text-based guidance. Extending open-vocabulary segmentation principles from natural images [9,17,18] to medical images introduces unique complexities. Medical datasets frequently suffer from limited annotated data, requiring innovative sampling strategies for robust model training. Moreover, the computational demands of open-vocabulary models challenge their feasibility on large, high-resolution medical volumes.

Further complicating medical image segmentation is the intrinsic diversity of medical imaging modalities. CT scans are volumetric with relatively coarse textures, whereas microscopic images reveal cellular-level details at substantially higher resolutions, involving vastly different texture patterns. Such variability, in dimensionality, resolution, and texturemakes it particularly challenging to develop a universally effective segmentation model. To overcome these hurdles, recent interactive medical segmentation methods such as SegVol [2], SAM-Med3D [15], VISTA3D [4], and nnInteractive [3] leverage user interactions for refinement but do not support open-ended text prompts. Text-guided segmentation approaches, by contrast, explicitly leverage natural language. BioMedParse [20] initiated this strategy for 2D biomedical images, while CAT [5] and SAT [21] have successfully extended text-guided open-vocabulary segmentation to 3D medical modalities.

Given the substantial diversity in medical imaging modalitiessuch as Computed Tomography (CT), Magnetic Resonance Imaging (MRI), Ultrasound, Microscopy, and Positron Emission Tomography (PET)developing a single universal segmentation model is highly challenging. Unlike natural images, these modalities vary significantly in dimensionality, texture, and resolution. Crucially, in clinical practice, clinicians inherently know the imaging modality being utilized, and this modality-specific information can be strategically leveraged to enhance segmentation performance. Therefore, rather than training one universal model, we propose training separate modality-specific models, explicitly tailored to the unique characteristics of each imaging type. Building upon the recently proposed SAT model [21], which has demonstrated strong performance in text-guided 3D medical segmentation, we develop five distinct SAT-based models [21], each fine-tuned with targeted sampling strategies optimized for their respective modality.

In this challenge, we leverage the provided text prompt to automatically infer the imaging modality. Once the modality is identified from the input prompt and image, the corresponding modality-specific model is dynamically selected and executed. This ensures optimized segmentation performance by automatically routing the task to the best-suited modality-specific SAT model, streamlining the segmentation process across diverse medical imaging scenarios.

2 Method

In our approach, we develop five independent models, one for each imaging modality (CT, MRI, PET, Ultrasound, and Microscopy), all based on the same SAT architecture [21] but trained with modality-specific data and weights.

2.1 Network Architecture

Figure 1 illustrates our modality-specific adaptation of the SAT architecture. Each model shares the same underlying structure but is independently trained on data from a specific imaging modality, allowing the architecture to specialize in the visual characteristics unique to that domain. During inference, a prompt parser identifies the modality from the input text, enabling automatic selection of the corresponding SAT model to perform segmentation. This design preserves architectural consistency while enabling tailored performance across diverse medical imaging modalities.

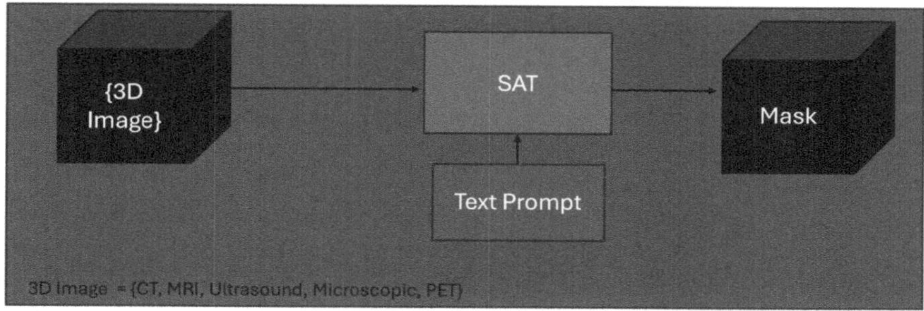

a) Training

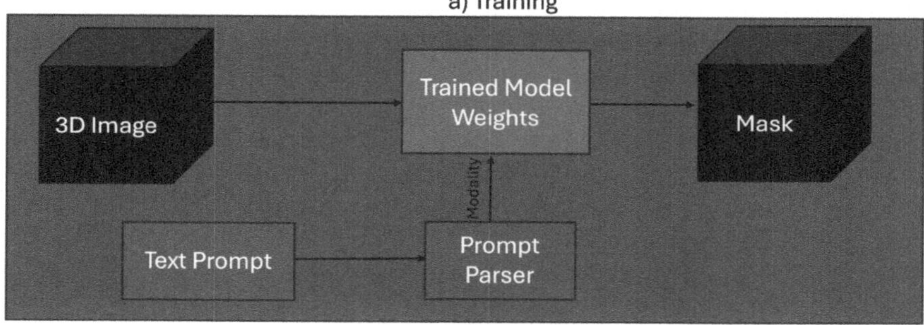

b) Inference

Fig. 1. (a) During training, we independently train five modality-specific models, one each for CT, MRI, PET, Ultrasound, and Microscopy, using the same SAT architecture, with separate weights for each modality.(b) During inference, a prompt parser module analyzes the input text to infer the imaging modality. Based on the inferred modality, the corresponding SAT model is selected and used to generate the segmentation mask.

2.2 Prompt Encoder and Decoder

Encoder. We are using the Text Encoder of SAT [21] that uses a BERT-based transformer trained on biomedical texts, further enhanced via contrastive learning using anatomical definitions and visual examples. It outputs a knowledge-rich embedding of the medical term.

Decoder. A transformer query decoder refines the text embedding by attending to image features. The final segmentation mask is generated by computing similarity between the refined text embedding and image features.

2.3 Loss Function

The SAT model uses a combination of Dice loss and Binary Cross-Entropy (BCE) loss [10]. Dice loss handles class imbalance by focusing on overlap between predicted and ground truth masks, while BCE ensures pixel-level accuracy.

2.4 Coreset Selection Strategy

For the Coreset Track, we were restricted to using only 10% of the full training dataset. To construct a representative and diverse subset, we designed a sampling strategy that ensures broad coverage across modalities and datasets while favoring samples rich in segmentation labels.

Our sampling process adhered to several key constraints: (1) the final subset must be approximately 8.2% of the total dataset size, (2) each dataset must contribute at least five samples to maintain diversity across sources, and (3) each imaging modality must be represented by at least fifty samples to preserve modality balance.

We first filtered out corrupted or invalid data and computed label presence for all usable files. Sampling was performed in two phases. In the first phase, we enforced the per-dataset and per-modality minimums through weighted random selection, where samples with more labeled structures were more likely to be chosen. In the second phase, we filled the remaining quota with globally sampled files, again guided by label richness. To ensure consistency and reproducibility, a fixed random seed was used throughout. The resulting subset was saved in a structured JSONL format and used to train our model.

2.5 Prompt-Based Modality Router (No Text Conditioning)

Scope. The prompt is used *only* to select the modality-specific SAT model at inference. We do *not* condition the decoder on text, and we do *not* parse organ names to alter outputs. Each modality-specific SAT predicts its predefined label set unchanged.

Procedure.

1. **Normalize & tokenize:** lowercase the prompt and tokenize with word boundaries to avoid spurious matches.
2. **Keyword detection:** search for modality keywords {`ct`, `mri`, `ultrasound`, `microscopy`, `pet`}.
3. **Model selection:** if a keyword is detected, load that modality's SAT weights and run segmentation; otherwise, **fallback to CT** (challenge default).

Notes. This router is rule-based (no learned parameters) and *does not* alter the segmentation network or its label heads. Any per-structure visualization uses the model's standard outputs; prompts are not used to gate or condition class predictions. Because the challenge enforced a strict per-case runtime limit, we intentionally kept the prompt parser lightweight and did not add extra complexity such as a separate image-based modality detector or a learned router.

3 Experiments

3.1 Dataset and Evaluation Metrics

The development set is an extension of the CVPR 2024 MedSAM on Laptop Challenge [12], including more 3D cases from public datasets[1] and covering commonly used 3D modalities, such as Computed Tomography (CT), Magnetic Resonance Imaging (MRI), Positron Emission Tomography (PET), Ultrasound, and Microscopy images. The hidden testing set is created by a community effort where all the cases are unpublished. The annotations are either provided by the data contributors or annotated by the challenge organizer with 3D Slicer [7] and MedSAM2 [13]. In addition to using all training cases, the challenge contains a coreset track, where participants can select 10% of the total training cases for model development.

The text-guided segmentation task contains both semantic segmentation and instance segmentation. For the semantic segmentation task, the evaluation metrics include Dice Similarity Coefficient (DSC) and Normalized Surface Distance (NSD) to evaluate the segmentation region overlap and boundary distance, respectively. For the instance segmentation task, we computed the F1 score at an overlapping threshold of 0.5 and DSC scores for true positives. In addition, the algorithm runtime will be limited to 60 s per class. Exceeding this limit will lead to all DSC and NSD metrics being set to 0 for that test case.

3.2 Implementation Details

Preprocessing. Following the practice in MedSAM [11], all images were processed to npz format with an intensity range of $[0, 255]$. Specifically, for CT images, we initially normalized the Hounsfield units using typical window width and level values: soft tissues (W:400, L:40), lung (W:1500, L:-160), brain (W:80,

[1] A complete list is available at https://medsam-datasetlist.github.io/.

L:40), and bone (W:1800, L:400). Subsequently, the intensity values were rescaled to the range of $[0, 255]$. For other images, we clipped the intensity values to the range between the 0.5th and 99.5th percentiles before rescaling them to the range of [0, 255]. If the original intensity range is already in $[0, 255]$, no preprocessing was applied.

Environment Settings. The development environments and requirements are presented in Table 1.

Table 1. Development environments and requirements.

System	Ubuntu 20
CPU	128 AMD EPYC 7000 series
RAM	1024 GB
GPU (number and type)	Four NVIDIA RTX A6000 48G
CUDA version	12.2
Programming language	Python 3.11.11
Deep learning framework	torch 2.6.0

Data Augmentation. We applied a diverse set of data augmentations, inspired by the nnU-Net framework [6], to improve model generalization and robustness. These included geometric (rotation, scaling, mirroring), intensity (contrast, brightness, gamma, noise, blur), and resolution-based transformations. Augmentations were applied probabilistically during training to simulate real-world variability in imaging conditions and anatomical presentations (Table 2).

Table 2. Training protocols.

Pre-trained Model	SAT Text Encoder
Batch size	1
Patch size	288×288×96
Total iterations	50000
Optimizer	Adam
Initial learning rate (lr)	1e-4 and 1e-5
Lr decay schedule	cosine annealing
Loss function	BCE and Dice
Number of model parameters	220.9M[4]

4 Results and Discussion

Table 3. Quantitative evaluation results of the **validation set** on the **coreset track**. Our proposed method, denoted as **SAT-{modality}**, trains a separate model for each imaging modality to better handle modality-specific characteristics. Microscopy metrics are unavailable for some cases due to evaluation errors.

Modality	Method	Sematic Segmentation		Instance Segmentation	
		DSC	NSD	F1	DSC TP
CT	CAT	**0.7443**	0.7444	0.2575	0.3148
	SAT	0.7028	0.7058	0.1128	0.1534
	SAT-CT(Ours)	0.3280	0.3043	0.04	0.12
MRI	CAT	**0.4831**	0.5472	0.1498	0.3127
	SAT	0.475	0.551	0.0575	0.175
	SAT-MRI(Ours)	0.305	0.349	0.0162	0.106
Microscopy	CAT	...	...	0.043	0.3224
	SAT	...	...	0.1741	0.5802
	SAT-Microscopy(Ours)	...	...	**0.5825**	**0.8254**
PET	CAT	...	...	0.1127	0.3382
	SAT	...	...	0.2736	0.7326
	SAT-PET(Ours)	...	...	**0.3105**	**0.7352**
Ultrasound	CAT	**0.818**	0.812	...	...
	SAT	0.7611	0.7268	...	...
	SAT-Ultrasound(Ours)	0.7656	0.7485	...	...

4.1 Quantitative Results on Validation and Test Set

Table 3 and Table 4 summarizes our modality-specific adaptation of SAT alongside the baseline SAT and CAT methods. Because we trained our models for far fewer iterations than the baselines, results remain below the performance of the fully trained SAT and CAT on CT and MR modality. However, for modalities with smaller datasets, namely microscopic images, ultrasound, and PET, the limited training still allowed the model to see every example, leading to strong segmentation performance. In fact, our adaptation outperforms both SAT and CAT on PET and microscopic image segmentation, as shown in the Table 3.

4.2 Qualitative Results on Validation Set

The qualitative results show that our open-vocabulary model can achieve strong performance on well-represented structures, e.g., lungs in CT, the prostate on T2-weighted MRI, and cardiac chambers in ultrasoundyielding high Dice scores

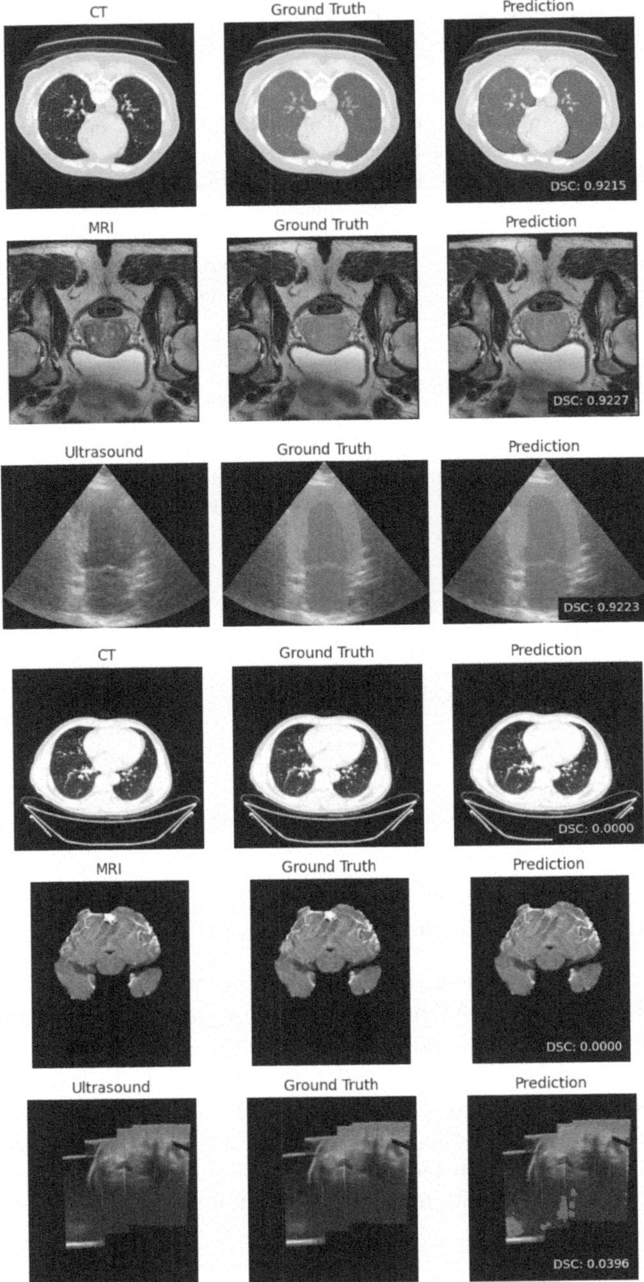

Fig. 2. Segmentation results for CT, MRI, and ultrasound modalities, showing both the best- and worst-performing cases (by Dice score) in each modality. The first three rows represent the best-performing cases, while the last three rows depict the worst-performing cases. In each row, the first column displays the original image slice; the second overlays the ground-truth segmentation; and the third overlays the models prediction with the corresponding Dice similarity coefficient (DSC) annotated.

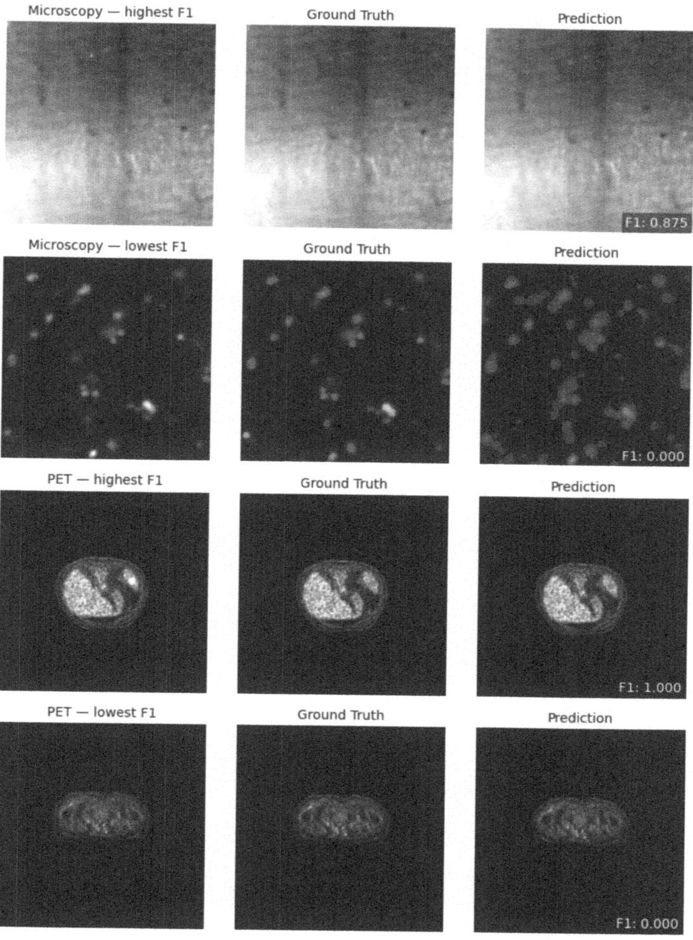

Fig. 3. Segmentation results for PET and Microscopy modality, showing both the best- and worst-performing cases (by F1 score) in each modality. The top and bottom two rows represent the best and worst performing cases for the Microscopy modality and PET modality respectively. In each row, the first column displays the original image slice; the second overlays the ground-truth segmentation; and the third overlays the models prediction with the corresponding F1 score annotated.

as shown on Fig. 2 and Fig. 3. At the same time, it entirely failed to delineate branching airway structures in CT and to segment brain tumors on MRI, both of which pose more complex anatomical and contextual challenges that the model couldnt learn in the limited training time. Likewise, limb segmentation in ultrasound was unsuccessful, reflecting the lack of similar examples in the training set. Altogether, these findings underscore the difficulty of open-vocabulary segmentation in medical imaging, where diverse modalities and intricate anatomy

Table 4. Quantitative evaluation results of the **test set** on the **coreset track**. Our proposed method, denoted as **SAT-{modality}**, trains a separate model for each imaging modality to better handle modality-specific characteristics.

Modality	Method	Sematic Segmentation		Instance Segmentation	
		DSC	NSD	F1	DSC TP
CT	CAT	0.3689	0.3500	...	...
	SAT	**0.4314**	0.3824	...	...
	SAT-CT(Ours)	0.2884	0.2114	...	...
MRI	CAT	0.2667	0.2701	0.0313	0.0398
	SAT	**0.3368**	0.3314	0.0884	0.1817
	SAT-MRI(Ours)	0.1644	0.1474	0.0154	0.0810
Microscopy	CAT	...	...	0.0110	0.3377
	SAT	...	...	0.3116	0.7609
	SAT-Microscopy(Ours)	...	...	**0.4502**	**0.7995**
PET	CAT	...	...	0.0000	0.0000
	SAT	...	...	**0.0886**	**0.2692**
	SAT-PET(Ours)	...	...	0.0728	0.1808

demand richer contextual knowledge than what models typically acquire from natural-image datasets.

4.3 Results on Final Testing Set

We participated in the Coreset Challenge, which was conducted on a subset of the full dataset to evaluate segmentation performance under limited data conditions. Our method, submitted under the team name **cvit**, achieved the 4th position in the final rankings. The official results released by the challenge organizers are summarized in Table 5.

Table 5. Final testing results of all participating teams. Our team, **cvit**, achieved the 4th position on the final testing set.

Rank	Team	Avg DSC	Avg NSD	Avg F1	Avg DSC_TP
1	mirthai-lab	0.402	0.3374	0.0283	0.082
2	zen	0.3457	0.3097	0.0533	0.1806
3	hanglok	0.3273	0.3175	0.0270	0.0412
4	**cvit**	**0.2378**	**0.1853**	**0.0314**	**0.108**
5	imiphdu	0.0803	0.0558	0.0094	0.0858
6	deepseg	0.0126	0.0147	0.0030	0.0076

4.4 Limitation and Future Work

We trained for approximately 10000 iterations. This limited schedule disproportionately affected **CT** and **MR**, which have larger data volume and tend to benefit from longer training and modest modality-specific tuning.

A major error source was **orientation heterogeneity** in the released `.npz` volumes: orientation metadata was not provided, preventing reliable normalization to a common convention (e.g., RAS/LPS). Under these conditions, standard spatial augmentations (flips/rotations) can inadvertently *mix left/right anatomy*, degrading structures with sidedness (e.g., left/right kidney, ribs).

Future work will: (i) add a deterministic orientation harmonization step; (ii) employ flip-aware labeling or sidedness-preserving augmentations; and (iii) incorporate left/right consistency checks to guard against such failures.

Our submission uses a **prompt-only, rule-based router** for modality selection at inference: keyword detection for {`ct`, `mri`, `ultrasound`, `microscopy`, `pet`}, with a **CT fallback** when the prompt lacks explicit modality cues (challenge default). This router performs *only* model selection and does not alter the segmentation network; no text-conditioned decoding is used in this work. **Future work** will strengthen routing by replacing fixed fallback with a lightweight image-based heuristic and a compact CNN modality classifier.

Given substantial heterogeneity across imaging types, we favor **five separate SAT models (one per modality)** over a single model. This enables modality-appropriate choices later (e.g., losses tuned for small structures; diffusion-style heads for tumor/pathology). These directions are **future work** and not part of the reported results.

5 Conclusion

In this work, we trained five separate models, each dedicated to a specific imaging modality, rather than relying on a single unified model. We believe this modality-specific strategy is more effective given the significant differences in data characteristics and anatomical structures across modalities.

Preliminary results indicate promising performance on modalities such as microscopy and ultrasound, where the models were able to converge well within the limited training period. However, for modalities like CT and MRI, which typically require more extensive training due to larger datasets and greater variability, convergence was not achieved within the restricted timeframe.

Disclosure of Interests. The authors have no competing interests to declare that are relevant to the content of this article.

Acknowledgements. We thank all the data owners for making the medical images publicly available and CodaLab [19] for hosting the challenge platform. This work was funded by the Center for Virtual Imaging Trials, NIH grants P41EB028744, R01EB001838, and R01CA261457.

References

1. Dahal, L., et al.: Xcat 3.0: A comprehensive library of personalized digital twins derived from CT scans. Medical Image Analysis p. 103636 (2025)
2. Du, Y., Bai, F., Huang, T., Zhao, B.: Segvol: Universal and interactive volumetric medical image segmentation. In: Advances in Neural Information Processing Systems, vol. 37, pp. 110746–110783 (2024)
3. Fabian, I., et al.: nninteractive: Redefining 3D promptable segmentation. arXiv preprint arXiv:2503.08373 (2025)
4. He, Y., et al.: VISTA3D: A unified segmentation foundation model for 3D medical imaging. In: Proceedings of the IEEE/CVF International Conference on Computer Vision and Pattern Recognition (2024)
5. Huang, Z., Jiang, Y., Zhang, R., Zhang, S., Zhang, X.: Cat: coordinating anatomical-textual prompts for multi-organ and tumor segmentation. In: Globerson, A., et al., (eds.) Advances in Neural Information Processing Systems, vol. 37, pp. 3588–3610 (2024)
6. Isensee, F., Jaeger, P.F., Kohl, S.A., Petersen, J., Maier-Hein, K.H.: nnu-net: a self-configuring method for deep learning-based biomedical image segmentation. Nat. Methods **18**(2), 203–211 (2021)
7. Kikinis, R., Pieper, S.D., Vosburgh, K.G.: 3D Slicer: a platform for subject-specific image analysis, visualization, and clinical support, pp. 277–289. Springer (2013)
8. Kirillov, A., et al.: Segment anything. In: Proceedings of the International Conference on Computer Vision, pp. 4015–4026 (2023)
9. Liang, F., et al.: Open-vocabulary semantic segmentation with mask-adapted clip. In: Proceedings of the IEEE/CVF Conference on Computer Vision and Pattern Recognition, pp. 7061–7070 (2023)
10. Ma, J., et al.: Loss odyssey in medical image segmentation. Med. Image Anal. **71**, 102035 (2021)
11. Ma, J., He, Y., Li, F., Han, L., You, C., Wang, B.: Segment anything in medical images. Nat. Commun. **15**, 654 (2024)
12. Ma, J., et al.: Efficient medsams: Segment anything in medical images on laptop. arXiv:2412.16085 (2024)
13. Ma, J., et al.: Medsam2: Segment anything in 3D medical images and videos. arXiv preprint arXiv:2504.03600 (2025)
14. Ravi, N., et al.: Sam 2: Segment anything in images and videos. In: International Conference on Learning Representations (2025)
15. Wang, H., et al.: Sam-med3d: Towards general-purpose segmentation models for volumetric medical images. arXiv preprint arXiv:2310.15161 (2024)
16. Wasserthal, J., et al.: Totalsegmentator: robust segmentation of 104 anatomic structures in CT images. Radiol.: Artif. Intell. **5**(5), e230024 (2023)
17. Xu, J., Liu, S., Vahdat, A., Byeon, W., Wang, X., De Mello, S.: Open-vocabulary panoptic segmentation with text-to-image diffusion models. In: Proceedings of the IEEE/CVF Conference on Computer Vision and Pattern Recognition, pp. 2955–2966 (2023)
18. Xu, J., et al.: Learning open-vocabulary semantic segmentation models from natural language supervision. In: Proceedings of the IEEE/CVF Conference on Computer Vision and Pattern Recognition, pp. 2935–2944 (2023)
19. Xu, Z., et al.: Codabench: Flexible, easy-to-use, and reproducible meta-benchmark platform. Patterns **3**(7), 100543 (2022)

20. Zhao, T., et al.: A foundation model for joint segmentation, detection and recognition of biomedical objects across nine modalities. Nat. Methods **22**, 166–176 (2025)
21. Zhao, Z., et al.: One model to rule them all: Towards universal segmentation for medical images with text prompt. arXiv preprint arXiv:2312.17183 (2023)
22. Zhu, C., Chen, L.: A survey on open-vocabulary detection and segmentation: past, present, and future. IEEE Transactions on Pattern Analysis and Machine Intelligence (2024)

Medal S: Spatio-Textual Prompt Model for Medical Segmentation

Pengcheng Shi[1], Jiawei Chen[1,4], Jiaqi Liu[1], Xinglin Zhang[1], Tao Chen[1,3], and Lei Li[1,2(✉)]

[1] Medical Image Insights, Shanghai, China
lenny.lilei.cs@gmail.com
[2] University of Washington, Seattle, WA, USA
[3] University of Waterloo, Waterloo, ON, Canada
[4] Xi'an Jiaotong University, Xi'an, China

Abstract. We introduce Medal S, a medical segmentation foundation model that supports native-resolution spatial and textual prompts within an end-to-end trainable framework. Unlike text-only methods lacking spatial awareness, Medal S achieves channel-wise alignment between volumetric prompts and text embeddings, mitigating inaccuracies from resolution mismatches. By preserving full 3D context, it efficiently processes multiple native-resolution masks in parallel, enhancing multi-class segmentation performance. A lightweight 3D convolutional module enables precise voxel-space refinement guided by both prompt types, supporting up to 243 classes across CT, MRI, PET, ultrasound, and microscopy modalities in the BiomedSegFM dataset. Medal S offers two prompting modes: a text-only mode, where model predictions serve as spatial prompts for self-refinement without human input, and a hybrid mode, incorporating manual annotations for enhanced flexibility. For 24-class segmentation, parallel spatial prompting reduces inference time by more than 90% compared to sequential prompting. We propose dynamic resampling to address target-patch ratio imbalance, extending SAT and nnU-Net for data augmentation. Furthermore, we develop optimized text preprocessing, a two-stage inference strategy, and post-processing techniques to improve memory efficiency, precision, and inference speed. On the five-modality average on the validation set, Medal S outperforms SAT with a DSC of 75.44 (vs. 69.83), NSD of 77.34 (vs. 71.06), F1 of 38.24 (vs. 24.88), and DSC TP of 65.46 (vs. 46.97). Medal S achieves excellent performance by harmonizing spatial precision with semantic textual guidance, demonstrating superior efficiency and accuracy in multi-class medical segmentation tasks compared to sequential prompt-based approaches. Medal S will be publicly available at https://github.com/yinghemedical/Medal-S.

Keywords: Medical Segmentation · Foundation Model · Spatial and Textual Prompts

X. Zhang—Project Lead

J. Ma et al. (Eds.): MedSegFM 2025, LNCS 16447, pp. 64–87, 2026.
https://doi.org/10.1007/978-3-032-23496-4_5

1 Introduction

Medical image segmentation, the precise delineation of anatomical structures and pathologies within medical volumes, is fundamental to computational healthcare. Despite its importance, challenges persist due to the diversity of imaging modalities and anatomical variations. Recent advances in foundation models, notably the Segment Anything Model (SAM) [13] and its successor, SAM 2 [19], have transformed natural image segmentation by introducing promptable models that generalize across various image distributions and tasks. However, directly applying these models to medical volumes is hindered by the intrinsic differences between natural and medical images (Fig. 1).

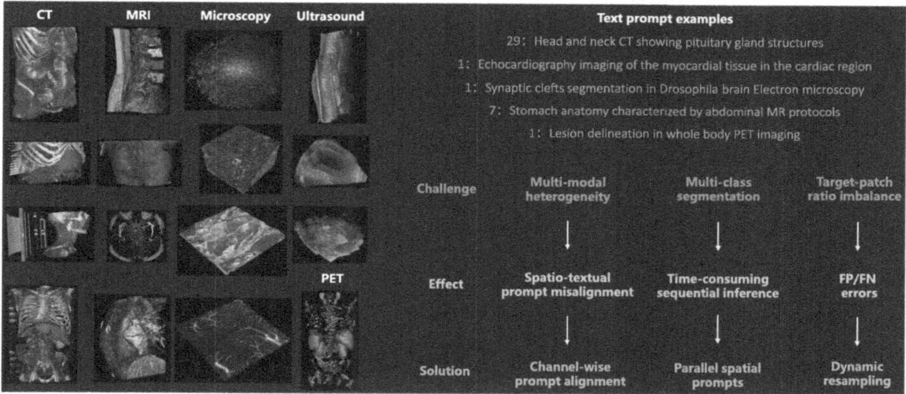

Fig. 1. Left: Example renders from the BiomedSegFM challenge dataset (original images and segmentation masks) covering five imaging modalities: CT, MRI, microscopy, PET, and ultrasound. Top-right: Sample text prompts. Bottom-right: Key challenges include (1) multi-modal heterogeneity, (2) multi-class segmentation, and (3) target-patch ratio imbalance, causing spatio-textual misalignment, sequential inference inefficiency, and FP/FN errors. Our solutions: channel-wise prompt alignment (2.3), parallel spatial prompts (2.3), and dynamic resampling (2.5).

Adaptations of foundation models for medical image segmentation have followed distinct strategies, each with inherent trade-offs. Early approaches, such as MedSAM [16], extended SAM's 2D capabilities to medical images, primarily using bounding box prompts. Similarly, ScribblePrompt [23], a 2D model, improved segmentation accuracy for unseen labels and image types by supporting flexible annotation styles, including bounding boxes, clicks, and scribbles. To overcome the limitations of 2D methods and leverage 3D spatial information, subsequent models incorporated 3D spatial prompts. For example, SAM-Med3D [22], SegVol [5], and VISTA3D [9] introduced dedicated 3D prompting mechanisms. VISTA3D [9] enabled automatic and interactive 3D segmentation with spatial prompts, facilitating efficient inspection and editing by clinicians. SegVol

[5] expanded prompt types to include spatial and semantic cues, improving precision and semantic disambiguation. Beyond this, MedSAM2 [18] advanced 3D segmentation by using intuitive 2D interactions to generate full 3D segmentations. MedSAM2 [18], akin to SAM 2 [19], supports segmentation of 3D medical images and videos, primarily using bounding box prompts and memory-conditioned features.

Most recently, nnInteractive [6], built on the nnU-Net [11] framework, introduced a comprehensive 3D interactive open-set segmentation method. This approach supports diverse spatial prompts, including points, scribbles, boxes, and a novel lasso prompt, leveraging 2D interactions to produce complete 3D segmentations with superior performance. Despite these advancements, current medical segmentation models face significant limitations with spatial prompts. Models like SegVol [5] and SAM-Med3D [22] often rely on multiple downsampling operations for spatial prompts, while VISTA3D [9] downsamples spatial point prompts, leading to substantial loss of voxel-level details. In contrast, nnInteractive [6] incorporates spatial prompts at the native resolution, preserving 3D spatial context. Moreover, existing spatial prompting methods process multiple classes sequentially rather than in parallel, reducing inference efficiency and limiting the model's ability to learn features across interrelated anatomical regions.

On the text prompt front, models like CLIP-Driven Universal Model [15] and SegVol [5] utilize simple semantic classes as prompts, while VISTA3D [9] employs similar class-based prompts. However, such categorical prompting often lacks flexibility in practice. More recent models, such as SAT [28] and BioMedParse [27], adopt text-only prompting paradigms. However, BioMedParse, a 2D model, remains limited in handling 3D medical images. These approaches often sacrifice 3D spatial context and lack spatial prompts, hindering self-iterative refinement and real-world correction capabilities. CAT [10] attempts to integrate spatial anatomical information with text prompts but embeds cropped regions after multiple downsampling steps, failing to utilize spatial prompts at native resolution. Additionally, its complex contrastive learning approach for inter-class relationships is less streamlined. This fragmentation creates a tension between preserving native-resolution spatial prompts and achieving efficient multimodal processing. Ideally, spatial prompts for different classes and their corresponding text should maintain one-to-one channel-wise correspondence at the native resolution. In text-guided controllable generation, several works have successfully integrated native-resolution segmentation masks with text prompts. Prior works like MakeAScene [7] and SpaText [1] have demonstrated effective fusion of segmentation masks and text for controllable generation. ControlNet [25] further enhances this through spatial conditioning of diffusion models. However, such joint textual and native-resolution spatial prompts approaches remain unexplored for medical image segmentation.

To address these challenges, we introduce Medal S, a medical segmentation foundation model that natively supports both spatial and textual prompts in an end-to-end framework. Medal S aligns with initiatives like ScaleMAI [14] and supports datasets including RadGenome-Chest CT [26] and RadGPT [2].

Our key contributions are:

- A novel channel-wise alignment between volumetric prompts and text embeddings through text embedding transformation and lightweight 3D convolution, addressing spatial prompt-text misalignment and enabling precise simultaneous refinement.
- Parallel spatial prompting at native resolution with simultaneous 3D spatial/textual input for multi-class segmentation. Maintains full fidelity and provides more than 10× faster inference (24 classes) vs. sequential processing.
- Dynamic resampling for target-patch ratio imbalance (building upon SAT [28] and nnU-Net [11]), with optimized text preprocessing, two-stage inference, and post-processing, achieving fast inference, memory efficiency, and excellent performance.
- Comprehensive support for 243 classes across CT, MRI, PET, ultrasound, and microscopy (BiomedSegFM dataset), featuring both text-only self-refinement and hybrid manual annotation modes for enhanced clinical flexibility.

2 Method

Our proposed **Medal S** framework presents a novel approach to universal medical image segmentation by synergistically integrating spatial prompts with text-driven feature adaptation. As illustrated in Fig. 2, the framework consists of three key components: (1) An image encoder that extracts multi-scale visual features, (2) A text encoder that processes prompt embeddings, and (3) A query decoder that fuses visual and textual features to produce adapted embeddings. Parallel spatial prompts–whether simulated, predicted, or annotated–are processed at native resolution and aligned with spatio-textual features through channel-wise alignment. The framework supports iterative self-refinement for precise segmentation, offering both robustness and flexibility in medical segmentation.

2.1 Prompt Encoder

The prompt encoder comprises two components: foreground spatial prompt encoding and textual prompt encoding, with implementations inspired by nnInteractive [6] and SAT [28] respectively.

Foreground Spatial Prompt Encoding. To enhance the model's focus on target foreground regions, we generate a foreground spatial prompt $\mathbf{S}_f \in \mathbb{R}^{1\times H\times W\times D}$ by aggregating parallel spatial prompts $\mathbf{S}_p \in \mathbb{R}^{N\times H\times W\times D}$ (obtained from either previous predictions or user annotations) through a binary thresholding operation:

$$\mathbf{S}_f = H\left(\sum_{i=1}^{N} \mathbf{S}_p^{(i)}\right) \tag{1}$$

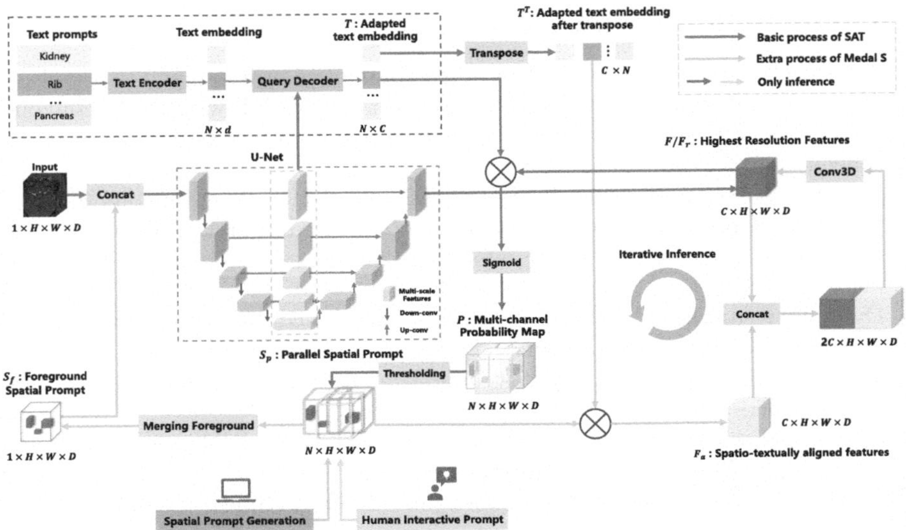

Fig. 2. Medal S framework pipeline. Multi-scale visual features from the image encoder and text embeddings from the text encoder are fused by a query decoder into adapted embeddings. Parallel spatial prompts (simulated, predicted, or annotated) are processed at native resolution and aligned via channel-wise matching, maintaining full fidelity. This achieves a greater than 10× speedup for 24-class segmentation versus sequential processing (see Fig. 4) and supports iterative self-refinement for precise segmentation.

where $H(\cdot)$ is the Heaviside step function:

$$H(x) = \begin{cases} 1 & \text{if } x > 0 \\ 0 & \text{otherwise} \end{cases} \quad (2)$$

The resulting $\mathbf{S}_f$ is concatenated with the input image as additional channels to the U-Net encoder, similar to the native resolution prompt in nnInteractive.

Textual Prompt Encoding. We employ a frozen pre-trained text encoder Φ_{text} from the SAT framework to process medical terminology prompts $\mathcal{T} = \{t_1, \ldots, t_N\}$:

$$\mathbf{z}_j = \Phi_{\text{text}}(t_j), \quad \mathbf{z}_j \in \mathbb{R}^d \quad (3)$$

where $\mathbf{z}_j$ represents the embedding for anatomical target t_j.

2.2 Spatial Prompt Generation

We introduce a spatial prompt generation method $\mathcal{G}_{\text{prompt}}$ that enhances segmentation robustness for both interactive applications and autonomous refinement. The generator produces realistic coarse segmentations from ground truth masks $\mathbf{M} \in 0, 1^{N \times H \times W \times D}$, where N represents semantic channels and (H, W, D) denote spatial dimensions. The method outputs two complementary binary prompts: a single-channel global foreground prompt $\mathbf{S}_f \in 0, 1^{1 \times H \times W \times D}$ and a multi-channel class-specific prompt $\mathbf{S}_p \in 0, 1^{N \times H \times W \times D}$.

The generation process applies controlled stochastic transformations through five key parameters. The drop probability range $[p_{\text{drop}}^{\min}, p_{\text{drop}}^{\max}] \in [0, 1]^2$ regulates false negative simulation by removing mask blocks, while the add probability range $[p_{\text{add}}^{\min}, p_{\text{add}}^{\max}]$ controls false positive generation through block additions. Channel-level variations are introduced via $p_{\text{chan-zero}}$, which nullifies entire channels in $\mathbf{S}_p$, and $pzero$ determines the probability of returning empty prompts. The block size set $\mathcal{B} \subset \mathbb{Z}_{\geq 1}^3$ defines the possible 3D block dimensions for these transformations.

As detailed in Algorithm 1, the process begins by potentially returning empty prompts when a random sample falls below p_{zero}. Otherwise, $\mathbf{M}_{\text{eff}}$ is created by randomly zeroing out channels in $\mathbf{M}$ according to $p_{\text{chan-zero}}$. The single-channel prompt $\mathbf{S}_f$ is generated by channel summation and binarization of $\mathbf{M}_{\text{eff}}$. For block operations, the method samples block dimensions $[b_h, b_w, b_d] \in \mathcal{B}$, establishing a transformation grid. Mutually exclusive drop and add masks ($\mathbf{B}_{\text{drop}}$ and $\mathbf{B}_{\text{add}}$) are generated using probabilistically sampled parameters, upsampled to full resolution, and applied to both prompt types. The multi-channel prompt additionally incorporates class-specific variations through random channel assignment of modified blocks. Final outputs undergo binarization to maintain strict 0,1 values.

This approach systematically simulates diverse input conditions ranging from coarse segmentations to imperfect user annotations, significantly improving model generalization across varying input qualities while maintaining anatomical plausibility. The stochastic yet controlled transformations enable robust handling of real-world scenarios where prompt quality may vary substantially.

2.3 Query Decoder

Our query decoder builds upon the architectures of SAM [13] and SAT [28], while incorporating key design principles from DETR [3] and MaskFormer [4] for segmentation tasks. Departing from conventional approaches that compress dense prompts into low-dimensional mask embeddings (e.g., SAM-Med3D [22], SegVol [5], and VISTA3D [9]), our method introduces a novel preservation of the complete 3D spatial context in volumetric prompts. This preservation proves particularly vital for 3D medical imaging applications, where the maintenance of native spatial resolution directly impacts diagnostic accuracy.

The decoder's architecture establishes precise channel-wise alignment between volumetric prompts and text embeddings, effectively mitigating the accuracy degradation typically caused by resolution mismatches. This design enables efficient parallel processing of multiple native-resolution masks, yielding significant improvements in multi-class segmentation performance. Furthermore, we incorporate a lightweight 3D convolutional module that jointly optimizes voxel-space features using both prompt modalities while maintaining their

Algorithm 1. Spatial Prompt Generation

Require: $\mathbf{M} \in \{0,1\}^{N\times H\times W\times D}$, $[p_{\text{drop}}^{\min}, p_{\text{drop}}^{\max}]$, $[p_{\text{add}}^{\min}, p_{\text{add}}^{\max}]$, $p_{\text{chan-zero}}$, $p_{\text{zero}} \in [0,1]$, $\mathcal{B} \subset \mathbb{Z}_{\geq 1}^{3}$
Ensure: $\mathbf{S}_f \in \{0,1\}^{1\times H\times W\times D}$, $\mathbf{S}_p \in \{0,1\}^{N\times H\times W\times D}$
if Random$(0,1) < p_{\text{zero}}$ **then**
  return $\mathbf{0}_{1\times H\times W\times D}$, $\mathbf{0}_{N\times H\times W\times D}$
end if
$\mathbf{M}_{\text{eff}} \leftarrow \mathbf{M} \odot \text{ChannelMask}(\mathbf{M}, p_{\text{chan-zero}})$
$\mathbf{S}_p \leftarrow \mathbf{M}_{\text{eff}}$
$\mathbf{S}_f \leftarrow (\sum_{c=1}^{N} \mathbf{M}_{\text{eff},c} > 0)$
if $p_{\text{drop}}^{\max} > 0$ or $p_{\text{add}}^{\max} > 0$ **then**
  $[b_h, b_w, b_d] \leftarrow \text{RandomChoice}(\mathcal{B})$
  $[n_h, n_w, n_d] \leftarrow [\lceil H/b_h \rceil, \lceil W/b_w \rceil, \lceil D/b_d \rceil]$
  $p_d \sim \mathcal{U}(p_{\text{drop}}^{\min}, p_{\text{drop}}^{\max})$, $p_a \sim \mathcal{U}(p_{\text{add}}^{\min}, p_{\text{add}}^{\max})$
  $\mathbf{B}_{\text{drop}} \leftarrow \text{Random}(n_h, n_w, n_d) < p_d$
  $\mathbf{B}_{\text{add}} \leftarrow (\text{Random}(n_h, n_w, n_d) < p_a) \wedge (\neg \mathbf{B}_{\text{drop}})$
  $\mathbf{U}_{\text{drop}}, \mathbf{U}_{\text{add}} \leftarrow \text{Upsample}(\mathbf{B}_{\text{drop}}, (H,W,D)), \text{Upsample}(\mathbf{B}_{\text{add}}, (H,W,D))$
  $\mathbf{S}_f \leftarrow \mathbf{S}_f \odot (1 - \mathbf{U}_{\text{drop}}) \vee \mathbf{U}_{\text{add}}$
  $\mathbf{C}_{\text{keep}} \leftarrow \text{AssignBlocksToChannels}(\neg \mathbf{B}_{\text{drop}}, N)$
  $\mathbf{C}_{\text{add}} \leftarrow \text{AssignBlocksToChannels}(\mathbf{B}_{\text{add}}, N)$
  $\mathbf{S}_p \leftarrow \mathbf{S}_p \odot \mathbf{C}_{\text{keep}} \vee \mathbf{C}_{\text{add}}$
end if
$\mathbf{S}_f \leftarrow (\mathbf{S}_f > 0)$, $\mathbf{S}_p \leftarrow (\mathbf{S}_p > 0)$
return $\mathbf{S}_f$, $\mathbf{S}_p$

channel-wise alignment, ensuring accurate and robust 3D segmentation across targets with varying semantics.

The query decoder operates on per-voxel features $\mathbf{F} \in \mathbb{R}^{C\times H\times W\times D}$, where (H,W,D) denote the voxel grid dimensions and C represents the feature channels. These features are derived through progressive upsampling of visual encoder outputs with skip connections in a U-Net-style architecture [20]. Concurrently, the decoder receives adapted text embeddings $\mathbf{T} \in \mathbb{R}^{N\times C}$ produced by a transformer-based query decoder [21], where N indicates the number of semantic queries (corresponding to anatomical targets). The query decoder adapts text embeddings $\mathbf{Z} \in \mathbb{R}^{N\times L}$ (with L as the text dimension) using multi-scale visual features $\mathbf{V} \in \mathbb{R}^{C_V\times H_V\times W_V\times D_V}$ according to:

$$\mathbf{T} = \Phi_{\text{query}}(\mathbf{V}, \mathbf{Z})$$

The core innovation of our approach lies in the spatial prompt refinement module. This module enhances per-voxel features $\mathbf{F}$ through an interaction mechanism between adapted text embeddings $\mathbf{T}$ and parallel spatial prompts $\mathbf{S}_p \in \mathbb{R}^{N\times H\times W\times D}$ (which originate from either previous predictions or user annotations during inference). The refinement process begins with the computation of spatio-textually aligned features $\mathbf{F}_a \in \mathbb{R}^{C\times H\times W\times D}$ via:

$$\mathbf{F}_a = \mathbf{T}^\top \mathbf{S}_p$$

where $\mathbf{T}^\top \in \mathbb{R}^{C\times N}$ denotes the transposed adapted text embeddings. We then concatenate $\mathbf{F}_a$ with the original features $\mathbf{F}$ along the channel dimension, resulting in a $\mathbb{R}^{2C\times H\times W\times D}$ tensor. This combined representation is processed by a lightweight 3D convolutional module inspired by nnU-Net's native-resolution skip connection architecture [11], producing refined features $\mathbf{F}_r \in \mathbb{R}^{C\times H\times W\times D}$:

$$\mathbf{F}_r = \mathrm{Conv}([\mathbf{F}; \mathbf{F}_a])$$

The final per-voxel prediction $\mathbf{P} \in \mathbb{R}^{N\times H\times W\times D}$ is obtained through voxel-wise correlation between queries and refined features, followed by sigmoid activation $\sigma(\cdot)$:

$$\mathbf{P} = \sigma\left(\mathbf{T}\mathbf{F}_r\right)$$

This approach produces a multi-channel probability map with dedicated channels for each anatomical structures and pathological region, facilitating complete 3D volumetric segmentation.

2.4 Iterative Inference

Our query decoder employs an iterative inference approach inspired by Masked Autoencoders (MAE) [8]. The algorithm progressively refines predictions through multiple iterations, where each output $\mathbf{P}^{(t)} \in \mathbb{R}^{N\times H\times W\times D}$ serves as the spatial prompt $\mathbf{S}_p$ for subsequent iterations. The random masking mechanism facilitates prediction in unprompted regions, with complementary masked predictions aggregated to improve robustness against input noise.

As detailed in Algorithm 2, each iteration t consists of four key components: (1) feature enhancement through cross-attention between text queries $\mathbf{T}$ and spatial prompts, (2) R rounds of random block masking using block sizes $\mathcal{B} = 4, 8$, (3) parallel prediction of both masked and unmasked regions, and (4) prediction averaging across all rounds.

Medal-S supports two distinct prompting strategies. The text-only mode initializes with zero tensors and relies solely on text prompts with self-refinement, while the hybrid mode incorporates external spatial cues such as manual annotations when configured. The inference pipeline orchestrates prompt generation and iterative refinement through coordinated function calls, dynamically updating spatial prompts to enhance segmentation accuracy throughout the process.

2.5 Dynamic Resampling

Dynamic resampling addresses the challenge of varying segmentation target sizes relative to a fixed patch size in medical image segmentation. When the target size significantly exceeds the patch size, partial visibility of the target within a patch can lead to false positives (FP), as the model lacks global context and

Algorithm 2. Iterative Query Decoder Inference

Require: Voxel features $\mathbf{F} \in \mathbb{R}^{C \times H \times W \times D}$, queries $\mathbf{T} \in \mathbb{R}^{N \times C}$, initial prompt $\mathbf{S}_p \in \mathbb{R}^{N \times H \times W \times D}$, iterations T, parameters Θ, block sizes $\mathcal{B} = \{4, 8\}$, repetitions $R = 1$
Ensure: Prediction $\mathbf{P} \in \mathbb{R}^{N \times H \times W \times D}$

$\mathbf{P}^{(0)} \leftarrow \mathbf{0}$
for $t = 1$ to T **do**
  $\mathbf{E}^{(t)} \leftarrow \mathbf{T}^\top \mathbf{S}_p^{(t-1)}$
  $\mathbf{F}_r^{(t)} \leftarrow \mathrm{Conv}([\mathbf{F}; \mathbf{E}^{(t)}]; \Theta)$
  $\mathbf{P}^{(t)} \leftarrow \sigma(\mathbf{T}\mathbf{F}_r^{(t)})$
  $\mathbf{S}_p^{(t)} \leftarrow \mathbf{P}^{(t)}$
  $\mathbf{P}_{\text{sum}} \leftarrow \mathbf{0}$
  for $r = 1$ to R **do**
    $b \leftarrow \mathrm{RandomChoice}(\mathcal{B})$
    $N_h \leftarrow \lceil H/b \rceil$, $N_w \leftarrow \lceil W/b \rceil$, $N_d \leftarrow \lceil D/b \rceil$
    $N_{\text{selected}} \leftarrow \max(1, \lfloor (N_h \cdot N_w \cdot N_d)/2 \rfloor)$
    $\mathbf{M}_b \leftarrow \mathrm{RandomMask}(N_h, N_w, N_d, N_{\text{selected}})$
    $\mathbf{M} \leftarrow \mathrm{Upsample}(\mathbf{M}_b, (H, W, D))$
    $\mathbf{M}_c \leftarrow 1 - \mathbf{M}$
    $\mathbf{P}_1 \leftarrow \mathrm{Model}(\mathbf{T}, \mathbf{P}^{(t)}, \mathbf{M}; \Theta)$
    $\mathbf{P}_2 \leftarrow \mathrm{Model}(\mathbf{T}, \mathbf{P}^{(t)}, \mathbf{M}_c; \Theta)$
    $\mathbf{P}_{\text{patch}} \leftarrow \mathbf{P}_1 \cdot \mathbf{M}_c + \mathbf{P}_2 \cdot \mathbf{M}$
    $\mathbf{P}_{\text{sum}} \leftarrow \mathbf{P}_{\text{sum}} + \mathbf{P}_{\text{patch}}$
  end for
  $\mathbf{P}^{(t)} \leftarrow \mathbf{P}_{\text{sum}}/R$
end for
return $\mathbf{P}^{(T)}$

may misinterpret background noise as part of the target. Conversely, when the target is much smaller than the patch, the imbalance between foreground and background can result in false negatives (FN), as the model struggles to focus on small, critical regions. To mitigate these issues, we propose a dynamic resampling strategy that adjusts the voxel spacing of the input image based on the physical size of the smallest foreground connected component or the smallest class-specific target, ensuring balanced representation within the fixed patch size used by the model.

Our approach begins by identifying the smallest foreground connected component or the smallest target class in each case, which serves as the reference for resampling. Ideally, each target would have a tailored resampling rate to optimize its representation within the patch. However, to balance computational efficiency during training and inference, we focus on the smallest target to determine the resampling parameters. The core idea is to adjust the current spacing $\mathbf{s} = [s_x, s_y, s_z]$ of the image to a target spacing $\mathbf{t} = [t_x, t_y, t_z]$ such that the physical dimensions of the target align with the patch size $\mathbf{p} = [p_x, p_y, p_z]$. The adjusted spacing for each dimension i is computed as:

$$s'_i = \begin{cases} \max\left(t_i, \frac{p_i \cdot \alpha \cdot t_i}{d_i}\right), & \text{if } s_i > t_i, \\ \min\left(t_i, \frac{p_i \cdot \alpha \cdot t_i}{d_i}\right), & \text{otherwise,} \end{cases}$$

where s'_i is the adjusted spacing, d_i is the image dimension, and α is a scale factor. This formula ensures that the physical size of the resampled image fits within the patch while preserving sufficient detail. To prevent excessive resampling, we impose constraints such that s'_i remains within practical bounds, depending on the target class and inference stage.

2.6 Two-Stage Inference

We propose a two-stage inference strategy to optimize computational efficiency and segmentation accuracy for medical imaging, particularly for localized regions like focal lesions or anatomical structures. The coarse-to-fine strategy first performs low-resolution segmentation to identify regions of interest (ROIs), followed by high-resolution refinement to capture fine details. This approach is efficient for datasets with small foreground regions, reducing inference time compared to full high-resolution processing.

The strategy trains two models: one for coarse segmentation at a voxel spacing of (1.5, 1.5, 3.0) and another for high-resolution segmentation at (1.0, 1.0, 1.0). In the first stage, images are processed using a sliding window with a crop size of (224, 224, 128), corresponding to a physical field of view of approximately (336, 336, 384). This coarse resolution enables rapid ROI detection. The output mask highlights potential target regions, but if no foreground is detected, the strategy defaults to full-volume high-resolution inference to avoid missing subtle targets.

In the second stage, the ROI is extracted based on the coarse segmentation's non-zero predictions, scaled by a factor (1.1 to 1.5) to include context. The image is resampled to a target spacing of (1.0, 1.0, 1.0) with a crop size of (192, 192, 192). To manage memory, the physical volume $V = \prod_{i=1}^{3} s_i \cdot d_i$ (where s_i and d_i are voxel spacing and dimension size) is constrained by a threshold $V_{\text{threshold}} = (1.8)^3 \cdot \prod_{i=1}^{3} c_i$, with c_i as the crop size. If exceeded, voxel spacing is adjusted to satisfy $s_i \cdot d_i \leq 1.9 \cdot c_i \cdot t_i$, where t_i is the target spacing, ensuring memory usage stays below 32 GB.

The second stage refines segmentation using the coarse predictions as spatial prompts, enhancing accuracy for small or intricate structures like synaptic clefts or micro-lesions. A sliding window approach ensures high precision despite increased computational cost. The strategy allows flexible use of either stage: the first for rapid analysis or the second for high-resolution segmentation when resources permit. This adaptability balances efficiency and accuracy, making the approach suitable for diverse medical imaging applications.

2.7 Text Prompts Preprocessing

To effectively preprocess text prompts from the BiomedSegFM dataset, a systematic approach is employed to extract modality and class-specific identifiers, enabling dynamic resampling and post-processing strategies. The methodology begins by parsing the text prompts JSON to generate a class mapping, which assigns unique identifiers to anatomical structures and lesions across modalities (CT, MRI, US, PET, Microscopy). This mapping is constructed by extracting modality information from dataset prefixes and standardizing class names, such as mapping "Left renal structure" to "Left kidney" or "Myocardium" to "Heart". The resulting class mapping, stored as a JSON file, ensures each class within a modality has a unique identifier, facilitating consistent encoding.

Next, a variant mapping is created to handle diverse terminologies in the prompts. This mapping accounts for anatomical and lesion variants, incorporating directionality (e.g., "left" or "right") and suffixes (e.g., "lesions", "tumors"). For instance, "hepatic lesions" is mapped to "Liver lesions" using predefined rules and regular expressions to detect directional patterns. The variant mapping prioritizes longer, more specific terms to avoid partial matches, ensuring "Brainstem" is distinguished from "Brain". This preprocess yields a comprehensive variant mapping JSON, covering all prompt variations.

For training and inference, a text preprocessing function extracts modality and class information from each prompt. Given a sentence s and instance label l (0 for anatomy, 1 for lesion), the function identifies the modality m (e.g., CT, MRI, US, PET, or Microscopy) by matching keywords. It then retrieves the class identifier c_{id} and canonical name c_{name} from the class mapping, using the variant mapping to handle term variations. The function prioritizes longer matches to ensure specificity, formalized as:

$$(c_{id}, c_{name}) = \arg\max_{k \in K} \left(\text{len}(k) \mid k \in s, k \in M_m^l \right),$$

where K is the set of terms (class names and variants), M_m^l is the modality-specific class dictionary for label l, and len(k) is the term length. Directional patterns are detected using regular expressions to refine matches, such as distinguishing "Left kidney" from "Kidney".

The extracted modality m and class identifier c_{id} are input to a text encoder, producing embeddings that guide dynamic resampling and post-processing. For example, the extracted modality m enables the text encoder to distinguish between different modalities, while resampling strategies leverage c_{id} to apply class-specific target spacing, or post-processing leverages c_{id} to apply class-specific segmentation refinements. This streamlined pipeline ensures robust handling of diverse text prompts, enhancing segmentation accuracy.

2.8 Loss Function

We employ a combined loss $\mathcal{L} = \mathcal{L}_{BCE} + \mathcal{L}_{Dice}$, standard in medical image segmentation. For N classes and C voxels:

$$\mathcal{L}_{BCE} = -\frac{1}{MC}\sum n, c\left[s_{n,c}\log p_{n,c} + (1 - s_{n,c})\log(1 - p_{n,c})\right]$$
$$\mathcal{L}_{Dice} = 1 - \frac{2\sum n, cp_{n,c}s_{n,c}}{\sum_{n,c} p_{n,c}^2 + \sum_{n,c} s_{n,c}^2}$$

where $p_{n,c}$ and $s_{n,c}$ are the predicted probability and ground truth (0 or 1) for class n at voxel c. This combination optimizes both pixel-level accuracy and region-based overlap.

2.9 Post-processing

Our post-processing method refines segmentation results by suppressing spurious predictions while preserving anatomically plausible structures, improving upon nnU-Net [11]. Unlike nnU-Net, which retains only the largest connected component across all classes in a single operation, our approach processes each class independently and leverages probability maps to prioritize components based on both probability and size. As outlined in Algorithm 3, given a probability map $\mathbf{P} \in \mathbb{R}^{N\times H\times W\times D}$, where N is the number of classes, the segmentation map $\mathbf{S} \in \mathbb{R}^{1\times H\times W\times D}$ is derived by computing the maximum probability across classes, $p_{\max} = \max_{j=1,\dots,N} \mathbf{P}_j$, and the corresponding class index, $c_{\max} = \arg\max_{j=1,\dots,N} \mathbf{P}_j$. Voxels are assigned class labels $l_j \in \{1, \dots, N\}$ where $p_{\max} \geq 0.5$, i.e., $\mathbf{S} = l_{c_{\max}}$ if $p_{\max} \geq 0.5$, otherwise $\mathbf{S} = 0$ (background).

For each class $l \in \{1, \dots, N\}$, a binary mask $M_l = (\mathbf{S} = l)$ is created. Connected components in M_l are labeled using 6-connectivity, yielding a labeled image C_l and component sizes $\Sigma_l = \{(c_i, s_i)\}$. The mean probability for component c_i is computed as the average of $\mathbf{P}_l$ over voxels where $C_l = c_i$. Among the top three largest components, those with mean probabilities within $\tau = 0.1$ of the maximum and above 0.86 are retained. If none qualify, the highest-probability component is kept if it is among the two largest and its size is at least 0.6 times the largest; otherwise, the largest component is selected. The refined mask M_l' updates $\mathbf{S}$ by setting $\mathbf{S} = 0$ where $M_l \wedge \neg M_l'$. This method enhances nnU-Net by processing classes individually and using probabilities to guide component selection, improving multi-class segmentation robustness.

3 Experimental Setup

3.1 Data and Evaluation Methodology

The development set builds upon the CVPR 2024 MedSAM on Laptop Challenge [17], incorporating additional 3D cases sourced from publicly available datasets[1]. This collection encompasses various standard 3D imaging modalities, including Computed Tomography (CT), Magnetic Resonance Imaging (MRI), Positron Emission Tomography (PET), Ultrasound, and Microscopy. The hidden

[1] Complete dataset details can be found at https://medsam-datasetlist.github.io/.

Algorithm 3. Post-processing

Require: $\mathbf{P} \in \mathbb{R}^{N \times H \times W \times D}$, labels $\{1, \ldots, N\}$, background $b = 0$, threshold $\tau = 0.1$, connectivity $k = 6$
Ensure: Refined segmentation $\mathbf{S} \in \mathbb{R}^{1 \times H \times W \times D}$
$p_{\max} \leftarrow \max_{j=1,\ldots,N} \mathbf{P}_j$, $c_{\max} \leftarrow \arg\max_{j=1,\ldots,N} \mathbf{P}_j$
$\mathbf{S} \leftarrow 0$, $\mathbf{S}[p_{\max} \geq 0.5] \leftarrow l_{c_{\max}}$
for $l = 1$ to N **do**
    $M_l \leftarrow (\mathbf{S} = l)$
    $C_l, \Sigma_l \leftarrow \text{ConnectedComponents}(M_l, k)$
    if $\Sigma_l = \emptyset$ **then continue**
    end if
    $T \leftarrow \text{SortBySize}(\Sigma_l)[:3]$
    $P_T \leftarrow \{(c_i, \text{mean}(\mathbf{P}_l[C_l = c_i])) \mid c_i \in T\}$
    $p_{\max} \leftarrow \max\{p_i \mid (c_i, p_i) \in P_T\}$
    $K \leftarrow \{c_i \mid (c_i, p_i) \in P_T, (p_{\max} - p_i) \leq \tau, p_i > 0.86\}$
    if $|K| \geq 2$ **then**
        $M'_l \leftarrow (C_l \in K)$
    else
        $c_{\max} \leftarrow \arg\max_{c_i} \{p_i \mid (c_i, p_i) \in P_T\}$
        $T_2 \leftarrow T[:2]$
        if $c_{\max} \in T_2$ and $\Sigma_l(c_{\max})/\Sigma_l(T[0]) > 0.6$ **then**
            $M'_l \leftarrow (C_l = c_{\max})$
        else
            $M'_l \leftarrow (C_l = T[0])$
        end if
    end if
    $\mathbf{S}[M_l \wedge \neg M'_l] \leftarrow b$
end for
return S

test set was collaboratively developed by the community, consisting exclusively of previously unpublished cases. All annotations were either supplied by data contributors or generated by the challenge organizers using 3D Slicer [12] and MedSAM2 [18]. Participants have the option to either use the full training set or participate in the coreset track, which permits model development using only 10% of the total training cases.

The text-guided segmentation task evaluates both semantic and instance segmentation performance. Semantic segmentation assessment employs two metrics: the Dice Similarity Coefficient (DSC) for measuring region overlap and Normalized Surface Distance (NSD) for evaluating boundary accuracy. Instance segmentation performance is quantified using the F1 score at a 0.5 overlap threshold, along with DSC scores for correctly identified instances. A runtime constraint of 60 s per class is enforced - submissions exceeding this limit will receive zero scores for all DSC and NSD metrics on the affected test cases.

3.2 Implementation Details

Data Preprocessing. Consistent with MedSAM [16], all medical images were converted to npz format and normalized to an intensity range of $[0, 255]$. For CT scans specifically, we performed Hounsfield unit normalization using standard window settings: soft tissues (width:400, level:40), lung (width:1500, level:-160), brain (width:80, level:40), and bone (width:1800, level:400). Following this normalization, the intensity values were linearly scaled to the target range of $[0, 255]$. For non-CT imaging modalities, we first truncated intensity values at the 0.5th and 99.5th percentiles before applying the same rescaling procedure. Images that already had native intensity values within the $[0, 255]$ range underwent no additional preprocessing steps.

Table 1. Training protocols.

Pre-trained Model	SAT
Batch size	4
Patch size	224×224×128
Spacing	(1.5, 1.5, 3.0)
Total steps	108600
Optimizer	AdamW
Initial learning rate (lr)	1e-4
Lr decay schedule	cosine
Training time	168 h
Loss function	BCE+Dice
Number of model parameters	221M

Training Protocols. To handle large-scale datasets for fast preprocessing and data loading, the dynamic resampling strategy mentioned in Sect. 2.5 is developed based on the latest version of the resampling function from the nnU-Net [11] framework. The resampling function in the latest version of nnU-Net significantly improves the efficiency of resampling large-scale data by leveraging CPU processing. Additionally, the latest Blosc2 compression format from nnU-Net is adopted to compress npz files, achieving a balance between file storage size and read speed during dataloader operations. For the preprocessing of 3D images, dataloader, and data augmentation, most of the functions and code from nnU-Net are retained with appropriate modifications.

For the text dataloader and simultaneous training across multiple datasets, different sampling rates are set for each dataset, along with adjustments to the positive-negative sample ratio and padding alignment for varying batch text prompt lengths. Multi-GPU training is primarily based on the SAT [28]. The optimal model selection criteria are also based on SAT, as the learning rate

Table 2. Training protocols for the 2nd model

Pre-trained Model	SAT
Batch size	8
Patch size	192×192×192
Spacing	(1.0, 1.0, 1.0)
Total steps	91300
Optimizer	AdamW
Initial learning rate (lr)	1e-4
Lr decay schedule	cosine
Training time	160 h
Loss function	BCE+Dice
Number of model parameters	221M

curve decreases gradually with each epoch; by default, the model from the final iteration is adopted.

The training configurations are as follows: for the 224224128 input size, we use a batch size of 2 per GPU across 2 GPUs (effective batch size of 4), while for the 192192192 input size, we employ a batch size of 2 per GPU across 4 GPUs (effective batch size of 8). The complete training process takes 7 days (168 h) to complete. Detailed environment settings and training protocols are presented in Table 3,Table 1, and Table 2.

Environment Settings. The development environments and requirements are presented in Table 3.

Table 3. Development environments and requirements.

System	Ubuntu 22.04.4 LTS (Jammy Jellyfish)
CPU	Intel(R) Xeon(R) Platinum 8468 CPU @2.10 GHz
RAM	2TB DDR (1.8TB available)
GPU (number and type)	Eight NVIDIA H100 80 GB HBM3
CUDA version	12.2
Programming language	Python 3.10.16
Deep learning framework	torch 2.2.0, torchvision 0.17.0

4 Results and Discussion

Table 4. Quantitative evaluation results of the validation set on the **all-data track**.

Modality	Method	Semantic Segmentation		Instance Segmentation	
		DSC	NSD	F1	DSC TP
CT	CAT	72.11	72.27	29.93	37.17
	BiomedParse-V	85.12	89.65	51.19	67.49
	SAT	67.80	67.26	25.17	39.54
	Medal S (w/o stage1)	80.36	79.28	29.66	47.14
	Medal S (w/o post)	81.87	81.59	38.46	49.97
	Medal S	81.90	81.61	39.97	50.94
MRI	CAT	54.15	61.93	13.75	28.13
	BiomedParse-V	73.96	86.64	53.17	70.53
	SAT	56.10	66.69	12.28	27.28
	Medal S (w/o stage1)	62.90	71.11	33.62	65.11
	Medal S (w/o post)	61.96	71.11	47.50	66.48
	Medal S	61.95	70.94	46.99	66.41
Microscopy	CAT	-	-	3.13	36.28
	BiomedParse-V	-	-	19.39	65.52
	SAT	-	-	20.06	42.43
	Medal S (w/o stage1)	-	-	33.03	70.49
	Medal S (w/o post)	-	-	33.82	72.12
	Medal S	-	-	33.44	72.39
PET	CAT	-	-	10.98	27.79
	BiomedParse-V	-	-	31.32	71.85
	SAT	-	-	42.00	78.63
	Medal S (w/o stage1)	-	-	28.30	72.92
	Medal S (w/o post)	-	-	33.89	70.89
	Medal S	-	-	32.57	72.11
Ultrasound	CAT	85.94	83.60	-	-
	BiomedParse-V	90.50	91.35	-	-
	SAT	85.58	79.24	-	-
	Medal S (w/o stage1)	77.99	73.04	-	-
	Medal S (w/o post)	82.37	79.16	-	-
	Medal S	82.45	79.48	-	-
Average	CAT	70.73	72.60	14.45	32.34
	BiomedParse-V	83.19	89.21	38.77	68.85
	SAT	69.83	71.06	24.88	46.97
	Medal S (w/o stage1)	73.75	74.48	31.15	63.91
	Medal S (w/o post)	75.40	77.28	38.42	64.87
	Medal S	75.44	77.34	38.24	65.46

4.1 Quantitative Results on Validation Set

Table 4 presents validation results on the all-data track. Our Medal S model consistently outperforms the CAT and SAT baselines, as well as the single-stage ablation Medal S (w/o stage1), across nearly all metrics and modalities. It falls below the concurrent BiomedParse-V in semantic segmentation but achieves comparable performance in instance segmentation.

On average, Medal S achieves 75.44 DSC, 77.34 NSD, 38.24 F1, and 65.46 DSC TP—representing gains of 4.71/4.74/23.79/33.12 over CAT and 5.61/6.28/13.36/18.49 over SAT. These improvements arise from two core innovations. Medal S advances beyond SAT through channel-wise spatial-textual alignment using lightweight 3D convolutions, preserving full-resolution fidelity. Combined with parallel prompt processing and optimized resampling, this enables superior boundary delineation and instance separation.

In ultrasound, Medal S lags behind SAT (82.45 vs. 85.58 DSC) due to large target-to-patch ratios, revealing that the current dynamic resampling strategy still has room for improvement to better adapt to more complex input sizes, spacings, and target proportions. While Medal S demonstrates the above advantages, it still lags behind BiomedParse-V in certain aspects, indicating room for further improvement in future work.

Ablation on Two-Stage Inference. The two-stage inference paradigm: low-resolution predictions from stage 1 provide global spatial prompts that effectively guide fine-grained refinement in stage 2. Ablation studies reveal average DSC gains of 1.69, NSD gains of 2.86, F1 gains of 7.09 and DSC TP gains of 1.55, with up to 13.37 F1 improvement in MRI—demonstrating that coarse-to-fine spatial guidance is essential for precise localization in complex, multi-organ scenes.

Ablation on Post-processing. Medal S with post-processing yields only marginal average gains over Medal S (w/o post): +0.04 DSC, +0.06 NSD, -0.18 F1, +0.59 DSC TP. This suggests that the current post-processing is not universally effective and may disrupt refined predictions in some cases.

In summary, Medal S establishes a new standard in universal medical segmentation by synergistically integrating global spatial cues with precise textual alignment in a two-stage, full-resolution framework—delivering superior accuracy and efficiency across diverse anatomies and imaging modalities.

4.2 Qualitative Results on Validation Set

As illustrated in Fig. 3, the qualitative results on the validation set provide insights into the performance of our proposed method, Medal S, across different modalities. Due to the unavailability of the CAT all-data Docker and the lack of updated qualitative results for CAT, a direct comparison with CAT on the all-data track for the validation set is not feasible. Consequently, our analysis focuses on comparing Medal S predictions against ground truth annotations across five modalities, presenting both successful and challenging segmentation cases for each.

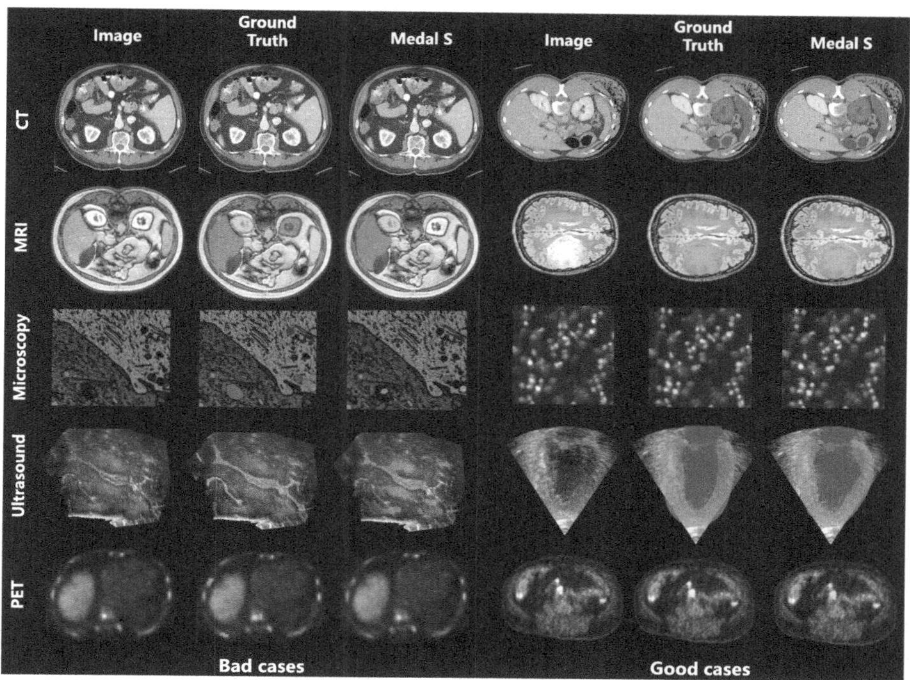

Fig. 3. Comparison of Medal S and ground truth results on the validation set for five different modalities. For each modality, we present both good segmentation results and bad segmentation results.

The qualitative results reveal that Medal S performs effectively in segmenting multi-class targets and regions with substantial volume across various modalities. In such cases, the model accurately delineates boundaries and captures structural details, benefiting from its channel-wise alignment of volumetric prompts and text embeddings, as well as its ability to process spatial prompts at native resolution. However, segmentation quality diminishes for smaller lesions, particularly in datasets with significant foreground-background imbalance or blurred boundaries, such as those involving tumors. These challenging cases often exhibit ambiguous edges and complex textures, which pose difficulties for precise segmentation.

A contributing factor to these failures is the inherent noise in the labels of such data, which increases segmentation difficulty. Small lesions and imbalanced datasets amplify the impact of label inaccuracies, making it harder for the model to distinguish between foreground and background. While Medal S's dynamic resampling and optimized preprocessing mitigate some of these issues, further improvements in handling noisy labels and refining boundary detection for small, ambiguous targets are necessary to enhance performance in these scenarios.

4.3 Spatial Prompt Ablation Study

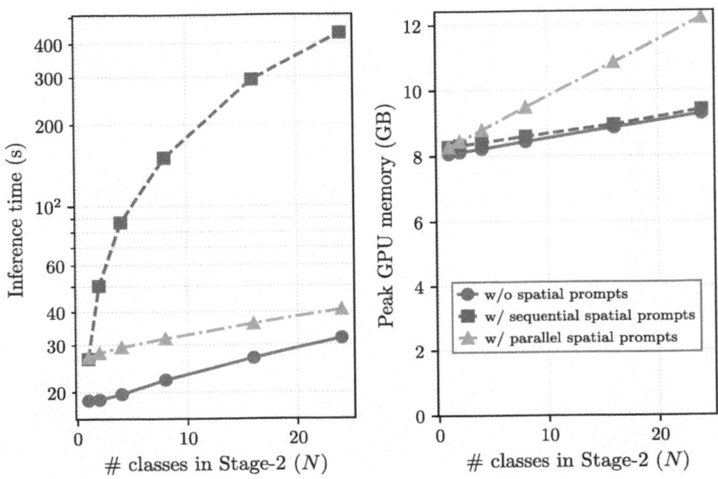

Fig. 4. Efficiency comparison of spatial prompting strategies. (a) Inference runtime and (b) peak GPU memory consumption versus the number of classes. Parallel prompting achieves minimal time complexity with respect to the number of classes, resulting in a greater than 10× speedup for 24-class segmentation over the sequential approach, whose runtime grows substantially. While parallel prompting requires moderately more memory, it remains within practical limits and offers a favorable trade-off for drastic time savings in multi-class scenarios.

Table 5. Quantitative ablation study on the effect of spatial prompts.

Variant	DSC	NSD
w/o spatial prompts	83.50	78.15
w/ stage1 spatial prompts	83.98	79.16
w/ GT spatial prompts	87.23	84.50

As shown in Fig. 5, we conduct a case study to analyze the impact of spatial prompts under three distinct settings: 1) without any spatial prompts, 2) using the Stage-1 segmentation prediction as the spatial prompt for Stage-2, and 3) using the ground-truth (GT) segmentation mask as the spatial prompt for Stage-2. The results qualitatively demonstrate that the model can dynamically adapt its predictions based on the presence and quality of spatial prompts. Specifically, when provided with more accurate spatial prompts (e.g., GT masks), the model generates significantly refined outputseffectively suppressing small-scale noise,

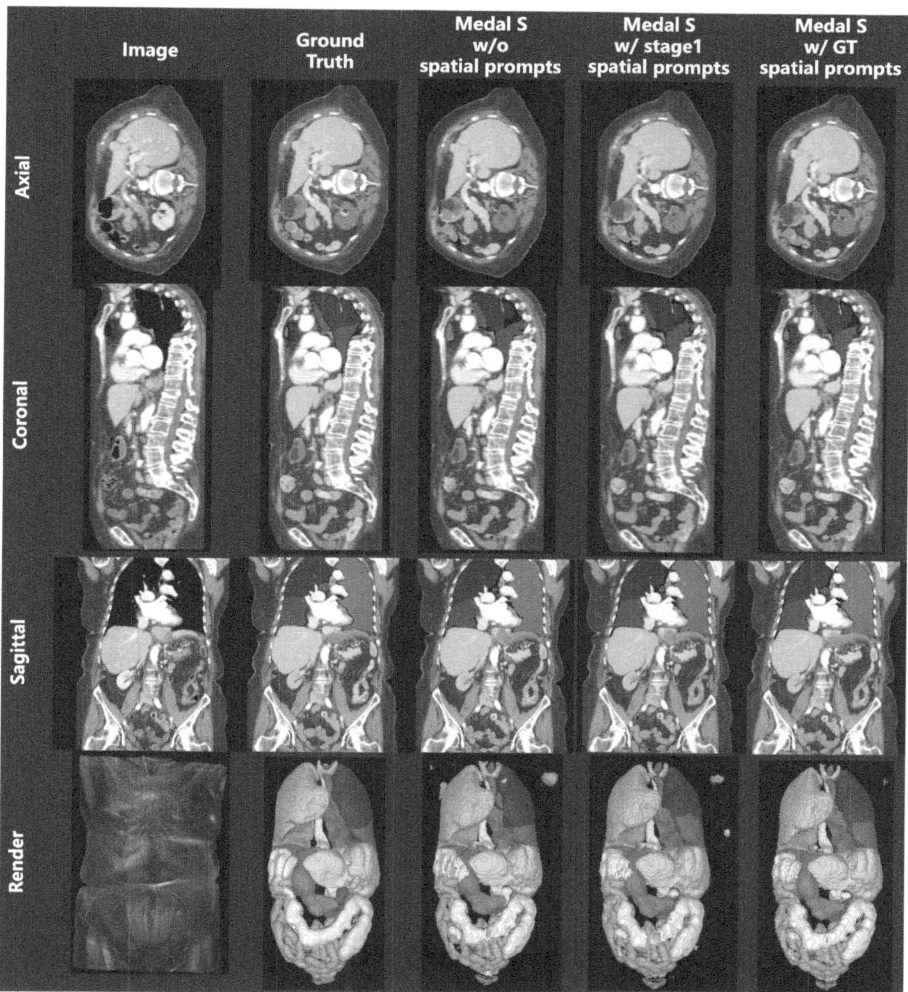

Fig. 5. Qualitative comparison of Medal S with different spatial prompt configurations. From left to right: (a) Input Image, (b) Ground Truth, (c) Medal S without spatial prompts, (d) Medal S with Stage-1 prediction as spatial prompts, and (e) Medal S with GT masks as spatial prompts. Each configuration is visualized in axial, coronal, sagittal views and 3D rendering, demonstrating the progressive improvement in segmentation quality with better spatial prompts - particularly in noise reduction, confusion resolution, and continuity enhancement.

resolving category confusion, and enhancing spatial continuity. These observations are quantitatively supported by the results in Table 5, where using GT spatial prompts yields the highest DSC and NSD, confirming that the model effectively leverages superior spatial prompts to produce more accurate segmentation results.

Based on the comprehensive analysis of spatial prompt effectiveness in Fig. 5 and Table 5, which is an analysis result for a single test data example, we further demonstrate the efficiency of our proposed parallel spatial prompting mechanism through runtime and memory evaluation. As shown in Fig. 4, our parallel spatial prompting approach achieves a remarkable balance between performance and efficiency when evaluated on the same single case. While providing significant segmentation quality improvements as evidenced by the 83.98 DSC and 79.16 NSD in Table 5, the parallel method only introduces moderate computational overhead compared to the no-prompt baseline. Crucially, as the number of classes increases from 1 to 24, the parallel approach maintains reasonable runtime (40.63 s vs 31.75 s baseline) and memory usage (12.5GB vs 9.49GB baseline), while sequential prompting exhibits substantial time growth (435.1 s), becoming practically infeasible for multi-class segmentation tasks. This efficiency advantage, combined with the proven effectiveness in enhancing segmentation quality, makes our parallel spatial prompting strategy highly promising for clinical applications where both accuracy and computational efficiency are paramount.

4.4 Results on Final Testing Set

The quantitative evaluation results on the test set for the all-data track, as shown in Table 6, demonstrate that our method Medal S achieves a Dice score of 58.06 and an NSD of 59.11, both of which are higher than those of the improved baseline model SAT (DSC: 54.13, NSD: 52.97). This indicates that Medal S is a promising approach. However, there remains a performance gap compared to the current leading method, BiomedParse-V (DSC: 74.97, NSD: 77.47), suggesting potential for further optimization in the future.

Table 6. Quantitative evaluation results of the testing set on the **all-data track**.

Method	Semantic Segmentation		Instance Segmentation	
	DSC	NSD	F1	DSC TP
CAT	33.04	31.53	1.94	4.66
BiomedParse-V	74.97	77.47	23.80	44.76
SAT	54.13	52.97	14.19	29.59
Medal S	58.06	59.11	10.54	17.86

4.5 Limitation and Future Work

While Medal S demonstrates strong performance across multiple modalities, certain limitations warrant further exploration. The dynamic resampling strategy, although effective in addressing target-patch ratio imbalances, requires additional refinement to better handle modalities like ultrasound, where large target sizes challenge the current patch-based approach. Expanding the variety of spatial prompts could further enhance performance. For instance, incorporating diverse spatial prompts, such as those in nnInteractive, including 2D spatial cues, could improve flexibility and precision in capturing complex anatomical structures.

Future work will focus on optimizing Medal S for challenging datasets, particularly those involving instance segmentation with small lesions, significant foreground-background imbalances, or blurred boundaries, such as tumor data. Additionally, addressing datasets with a high number of classes and intricate anatomical relationships will be a priority. To align with clinical scenarios, we aim to develop robust solutions for diverse, complex datasets with numerous lesions, ensuring the model's applicability in real-world medical imaging tasks.

5 Conclusion

This study introduces Medal S, a novel medical image segmentation foundation model that achieves superior performance across diverse modalities. Its end-to-end trainable framework uniquely harmonizes spatial precision with semantic textual guidance by supporting native-resolution spatial and textual prompts. A key innovation is the channel-wise alignment of spatial prompts and text embeddings, which successfully mitigates inaccuracies from resolution mismatchesa critical limitation of text-only methods. Crucially, this parallel processing of spatial prompts yields a 10× speedup for 24-class segmentation over sequential methods, with even greater efficiency gains for more classes. This advancement is further enabled by a lightweight 3D convolutional module for precise voxel-space refinement.

Medal S demonstrates superior efficiency and accuracy in multi-class 3D medical segmentation. On the five-modality average on the validation set, it outperforms SAT with a DSC of 75.44 (vs. 69.83), NSD of 77.34 (vs. 71.06), F1 of 38.24 (vs. 24.88), and DSC TP of 65.46 (vs. 46.97). Supporting up to 243 classes across CT, MRI, PET, ultrasound, and microscopy, Medal S offers two versatile prompting modes: text-only for self-refinement and hybrid for incorporating manual annotations. Future work will focus on improving robustness for complex, imbalanced datasets and small lesions, and refining the dynamic resampling strategy to address the current performance lag in ultrasound. Overall, Medal S represents a significant advancement for high-speed, memory-efficient, and accurate medical image segmentation.

Disclosure of Interests. The authors have no competing interests to declare that are relevant to the content of this article.

Acknowledgements. We thank all the data owners for making the medical images publicly available and CodaLab [24] for hosting the challenge platform.

References

1. Avrahami, O., et al.: Spatext: Spatio-textual representation for controllable image generation. In: Proceedings of the IEEE/CVF Conference on Computer Vision and Pattern Recognition, pp. 18370–18380 (2023)
2. Bassi, P.R., et al.: Radgpt: Constructing 3D image-text tumor datasets. In: Proceedings of the IEEE/CVF International Conference on Computer Vision, pp. 23720–23730 (2025)
3. Carion, N., Massa, F., Synnaeve, G., Usunier, N., Kirillov, A., Zagoruyko, S.: End-to-end object detection with transformers. In: European Conference on Computer Vision, pp. 213–229. Springer (2020)
4. Cheng, B., Schwing, A., Kirillov, A.: Per-pixel classification is not all you need for semantic segmentation. Adv. Neural. Inf. Process. Syst. **34**, 17864–17875 (2021)
5. Du, Y., Bai, F., Huang, T., Zhao, B.: Segvol: Universal and interactive volumetric medical image segmentation. In: Advances in Neural Information Processing Systems, vol. 37, pp. 110746–110783 (2024)
6. Fabian, I., et al..: nninteractive: Redefining 3D promptable segmentation. arXiv preprint arXiv:2503.08373 (2025)
7. Gafni, O., Polyak, A., Ashual, O., Sheynin, S., Parikh, D., Taigman, Y.: Make-a-scene: Scene-based text-to-image generation with human priors. In: European Conference on Computer Vision, pp. 89–106. Springer (2022). https://doi.org/10.1007/978-3-031-19784-0_6
8. He, K., Chen, X., Xie, S., Li, Y., Dollár, P., Girshick, R.: Masked autoencoders are scalable vision learners. In: Proceedings of the IEEE/CVF Conference on Computer Vision and Pattern Recognition, pp. 16000–16009 (2022)
9. He, Y., et al.: VISTA3D: A unified segmentation foundation model for 3D medical imaging. In: Proceedings of the IEEE/CVF International Conference on Computer Vision and Pattern Recognition (2024)
10. Huang, Z., Jiang, Y., Zhang, R., Zhang, S., Zhang, X.: Cat: coordinating anatomical-textual prompts for multi-organ and tumor segmentation. In: Globerson, A., et al., (eds.) Advances in Neural Information Processing Systems, vol. 37, pp. 3588–3610 (2024)
11. Isensee, F., Jaeger, P.F., Kohl, S.A., Petersen, J., Maier-Hein, K.H.: nnu-net: a self-configuring method for deep learning-based biomedical image segmentation. Nat. Methods **18**(2), 203–211 (2021)
12. Kikinis, R., Pieper, S.D., Vosburgh, K.G.: 3D Slicer: a platform for subject-specific image analysis, visualization, and clinical support, pp. 277–289. Springer (2013)
13. Kirillov, A., et al.: Segment anything. In: Proceedings of the International Conference on Computer Vision, pp. 4015–4026 (2023)
14. Li, W., et al.: Scalemai: Accelerating the development of trusted datasets and ai models. arXiv preprint arXiv:2501.03410 (2025)
15. Liu, J., et al.: Clip-driven universal model for organ segmentation and tumor detection. In: Proceedings of the IEEE/CVF International Conference on Computer Vision, pp. 21152–21164 (2023)
16. Ma, J., He, Y., Li, F., Han, L., You, C., Wang, B.: Segment anything in medical images. Nat. Commun. **15**, 654 (2024)
17. Ma, J., et al.: Efficient medsams: Segment anything in medical images on laptop. arXiv:2412.16085 (2024)
18. Ma, J., et al.: Medsam2: Segment anything in 3d medical images and videos. arXiv preprint arXiv:2504.03600 (2025)

19. Ravi, N., et al.: Sam 2: Segment anything in images and videos. In: International Conference on Learning Representations (2025)
20. Ronneberger, O., Fischer, P., Brox, T.: U-net: convolutional networks for biomedical image segmentation. In: International Conference on Medical Image Computing and Computer-Assisted Intervention, pp. 234–241 (2015)
21. Vaswani, A., et al.: Attention is all you need. In: Advances in Neural Information Processing Systems, vol. 30 (2017)
22. Wang, H., et al.: Sam-med3d: towards general-purpose segmentation models for volumetric medical images. In: European Conference on Computer Vision, pp. 51–67. Springer (2024)
23. Wong, H.E., Rakic, M., Guttag, J., Dalca, A.V.: Scribbleprompt: fast and flexible interactive segmentation for any biomedical image. In: European Conference on Computer Vision, pp. 207–229. Springer (2024)
24. Xu, Z., et al.: Codabench: Flexible, easy-to-use, and reproducible meta-benchmark platform. Patterns **3**(7), 100543 (2022)
25. Zhang, L., Rao, A., Agrawala, M.: Adding conditional control to text-to-image diffusion models. In: Proceedings of the IEEE/CVF International Conference on Computer Vision, pp. 3836–3847 (2023)
26. Zhang, X., et al.: Development of a large-scale grounded vision language dataset for chest CT analysis. Sci. Data **12**(1), 1636 (2025)
27. Zhao, T., et al.: A foundation model for joint segmentation, detection and recognition of biomedical objects across nine modalities. Nat. Methods **22**, 166–176 (2025)
28. Zhao, Z., et al.: Large-vocabulary segmentation for medical images with text prompts. NPJ Digital Med. **8**(1), 566 (2025)

From Single-Round to Sequential: Building Stateful Interactive Medical Image Segmentation with SegVol and GRU Corrector

Chuanyi Huang, Jinlong Huang, and Lisheng Wang(✉)

School of Automation and Intelligent Sensing, Shanghai Jiao Tong University, Shanghai 200240, China
lswang@sjtu.edu.cn

Abstract. Medical image segmentation has advanced considerably with foundational models like the Segment Anything Model (SAM) and its medical variants, yet real-world clinical deployment remains constrained by heterogeneous imaging protocols, limited data generalization, and the inefficiency of manual interaction. While recent SAM-based frameworks (e.g., SAM2, MedSAM2) introduce memory-aware mechanisms, they still rely on dense re-encoding and lack targeted correction strategies. We propose **"From Single-Round to Sequential: Building Stateful Interactive Segmentation with SegVol and GRU Corrector"**, a lightweight framework that reformulates interactive segmentation as a sequential refinement process guided by uncertainty and error heuristics. Specifically, we design: (1) a GRU-based temporal module to encode interaction history and enable stateful correction, and (2) an uncertainty-driven region adaptation scheme that selectively focuses refinement on ambiguous or mis-segmented areas, reducing redundant computation while improving correction efficiency. On validation data, our framework achieves a progressive Dice coefficient improvement from 0.661 (single-box prompt) to 0.671 after three refinement rounds, showing a 1.5% absolute gain with diminishing returns in later interactions. These results highlight that uncertainty-guided, memory-efficient refinement offers a promising direction for practical interactive medical segmentation.

Keywords: Interactive Medical Image Segmentation · Uncertainty-Driven Refinement · Sequential State Modeling · Lightweight GRU Correction

1 Introduction

1.1 Background

Medical image segmentation has undergone a paradigm shift with the emergence of foundation models such as the Segment Anything Model (SAM) [5] and its medical extensions [6,8]. By leveraging large-scale pretraining, these

J. Ma et al. (Eds.): MedSegFM 2025, LNCS 16447, pp. 88–108, 2026.
https://doi.org/10.1007/978-3-032-23496-4_6

models demonstrate remarkable generalization across diverse anatomical structures. However, their clinical translation remains hindered by substantial domain heterogeneity—multi-center imaging data vary widely in acquisition protocols, contrast levels, and patient populations [8]. Existing segmentation frameworks still struggle with small or irregular structures that violate shape priors and intensity uniformity [3]. Such limitations undermine clinical tasks that rely on accurate lesion boundaries, including quantitative diagnosis, treatment response assessment, and longitudinal monitoring [1]. These challenges underscore the need for interactive and adaptable segmentation systems that can efficiently integrate human feedback while remaining computationally feasible for routine use.

1.2 Related Work and Limitations

Interactive segmentation offers a promising way to bridge the gap between automated inference and clinical reliability. Foundation models such as SAM/SAM2 [5,9] and MedSAM/MedSAM2 [6,8] have demonstrated the potential of general-purpose visual prompts for medical imaging. Notably, recent versions already incorporate *memory-aware processing*, enabling limited contextual understanding across multiple prompts. Yet, their refinement process remains computationally expensive, as each correction still triggers dense re-encoding of the entire volume. Moreover, these models treat all regions uniformly during refinement, without explicitly prioritizing areas of high uncertainty or segmentation error. This results in redundant computation and limited gains with repeated interaction, particularly in volumetric 3D settings where localized corrections are more desirable.

Beyond SAM-based designs, frameworks such as VISTA3D [3] and nnInteractive [2] improve volumetric reasoning but largely preserve the stateless nature of interaction, handling each prompt independently. Consequently, they struggle to capture users' sequential intent—how each feedback relates to prior corrections—and fail to balance efficiency with accuracy [1]. These gaps motivate a new perspective: treating interactive segmentation not as isolated refinements, but as a sequential decision process guided by uncertainty and prior state information.

1.3 Contributions

To address these limitations, we propose **"From Single-Round to Sequential: Building Stateful Interactive Segmentation with SegVol and GRU Corrector"**, a lightweight framework that models interactive refinement as a temporally coherent process. Our main contributions are as follows.

First, we introduce a **GRU-based temporal corrector** that encodes the history of user interactions and segmentation states. Instead of reprocessing the full volume after each prompt, the model selectively updates predictions based on the accumulated context, effectively capturing user intent over time.

Second, we develop an **uncertainty-driven region adaptation** mechanism that heuristically identifies ambiguous or error-prone regions for targeted correction. By focusing computation on these uncertain areas—typically near boundary inconsistencies or low-confidence voxels—the model reduces redundant processing while maintaining segmentation precision. This makes our approach particularly efficient for repeated interactions in complex cases such as irregular tumor margins or fine vascular networks.

Through these designs, our framework enables progressive, memory-efficient refinement in a stateful manner, achieving effective correction with minimal overhead. Unlike existing memory-heavy systems, our approach leverages uncertainty as an implicit guide for interaction, providing a practical and interpretable path toward adaptive clinical segmentation.

2 Method

Our framework, illustrated in Fig. 1, reformulates interactive medical image segmentation as a sequential refinement process. It integrates three main components: (1) **Box-Initialized Segmentation**, (2) **Uncertainty-Aware Interaction Sampling**, and (3) **GRU-Based Sequential Correction**. Together, these modules enable efficient, memory-aware refinement by focusing computation on uncertain and error-prone regions.

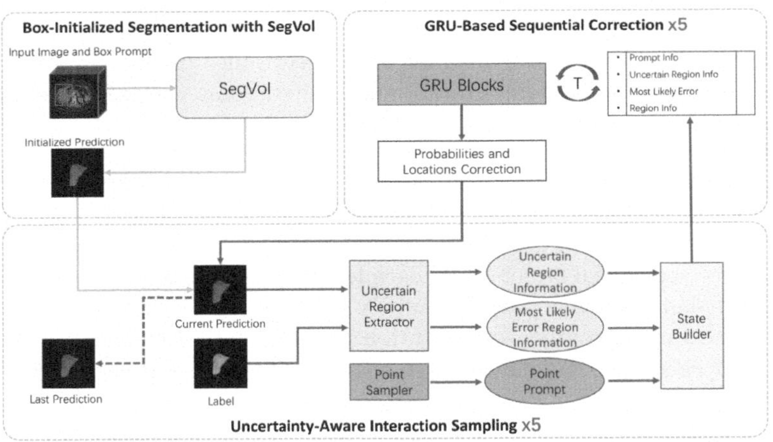

Fig. 1. Overview of the proposed framework. (a) SegVol produces an initial mask from a box prompt. (b) Uncertain and erroneous regions are sampled to build the sequential state tensor. (c) The GRU Corrector refines predictions based on accumulated interaction history.

2.1 Box-Initialized Segmentation with SegVol

Given a volumetric medical image $\mathbf{I} \in \mathbb{R}^{D \times H \times W}$ and a user-specified bounding box $\mathbf{B} \in \mathbb{R}^6$, the SegVol module generates an initial probability map $\mathbf{P}_0 \in$

$[0, 1]^{D\times H\times W}$ and a corresponding binary mask:

$$\mathbf{M}_0 = \text{SegVol}(\mathbf{I}, \mathbf{B}), \quad \hat{y}_0 = \mathbb{I}(\mathbf{M}_0 > 0.5), \tag{1}$$

where $\mathbb{I}(\cdot)$ denotes the indicator function and $\hat{y}_0$ is the binarized segmentation output. This serves as the initial state for interactive refinement.

2.2 Uncertainty-Aware Interaction Sampling

To avoid reprocessing the full volume after every interaction, we design a lightweight sampling mechanism that identifies only the regions most in need of correction.

At iteration t, the current prediction produces a voxel-wise probability map $\mathbf{P}_t = \sigma(\mathbf{Z}_t)$, where $\mathbf{Z}_t$ denotes the raw logits from SegVol and $\sigma(\cdot)$ the sigmoid activation. We define the voxel-wise probability $p_t(i, j, k)$ as:

$$p_t(i, j, k) = \sigma(z_t(i, j, k)) = \frac{1}{1 + e^{-z_t(i,j,k)}}, \tag{2}$$

representing the model's confidence that voxel (i, j, k) belongs to the foreground.

Uncertainty is quantified by the proximity of $p_t(i, j, k)$ to a confidence threshold $\tau \in (0, 0.5]$, which measures the distance from the decision boundary $(p = 0.5)$. Voxels near this boundary correspond to ambiguous predictions:

$$\mathcal{U}_t = \{(i, j, k) \mid |p_t(i, j, k) - 0.5| < \tau\}. \tag{3}$$

In practice, τ is empirically set to 0.1, indicating that voxels with probabilities between 0.4 and 0.6 are treated as uncertain.

To incorporate user feedback, corrective clicks are simulated as $\mathbf{c}_n = (x_n, y_n, z_n)$ with associated labels $l_n \in \{0, 1\}$ (positive for inclusion, negative for exclusion). The corresponding error region is defined by the mismatch between the current prediction $\hat{y}_t$ and user intent:

$$\mathcal{E}_t = \bigcup_n \left\{(i, j, k) \mid \|\mathbf{x} - \mathbf{c}_n\|_2 \leq r \text{ and } \hat{y}_t(i, j, k) \neq l_n\right\}, \tag{4}$$

where r denotes the local radius for sampling around each click. The union of uncertainty and error regions forms the candidate correction set.

Both $\mathcal{U}_t$ and $\mathcal{E}_t$ are ranked by confidence and truncated or zero-padded to a fixed number K (default $K = 200$) to balance GPU memory usage. Algorithm 1 summarizes the procedure.

2.3 State Tensor Construction

After sampling uncertainty points $\mathcal{U}_t$ and error points $\mathcal{E}_t$, we construct a structured state tensor for GRU-based sequential correction. The process for constructing the sequential state tensor is illustrated in Fig. 2. It consists of three horizontally arranged modules: the top module extracts **Uncertain Region**

Algorithm 1 Uncertainty- and Error-Guided Sampling at Iteration t

Require: Probability map $\mathbf{P}_t$, binary mask $\hat{y}_t$, user clicks $\{\mathbf{c}_n, l_n\}$, threshold τ, radius r, limit K

Ensure: Sets $\mathcal{U}_t$, $\mathcal{E}_t$

$\mathcal{U}_t \leftarrow \emptyset$, $\mathcal{E}_t \leftarrow \emptyset$
for each voxel (i, j, k) **do**
    if $|p_t(i, j, k) - 0.5| < \tau$ **then**
        $\mathcal{U}_t \leftarrow \mathcal{U}_t \cup \{(i, j, k, |p_t(i, j, k) - 0.5|)\}$
    end if
end for
for each click $\mathbf{c}_n$ with label l_n **do**
    for voxels $\mathbf{x}$ within radius r of $\mathbf{c}_n$ **do**
        if $\hat{y}_t(\mathbf{x}) \neq l_n$ **then**
            $\mathcal{E}_t \leftarrow \mathcal{E}_t \cup \{\mathbf{x}\}$
        end if
    end for
end for
Rank $\mathcal{U}_t$ by $|p_t - 0.5|$ and select top K entries
Randomly sample or pad $\mathcal{E}_t$ to size K

Information, the middle module extracts **Most Likely Error Region Information**, and the bottom module constructs the combined **State Tensor**.

Each sampled voxel is represented by an 8-dimensional feature vector that encodes spatial, probabilistic, and interaction information. Specifically, the first three dimensions correspond to the voxel's normalized spatial coordinates $(i/D, j/H, k/W)$, capturing its relative position within the volumetric input. The fourth dimension stores either the model's predicted probability $p_t(i, j, k)$ for uncertainty points or the user-provided label $y_{\text{user}} \in \{0, 1\}$ for error points. The fifth dimension is a binary validity flag $m \in \{0, 1\}$, which distinguishes real voxels from padding entries introduced to maintain a fixed tensor size. The final three dimensions encode the coordinates of the initial user click (x_0, y_0, z_0), providing global contextual information that is repeated for all sampled points.

Concatenating these components gives the final 8-dimensional feature vector for each voxel. Features from uncertainty and error points are separately organized as tensors:

$$\mathbf{F}_t^{\text{unc}} \in \mathbb{R}^{K \times 8}, \tag{5}$$

$$\mathbf{F}_t^{\text{err}} \in \mathbb{R}^{K \times 8}, \tag{6}$$

and then vertically concatenated to form the combined input:

$$\mathbf{X}_t = [\mathbf{F}_t^{\text{unc}}; \mathbf{F}_t^{\text{err}}] \in \mathbb{R}^{2K \times 8}. \tag{7}$$

For geometric alignment during refinement, the original spatial coordinates are stored separately as

$$\mathbf{C}_t = [\text{coordinates}(\mathcal{U}_t); \text{coordinates}(\mathcal{E}_t)] \in \mathbb{R}^{2K \times 3}. \tag{8}$$

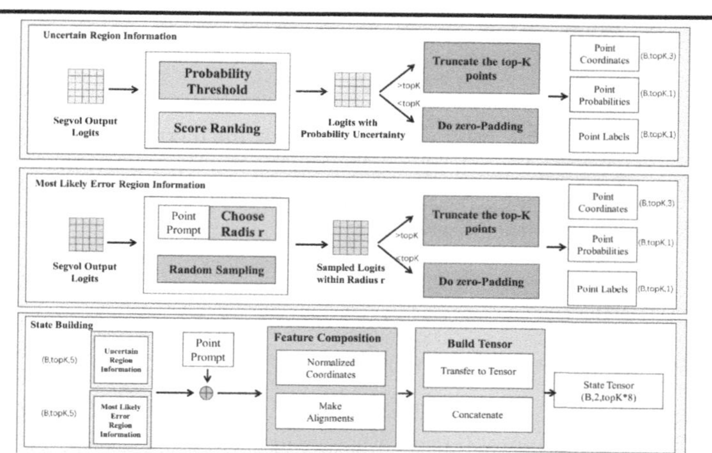

Fig. 2. Workflow for constructing the sequential state tensor from interaction points. The top horizontal container illustrates the extraction of **Uncertain Region Information**, where voxels with probabilities near the segmentation threshold (τ) are identified. The middle container depicts the extraction of **Most Likely Error Region Information**, highlighting regions around user-provided corrective clicks where the current prediction disagrees with the user label. The bottom container shows the **State Construction** process, where features from both uncertainty and error regions are combined into a structured tensor suitable for GRU-based sequential correction.

This tensor $\mathbf{X}_t$ together with $\mathbf{C}_t$ is passed to the GRU network at step t, allowing the model to incorporate both local uncertainty/error cues and global contextual information while maintaining a fixed-size, memory-efficient representation.

2.4 GRU-Based Sequential Correction

To capture temporal dependencies across interactions, we employ a Gated Recurrent Unit (GRU) network parameterized by θ. At each iteration t, it processes the current feature tensor $\mathbf{X}_t$ and hidden state $\mathbf{h}_{t-1}$ to output probability and coordinate adjustments:

$$\Delta p_t, \Delta \mathbf{C}_t = \mathrm{GRU}_\theta(\mathbf{X}_t, \mathbf{h}_{t-1}), \tag{9}$$

where $\Delta p_t \in \mathbb{R}^{2K}$ denotes the predicted probability offsets for the selected voxels, and $\Delta \mathbf{C}_t \in \mathbb{R}^{2K \times 3}$ represents the coordinate refinements. The updated hidden state $\mathbf{h}_t$ encodes accumulated interaction history.

2.5 Iterative Refinement

After each iteration, voxel probabilities at sampled coordinates $\mathcal{C}_t$ are updated by:

$$p_{t+1}(i,j,k) = p_t(i,j,k) + \Delta p_t^{(n)}, \quad \text{for } (i,j,k) \in \mathcal{C}_t, \tag{10}$$

followed by mask binarization:

$$\hat{y}_{t+1} = \mathbb{I}(p_{t+1} > 0.5). \tag{11}$$

This process continues for T interaction rounds or until convergence. In contrast to previous memory-heavy methods, only a sparse set of uncertain or erroneous voxels is refined at each step, significantly improving computational efficiency while maintaining segmentation accuracy.

3 Experiments

3.1 Dataset and Evaluation Metrics

The development set is an extension of the CVPR 2024 MedSAM on Laptop Challenge [7], including more 3D cases from public datasets[1] and covering commonly used 3D modalities, such as Computed Tomography (CT), Magnetic Resonance Imaging (MRI), Positron Emission Tomography (PET), Ultrasound, and Microscopy images. The hidden testing set is created by a community effort where all the cases are unpublished. The annotations are either provided by the data contributors or annotated by the challenge organizer with 3D Slicer [4] and MedSAM2 [8]. In addition to using all training cases, the challenge contains a coreset track, where participants can select 10% of the total training cases for model development.

For each iterative segmentation, the evaluation metrics include Dice Similarity Coefficient (DSC) and Normalized Surface Distance (NSD) to evaluate the segmentation region overlap and boundary distance, respectively. The final metrics used for the ranking are:

DSC_AUC and NSD_AUC Scores The **AUC (Area Under the Curve)** for DSC and NSD measures cumulative improvement across interactions. This metric quantifies performance gains over the five click predictions, offering a comprehensive view of segmentation refinement. Notably, the AUC is computed solely based on click predictions, excluding the initial bounding box prediction (which is optional).

Final DSC and NSD Scores. These scores reflect the model's segmentation performance after all refinements, representing the ultimate accuracy achieved. In addition, the algorithm runtime will be limited to 90 s per class. Exceeding this limit will lead to all DSC and NSD metrics being set to 0 for that test case.

3.2 Implementation Details

Preprocessing. Following the practice in MedSAM [6], all images were processed to npz format with an intensity range of $[0, 255]$. Specifically, for CT images, we initially normalized the Hounsfield units using typical window width

[1] A complete list is available at https://medsam-datasetlist.github.io/.

and level values: soft tissues (W:400, L:40), lung (W:1500, L:-160), brain (W:80, L:40), and bone (W:1800, L:400). Subsequently, the intensity values were rescaled to the range of $[0, 255]$. For other images, we clipped the intensity values to the range between the 0.5th and 99.5th percentiles before rescaling them to the range of [0, 255]. If the original intensity range is already in $[0, 255]$, no preprocessing was applied.

Following the practice in SegVol-for-SegFM, to enhance foreground contrast, we implemented dynamic intensity normalization through the `ForegroundNorm` method, which first identifies foreground voxels using an adaptive mean-intensity threshold. The intensities are then clipped to the 0.05th and 99.95th percentiles of the foreground distribution before standardization, reducing sensitivity to extreme outliers while preserving tissue contrast. For multi-class segmentation tasks, ground truth masks are automatically decomposed into binary channels for each non-background category, with explicit validation of spatial alignment between image and mask dimensions.

For memory-efficient processing of high-resolution volumetric data, we utilize sparse matrix storage (NPZ format) for ground truth masks during loading, converting to dense arrays only when necessary for computational operations. The preprocessing pipeline supports both file-based and direct array inputs, allowing flexible integration with different data sources while maintaining consistent internal representations. All spatial transformations, including resizing and cropping, are applied after initial intensity normalization to minimize intermediate memory allocation. During training, stochastic patch extraction is performed through a weighted augmentation strategy that balances computational cost and diversity, prioritizing positive-negative sampling crops where appropriate.

Environment Settings. The development environments and requirements are presented in Table 1.

Table 1. Development environments and requirements. (mandatory table)

System	Ubuntu 22.04.2 LTS
CPU	Intel(R) Core(TM) i9-10920X CPU @ 3.50GHz
RAM	16×32 GB; 3200MT/s
GPU (number and type)	Two NVIDIA GeForce RTX 4090 24G
CUDA version	12.4
Programming language	Python 3.10.16
Deep learning framework	torch 2.7.0+cu126;torchvision 0.14.1+cu117

Training Protocols. Building upon the successful practices established in SegVol [1], we have developed an enhanced training methodology with optimized data augmentation and sampling strategies.

Data Augmentation: The training pipeline incorporates several spatial and intensity transformations to improve model generalization. Spatial augmentations include random flipping along all three axes (sagittal, coronal, and axial planes) with a probability of 0.2 for each orientation. For volumetric data, we employ a mixed strategy of either full-volume resizing or patch extraction through positive-negative sampling, with sampling weights favoring the latter (3:1 ratio). The patch extraction uses `RandCropByPosNegLabeld` with 3 positive samples for every negative sample, ensuring adequate representation of both foreground and background regions. Intensity augmentations consist of random scaling (factor range ±20%) and shifting (±20% of intensity range), each applied with 20% probability.

Data Sampling Strategy: We implement a dynamic sampling approach that adapts to the multi-class nature of segmentation tasks. During batch construction, the system automatically balances class representation by: 1) Preserving all available foreground classes in each sample through binary mask decomposition 2) Applying foreground cropping to concentrate computation on relevant regions 3) Using sparse storage formats for ground truth masks during loading to enable memory-efficient handling of large 3D volumes 4) Supporting both whole-volume processing and patch-based training, with the latter preferentially sampling regions containing segmentation targets when available. The sampling weights for patch extraction favor positive regions (3:1 positive-to-negative ratio) to address class imbalance while maintaining context. For inference, we process full volumes with optional overlapping sliding window when necessary for large scans.

Interactive Optimization Strategy. We present a two-stage training strategy that harmonizes global shape consistency with local detail refinement to achieve an optimal balance between interaction efficiency and segmentation accuracy in medical image analysis. The framework employs box prompt losses in the first stage to establish topological validity through global similarity metrics, followed by a second stage that combines both box and point prompt losses to enable precise boundary refinement using distance metrics, thereby preventing overfitting to initial prompts while ensuring robust convergence.

To accurately reflect clinical workflows where users typically perform limited refinements, we implement a weighted training protocol that prioritizes 2–3 GRU-based refinement iterations as the most frequent scenario, with 1 and 4 iterations occurring less frequently, and 0 or 5 iterations representing rare cases. This distribution ensures the model learns predominant interaction patterns while maintaining adaptability to extreme cases. The optimization process incorporates sequential refinement mechanisms that maintain memory states between iterations, coupled with a composite loss function that simultaneously optimizes global structural similarity, voxel-wise prediction accuracy, and consistency between initial and refined outputs. The conditional execution architecture enables differentiated processing of multimodal interaction prompts while ensuring stable gradient flow throughout the refinement cascade, providing both the efficiency required for clinical practice and the flexibility needed for complex segmentation tasks (Table 2).

Table 2. Training protocols. (mandatory table)

Pre-trained Model	SegVol (for SegFM)
Batch size	4
Patch size	256×256×32
Total epochs	25
Optimizer	AdamW
Initial learning rate (lr)	1e-5
Lr decay schedule	None
Training time	2 days 9 h
Loss function	Dice loss + BCE loss
Number of model parameters	295.35M[a]
Number of flops	264.18G[b]

[a]https://github.com/sksq96/pytorch-summary
[b]https://github.com/facebookresearch/fvcore.

4 Results

4.1 Analysis of the Iterative Refinement Mechanism

Our framework is fundamentally designed to enhance segmentation accuracy through a progressive, multi-stage correction process. To validate the effectiveness of this core mechanism, we first conducted an analysis focused on the performance gains achieved at each step of the iterative refinement. This evaluation was performed on a representative 5% subset of the validation set to enable rapid prototyping and assessment of the iterative dynamics.

As detailed in Table 3, the model demonstrates a clear and consistent pattern of improvement with each correction iteration. Starting from an initial segmentation generated by the first prompt, which achieved a Dice Similarity Coefficient (DSC) of 0.661, the model's performance steadily increases. The first correction step yields the most substantial improvement, boosting the DSC to 0.669 relative gain of 1.18%. Subsequent corrections continue to fine-tune the segmentation boundaries, with the second and third iterations contributing further incremental gains of +0.17% and +0.11%, respectively. After three refinement stages, the final DSC score stabilized at 0.671, achieving a total absolute improvement of approximately +0.01 over the initial baseline.

This iterative enhancement pattern confirms that our proposed correction module effectively identifies and rectifies initial segmentation errors. The diminishing returns in later stages suggest that the model converges towards a more accurate solution. Having established the internal validity and efficacy of our iterative approach, we then proceeded to conduct a comprehensive comparative evaluation against state-of-the-art methods across the full spectrum of imaging modalities to benchmark its overall performance.

Table 3. Performance Improvement Through Iterative Refinement (based on 5% validation set)

Iteration	DSC Value	Absolute Improvement	Relative Improvement (%)
Initial Prompt	0.661081	-	-
First Correction	0.668906	+0.00783	+1.18%
Second Correction	0.670053	+0.00115	+0.17%
Third Correction	0.670816	+0.00076	+0.11%

4.2 Comparative Evaluation on Multi-modal Datasets

We conducted a comprehensive comparative evaluation to benchmark our framework against several state-of-the-art (SOTA) interactive segmentation methods, including SAM-Med3D, VISTA3D, SegVol and nnInteractive. The evaluation was performed across a diverse range of five medical imaging modalities: Computed Tomography (CT), Magnetic Resonance Imaging (MRI), Microscopy, Positron Emission Tomography (PET), and Ultrasound (US). The objective was to assess the generalization capability and overall performance of our method in various clinical and research scenarios.

The quantitative results on validation sets, summarized in Table 4, reveal a highly competitive performance landscape. Our method consistently places among the top performers, demonstrating particular strength in clinically prevalent modalities. Notably, it achieves state-of-the-art results in MRI, securing the highest scores in both DSC AUC (2.960) and NSD AUC (3.449). Furthermore, our framework delivers top-tier performance in CT and US modalities, outperforming most competing approaches and underscoring its robustness and versatility.

This quantitative superiority is directly corroborated by a qualitative analysis of the segmentation results. For modalities with well-defined structures, such as CT scans with clear anatomical boundaries, our method consistently produces high-fidelity segmentations. As shown in Fig. 3, our approach (l) successfully renders a smooth and coherent 3D model that is visibly more complete than that of SegVol (i), directly explaining its improved accuracy reported in Table 4.

The advantages of our framework are even more pronounced in MRI datasets, which are characterized by high soft-tissue contrast. This environment is particularly well-suited for our iterative refinement mechanism. As illustrated in Fig. 5, our method (l) excels at producing a remarkably complete and detailed

3D segmentation, overcoming the challenges of ambiguous tissue boundaries that lead to fragmented results in other models like SegVol (i). This superior capability to handle complex soft-tissue anatomy is the primary driver behind our state-of-the-art quantitative scores in the MRI category.

Conversely, the evaluation highlights the shared challenges posed by modalities with inherent physical limitations. The primary failure cases for all methods occur in PET images with low spatial resolution, where the limited anatomical detail and inherent blurriness hinder the accurate delineation of fine structures (Fig. 6). Similarly, while our method performs well quantitatively on Ultrasound data, the presence of speckle noise and acoustic shadowing artifacts remains a challenge for achieving perfect boundary precision (Fig. 7), an area for future improvement for all segmentation algorithms.

In summary, the comprehensive benchmark validates our framework's position as a robust and high-performing interactive segmentation tool. The analysis confirms that our iterative refinement strategy is particularly effective in complex clinical modalities like MRI and CT, while soberly acknowledging the shared challenges faced by all current methods in lower-quality imaging environments (Fig. 4).

This strong quantitative performance is directly corroborated by a qualitative analysis of the segmentation results, which reveals the underlying reasons for our method's success and limitations in different imaging environments (Table 5).

For modalities with well-defined structures, such as CT scans with clear anatomical boundaries, our method consistently produces high-fidelity segmentations. As shown in Fig. 3, our approach (l) successfully renders a smooth and coherent 3D model. Compared to SegVol (i), which misses several smaller anatomical components, our method's result is visibly more complete, which directly explains its improved segmentation accuracy reported in Table 4.

The advantages of our framework are even more pronounced in MRI datasets, which are characterized by high soft-tissue contrast. This environment is particularly well-suited for our iterative refinement mechanism. As illustrated in Fig. 4 and Fig. 5, our method (l) excels at producing a remarkably complete and detailed 3D reconstruction, overcoming the challenges of ambiguous tissue boundaries that lead to fragmented results in other models like SegVol (i). This superior capability to handle complex soft-tissue anatomy is the primary driver behind our state-of-the-art quantitative scores in the MRI category.

Conversely, the model's performance, along with that of all competing methods, is challenged by modalities with inherent physical limitations. The primary failure cases occur in: PET images with low spatial resolution: As seen in Fig. 6, the limited anatomical detail and inherent blurriness of PET scans hinder the accurate delineation of fine structures, a fundamental challenge for any segmentation algorithm. Ultrasound artifacts: Despite achieving strong quantitative results, ultrasound imaging (Fig. 7) remains a difficult modality. The presence of speckle noise and acoustic shadowing effects can occasionally compromise the model's robustness, leading to less precise boundaries compared to CT or MRI. The strong performance reported in Table 4 highlights our model's notable resilience to these artifacts compared to other methods, though it remains an area for future improvement. In summary, the comprehensive benchmark across five distinct modalities validates our framework's position as a robust, versatile, and high-performing interactive segmentation tool. The qualitative analysis confirms that our iterative refinement strategy is particularly effective in complex clinical modalities like MRI and CT, while soberly acknowledging the shared challenges faced by all current methods in lower-quality imaging environments.

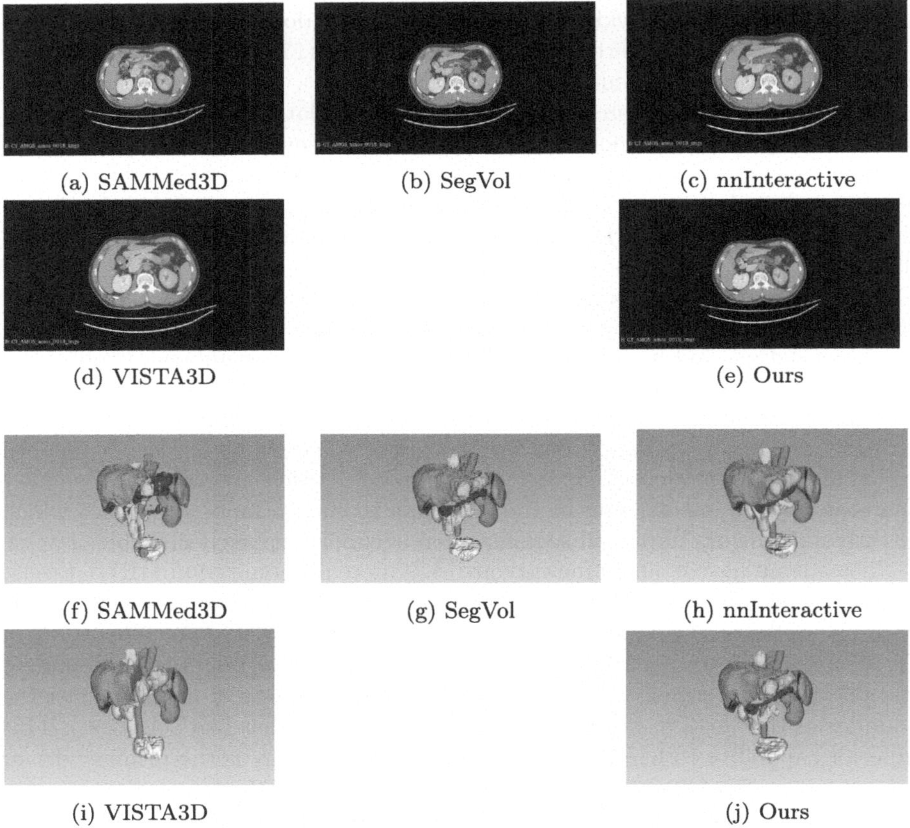

Fig. 3. Qualitative comparison of different segmentation methods on an abdominal CT scan. The first row (a-e) shows the 2D cross-sectional segmentation results from SAMMed3D, SegVol, nnInteractive, VISTA3D, and our method, respectively. The second row (f-j) shows the corresponding 3D rendered visualizations.

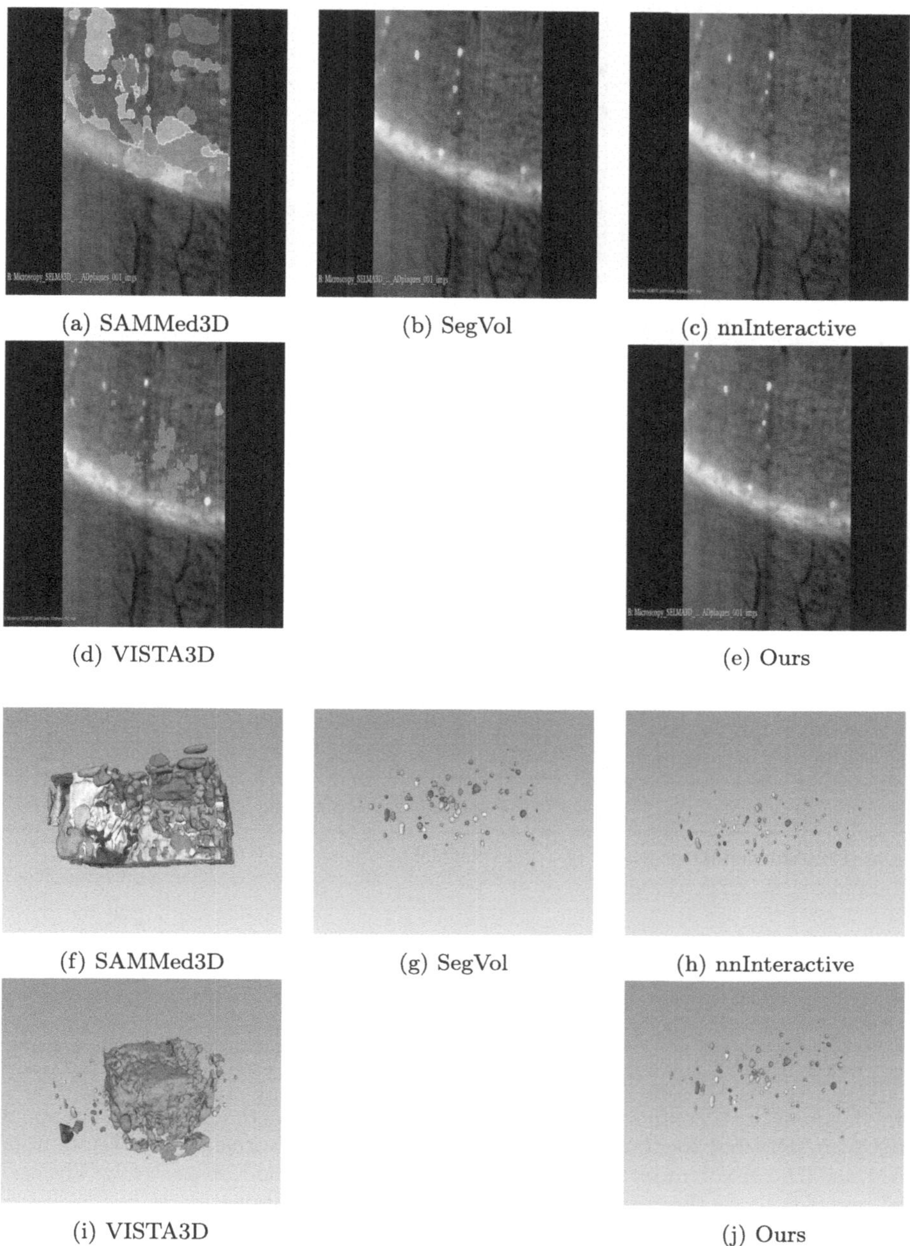

(a) SAMMed3D (b) SegVol (c) nnInteractive
(d) VISTA3D (e) Ours
(f) SAMMed3D (g) SegVol (h) nnInteractive
(i) VISTA3D (j) Ours

Fig. 4. Qualitative comparison of different segmentation methods on an abdominal Microscopy scan. The first row (a-e) shows the 2D cross-sectional segmentation results from SAMMed3D, SegVol, nnInteractive, VISTA3D, and our method, respectively. The second row (f-j) shows the corresponding 3D rendered visualizations.

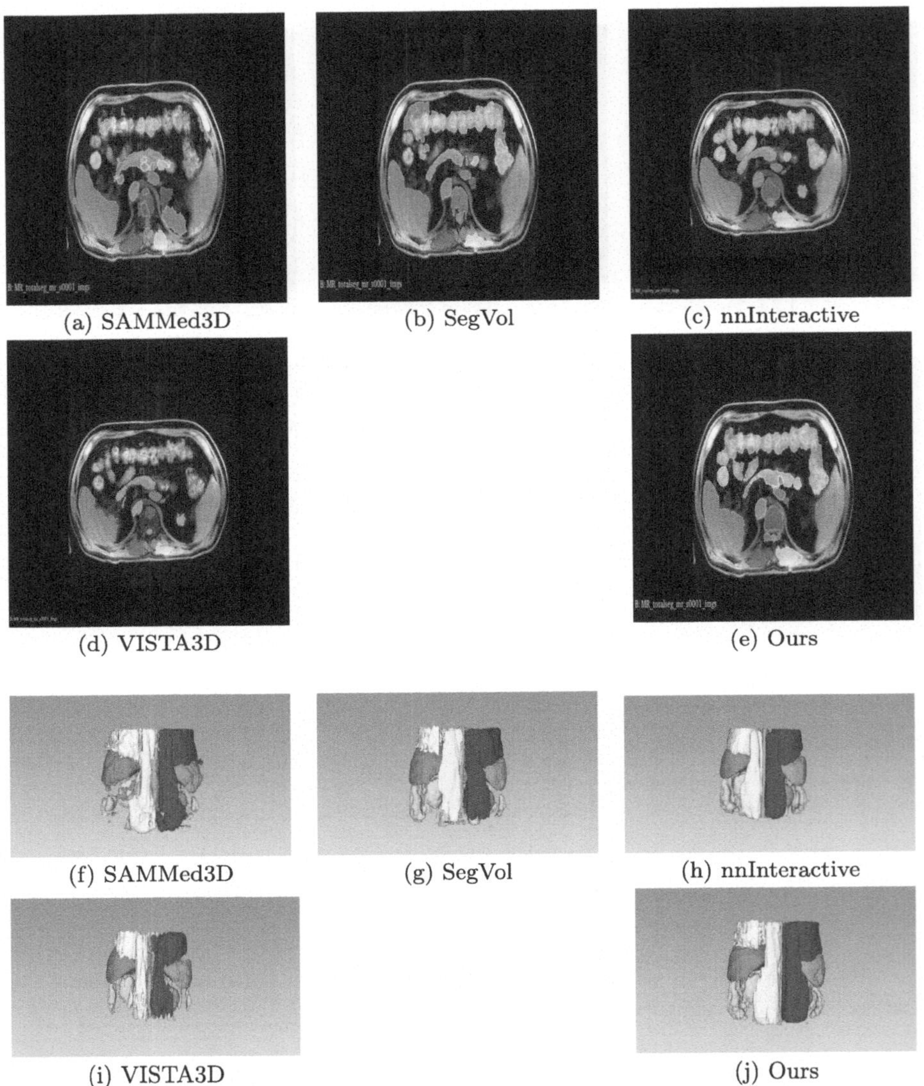

(a) SAMMed3D (b) SegVol (c) nnInteractive (d) VISTA3D (e) Ours

(f) SAMMed3D (g) SegVol (h) nnInteractive (i) VISTA3D (j) Ours

Fig. 5. Qualitative comparison of different segmentation methods on an abdominal MRI scan. The first row (a-e) shows the 2D cross-sectional segmentation results from SAMMed3D, SegVol, nnInteractive, VISTA3D, and our method, respectively. The second row (f-j) shows the corresponding 3D rendered visualizations.

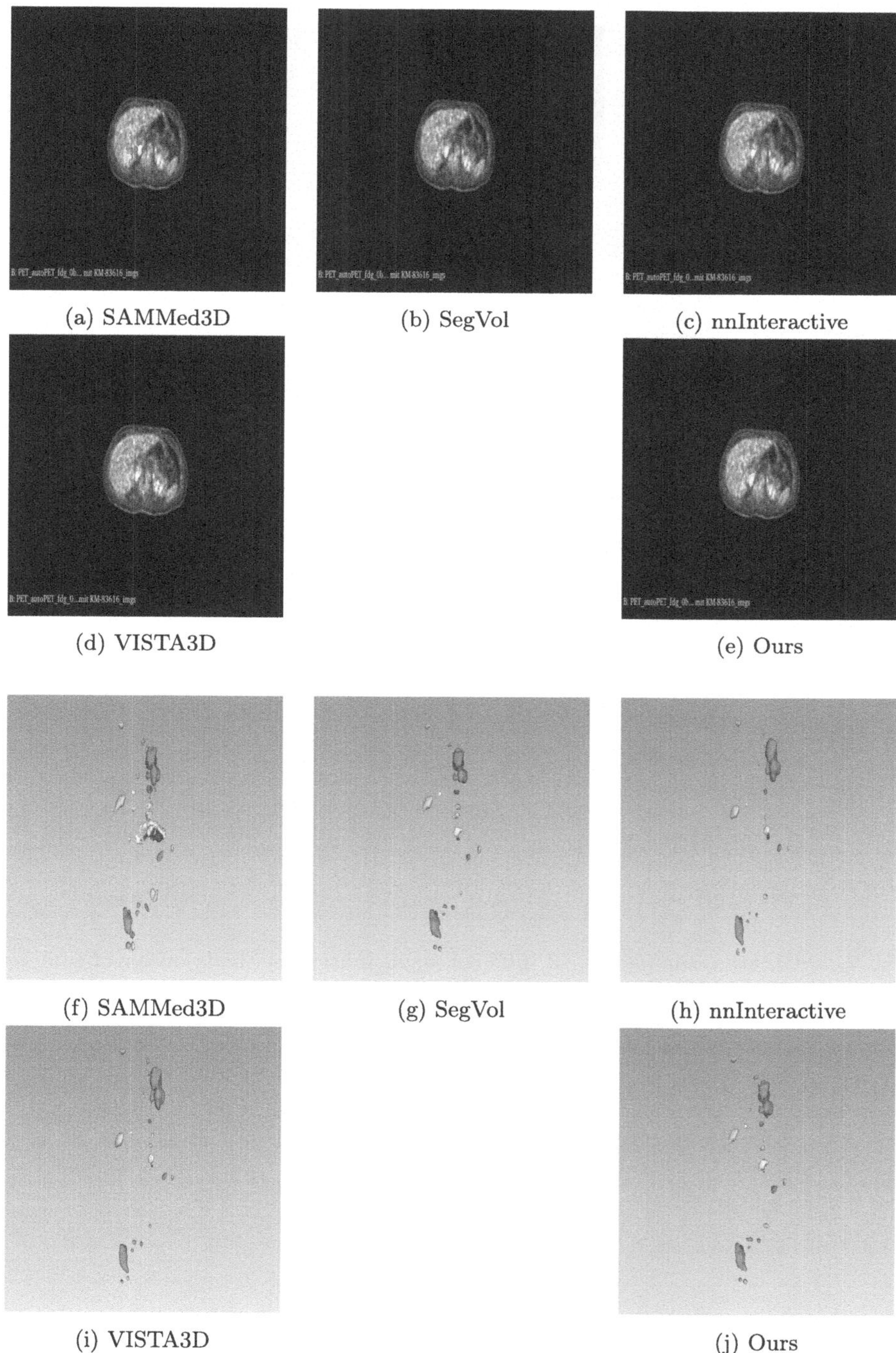

Fig. 6. Qualitative comparison of different segmentation methods on an abdominal PET scan. The first row (a-e) shows the 2D cross-sectional segmentation results from SAMMed3D, SegVol, nnInteractive, VISTA3D, and our method, respectively. The second row (f-j) shows the corresponding 3D rendered visualizations.

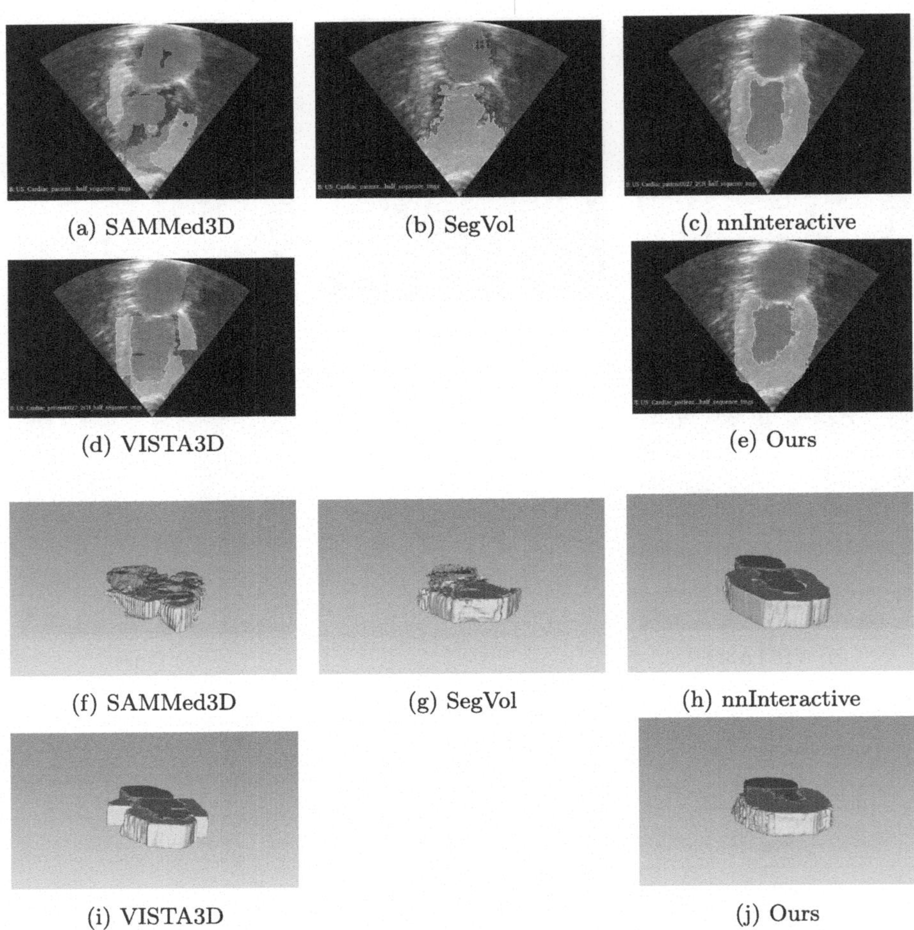

Fig. 7. Qualitative comparison of different segmentation methods on an abdominal US scan. The first row (a-e) shows the 2D cross-sectional segmentation results from SAMMed3D, SegVol, nnInteractive, VISTA3D, and our method, respectively. The second row (f-j) shows the corresponding 3D rendered visualizations.

Table 4. Comparison of segmentation methods on validation sets.

Modality	Method	DSC_AUC	NSD_AUC	DSC_Final	NSD_Final
CT	SAM-Med3D	2.2408	2.2213	0.5590	0.5558
	VISTA3D	3.1689	3.2652	0.8041	0.8344
	SegVol	2.9809	3.1235	0.7452	0.7809
	nnInteractive	3.4337	3.5743	0.8764	0.9165
	Our	3.155	3.383	0.789	0.846
MR	SAM-Med3D	1.5222	1.5226	0.3903	0.3964
	VISTA3D	2.5895	2.9683	0.6545	0.7493
	SegVol	2.6719	3.1535	0.6680	0.7884
	nnInteractive	2.6975	3.0292	0.7302	0.8227
	Our	2.960	3.449	0.743	0.879
Microscopy	SAM-Med3D	0.1163	0.0000	0.0291	0.0000
	VISTA3D	2.1196	3.2259	0.5478	0.8243
	SegVol	1.6846	2.9716	0.4211	0.7429
	nnInteractive	2.3311	3.1109	0.5943	0.7890
	Our	2.108	3.107	0.526	0.776
PET	SAM-Med3D	2.1304	1.7250	0.5344	0.4560
	VISTA3D	2.6398	2.3998	0.6779	0.6227
	SegVol	2.9683	2.8563	0.7421	0.7141
	nnInteractive	3.1877	3.0722	0.8156	0.7915
	Our	2.923	2.805	0.730	0.701
US	SAM-Med3D	1.4347	1.9176	0.4102	0.5435
	VISTA3D	2.8655	2.8441	0.8105	0.8079
	SegVol	1.2438	1.8045	0.3109	0.4511
	nnInteractive	3.3481	3.3236	0.8547	0.8494
	Our	3.038	3.146	0.759	0.786

*All methods exclude failed cases from metrics. Empty segmentations receive score 0 in official evaluation.

Table 5. Performance comparison across modalities and methods on test sets.

Modality	Method	DSC_AUC	NSD_AUC	DSC_Final	NSD_Final
CT	SAM-Med3D	2.1944	1.7887	0.5711	0.4681
	VISTA3D	2.3141	2.1127	0.6090	0.5595
	SegVol	2.5460	2.5083	0.6365	0.6271
	nnInteractive	3.2866	3.3022	0.8544	0.8715
	our	2.4208	2.3965	0.6075	0.6010
MR	SAM-Med3D	2.1064	2.0427	0.5317	0.5169
	VISTA3D	2.4891	2.5825	0.6516	0.6859
	SegVol	2.8377	3.1261	0.7094	0.7815
	nnInteractive	3.3866	3.6611	0.8680	0.9416
	our	2.7898	3.0283	0.6984	0.7576
Microscopy	SAM-Med3D	0.3115	0.1726	0.0778	0.0431
	VISTA3D	2.4526	3.4035	0.6231	0.8528
	SegVol	2.9603	3.9472	0.7401	0.9868
	nnInteractive	3.4580	3.9895	0.8743	0.9980
	our	3.0123	3.9737	0.7551	0.9942
PET	SAM-Med3D	1.3004	0.7297	0.3285	0.1844
	VISTA3D	1.8687	1.3919	0.4688	0.3523
	SegVol	2.9844	2.5108	0.7461	0.6277
	nnInteractive	3.2230	3.0753	0.8170	0.7854
	our	2.9323	2.4794	0.7329	0.6202
US	SAM-Med3D	0.8313	0.7004	0.2078	0.1751
	VISTA3D	0.9072	1.2257	0.2953	0.4789
	SegVol	0.9429	1.4435	0.2357	0.3609
	nnInteractive	2.4088	3.0407	0.7073	0.8886
	our	0.9949	1.5788	0.2652	0.4112

5 Discussion and Limitation

Our framework redefines interactive 3D medical image segmentation by emphasizing targeted, lightweight correction based on uncertainty and error heuristics. Unlike prior works that rely on memory-aware backbone architectures or multimodal generalization strategies, our method selectively processes only those regions with high uncertainty or localized label disagreements, substantially reducing computational overhead while maintaining effective refinement. This approach enables progressive improvement in segmentation accuracy with each interaction, demonstrating diminishing yet consistent gains over successive iterations.

Despite its effectiveness, several limitations remain. First, the notion of uncertainty—voxels with probabilities near the decision threshold—is useful for identifying ambiguous regions but is not explicitly calibrated; it does not guarantee coverage of all true error regions. Similarly, the "error" set, defined by local disagreement with user-provided clicks, may overlook systematic or spatially distributed prediction errors. Consequently, the GRU corrector can only address a subset of potential errors, and comprehensive volumetric correction is not ensured.

Additional limitations include memory-constrained input sampling and the external nature of sequential modeling. At each interaction step, only a fixed number of points (e.g., 200) are sampled due to GPU constraints, limiting the model's ability to capture long-range spatial context. Moreover, the GRU operates outside the segmentation backbone, receiving low-dimensional features rather than full encoder-decoder representations. This separation restricts deeper temporal context modeling and may constrain correction potential in complex anatomical regions.

To address these limitations, several avenues for future work are envisioned. Scaling up the number of sampled points would allow richer contextual cues from both uncertainty and error distributions. Integrating the GRU directly into the segmentation backbone could enable prompt-aware, temporally consistent refinement within high-dimensional feature space. Finally, end-to-end temporal learning would allow joint optimization of segmentation and memory updates, potentially improving both convergence and overall accuracy.

6 Conclusion

We have presented a novel framework for interactive 3D medical image segmentation that leverages sequential, history-aware refinement driven by uncertainty and error heuristics. By focusing computation on the most informative regions, our approach achieves a lightweight yet effective correction mechanism, improving segmentation accuracy progressively over multiple interactions.

Extensive evaluation across diverse imaging modalities—CT, MRI, Microscopy, PET, and Ultrasound—demonstrates that our method consistently enhances segmentation quality, particularly in anatomically complex regions or modalities with challenging contrast. While our current heuristics may not guarantee exhaustive coverage of all error regions, the approach provides a practical balance between efficiency, memory usage, and interactive performance.

Overall, this work underscores the value of targeted, iterative correction in interactive segmentation, offering a robust and versatile tool that can accelerate medical image annotation and support precise, clinically relevant analyses.

Disclosure of Interests. The authors have no competing interests to declare that are relevant to the content of this article.

Acknowledgements. We thank all the data owners for making the medical images publicly available and CodaLab [10] for hosting the challenge platform.

References

1. Du, Y., Bai, F., Huang, T., Zhao, B.: Segvol: Universal and interactive volumetric medical image segmentation. In: Advances in Neural Information Processing Systems, vol. 37, pp. 110746–110783 (2024)
2. Fabian, I., et al.: nninteractive: Redefining 3D promptable segmentation. arXiv preprint arXiv:2503.08373 (2025)
3. He, Y., et al.: VISTA3D: A unified segmentation foundation model for 3D medical imaging. In: Proceedings of the IEEE/CVF International Conference on Computer Vision and Pattern Recognition (2024)
4. Kikinis, R., Pieper, S.D., Vosburgh, K.G.: 3D Slicer: a platform for subject-specific image analysis, visualization, and clinical support, pp. 277–289. Springer (2013)
5. Kirillov, A., et al.: Segment anything. In: Proceedings of the International Conference on Computer Vision, pp. 4015–4026 (2023)
6. Ma, J., He, Y., Li, F., Han, L., You, C., Wang, B.: Segment anything in medical images. Nat. Commun. **15**, 654 (2024)
7. Ma, J., et al.: Efficient medsams: Segment anything in medical images on laptop. arXiv:2412.16085 (2024)
8. Ma, J., et al.: Medsam2: Segment anything in 3d medical images and videos. arXiv preprint arXiv:2504.03600 (2025)
9. Ravi, N., et al.: Sam 2: segment anything in images and videos. In: International Conference on Learning Representations (2025)
10. Xu, Z., et al.: Codabench: Flexible, easy-to-use, and reproducible meta-benchmark platform. Patterns **3**(7), 100543 (2022)

BiomedParse-V: Scaling Foundation Model for Universal Text-Guided Volumetric Biomedical Image Segmentation

Theodore Zhao[1], Ho Hin Lee[1], Alberto Santamaria-Pang[1,2], Noel C. Codella[1], Sid Kiblawi[1], Yu Gu[1], Yu Fang[1], Wen Xuan Teng[1], Naiteek Sangani[1], Ivan Tarapov[1], Matthew P. Lungren[1], Matthias Blondeel[1], Tristan Naumann[1], Naoto Usuyama[1], Sheng Wang[1,3], Paul Vozila[1], Hoifung Poon[1], and Mu Wei[1(✉)]

[1] Microsoft, Redmond, WA 98052, USA
MuHsin.Wei@microsoft.com
[2] Johns Hopkins Medicine, Baltimore, MD 21205, USA
[3] University of Washington, Seattle, WA 98195, USA

Abstract. Three-dimensional (3D) image segmentation plays a pivotal role in clinical diagnosis, therapy planning, and drug discovery by enabling the precise delineation of anatomical structures, pathological lesions, and cellular features in medical imaging modalities such as CT and MRI, as well as in biomedical microscopy. Despite its central importance, 3D segmentation remains a formidable technical challenge due to high computational requirements, the vast diversity of segmentation tasks across clinical and research domains, and the lack of interoperability among existing models, which are typically developed for specific modalities and tasks. To address these limitations, we introduce *BiomedParse-V*, a scalable and generalizable multimodal foundation model that leverages pretrained 2D foundation models to enable accurate, text-prompted 3D image segmentation. Our method features a novel Fractal Volumetric Encoding (FVE) scheme, which hierarchically compresses volumetric data by capturing self-similarity across slices into a compact fractal-based 2.5D representation. This design allows the effective use of powerful 2D foundation models while preserving essential 3D spatial context. We further propose the Independent Segmentation Discriminator (ISD) module to promote robust and consistent object localization throughout the segmented volume, addressing the challenges of maintaining spatial coherence in text-guided segmentation. Extensive experiments conducted across diverse biomedical imaging modalities demonstrate that *BiomedParse-V* consistently achieves state-of-the-art performance, significantly surpassing leading supervised 3D segmentation models. Our approach delivers a prompt-driven, computationally efficient, and broadly applicable solution for 3D biomedical image segmentation, advancing the accessibility and impact of segmentation technologies in real-world clinical and research environments.

Code available at https://github.com/microsoft/BiomedParse.

J. Ma et al. (Eds.): MedSegFM 2025, LNCS 16447, pp. 109–138, 2026.
https://doi.org/10.1007/978-3-032-23496-4_7

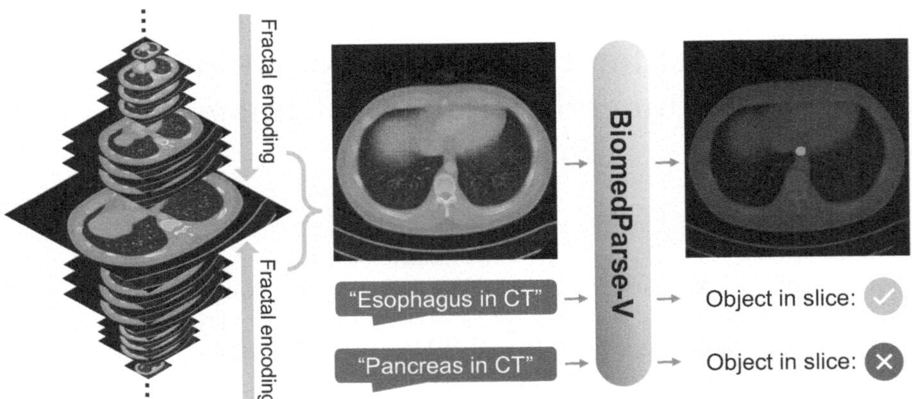

Fig. 1. Overview of *BiomedParse-V*. Volumetric medical data is encoded using Fractal Volumetric Encoding, compressing rich 3D context into an RGB format. Text-prompted segmentation is performed on the encoded slices, and the presence of the prompted object within each slice is predicted by the Independent Segmentation Discriminator.

1 Introduction

Biomedical image segmentation is the cornerstone of both clinical medicine and biomedical research, allowing accurate diagnosis, therapy planning, and disease monitoring. In radiology, three-dimensional (3D) segmentation of modalities such as Computed Tomography (CT) and Magnetic Resonance Imaging (MRI) provides detailed anatomical and pathological insights, while in microscopy, 3D segmentation is critical for cellular and subcellular analysis. However, the diversity of imaging modalities and segmentation targets introduces substantial technical challenges. Existing models are typically developed for specific modalities, resulting in limited generalization and poor interoperability across domains, a significant barrier in multidisciplinary settings where seamless integration of radiology and microscopy data is essential.

Recent advances in foundation models have shown promise for unified, prompt-driven segmentation frameworks that use natural language guidance to address multiple tasks. Methods such as MedSAM [15] leverage large-scale pretrained models to generalize across a variety of segmentation scenariosthrough interactive prompting. However, adapting these models to 3D volumetric data is hampered by increasing interaction demands from the users. Furthermore, promptable 3D segmentation approaches such as SegVol [3] often underperform when using textual prompts alone, due to difficulties in contextually aligning language with volumetric image data. Addressing these challenges is crucial for developing scalable and interoperable segmentation solutions applicable across the full spectrum of biomedical imaging modalities.

To address these challenges, we argue that traditional volumetric processing at a fixed spatial scale is inefficient, necessitating carefully designed network architectures that implicitly learn transformations equivalent to data encodings. We challenge the assumption that volumetric information cannot be utilized by 2D model architectures. We drew inspiration from the mathematical concept of fractal, where infinity can be encoded in a finite space, such as the Sierpiński carpet [21] and the Koch curve [22], defying the traditional notion of dimensionality. Inspired by this insight, we introduce *Fractal Volumetric Encoding (FVE)*, a novel encoding strategy that recursively compresses 3D volumes into patterns of reducing scale on the 2D plane and enables leveraging pretrained 2D foundation models.

Another major challenge in text-prompted 3D segmentation is accurately determining whether the prompted anatomical structures are present in each individual slice, as errors can result in numerous false-positive predictions. To address this, we propose an *Independent Segmentation Discriminator (ISD)* module, which independently verifies the presence of the prompted structures per slice basis. By effectively filtering irrelevant slices, the ISD significantly reduces false positives and enhances the overall reliability of text-prompted segmentation. Our key contributions are summarized as follows:

- We propose **Fractal Volumetric Encoding (FVE)**, a novel method that efficiently encodes the 3D volumetric context into a compact 2.5D representation, allowing the use of powerful and efficient 2D foundation models for volumetric segmentation while preserving rich spatial information.
- We introduce the Independent Segmentation Discriminator (ISD) module to robustly determine slice-level segmentation relevance, enhancing the accuracy of text-promptable segmentation in 3D volumes.
- We present *BiomedParse-V*, a single multimodal segmentation foundation model that brings the power of BiomedParse to volumetric segmentation using FVE and ISD, and show through extensive validation of various 3D modalities that *BiomedParse-V* achieves superior segmentation accuracy compared to current state-of-the-art 3D segmentation methods.

2 Related Work

Medical image segmentation has continually advanced to improve accuracy across diverse imaging modalities and clinical challenges. Early advances, such as the introduction of U-Net and its 3D variants [1,20], established a robust foundation for supervised dense segmentation. These led to specialized architectures, including UNet++ [30], H-DenseUNet [12], and SegResNet [18], optimized for specific anatomical and modality-driven contexts. More recently, frameworks such as nnU-Net [7] introduced comprehensive hierarchical designs to improve coarse-to-fine learning.

Alongside these developments, transformer-based architectures have gained prominence driven by their capacity for modeling long-range dependencies. Models such as UNETR [5] leverage vision transformers (ViTs) to capture broad spatial relationships across medical images, at the cost of significant computational overhead. To mitigate this, hierarchical transformer designs such as the Swin

Transformer, used in SwinUNETR [4], employ efficient sliding-window strategies for localized attention. Depthwise convolution-based architectures, such as 3D UX-Net [11], offer an alternative path to computational efficiency, nevertheless their performance remains limited when addressing anatomical structures that vary across multiple spatial scales. Foundation models have recently transformed medical image segmentation, enabling flexible, task-agnostic segmentation guided by diverse prompts, including natural language. Notable examples include MedSAM [15] and BiomedParse [27], which build upon large-scale pre-trained general-domain models to achieve remarkable segmentation performance. However, extending these prompt-driven models to 3D volumetric imaging remains challenging due to significantly increased computational and memory demands.

Prompt-based segmentation frameworks specifically targeting 3D modalities, such as SegVol [3], have employed spatial prompts such as bounding boxes and points to guide the model and improve segmentation accuracy. However, their effectiveness decreases when relying solely on textual prompts. This limitation arises due to inherent challenges in aligning linguistic semantics with complex 3D volumetric structures, revealing a critical gap for text-based prompting methods in volumetric contexts. Effective data encoding strategies are crucial to improve segmentation efficiency and accuracy. Recent advances in representation learning, particularly transformer-based architectures and self-supervised methods, have greatly enriched feature expressiveness and quality. Despite these advances, explicit and efficient encoding of volumetric medical data within prompt-driven segmentation frameworks remains largely unexplored, representing an important research frontier.

In general, current segmentation methods exhibit critical limitations: specialized modality-specific models lack interoperability, computational complexity restricts practical deployment, and existing prompt-based methods struggle to contextually align textual prompts in 3D data. Addressing these gaps requires novel approaches capable of efficiently compressing volumetric information, enhancing contextual semantic alignment, and promoting interoperability across imaging modalities. In contrast, *BiomedParse-V* directly addresses these challenges by introducing fractal-informed representations, efficiently compressing volumetric data, and allowing robust text-based prompt segmentation in a unified framework.

3 Method

Our proposed *BiomedParse-V* framework addresses the computational and scalability challenges inherent in volumetric biomedical image segmentation by leveraging efficient fractal-informed encoding and robust prompt-driven segmentation. The general architecture is illustrated in Fig. 1. Specifically, using FVE, a focal slice is encoded along with its corresponding 3D context into a compact RGB representation, enabling effective segmentation guided by text prompts without additional computational overhead. To further improve segmentation

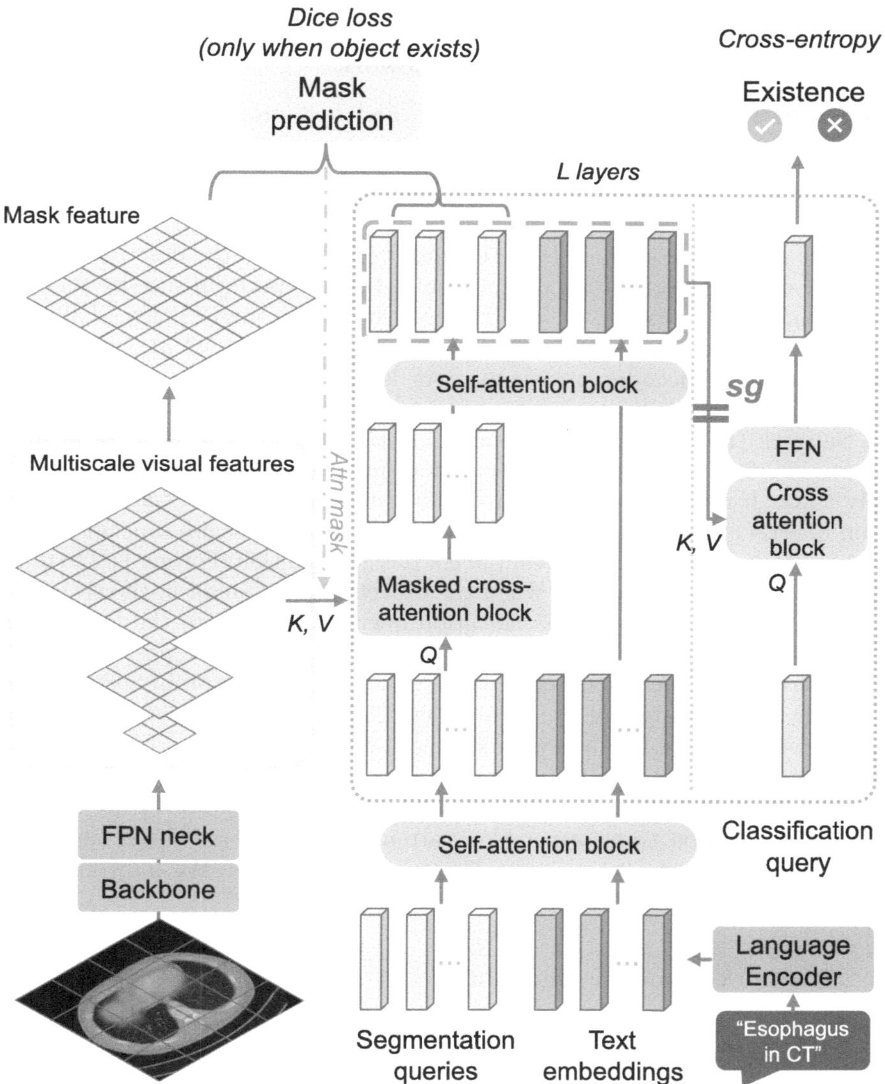

Fig. 2. The model architecture of *BiomedParse-V*. For each slice in the 3D volume, we encode spatial context around the slice into an RGB image (bottom left) and feed it into the model. The model then performs segmentation on the slice based on the given text prompt (bottom right). A transformer mask decoder processes the image features and text embeddings along with learnable segmentation queries and a classification query to produce the mask prediction and verify the existence of the prompted object.

reliability, we predict the presence of the prompted object within encoded slices using the dedicated ISD classification module.

3.1 Promptable Segmentation Framework

Given a 3D image volume $\mathcal{V} \in \mathbb{R}^{H \times W \times D}$ and text prompt $\mathcal{P}$ describing the desired object, the promptable segmentation problem is to output a binary mask

$$M = f(\mathcal{V}, \mathcal{P}) \in \{0, 1\}^{H \times W \times D},$$

where the set of 1's corresponds to the voxels occupied by the described object.

We leverage 2D foundation model architectures to perform slice-by-slice segmentation, while encoding volumetric context into a single image. Following recent advances in segmentation foundation models [10,15,27,31], we adopt a transformer-based decoder architecture. As depicted in Fig. 2, we utilize a vision backbone to extract multi-scale visual features further refined by a Feature Pyramid Network (FPN) [13]. Text prompts are transformed into text embeddings and combined with learnable segmentation queries, which are processed iteratively through multiple transformer blocks. In each transformer layer, segmentation queries cross-attend to visual features at different scales. Specifically, we adopt the Boltzmann attention sampling strategy from BoltzFormer [28] to maintain segmentation quality even when the object appears small in the slice.

Additionally, a dedicated classification query in parallel to the transformer decoder independently assesses object existence, reducing false positives in text prompt-driven segmentation tasks, which is discussed in detail in Sect. 3.4.

In our experiments, we used FocalNet [25] as the image backbone which outputs four scales of features with strides 4, 8, 16 and 32. The FPN takes the multiscale backbone features to output multiscale visual features of strides 4, 8, 16 and 32. The multiscale visual features convolute to mask feature of stride 4. The segmentation transformer block attends to multiscale visual features of strides 16, 8, and 4 in 3 loops, totaling up to nine layers. We interpolated to original resolution of the image shape.

3.2 Fractal Volumetric Encoding

To efficiently embed volumetric medical data into a compact representation suitable for 2D foundation models, we propose fractal volumetric encoding. Formally, this fractal encoding process is expressed as

$$\mathcal{E}(\mathcal{V}, i) : \mathbb{R}^{H \times W \times D} \otimes \mathbb{N} \to \mathbb{R}^{H \times W \times C},$$

where $\mathcal{E}$ transforms the 3D voxel data $\mathcal{V}$ into a multi-channel 2D image, centered around the i-th slice. Although this encoding scheme is general and supports arbitrary channel dimensions, we specifically focus on encoding into RGB channels ($C = 3$) so to leverage and be compatible with common 2D vision architectures.

Specifically, the focal slice $\mathcal{V}_i$ (target segmentation plane) is stored in one RGB channel at full resolution, while adjacent upper and lower context slices are

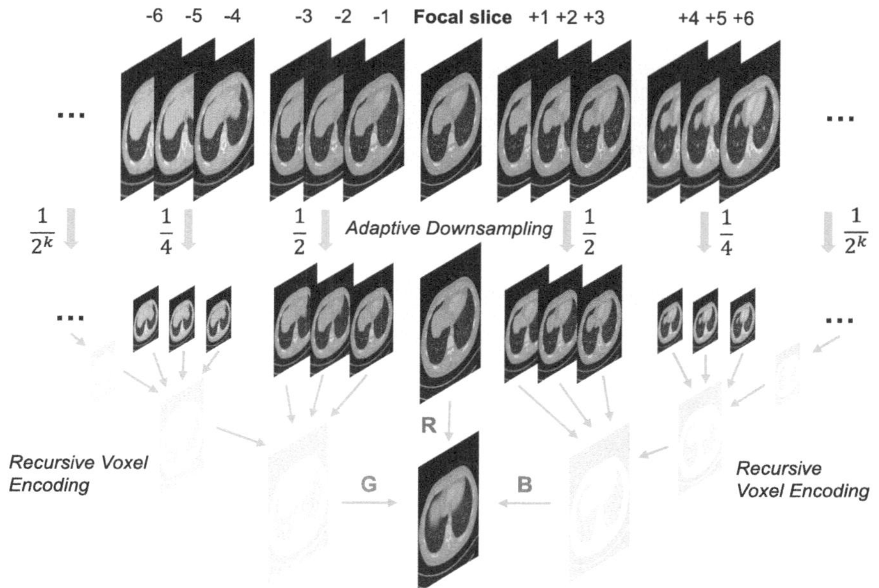

Fig. 3. Illustration of the fractal volumetric encoding process. A focal slice is combined with its surrounding 3D context. The focal slice maintains full resolution, while the context is adaptively downsampled and encoded recursively into compact channels, ensuring efficient spatial representation.

compressed into the other two channels via fractal-based hierarchical compression. This recursive encoding partitions slices into hierarchical groups, applying adaptive downsampling proportional to their distance from the focal slice. The process, depicted in Fig. 3, efficiently preserves critical spatial coherence with a limited channel bandwidth. The pseudo code to encode one side of the 3D context into a single channel is described in Algorithm 1. The fractal encoding order k determines the number of slices used.

To construct a fractal-encoded image, we define the pixel_mix function that combines 4 images into a single image with twice the resolution:

$$\mu' = \text{pixel\_mix}(\mu_1, \mu_2, \mu_3, \mu_4),$$

where $\mu_1, \mu_2, \mu_3, \mu_4 \in \mathbb{R}^{h \times w}$ and $\mu' \in \mathbb{R}^{2h \times 2w}$. The pixel-level mapping is as follows:

$$\begin{aligned} \mu'(2x, 2y) &= \mu_1(x, y) \\ \mu'(2x, 2y+1) &= \mu_2(x, y) \\ \mu'(2x+1, 2y) &= \mu_3(x, y) \\ \mu'(2x+1, 2y+1) &= \mu_4(x, y), \end{aligned}$$

Algorithm 1. Fractal Volumetric Encoding

```
Input: A list of image slices imgs = [s1, s2, ···], ordered by their distance to the focal slice. Fractal encoding order k.
Output: A single image of the same resolution as the slices.
def fractal_encode(imgs, k):
  if k > 1:
    imgs_low = Downsample imgs by half
    μ1, μ2, μ3 = imgs_low[:3]
    μ4 = fractal_encode(imgs_low[3:], k − 1)
    return pixel_mix(μ1, μ2, μ3, μ4)
  else:
    return imgs[0]
```

for $x = 0, \cdots, h-1$ and $y = 0, \cdots, w-1$.

For an encoding of order k, the total number of slices encoded per side is $N(k) = 3k - 2$. Including the focal slice, the RGB-encoded image represents a total of $N_{rgb}(k) = 6k - 3$ slices. Padding is applied by repeating the last available slice if needed.

3.3 Mathematical Equivalence to 3D Convolution

To theoretically justify the proposed fractal encoding, we establish its mathematical equivalence to traditional 3D convolution operations commonly employed in volumetric segmentation methods.

Patch-based vision models, such as ViT [2] and FocalNet [25], typically process an input image by dividing it into disjoint patches (resolution $p \times p$). Each patch $P_{ij} \in \mathbb{R}^{p \times p \times C}$ is embedded with a linear projection as follows:

$$e_{ij} = \text{Linear}\left(\text{Flatten}(P_{ij})\right),$$

where (i, j) denotes the spatial indices of the patch. The network then processes the patch embeddings e_{ij} in units.

Within our fractal encoding, each 2D patch aggregates voxels aligned along the depth dimension (z-axis), forming compact neighborhoods we refer to as "super pixels". Mathematically, each patch P captures a voxel neighborhood V, as illustrated in Fig. 4.

We formally establish the mathematical equivalence between applying linear transformations (patch embeddings) on fractal-encoded patches and performing an adaptive-resolution 3D convolution operation.

Theorem 1 (Equivalence to 3D Convolution). *Given a fractal encoding function ($\mathcal{E}$), defined as*

$$\mathcal{E}(\mathcal{V}, i) : \mathbb{R}^{H \times W \times D} \otimes \mathbb{N} \rightarrow \mathbb{R}^{H \times W \times C}, \tag{1}$$

applying a linear embedding operator on patches of the encoded image corresponds mathematically to performing an adaptive-resolution 3D convolution on the original volume.

Proof. We leave the formal proof to the appendix.

To ensure equivalence, each "super pixel" must be fully contained within a single model patch. Consequently, the minimum patch size is determined by the encoding order k and is given by 2^{k-1}.

This analysis demonstrates that fractal encoding inherently represents an adaptive, multi-scale 3D convolution operation, efficiently rearranged into a patch-compatible multi-channel (e.g., RGB) format suitable for standard 2D vision architectures.

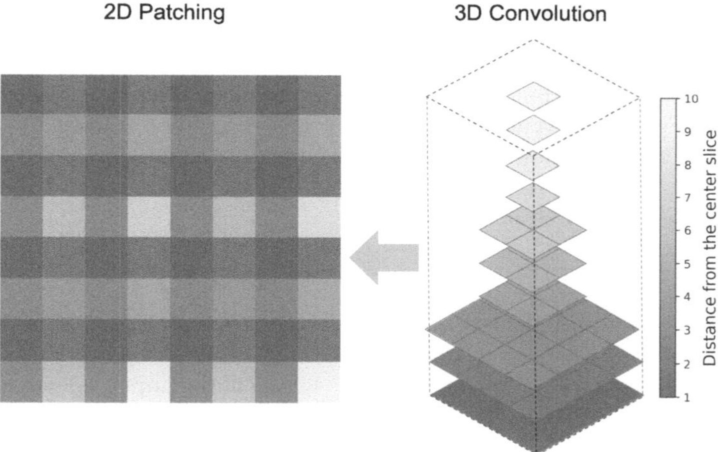

Fig. 4. The 2D patching process on fractal-encoded channels is mathematically equivalent to adaptive-resolution 3D convolution. Each colored square represents a pixel/voxel within a 2D patch or corresponding 3D voxel neighborhood. Pixel colors indicate distance from the focal slice. This visualization depicts the encoding of one side of the 3D context.

3.4 Independent Segmentation Discriminator (ISD)

A major challenge for purely text-prompted segmentation in 3D is to reliably determine the presence of prompted objects within each slice. To overcome this, we propose the Independent Segmentation Discriminator (ISD), which uses a dedicated classification query vector q in parallel to the segmentation transformer decoder, as shown on the right side in Fig. 2. q cross-attends to the hidden state of the segmentation queries and text embeddings at the end of each transformer block and then updates itself through a feed-forward network (FFN).

After the last transformer block, the q produces a binary classification probability $\omega \in [0, 1]$ through a linear layer, representing the existence of the prompted object. At inference time, the final segmentation mask prediction $\hat{M}$ for a given slice is computed as:

$$\hat{M} = \hat{M}_{raw} \cdot (\omega > 0.5). \tag{2}$$

The ISD is trained jointly with the segmentation module to classify the existence of the prompted object based on the transformer's hidden states during segmentation. ω is supervised jointly with the segmentation prediction $\hat{M}_{raw}$ through the following loss function:

$$\mathcal{L}(\hat{M}_{raw}, \omega; M) = \begin{cases} \mathcal{S}(\hat{M}_{raw}, M) - \log(\omega), & M \neq 0 \\ -\log(1 - \omega), & M = 0. \end{cases} \tag{3}$$

Since segmentation masks are supervised only on positive slices using segmentation loss $\mathcal{S}$, training with additional negative slices introduces gradients unrelated to accurate mask boundary detection, negatively impacting segmentation performance. To mitigate this issue, we implemented the gradient cut-off design (see Fig. 2), preventing irrelevant negative gradients from propagating back into the segmentation module, thus ensuring segmentation quality remains consistent despite the presence of numerous negative slices. The classification query vector q is updated in each layer as

$$q_{l+1} = \text{FFN}(\text{LN}(q_l + \text{CrossAttn}(q_l, sg([S_l, T_l])))), \tag{4}$$

where LN is layer normalization, S_l and T_l are segmentation queries and text embeddings after the l-th layer, and sg is the stop-gradient operator. We show in Sect. 4.3 that the gradient cut-off strategy significantly improved segmentation performance.

3.5 Inference on 3D Volumes

During training, all 3D volumes were processed into 2D images with FVE. Images from different volumes were mixed together in batches, and we randomly sampled a fixed number of prompts for each image per training iteration. During inference time, we leveraged the information shared in a 3D volume to achieve efficient inference. Given a 3D image and a list of prompts, we first computed the text embeddings for the prompts. The same embeddings were expanded for all 2D FVE-encoded images in the volume. We also repeat-interleaved the multiscale visual features and the mask features from each slice in the batch dimension to match the number of prompts. The image features and text embeddings for all slice-prompt pairs are then fed into the segmentation and classification module (upper right box in Fig. 2).

After the model outputs the segmentation masks and existence probabilities for each slice, we simply stacked the 2D masks together into the 3D volume. When multiple prompts for disjoint objects were presented, we first applied slice-level non-maximum suppression to remove overlapping objects and assigned each voxel to the class with the highest probability. We did not perform any further smoothing or processing in this work.

In order to provide options for better instance splitting, *BiomedParse-V* was able to output the edge of the prompted object in addition to the full segmentation mask. We used part of the segmentation queries to predict the edge while keeping the others for the original segmentation task. The same set of losses was used for the two targets during training. During instance segmentation inference, the user could optionally remove the edge from the predicted masks so that adjacent instances were separable. The masks expanded to their original area after being split into single-connected components. All operations were performed in stacked 3D volume. Due to the trade-off in removing small objects, we did not incorporate edge removal in our main experiments.

4 Preliminary Studies

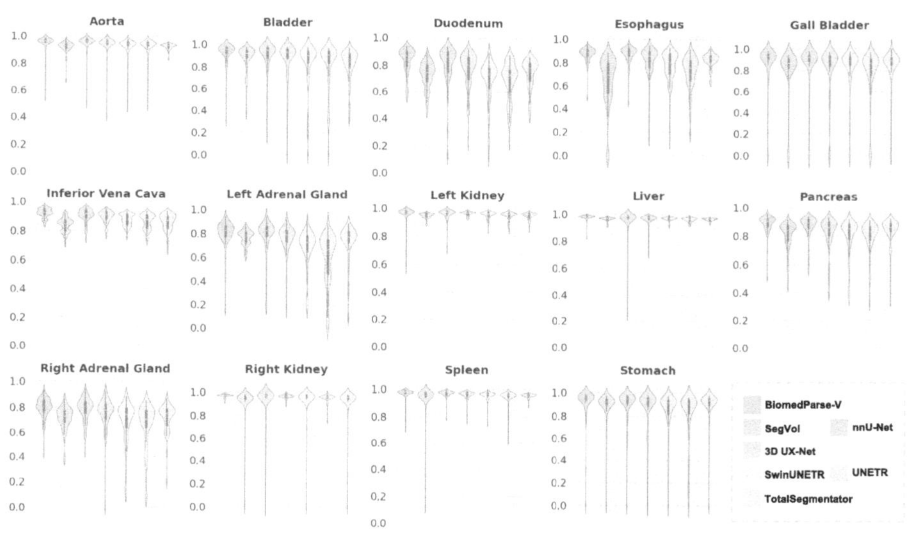

Fig. 5. Violin plots of Dice score evaluation for anatomies in CT, with *BiomedParse-V* compared with baseline models.

To investigate the 3D text-guided segmentation capability of *BiomedParse-V* before training at scale, we conducted preliminary experiments on abdominal CT and MRI data with multiple anatomies. We focused our training and evaluation for cross-modality experiments on AMOS22 [8] and compared to supervised models and universal medical image segmentation models. We also performed ablation studies to understand the effectiveness of each component in *BiomedParse-V*.

Table 1. Quantitative results of CT segmentation performance in Dice score (%) across *BiomedParse-V* and state-of-the-art models.

Target	*BiomedParse-V*	SegVol	nnU-Net	3DUX-Net	SwinUNETR	UNETR	TotalSeg.
Aorta	**95.27**	92.07	95.20	94.00	92.85	92.84	92.53
Bladder	**90.17**	88.03	87.52	84.85	82.39	81.74	82.82
Duodenum	**83.27**	72.49	80.72	76.46	68.13	67.85	74.10
Esophagus	87.11	64.47	**87.31**	81.58	76.27	72.07	82.68
Gallbladder	**85.96**	79.05	83.06	81.59	81.28	76.98	83.85
Left A.G.	**79.48**	76.31	78.06	75.26	68.21	58.64	74.03
Left Kid.	**96.39**	94.58	95.39	96.30	95.20	94.64	94.88
Liver	**97.71**	96.24	96.09	95.83	96.89	96.50	96.70
Pancreas	**88.42**	80.97	86.57	82.53	79.42	79.60	84.29
IVC	**92.02**	83.65	90.38	89.56	87.30	85.99	85.79
Right A.G.	**79.39**	71.07	78.24	75.06	69.33	65.86	71.70
Right Kid.	**96.88**	92.92	93.19	96.38	93.46	95.30	93.22
Spleen	**96.91**	94.03	**96.91**	95.83	95.73	95.02	95.54
Stomach	**91.49**	88.82	89.79	86.96	84.32	82.34	89.68
Average	**90.03**	83.91	88.35	86.59	83.63	81.81	85.84

4.1 Setup

We processed all 3D volumes into RGB images with the proposed fractal encoding technique. Each RGB image corresponds to one encoded slice in the volume, and we perform segmentation on the image. In this experiment we used default resolution of 1024×1024 to cover the highest resolution in AMOS22. We pair encoded images with text prompts following BiomedParse [27], and used the same data splits. Example prompts include "esophagus in abdominal computed tomography" and "stomach in abdominal magnetic resonance imaging". An empty mask prediction is expected where the prompted object is absent.

In terms of model architecture, we followed BiomedParse [27] and used FocalNet [25] as the image backbone. We adapted BoltzFormer [28] as the segmentation decoder head, adding the ISD module for object existence classification. The language encoder is a lightweight UniCL [26] architecture trained together with all other parts of the model. We initialized the image backbone from the pretrained SEEM [31] model, and all other parts trained from scratch.

4.2 Baseline Comparisons

We compared *BiomedParse-V* with two types of baseline 3D segmentation models: (1) pretrained 3D segmentation foundation models, including SegVol [3] and TotalSegmentator [23]; and (2) supervised task-specific models, including nnU-Net [7], 3D UX-Net [11], SwinUNETR [4], and UNETR [5]. Table 1 presents the Dice scores for 14 anatomical structures in the CT dataset, as well as the

Table 2. Quantitative results of MRI segmentation performance in Dice score (%) across *BiomedParse-V* and state-of-the-arts.

Target	*BiomedParse-V*	nnU-Net	3DUX-Net	SwinUNETR	UNETR	TotalSeg.
Aorta	95.73	95.64	**96.23**	96.13	94.66	85.71
Duodenum	**76.03**	66.78	69.58	66.40	62.44	55.50
Esophagus	81.38	73.62	**82.76**	81.40	74.12	79.26
Gallbladder	**66.58**	66.32	60.29	64.87	55.23	60.62
Left A.G.	63.35	57.15	**68.88**	64.90	62.11	57.79
Left Kid.	**96.92**	95.82	96.58	96.11	93.04	91.11
Liver	97.66	97.25	**97.84**	97.79	96.71	91.89
Pancreas	**88.70**	79.29	83.68	85.35	81.47	76.02
IVC	87.26	**90.66**	87.76	86.19	82.88	67.42
Right A.G.	68.14	53.29	**69.61**	65.94	56.44	56.85
Right Kid.	**96.69**	85.48	96.48	96.09	95.57	92.97
Spleen	96.88	96.66	97.13	**97.16**	94.20	89.91
Stomach	**88.93**	88.80	86.87	88.91	83.63	88.48
Average	**84.94**	80.52	84.13	83.63	79.42	76.43

average Dice scores for *BiomedParse-V* and all baseline models. Figure 5 shows the violin plots of the Dice score distribution for the models on all anatomies. We present Dice scores on the MRI dataset in Table 2.

Pretrained 3D Segmentation Foundation Models. We evaluated the performance of large-scale pretrained models SegVol and TotalSegmentator. SegVol originally trained exclusively on CT data and utilized here in text-prompt mode, achieved an average Dice score of 83.91. TotalSegmentator, benefiting from multi-class pretraining on the AMOS22 dataset, achieved an average Dice score of 85.84 on the CT dataset and 76.43 on the MRI dataset. Although both models leverage the advantages of extensive pretraining to generate robust generic representations, the inference performance demonstrates the gap between pretraining tasks and task-specific segmentation. This comparison underscores that while large-scale pretraining provides a strong starting point, tailoring the network architecture and task-specific training regimen is crucial to achieve state-of-the-art performance.

Supervised Task-Specific Models. In addition to foundation models, we benchmarked *BiomedParse-V* against state-of-the-art supervised architectures, including nnU-Net, 3D UX-Net, SwinUNETR, and UNETR. For CT data, nnU-Net and 3D UX-Net achieved average Dice scores of 88.35 and 86.59, respectively, with SwinUNETR and UNETR slightly behind. *BiomedParse-V* surpassed the performance of all supervised approaches by achieving the highest average Dice score of 90.03 in all anatomical structures. In the MRI dataset, *BiomedParse-V* maintained its leading performance with an average Dice score of 84.94, outperforming its supervised counterparts by a significant margin.

Quantitative Evaluation Across Anatomies. A detailed examination of the segmentation performance across varied anatomical structures reveals distinct performance gradients among the seven methods. The violin plots in Fig. 5 indicate that *BiomedParse-V* and nnU-Net exhibit higher median Dice scores with tighter distributions, suggesting a more refined and consistent segmentation performance across different organs. In contrast, the foundation models, TotalSegmentator and SegVol, show lower median values and higher variability, reflecting less robust segmentation performance. 3D UX-Net and SwinUNETR, demonstrate a gradual improvement in their performance distributions. This quantitative evaluation confirms that *BiomedParse-V* not only achieves the highest overall Dice scores, but also delivers consistent performance across diverse anatomical regions.

4.3 Ablation Studies

We conducted ablation studies on the components of *BiomedParse-V* to assess their impact on segmentation performance. Unless otherwise specified, we used the default setting with a fractal encoding order of $k = 1$ and all modules enabled. For ablation experiments requiring additional training, we downsampled images to 512×512 to generate lower-resolution masks, which were then interpolated to match the ground truth size. This resulted in a slight overall performance drop compared to the main results.

Fractal Encoding Order. To explore the effect of different orders of fractal encoding and validate the need for spatial context, we trained the model in settings that range from no encoding (single slice) to encoding order of up to 3. We report the averaged Dice score reported in Table 3. We can see that the segmentation performance dropped when there was no extra encoded spatial context. The performance change is small when the order of encoding is changed from 1 to 3. This could be explained by the trade-off of more context on the z axis versus less resolution on the x-y plane. We also note that the advantage of the fractal encoding was greater on MRI than on CT, possibly due to the spacing between adjacent slices from the two different imaging techniques.

Table 3. Segmentation performance in Dice score (%), without and with FVE of different orders k.

Modality	No FVE	$k = 1$	$k = 2$	$k = 3$
CT	88.24	**88.94**	88.65	88.61
MRI	82.49	83.80	**83.92**	83.22

Independent Segmentation Discriminator. To demonstrate the necessity of the ISD module, we configured *BiomedParse-V* to produce raw 2D segmentation masks without applying the slice filtering process in Eq. (2). As shown in Table 4, removing the ISD module led to a substantial drop in segmentation performance, particularly for CT. The performance decrease for MRI was notably smaller, likely because MRI volumes generally contain fewer empty slices. In contrast, CT scans typically cover a larger anatomical region, making slice filtering more impactful.

Table 4. Volumetric segmentation performance in Dice score (%), with raw 2D mask prediction and with the ISD slice filtering.

Modality	Raw mask	ISD (ours)
CT	73.87	**90.03**
MRI	82.31	**84.94**

Gradient Cut-Off. To validate the effectiveness of the gradient cut-off design in the ISD module, we trained and evaluated the model with free back-propagation, and compared it with our proposed approach in Table 5. The volumetric segmentation performance decreased significantly when there was no stop-gradient operation from the segmentation module to the classification module, indicating the necessity of the design.

Table 5. Volumetric segmentation performance in Dice score (%), with and without gradient cut-off in the ISD module.

Modality	No cut-off	With cut-off (ours)
CT	86.40	**88.94**
MRI	80.68	**83.80**

5 Experiments

In our main training experiment, we trained *BiomedParse-V* at scale on five different 3D modalities, and compared with other text-guided segmentation models.

5.1 Dataset and Evaluation Metrics

The development set is an extension of the CVPR 2024 MedSAM on Laptop Challenge [16], including more 3D cases from public datasets[1] and covering commonly used 3D modalities, such as Computed Tomography (CT), Magnetic Resonance Imaging (MRI), Positron Emission Tomography (PET), Ultrasound, and Microscopy images. The hidden testing set is created by a community effort in which all the cases are unpublished. The annotations are provided by the data contributors or annotated by the challenge organizer with 3D Slicer [9] and MedSAM2 [17]. In addition to using all training cases, the challenge contains a coreset track, where participants can select 10% of the total training cases for model development.

The text-guided segmentation task contains both semantic segmentation and instance segmentation. For the semantic segmentation task, the evaluation metrics include the Dice Similarity Coefficient (DSC) and Normalized Surface Distance (NSD) to evaluate the segmentation region overlap and boundary distance, respectively. For the instance segmentation task, we computed the F1 score at an overlapping threshold of 0.5 and DSC scores for true positives. In addition, the algorithm runtime will be limited to 60 s per class. Exceeding this limit will cause all DSC and NSD metrics to be set to 0 for that test case.

5.2 Implementation Details

Preprocessing. Following the practice in MedSAM [15], all images were processed to npz format with an intensity range of $[0, 255]$. Specifically, for CT images, we normalized Hounsfield units using typical window width and level values: soft tissues (W:400, L:40), lung (W:1500, L:-160), brain (W:80, L:40), and bone (W:1800, L:400). Subsequently, the intensity values were rescaled to the range of $[0, 255]$. For other images, we clipped the intensity values in the range between the 0.5th and 99.5th percentiles before rescaling them to the range of $[0, 255]$. If the original intensity range is already in $[0, 255]$, no preprocessing was applied.

For the training data, we followed Sect. 3.2 to process all 3D volumes into 2D RGB images. Based on ablation study, Sect. 4.3, we chose the fractal order $k = 1$ to balance the encoding depth and neighboring details. The smaller fractal order also allows more aggressive data augmentation while satisfying the conditions for Theorem 1, as the size of the encoded "super pixels" are smaller.

We adaptively chose the optimal views for slicing. For 3D image of shape $H \times W \times D$ on $x - y - z$ coordinate, we select the axial view ($x - y$ plane) by default if the ratio $\frac{2|H-W|}{H+W} < 0.5$, otherwise we select the view with the lowest ratio. We incorporate additional views during training if the ratio is less than 0.5 for all views and if the voxel spacing differs less than 10% across the dimensions. We converted all sliced images and masks to 512×512 resolution in 8-bit RGB format for efficient data processing, storage, and loading.

[1] A complete list is available at https://medsam-datasetlist.github.io/.

Environment Settings. The development environments and requirements are presented in Table 6.

Table 6. Development environments and requirements.

System	Ubuntu 22.04
CPU	AMD EPYC 7V12
RAM	900 GiB
GPU	40 NVIDIA A100 40G
CUDA version	11.8
Programming language	Python 3.10
Deep learning framework	torch 2.3.1, torchvision 0.18.1

Training Protocols. We trained *BiomedParse-V* on 40 NVIDIA A100 GPUs with 40 GB memory per GPU. The effective batch size counts to 320. For each 2D image example, we sample 4 classes from the feasible list of the source dataset, and randomly select one prompt for each class. The masks corresponding to the sampled classes were used as the ground truth for prediction, with absent classes resulting in empty masks (all-zero). We duplicated the image features across the 4 prompts for efficient computation.

We used AdamW [14] as the optimizer with the same segmentation loss and slice level classification loss. The segmentation loss was equally weighted Dice loss and pixel-wise binary cross-entropy loss. The classification loss was a slice-level binary cross-entropy loss with a positive class weight equal to 3. We used learning rate 1×10^{-5} and weight decay 10^{-2}. We applied an additional

Table 7. Training protocols.

Pre-trained Model	SEEM
Batch size	320
Patch size	4×4×3
Total epochs	80
Optimizer	AdamW
Initial learning rate (lr)	1×10^{-5}
Lr decay schedule	Cosine
Training time	240 h
Loss function	Dice, Pixel BCE, Slice BCE
Number of model parameters	371M
Number of flops	8612G per slice

segmentation loss with the same setting on the edge of the masks for instance edge prediction (Table 7).

6 Results and Discussion

We evaluated *BiomedParse-V* and compared with baseline text-guided 3D biomedical image segmentation models CAT [6] and SAT [29]. We compared with the baseline model trained on all data as well as the core set.

Table 8. Quantitative evaluation results of the validation set on the **all-data track**.

Modality	Method	Sematic Segmentation		Instance Segmentation	
		DSC	NSD	F1	DSC TP
CT	CAT	0.7211	0.7227	0.2993	0.3717
	SAT	0.6780	0.6726	0.2517	0.3954
	BiomedParse-V	**0.8512**	**0.8965**	**0.5119**	**0.6749**
MRI	CAT	0.5415	0.6193	0.1375	0.2813
	SAT	0.5610	0.6669	0.1228	0.2728
	BiomedParse-V	**0.7396**	**0.8664**	**0.5317**	**0.7053**
Microscopy	CAT	-	-	0.0313	0.3628
	SAT	-	-	**0.2006**	0.4243
	BiomedParse-V	-	-	0.1939	**0.6552**
PET	CAT	-	-	0.1098	0.2779
	SAT	-	-	**0.4200**	**0.7863**
	BiomedParse-V	-	-	0.3132	0.7185
Ultrasound	CAT	0.8594	0.8360	-	-
	SAT	0.8558	0.7924	-	-
	BiomedParse-V	**0.9050**	**0.9135**	-	-

6.1 Quantitative Results on Validation Set

As shown in Fig. 6, 7, 8, 9, and Table 8, *BiomedParse-V* outperformed baseline models in most modalities and metrics. The advantage is dominating for CT, MRI and ultrasound, where the margin ranges from 5–43%. For microscopy, *BiomedParse-V* outperforms all baseline models by 23–29% in terms of DSC on true positive instances, and on par with the best competing method with less than 1% difference in F1 score. *BiomedParse-V* outperforms CAT significantly, but lags behind SAT on PET with a 7–11% difference between metrics. In terms of computation, the average raw model inference time per volume on the validation set was 5.3 s, and 20.5 s including full environment and model loading.

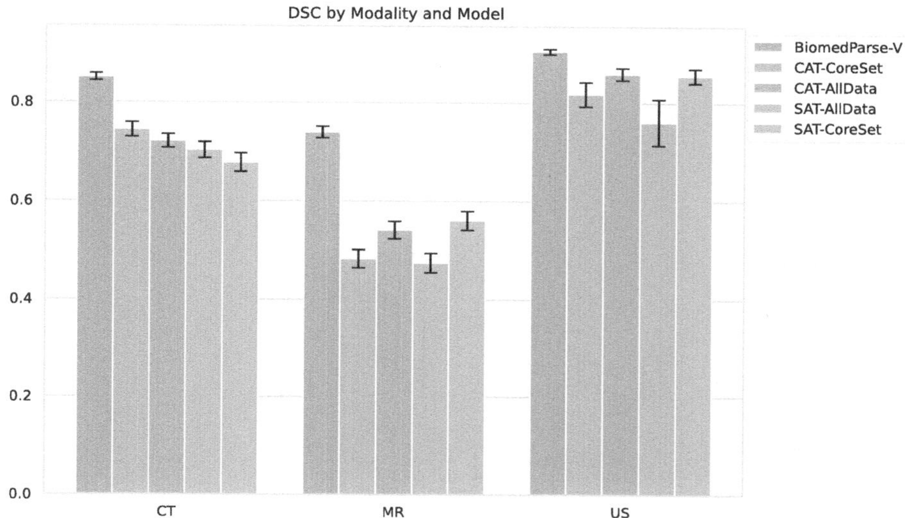

Fig. 6. Bar plot of semantic segmentation Dice Similarity Coefficients for *BiomedParse-V* and baseline models on different modalities.

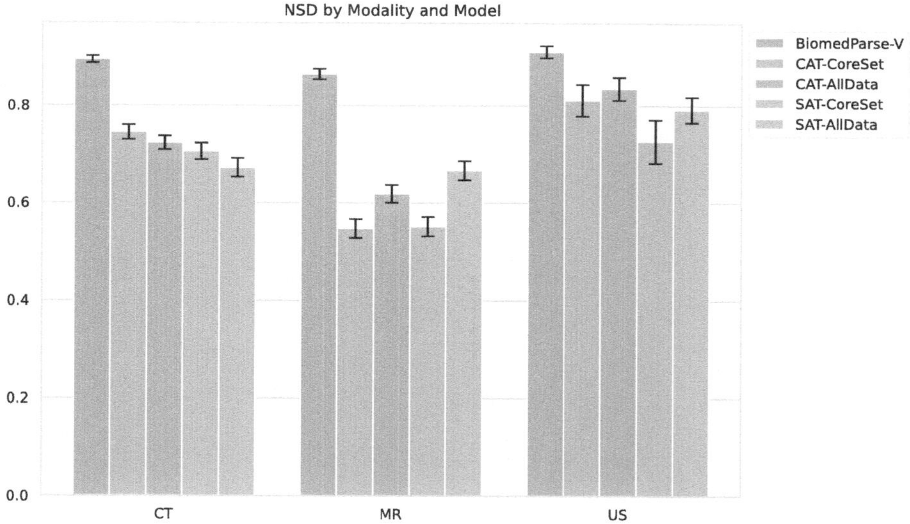

Fig. 7. Bar plot of semantic segmentation Normalized Surface Distances for *BiomedParse-V* and baseline models on different modalities.

6.2 Qualitative Results on Validation Set

Representative visualizations are shown in Figs. 10, 11, 12, and 13, including two successful and two suboptimal cases. In the first two, *BiomedParse-V* correctly segments all prompted objects despite cluttered scenes or low image quality.

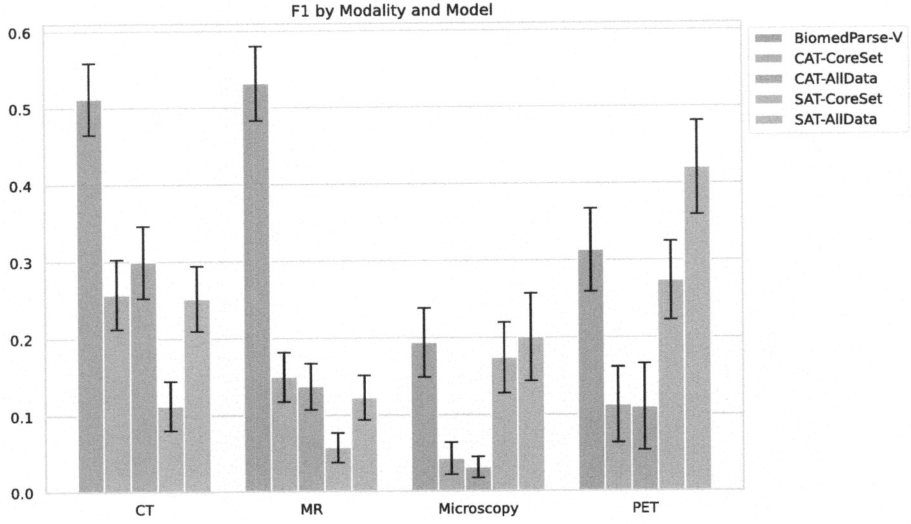

Fig. 8. Bar plot of instance segmentation F1 scores for *BiomedParse-V* and baseline models on different modalities.

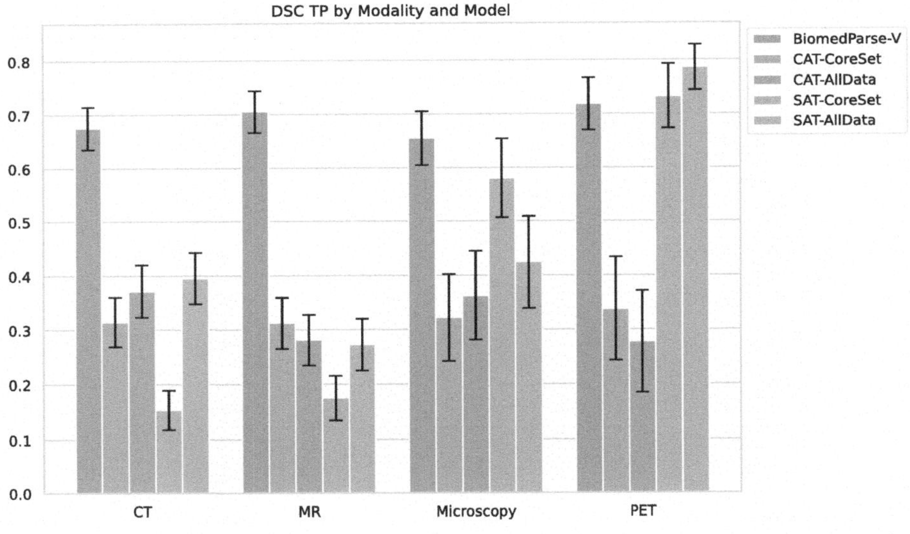

Fig. 9. Bar plot of instance segmentation Dice Similarity Coefficients on true positives for *BiomedParse-V* and baseline models on different modalities.

In Fig. 12, *BiomedParse-V* recovers most annotated nuclei but tends to under-segment low-intensity nuclei. Touching or overlapping nuclei are sometimes merged, which complicates downstream instance separation. In our experiments, edge-removal post-processing alleviated some merges but occasionally removed small true positives as a trade-off.

In Fig. 13, *BiomedParse-V* was prompted to segment the right humerus, yet the ISD module predicted absence in the slice. A likely failure mode is anatomical symmetry, which makes laterality ambiguous. Because *BiomedParse-V* operates on locally encoded 2D slices with limited 3D context, and training includes image-level augmentations (e.g., leftright flips), laterality cues can be weakened, leading to such false negatives.

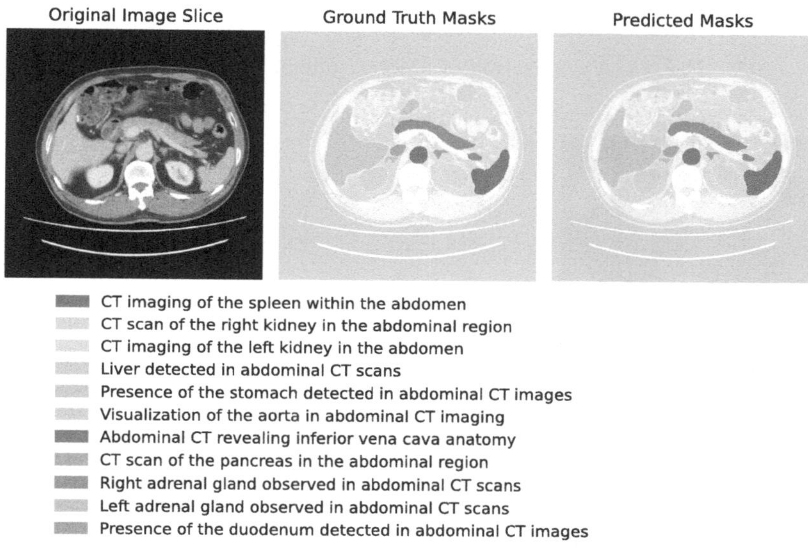

Fig. 10. Visualization of organ segmentation in abdominal CT.

6.3 Results on Final Testing Set

In the hidden testing set, *BiomedParse-V* consistently outperformed all baseline methods across all metrics. As shown in Table 9, *BiomedParse-V* exhibits a 10–46% advantage. As an overall observation, instance segmentation is still a challenging task compared to semantic segmentation, as it involves more tumor and lesion segmentation cases, which are typically small in size and exhibit high variance in location.

6.4 Limitation and Future Work

While *BiomedParse-V* tackles the 3D segmentation problem by encoding 3D context into 2D images with FVE, the total amount of spatial information is upper bounded by a native 3D architecture. As a result, it still lags behind the

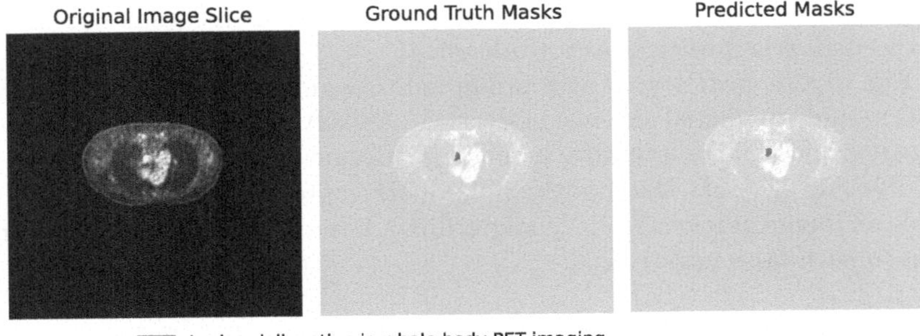

Fig. 11. Visualization of lesion segmentation in PET.

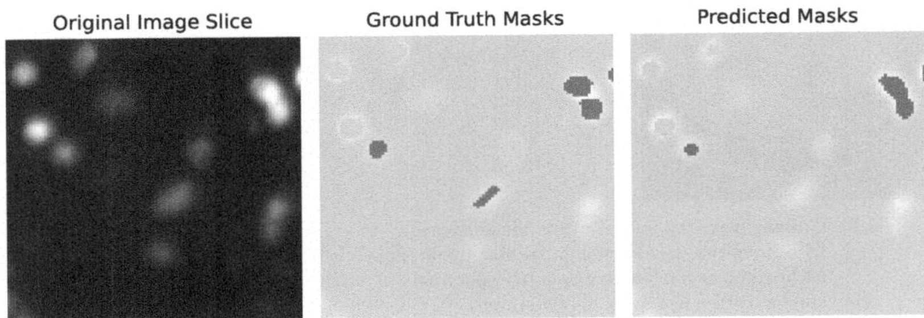

Fig. 12. Visualization of nuclei segmentation in microscopy.

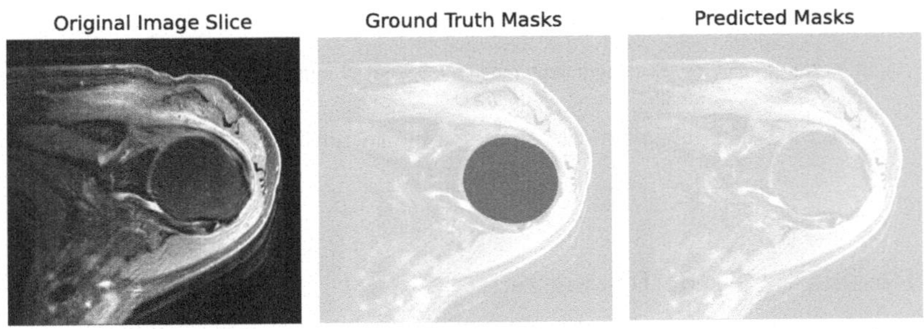

Fig. 13. Visualization of humerus segmentation in MRI.

Table 9. Quantitative evaluation results of the testing set on the **all-data track**.

Method	Sematic Segmentation		Instance Segmentation	
	DSC	NSD	F1	DSC TP
CAT	0.3304	0.3153	0.0194	0.0466
SAT	0.5413	0.5297	0.1419	0.2959
BiomedParse-V	**0.7497**	**0.7747**	**0.2380**	**0.4476**

best competing model when the full volumetric context is essential. We envision future models to be able to efficiently encode richer 3D context, or take the BoltzFormer segmentation framework to the native 3D domain.

On the other hand, since *BiomedParse-V* only outputs binary segmentation masks, the heuristic instance splitting approach limits its performance, as shown in the instance segmentation results. We envision the model architecture to be expanded to produce more direct and precise instance predictions, or to combine with existing instance segmentation tools to achieve best performance.

6.5 Discussions

In order to tackle the problem of 3D medical image segmentation driven by text prompting, we presented generic applicable approaches to utilize 2D foundation models for 3D images. With a rich spatial context encoded in a single image, vision models with downstream applications such as classification, text generation, and question answering could be directly applied to solve 3D problems.

In addition, our fractal-based encoding approach is not limited to 3D medical images but can extend to other vision domains that involve sequential or volumetric data, such as video-based analysis. Thus, Fractal Volumetric Encoding (FVE) provides a versatile and efficient solution, unleashing the power of vision foundation models across various application domains.

The Independent Segmentation Discriminator (ISD) module with gradient cut-off was proven to be effective in determining object existence while maintaining coherence segmentation performance. The same idea could be applied to applications such as video segmentation, where object existence is also a challenge [19].

7 Conclusion

We presented *BiomedParse-V*, a novel and efficient multimodal model for 3D medical image segmentation that leverages the strengths of pretrained 2D foundation models. By employing Fractal Volumetric Encoding (FVE), our method compresses 3D volumes into compact 2.5D representations that preserve essential spatial context and readily fit common vision foundation models. Complemented by an Independent Segmentation Discriminator (ISD) with gradient cut-off, *BiomedParse-V* achieves enhanced volumetric segmentation accuracy. Extensive experiments on CT and MRI datasets demonstrate that our approach outperforms current state-of-the-art pretrained models and supervised expert models. We envision our work opening a promising direction for practically deploying robust foundation models in clinical medical imaging, addressing critical scalability and resource-constraint challenges inherent to volumetric segmentation.

Acknowledgements. We thank all the data owners for making the medical images publicly available and CodaLab [24] for hosting the challenge platform.

Disclosure of Interests. The authors have no competing interests to declare that are relevant to the content of this article.

A Proof of Theorem

Theorem 1 (Equivalence to 3D Convolution). *Given a fractal encoding function ($\mathcal{E}$), defined as*

$$\mathcal{E}(\mathcal{V}, i) : \mathbb{R}^{H\times W\times D} \otimes \mathbb{N} \rightarrow \mathbb{R}^{H\times W\times C}, \tag{5}$$

applying a linear embedding operator on patches of the encoded image corresponds mathematically to performing an adaptive-resolution 3D convolution on the original volume.

Proof. We will show that for any spatial patch of the fractal encoded image, the linear projection on that patch reproduces exactly an adaptive-resolution 3D convolution on the original volume.

- Volume $\mathcal{V} \in \mathbb{R}^{H\times W\times D}$, focal index i.
- Encoding order k induces patch size $p = 2^{k-1}$ and depth-extent $\Delta_k = 3k-2$.
- Encoded image $\mathcal{I} = \mathcal{E}(\mathcal{V}, i) \in \mathbb{R}^{H\times W\times C}$, $C = 3$.
- Fix a 2D patch

$$P = \{\mathcal{I}_{i_0+u,\, j_0+v,\, c} \mid 0 \leq u, v < p,\ 0 \leq c < C\}.$$

- Flattening $\boldsymbol{P} \in \mathbb{R}^{p^2 C}$; linear weights $W \in \mathbb{R}^{M\times(p^2 C)}$; embedding $e = W\boldsymbol{P} \in \mathbb{R}^M$.

By the fractal encoding and pixel mixing construction, each element of $\boldsymbol{P}$ is exactly one voxel $\mathcal{V}_{x,y,z}$with$(x - i_0, y - j_0) \in \mathcal{U}(z - i)$, $z \in \{i - \Delta_k, \ldots, i + \Delta_k\}$. Here $\mathcal{U}(z - i)$ is the set of voxel points in the downsampled slice at z, relative to focal index i. We have

An adaptive-resolution 3D convolution at spatial location (i_0, j_0, i) with kernel $K \in \mathbb{R}^{p\times p\times(2\Delta_k+1)}$ computes

$$(K * \mathcal{V})_{i_0,j_0,i} = \sum_{d=-\Delta_k}^{\Delta_k} \sum_{(u,v)\in\mathcal{U}(d)} K_{u,v,d+\Delta_k}\, \mathcal{V}_{i_0+u,\, j_0+v,\, i+d}.$$

As the voxels in the neighborhood of (i_0, j_0, i) are the same as the elements in the flattened 2D patch after fractal encoding, learning a 3D convolutional kernel K is equivalent to learning a patch embedding W, as long as the 2D patches do not overlap.

B Fractal Encoding Examples

We visualize the encoded RGB images from FVE in Fig. 14 and 15. An encoding-decoding example is shown in Fig. 16. We show the voxel allocation with different orders of fractal encoding in Fig. 17. The majority portion of the voxels is from the slices close to the center slice. As the order increases, the size of a "super pixel" also increases. The ratio of the voxels from the close layers keeps the same when increasing the encoding order.

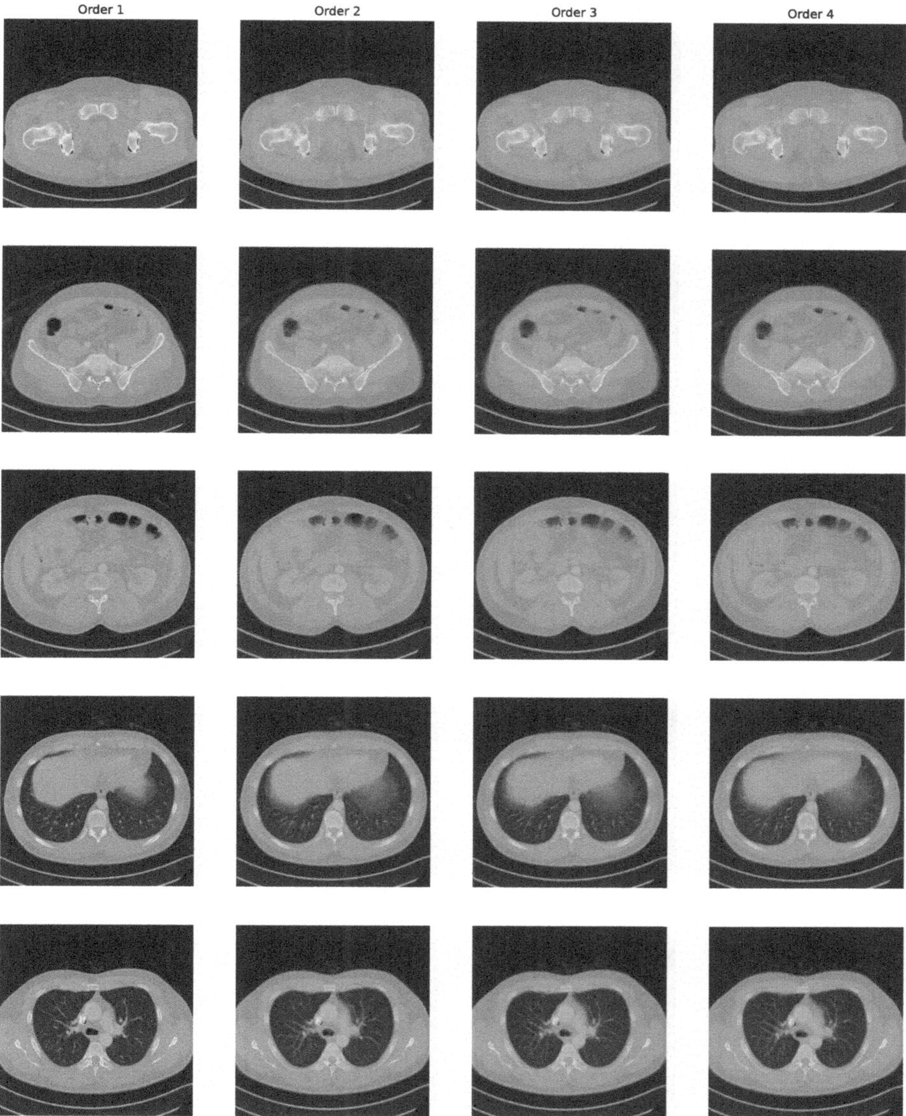

Fig. 14. Fractal encoded RGB image for CT with different encoding order. Each row corresponds to encoding around the same focal slice.

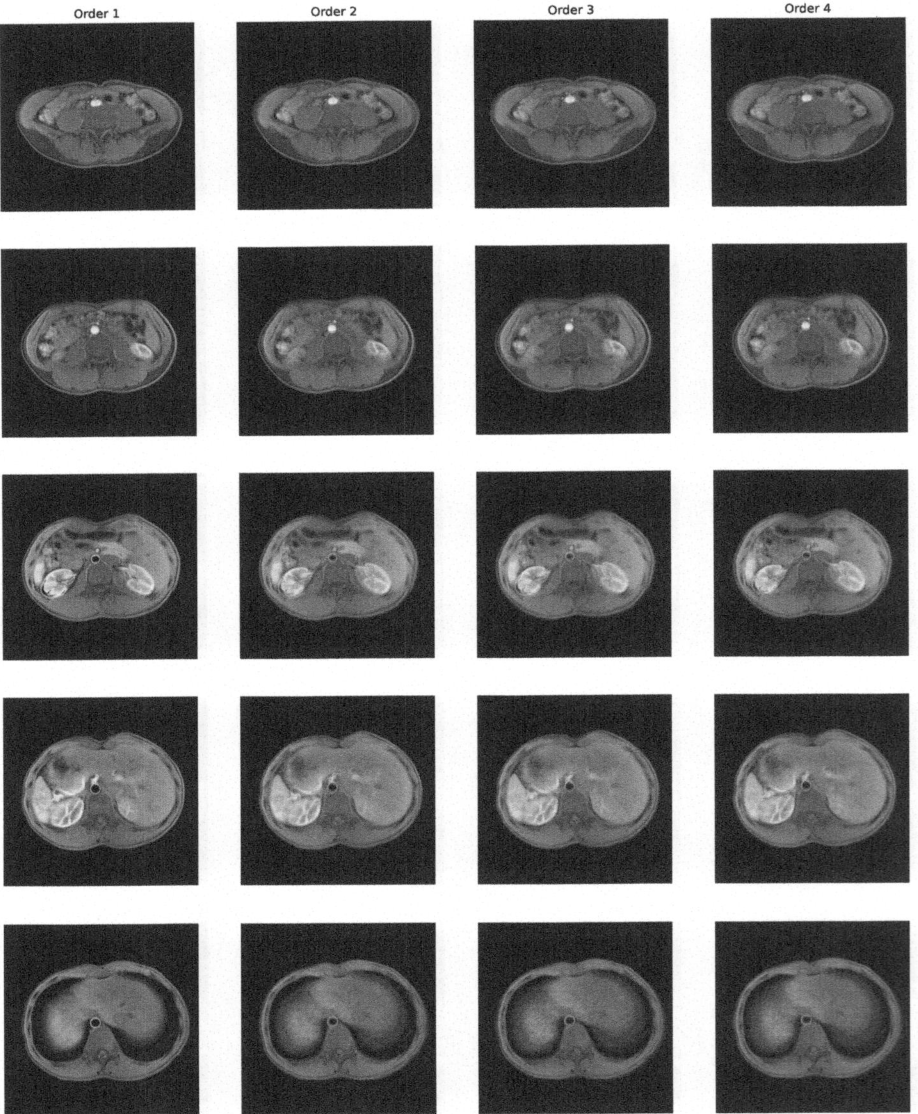

Fig. 15. Fractal encoded RGB image for MRI with different encoding order. Each row corresponds to encoding around the same focal slice.

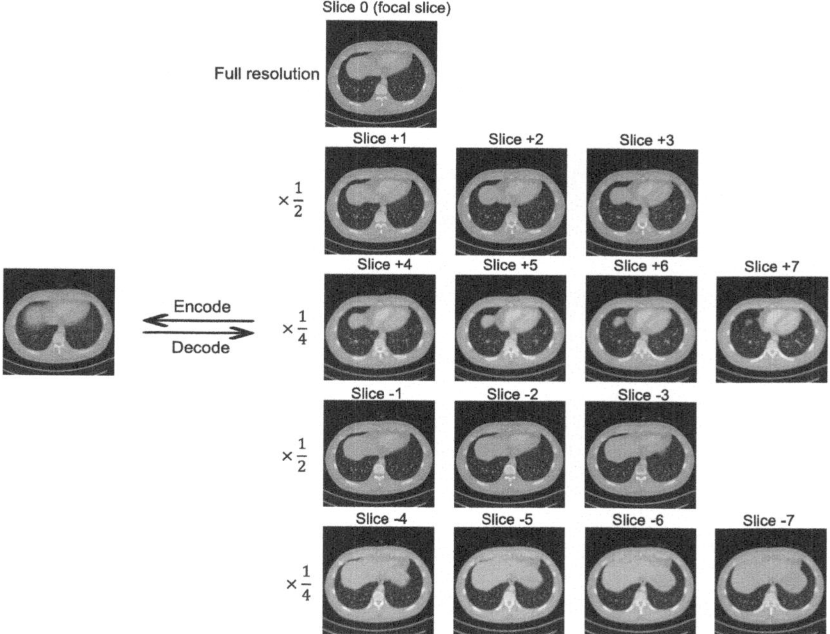

Fig. 16. Example encoding-decoding around a focal slice. The FVE encoded image on the left contains a full resolution focal slice along with adaptively downsampled context slices. The encoded slice can decode back to the slices on the right losslessly.

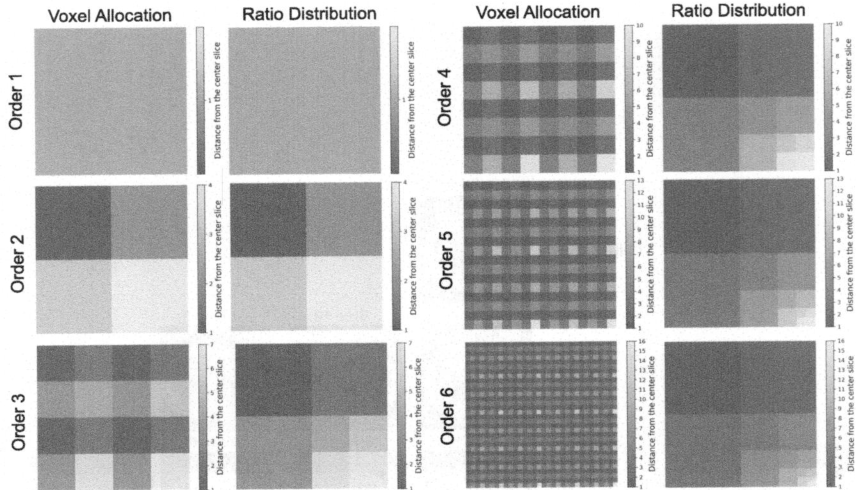

Fig. 17. The voxel allocation pattern for FVE of order 1 through 6. We show the minimal unit of neighborhood encoding (super pixel) for each order. The color represents the distance from the voxel to the focal slice in the original volume. The right side of each column shows the overall ratio distribution of the encoded voxels in terms of their distances to the focal slice.

References

1. Çiçek, Ö., Abdulkadir, A., Lienkamp, S.S., Brox, T., Ronneberger, O.: 3D U-Net: learning dense volumetric segmentation from sparse annotation. In: International Conference on Medical Image Computing and Computer-Assisted Intervention, pp. 424–432. Springer (2016)
2. Dosovitskiy, A., et al.: An image is worth 16x16 words: transformers for image recognition at scale. arXiv preprint arXiv:2010.11929 (2020)
3. Du, Y., Bai, F., Huang, T., Zhao, B.: Segvol: universal and interactive volumetric medical image segmentation. Adv. Neural. Inf. Process. Syst. **37**, 110746–110783 (2025)
4. Hatamizadeh, A., Nath, V., Tang, Y., Yang, D., Roth, H.R., Xu, D.: Swin UNETR: swin transformers for semantic segmentation of brain tumors in MRI images. In: International MICCAI Brain Lesion Workshop, pp. 272–284. Springer (2022)
5. Hatamizadeh, A., et al.: UNETR: transformers for 3D medical image segmentation. In: Proceedings of the IEEE/CVF Winter Conference on Applications of Computer Vision, pp. 574–584 (2022)
6. Huang, Z., Jiang, Y., Zhang, R., Zhang, S., Zhang, X.: Cat: coordinating anatomical-textual prompts for multi-organ and tumor segmentation. Adv. Neural. Inf. Process. Syst. **37**, 3588–3610 (2024)
7. Isensee, F., et al.: nnU-Net revisited: a call for rigorous validation in 3D medical image segmentation. In: International Conference on Medical Image Computing and Computer-Assisted Intervention, pp. 488–498. Springer (2024)

8. Ji, Y., et al.: Amos: a large-scale abdominal multi-organ benchmark for versatile medical image segmentation. Adv. Neural. Inf. Process. Syst. **35**, 36722–36732 (2022)
9. Kikinis, R., Pieper, S.D., Vosburgh, K.G.: 3D Slicer: a platform for subject-specific image analysis, visualization, and clinical support, pp. 277–289. Springer (2013)
10. Kirillov, A., et al.: Segment anything. In: Proceedings of the IEEE/CVF International Conference on Computer Vision, pp. 4015–4026 (2023)
11. Lee, H.H., Bao, S., Huo, Y., Landman, B.A.: 3D UX-Net: a large kernel volumetric convnet modernizing hierarchical transformer for medical image segmentation. In: The Eleventh International Conference on Learning Representations (2022)
12. Li, X., Chen, H., Qi, X., Dou, Q., Fu, C.W., Heng, P.A.: H-DenseUNet: hybrid densely connected unet for liver and tumor segmentation from CT volumes. IEEE Trans. Med. Imaging **37**(12), 2663–2674 (2018)
13. Lin, T.Y., Dollár, P., Girshick, R., He, K., Hariharan, B., Belongie, S.: Feature pyramid networks for object detection. In: Proceedings of the IEEE Conference on Computer Vision and Pattern Recognition, pp. 2117–2125 (2017)
14. Loshchilov, I.: Decoupled weight decay regularization. arXiv preprint arXiv:1711.05101 (2017)
15. Ma, J., He, Y., Li, F., Han, L., You, C., Wang, B.: Segment anything in medical images. Nat. Commun. **15**(1), 654 (2024)
16. Ma, J., et al.: Efficient medsams: segment anything in medical images on laptop. arXiv:2412.16085 (2024)
17. Ma, J., et al.: Medsam2: segment anything in 3D medical images and videos. arXiv preprint arXiv:2504.03600 (2025)
18. Myronenko, A.: 3D MRI brain tumor segmentation using autoencoder regularization. In: Brainlesion: Glioma, Multiple Sclerosis, Stroke and Traumatic Brain Injuries: 4th International Workshop, BrainLes 2018, Held in Conjunction with MICCAI 2018, Granada, Spain, September 16, 2018, Revised Selected Papers, Part II 4, pp. 311–320. Springer (2019)
19. Ravi, N., et al.: Sam 2: segment anything in images and videos. In: International Conference on Learning Representations (2025)
20. Ronneberger, O., Fischer, P., Brox, T.: U-Net: convolutional networks for biomedical image segmentation. In: Medical Image Computing and Computer-Assisted Intervention–MICCAI 2015: 18th International Conference, Munich, Germany, 5–9 October 2015, Proceedings, Part III 18, pp. 234–241. Springer (2015)
21. Sierpinski, W.: Sur une courbe cantorienne qui contient une image biunivoque et continue de toute courbe donnée. CR Acad. Sci. Paris **162**(25), 629–632 (1916)
22. Von Koch, H.: On a continuous curve without tangents constructive from elementary geometry. In: Classics on Fractals, pp. 24–45. CRC Press (2019)
23. Wasserthal, J., et al.: Totalsegmentator: robust segmentation of 104 anatomic structures in CT images. Radiol. Artif. Intell. **5**(5) (2023)
24. Xu, Z., et al.: Codabench: flexible, easy-to-use, and reproducible meta-benchmark platform. Patterns **3**(7), 100543 (2022)
25. Yang, J., Li, C., Dai, X., Gao, J.: Focal modulation networks. Adv. Neural. Inf. Process. Syst. **35**, 4203–4217 (2022)
26. Yang, J., et al.: Unified contrastive learning in image-text-label space. In: Proceedings of the IEEE/CVF Conference on Computer Vision and Pattern Recognition, pp. 19163–19173 (2022)
27. Zhao, T., et al.: A foundation model for joint segmentation, detection and recognition of biomedical objects across nine modalities. Nat. Methods **22**(1), 166–176 (2025)

28. Zhao, T., et al.: Boltzmann attention sampling for image analysis with small objects. In: Proceedings of the Computer Vision and Pattern Recognition Conference, pp. 25950–25959 (2025)
29. Zhao, Z., et al.: One model to rule them all: towards universal segmentation for medical images with text prompts. arXiv preprint arXiv:2312.17183 (2023)
30. Zhou, Z., Siddiquee, M.M.R., Tajbakhsh, N., Liang, J.: UNet++: redesigning skip connections to exploit multiscale features in image segmentation. IEEE Trans. Med. Imaging **39**(6), 1856–1867 (2019)
31. Zou, X., et al.: Segment everything everywhere all at once. Adv. Neural Inf. Process. Syst. **36** (2024)

Enhancing a 3D Foundation Model with Gaussian Sampling for Interactive Biomedical Image Segmentation

Jianhang Ji[1], Tingyi Lin[1], Junchen Xiong[1], and Tao Han[1,2](✉)

[1] The Hanglok-Tech Company, Ltd., Hengqin, China
107000292@seu.edu.cn
[2] The Department of Radiology, Zhongda Hospital, Medical School, Center of Interventional Radiology and Vascular Surgery, Southeast University, Nanjing, China

Abstract. Interactive segmentation of 3D medical images seeks to produce accurate object masks with minimal user input, substantially alleviating the burden of manual annotation. For the CVPR 2025 Foundation Models for Interactive 3D Biomedical Image Segmentation Challenge, we extend the VISTA3D foundation modela state-of-the-art 3D segmentation network supporting both automatic and interactive modesby introducing several targeted improvements for robust interactive segmentation. First, we propose a Gaussian Edge-Center point sampling strategy, which leverages Gaussian-weighted randomness combined with center/edge distance transforms to preferentially sample points at object centers and boundaries. This yields more realistic and effective foreground/background click simulations during training. Second, we integrate this sampler into a two-stage fine-tuning pipeline: initial conventional fine-tuning with provided pre-trained weights, followed by prompt-focused fine-tuning using our improved sampling strategy. Third, to meet the challenges 90-second runtime limit, we optimize inference by dynamically adjusting the region of interest (ROI) size and resolution based on input voxel spacing, including adaptive downsampling and ROI cropping. We trained models for both tracksusing 4A100 GPUs for the full dataset and 4A800 GPUs for the 10% core datasetunder identical protocols. On the validation set, our full-data model achieved a Dice Similarity Coefficient (DSC) Final of 0.7194, while the core-data model achieved 0.6782. These results demonstrate that our enhanced approach effectively leverages the capabilities of foundation models for interactive 3D segmentation, delivering accurate results with efficient user interaction. Code is available at https://github.com/M4cheal/GS_MedSegFM.

Keywords: Interactive segmentation · 3D biomedical image analysis · Prompt sampling

1 Introduction

3D biomedical image segmentation is essential for clinical diagnosis, surgical planning, and biomedical research [4,8,15]. The advent of high-resolution imag-

J. Ma et al. (Eds.): MedSegFM 2025, LNCS 16447, pp. 139–154, 2026.
https://doi.org/10.1007/978-3-032-23496-4_8

ing modalities such as CT, MRI, PET, and ultrasound has created an urgent need for segmentation models that are accurate, robust, and broadly applicable to diverse anatomical structures and imaging protocols [13,16]. However, manual annotation of 3D medical images is extremely labor-intensive and time-consuming, especially for complex structures or rare pathologies [1,9]. This challenge has motivated the development of interactive segmentation algorithms, where the model iteratively refines its predictions based on sparse user prompts (such as points or bounding boxes), thereby minimizing the annotation burden while maintaining high accuracy [7,9,12].

The CVPR 2025 Foundation Models for Interactive 3D Biomedical Image Segmentation Challenge further raises the bar by requiring universal models capable of segmenting a wide variety of anatomical structures across multiple imaging modalities, with efficient and accurate human-in-the-loop refinement. This goal is complicated by heterogeneous data, anatomical variability, class imbalance, and strict computational constraints such as a 90-second runtime limit per case.

Recent years have witnessed rapid progress in foundation models for both natural and medical image segmentation. The Segment Anything Model (SAM) [7] and its successors [14] have pioneered promptable segmentation, enabling user-driven object extraction via points, boxes, or text prompts. Inspired by these advances, the medical imaging community has developed powerful 3D segmentation foundation models such as MedSAM [9], MedSAM2 [11], SegVol [2], SAM-Med3D [17], and nnInteractive [5]. These approaches extend promptable segmentation to 3D medical images, leverage large and diverse datasets, and support interactive correction, but often still face limitations: many methods rely on 2D interaction strategies, require slice-by-slice annotation, or struggle with efficient and robust refinement in volumetric settings. VISTA3D [3] addresses several of these challenges with a unified 3D foundation model supporting both automatic and interactive segmentation. However, open problems remain regarding realistic user prompt simulation and strict clinical runtime constraints.

To address these challenges, our motivation is two-fold: (1) to design a prompt sampling strategy that more realistically mimics human correctionsparticularly at object centers and boundaries where segmentation errors are most common; and (2) to optimize the inference pipeline to reliably meet tight runtime requirements in real-world scenarios. Building on the strong foundation of VISTA3D, we introduce the following key contributions:

- **Gaussian Edge-Center Point Sampling:** We propose a novel prompt generation strategy that samples foreground and background clicks using a Gaussian-weighted distance map, focusing on object centers and edges to encourage more informative and realistic training interactions.
- **Two-Stage Fine-Tuning:** Utilizing the official VISTA3D challenge weights, we employ a two-phase fine-tuning protocol: the first stage focuses on general segmentation adaptation, while the second stage incorporates our new prompt simulation to specifically enhance interactive refinement capability.

- **Adaptive Inference with ROI and Resolution Selection:** We develop an automatic region-of-interest cropping and adaptive downsampling scheme at inference, ensuring the model processes only the relevant image region and always meets the 90-second runtime limit required for clinical usability.

Through comprehensive experiments on both the full-data and core-data challenge tracks, we demonstrate that our approach delivers both high segmentation accuracy and efficient refinement, further narrowing the gap between the capabilities of foundation models and the requirements of practical, interactive 3D medical annotation.

2 Method

2.1 Network Architecture

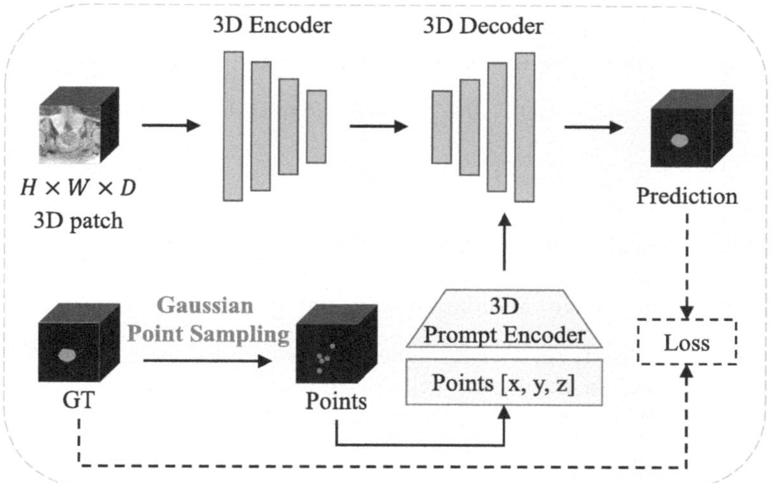

Fig. 1. Overview of our method. The framework consists of a 3D encoder, a 3D decoder, and a 3D prompt encoder. Given a 3D image and its ground truth mask (during training) or user prompts (during inference), foreground and background points are sampled using a Gaussian edge-center strategy to simulate or collect user input. The 3D encoder extracts volumetric image features, while the prompt encoder encodes the sampled points into spatial representations. The decoder then fuses image features and prompt encodings to produce the segmentation mask, which can be iteratively refined as new prompts are provided. ROI cropping and downsampling are applied as needed for efficient processing.

Our solution builds upon the VISTA3D foundation model [3], a unified segmentation framework designed for both automatic and interactive 3D medical image segmentation. As illustrated in Fig. 1, the model follows a dual-branch architecture: a shared 3D encoder based on a U-Net-style or SegResNet backbone, and two task-specific decodersone for fully automatic segmentation (prompted by class index) and another for interactive segmentation with point prompts. In this challenge, we focus on the interactive branch.

The encoder extracts hierarchical volumetric features from the input 3D patch (e.g., $H \times W \times D$ CT/MRI block), passing them to both decoders. The interactive decoder fuses these features with prompt encodings and progressively refines segmentation predictions conditioned on user input. To improve clinical practicality, we implement patch-based training and sliding window inference, cropping regions of interest (ROI) around user prompts to efficiently handle large volumes.

2.2 Prompt Encoder and Interaction Simulation

Prompt encoding is central to interactive segmentation. We simulate realistic user corrections during training using a Gaussian edge-center point sampling strategy. For each object (foreground class) in the ground truth mask, we first compute the Euclidean distance transform and define center and edge regions:

$$d = \mathrm{EDT}(M), \qquad d_{\max} = \max_u d(u), \tag{1}$$

$$\mathcal{C} = \{\, u \mid d(u) > \tau_c\, d_{\max} \,\}, \qquad \mathcal{E} = \{\, u \mid \tau_e\, d_{\max} < d(u) \le \tau_c\, d_{\max} \,\}, \tag{2}$$

where $M \in \{0,1\}^{H \times W \times D}$ is the binary ground-truth mask. The variable u denotes a voxel location in the distance field. We use fixed thresholds $\tau_e, \tau_c \in (0, 1)$ with $\tau_c = 0.5$ and $\tau_e = 0.1$ based on empirical practice. The sets $\mathcal{C}$ and $\mathcal{E}$ denote the center and edge candidate regions. Points are then sampled as follows:

- **Foreground (Positive) Points:** One point is sampled from the center region $\mathcal{C}$ (distance above a fixed percentile of the maximum, i.e., deep inside the object), and the remaining points are sampled from the edge region $\mathcal{E}$ (distance within a percentile range near the boundary).
- **Background (Negative) Points:** Randomly sampled outside the object mask.
- **Number of Points:** The total number of positive/negative prompts is drawn from a Gaussian distribution centered at half the maximum allowed, introducing variability.

If not enough candidates exist in a region, random points are used to fill up the quota. Each point is encoded as a 3D coordinate $[x, y, z]$ with an associated label (foreground/background).

During training, this sampled prompt set is provided to the interactive decoder. The decoder predicts segmentation masks conditioned on both the image and prompts, supporting robust iterative correction. The edge-center sampling ensures exposure to both easy (center) and hard (boundary) refinement scenarios, which better simulates clinical corrections compared to purely random clicks.

2.3 Decoder and Loss Function

The interactive decoder mirrors the encoder with 3D upsampling and skip connections, similar to standard U-Net architectures. Prompt features are fused into the decoding path at multiple scales using cross-attention or concatenation, allowing the network to leverage both image context and user guidance.

For optimization, we adopt a compound loss function combining Dice loss and cross-entropy loss:

$$\mathcal{L} = \mathcal{L}_{\text{Dice}} + \mathcal{L}_{\text{CE}} \tag{3}$$

This loss balances region overlap and voxel-wise classification, providing robust performance across varied structures.

To efficiently handle large 3D images, two strategies are adopted:

- **ROI Cropping:** During both training and inference, we crop a ROI around prompts/targets, reducing memory and computation.
- **Adaptive Downsampling:** For very high-resolution inputs, we dynamically downsample the ROI (using interpolation) to ensure the processed patch fits into GPU memory and meets runtime constraints.

2.4 Coreset Selection Strategy

For the coreset track, we simply follow the official rules and randomly sample 10% of the training data as the coreset. The same pipeline, prompt simulation, and training recipes are used for both tracks, allowing for fair comparison of model generalization under limited data.

2.5 Post-processing and Inference Acceleration

In the inference stage, we apply minimal post-processing: the predicted segmentation mask is resampled to the original image resolution (if downsampling was used), and the cropped ROI is placed back into the full volume. No further morphological operations are applied. To accelerate inference and comply with the strict 90-second runtime limit, the ROI and downsampling factor are dynamically selected based on prompt location and input size.

3 Experiments

3.1 Dataset and Evaluation Metrics

The development set is an extension of the CVPR 2024 MedSAM on Laptop Challenge [10], including more 3D cases from public datasets[1] and covering commonly used 3D modalities, such as Computed Tomography (CT), Magnetic Resonance Imaging (MRI), Positron Emission Tomography (PET), Ultrasound,

[1] A complete list is available at https://medsam-datasetlist.github.io/.

and Microscopy images. The hidden testing set is created by a community effort where all the cases are unpublished. The annotations are either provided by the data contributors or annotated by the challenge organizer with 3D Slicer [6] and MedSAM2 [11]. In addition to using all training cases, the challenge contains a coreset track, where participants can select 10% of the total training cases for model development.

For each iterative segmentation, the evaluation metrics include Dice Similarity Coefficient (DSC) and Normalized Surface Distance (NSD) to evaluate the segmentation region overlap and boundary distance, respectively. The final metrics used for the ranking are:

- DSC_AUC and NSD_AUC Scores: AUC (Area Under the Curve) for DSC and NSD is used to measure cumulative improvement with interactions. The AUC quantifies the cumulative performance improvement over the five click predictions, providing a holistic view of the segmentation refinement process. It is computed only over the click predictions without considering the initial bounding box prediction as it is optional.
- Final DSC and NSD Scores after all refinements, indicating the model's final segmentation performance.

In addition, the algorithm runtime will be limited to 90 s per class. Exceeding this limit will lead to all DSC and NSD metrics being set to 0 for that test case.

3.2 Implementation Details

Preprocessing. Following the practice in MedSAM [9], all images were processed to npz format with an intensity range of $[0, 255]$. Specifically, for CT images, we initially normalized the Hounsfield units using typical window width and level values: soft tissues (W:400, L:40), lung (W:1500, L:-160), brain (W:80, L:40), and bone (W:1800, L:400). Subsequently, the intensity values were rescaled to the range of $[0, 255]$. For other images, we clipped the intensity values to the range between the 0.5th and 99.5th percentiles before rescaling them to the range of [0, 255]. If the original intensity range is already in $[0, 255]$, no preprocessing was applied.

Environment Settings. The development environments and requirements are presented in Table 1.

Training Protocols. We describe our training protocols in detail, including data augmentation, sampling strategy, and model selection. The main hyperparameters and training details are summarized in Table 2 (coreset track) and Table 3 (all-data track).

1. Data augmentation To improve generalization and robustness, we employ a comprehensive suite of data augmentations for each input patch during training. Specifically, we apply:

Table 1. Development environments and requirements.

System	Ubuntu 20.04.6 LTS
CPU	Intel(R) Xeon(R) Platinum 8358 CPU @ 2.60GHz
RAM	8×64GB; 3200 MT/s
GPU (number and type)	Four NVIDIA A800-SXM4-80GB and A100-SXM4-80GB
CUDA version	12.2
Programming language	Python 3.10
Deep learning framework	torch 2.6, torchvision 0.21.0

Table 2. Training protocols for the coreset track.

Pre-trained Model	VISTA3D
Batch size	1
Patch size	128×128×128
Total epochs	200
Optimizer	AdamW
Initial learning rate (lr)	2e-5
Lr decay schedule	WarmupCosineSchedule
Training time	4 h per epoch
Loss function	DiceCELoss
Number of model parameters	196.51 M
Number of flops	4388.97G

- **Intensity normalization**: Image intensities are linearly scaled to the [0, 1] range using percentile-based clipping (1st and 99th percentiles).
- **Spatial padding and random cropping**: All images and masks are padded to at least 128 × 128 × 128 voxels, then randomly cropped into patches of the same size using label-aware cropping, ensuring each patch contains foreground.
- **Intensity perturbations**: With probability 0.2, we apply random intensity scaling (±0.2), random intensity shifting (±0.2), and random Gaussian noise (std=0.2).
- **Spatial augmentations**: Each patch is randomly flipped along each axis (x, y, z) with probability 0.2. We also apply random 90-degree rotations (up to 3 times) along random axes with probability 0.2.

These augmentations are implemented via the MONAI framework and are applied online during data loading, increasing the diversity of the training data and helping to mitigate overfitting.

2. Data sampling strategy Our training is patch-based: for each 3D image, we extract four 128^3 patches per sample, with each patch centered on regions containing foreground classes (as ensured by label-aware cropping). For each

Table 3. Training protocols for the all-data track.

Pre-trained Model	VISTA3D
Batch size	1
Patch size	128×128×128
Total epochs	100
Optimizer	AdamW
Initial learning rate (lr)	2e-5
Lr decay schedule	WarmupCosineSchedule
Training time	10 h per epoch
Loss function	DiceCELoss
Number of model parameters	196.51 M
Number of flops	4388.97G

patch, we employ a Gaussian edge-center point sampling strategy to generate interactive prompts.

3. Model selection criteria We use a two-stage fine-tuning protocol. The model is initialized with the official VISTA3D challenge weights and trained for a fixed number of epochs (e.g., 100180, depending on the track) using the AdamW optimizer and cosine learning rate scheduling. During training, checkpoints are saved at each epoch. We use the final checkpoint for all evaluations.

4 Results and Discussion

We present both quantitative and qualitative results of our method on the challenge validation set, followed by an analysis of failure cases and a discussion of limitations.

4.1 Quantitative Results on Validation Set

Tables 4 and 5 summarize the quantitative performance of our method and several recent baselines (SAM-Med3D, VISTA3D, SegVol, nnInteractive) on the coreset and all-data tracks, respectively. Metrics include DSC AUC, NSD AUC, final DSC, and final NSD, averaged across different imaging modalities.

Our method consistently outperforms or matches strong baselines on both tracks and all modalities, with particularly notable results on the coreset track. For example, on the coreset track, our approach achieves the highest DSC Final and NSD Final on CT, MRI and ultrasound, and competitive results on Microscopy and PET. This demonstrates that the proposed Gaussian edge-center prompt sampling strategy is especially effective when labeled data is limited, as it encourages the model to fully leverage informative user interactions and generalize from fewer examples.

Table 4. Quantitative evaluation results of the validation set on the **coreset track**.

Modality	Methods	DSC AUC	NSD AUC	DSC Final	NSD Final
CT	SAM-Med3D	2.2408	2.2212	0.5590	0.5558
	VISTA3D	2.7975	2.8155	0.7147	0.7243
	SegVol	2.8987	3.0373	0.7247	0.7593
	nnInteractive	-	-	-	-
	Ours	2.9638	3.0037	0.7562	0.7739
MRI	SAM-Med3D	1.5191	1.5195	0.3895	0.3956
	VISTA3D	2.2901	2.5783	0.5777	0.6479
	SegVol	1.1131	1.3137	0.2783	0.3284
	nnInteractive	-	-	-	-
	Ours	2.3980	2.7477	0.6046	0.6944
Microscopy	SAM-Med3D	0.3042	0.0169	0.0768	0.0042
	VISTA3D	1.7183	2.7084	0.4455	0.6931
	SegVol	2.0355	3.4730	0.5089	0.8682
	nnInteractive	-	-	-	-
	Ours	1.8252	2.8487	0.4665	0.6827
PET	SAM-Med3D	2.1304	1.8150	0.5344	0.4560
	VISTA3D	2.3878	2.0984	0.6123	0.5430
	SegVol	2.9683	2.8563	0.7421	0.7141
	nnInteractive	-	-	-	-
	Ours	2.3949	2.1673	0.6089	0.5501
Ultrasound	SAM-Med3D	1.3434	1.7956	0.3841	0.5090
	VISTA3D	2.5803	2.5886	0.7074	0.7174
	SegVol	1.2325	1.7881	0.3081	0.4470
	nnInteractive	-	-	-	-
	Ours	2.5513	2.5333	0.7486	0.7497

However, on the all-data track, although our method remains competitive, it does not achieve the absolute best results across all modalities. A possible reason is that the increased data scale requires longer or more carefully tuned training schedules to fully realize the models capacity; in our experiments, the number of training epochs for the all-data track was not significantly increased due to computational resource and time constraints. As a result, the model may not have fully converged or exploited the richer supervision available in the larger dataset. In addition, the hyperparameters (such as prompt sampling, learning rate, and regularization) were not extensively re-optimized for the all-data setting, which may have affected the ultimate performance. Future work will investigate longer training, more aggressive data augmentation, and track-

Table 5. Quantitative evaluation results of the validation set on the **all-data track**.

Modality	Methods	DSC AUC	NSD AUC	DSC Final	NSD Final
CT	SAM-Med3D	2.2615	2.1533	0.5676	0.5421
	VISTA3D	3.1689	3.2652	0.8041	0.8344
	SegVol	2.9860	3.1191	0.7465	0.7798
	nnInteractive	3.4337	3.5743	0.8764	0.9165
	Ours	3.0983	3.1734	0.7897	0.8160
MRI	SAM-Med3D	1.6351	1.6106	0.4208	0.4193
	VISTA3D	2.5895	2.9683	0.6545	0.7493
	SegVol	1.2720	1.4629	0.3180	0.3657
	nnInteractive	2.6975	3.0292	0.7302	0.8227
	Ours	2.6072	2.9929	0.6593	0.7560
Microscopy	SAM-Med3D	0.3041	0.0168	0.0768	0.0042
	VISTA3D	2.0229	3.0150	0.5286	0.7701
	SegVol	2.2851	3.5661	0.5713	0.8915
	nnInteractive	3.0801	3.9027	0.7836	0.9813
	Ours	2.1634	3.3163	0.5601	0.8500
PET	SAM-Med3D	1.2879	0.7779	0.3219	0.1945
	VISTA3D	2.6398	2.3998	0.6779	0.6227
	SegVol	3.0225	2.9132	0.7556	0.7283
	nnInteractive	3.1877	3.0722	0.8156	0.7915
	Ours	2.6225	2.3821	0.6773	0.6199
Ultrasound	SAM-Med3D	1.7246	2.1188	0.4613	0.5597
	VISTA3D	2.8655	2.8441	0.8105	0.8079
	SegVol	3.4116	3.4167	0.8529	0.8542
	nnInteractive	3.3481	3.3236	0.8547	0.8494
	Ours	2.3970	2.4091	0.7112	0.7211

specific hyperparameter tuning to further improve performance on the full-data track.

Overall, these results highlight the robustness and data efficiency of our approach in low-data regimes, while also suggesting directions for improvement when scaling to very large training sets.

4.2 Qualitative Results on Validation Set

Figure 2 presents qualitative results for each modality on the validation set, including both well-segmented (Good) and poorly-segmented (Bad) cases. Each row shows representative slices from different imaging modalities: CT, MRI, microscopy, PET, and ultrasound. For each case, we display the input image, ground truth (GT) mask, and our models prediction (Ours).

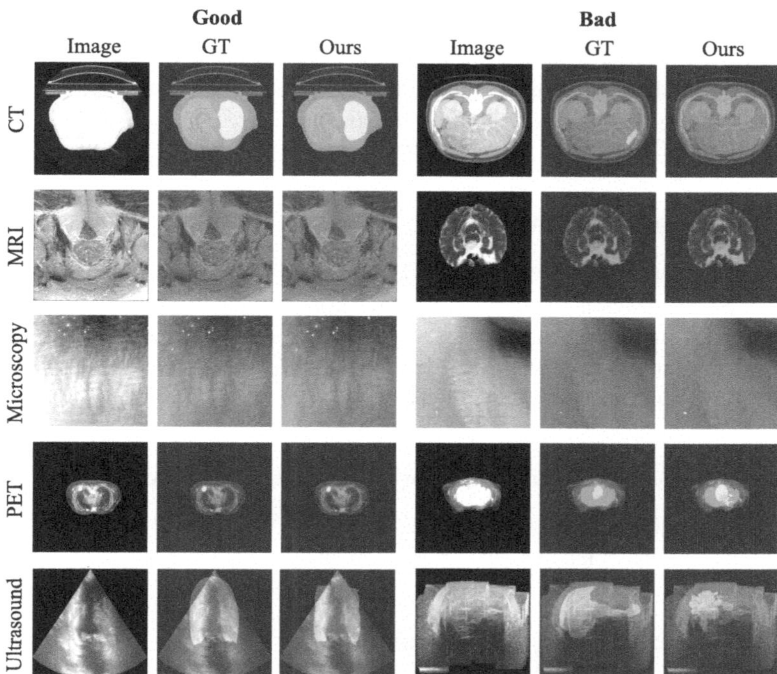

Fig. 2. Qualitative examples on the validation set. For each modality, we show both a successful (Good) and a failure (Bad) case. Columns are: input image, ground truth (GT), and our prediction (Ours).

Cases Where the Proposed Method Works Well: As shown in the left (Good) columns, our method achieves accurate segmentation across a variety of modalities and organs. For example, in CT and MRI, both multi-class organ boundaries and object shapes are well captured, even for relatively small or thin structures. In microscopy and PET, our model correctly identifies target regions despite low contrast and heterogeneous backgrounds. In ultrasound, our approach produces anatomically plausible masks that closely match the ground truth.

Analysis of Failure Cases: On the right (Bad) columns, we illustrate typical failure modes. These include missed or partially segmented targets (e.g., under-segmentation of small lesions in CT and MRI), false positive predictions (e.g., spurious objects in PET and microscopy), and shape distortions in challenging ultrasound images. Common reasons for these failures include:

- **Low image contrast or artifacts**: Especially in PET and ultrasound, poor image quality or heavy noise can confuse the model.
- **Class imbalance and small targets**: The model tends to miss small or rare objects that are underrepresented during training.

- **Ambiguous boundaries**: Weak or unclear object boundaries, especially in microscopy and ultrasound, often lead to over- or under-segmentation.
- **Out-of-distribution cases**: Extremely rare or complex anatomies not well covered by the training set remain challenging.

4.3 Results on Final Testing Set

On the test set of the CVPR 2025 Foundation Models for Interactive 3D Biomedical Image Segmentation Challenge, our method was submitted under the team name **hanglok**. In the All-data Track, our approach ranked 4th, and in the Coreset Track, it ranked 6th. The official leaderboard for both tracks is summarized in Table 6, and the modality-wise results are reported in Tables 7 and 8.

Table 6. Leaderboard on the test set for both tracks. The **bold** rows indicate our method (hanglok).

Track	Rank	Team	DSC AUC	NSD AUC	DSC Final	NSD Final
All-data Track	1	aim	3.129	3.258	0.805	0.842
	2	yiooo	2.981	3.009	0.767	0.779
	3	sjtu-426lab	2.552	2.645	0.640	0.664
	4	**hanglok**	**2.372**	**2.296**	**0.632**	**0.624**
	5	sail	1.950	1.907	0.487	0.477
	6	medibot	0.098	0.109	0.025	0.027
Coreset Track	1	aim	3.104	3.232	0.801	0.838
	2	norateam	2.911	2.970	0.754	0.775
	3	yiooo	2.896	2.898	0.745	0.749
	4	lexor	2.501	2.572	0.625	0.643
	5	ahus	2.404	2.266	0.627	0.597
	6	**hanglok**	**2.120**	**2.012**	**0.553**	**0.533**
	7	cemrg	1.885	1.624	0.476	0.410
	8	sail	1.654	1.593	0.413	0.398
	9	dtftech	1.591	1.079	0.417	0.284
	10	owwwen	0.956	0.496	0.239	0.124

4.4 Limitation and Future Work

Despite strong overall performance, our approach still has several limitations. First, segmentation quality degrades on very small, low-contrast, or highly variable targets, particularly in modalities with poor signal-to-noise ratios (e.g., ultrasound, PET). Second, while the Gaussian edge-center prompt strategy improves robustness, it is still based on simulated points; the model might not fully generalize to unpredictable real user corrections. Third, inference acceleration via ROI cropping and downsampling may occasionally lead to the loss of fine details for large or elongated structures. In future work, we plan to incorporate

Table 7. Modality-wise results on the test set (All-data Track).

Modality	Team	DSC AUC	NSD AUC	DSC Final	NSD Final
CT	aim	3.084	3.089	0.792	0.798
	yiooo	2.904	2.760	0.747	0.716
	sjtu-426lab	2.421	2.396	0.608	0.601
	hanglok	**2.400**	**2.134**	**0.640**	**0.577**
	sail	1.984	1.707	0.496	0.427
	medibot	0.386	0.495	0.096	0.124
MRI	aim	3.246	3.556	0.833	0.912
	yiooo	3.133	3.405	0.802	0.873
	sjtu-426lab	2.790	3.028	0.698	0.758
	hanglok	**2.510**	**2.638**	**0.658**	**0.703**
	sail	1.933	2.089	0.483	0.522
	medibot	0.185	0.211	0.046	0.053
PET	aim	2.953	2.581	0.783	0.698
	yiooo	3.148	2.884	0.799	0.746
	sjtu-426lab	2.932	2.479	0.733	0.620
	hanglok	**2.194**	**1.676**	**0.543**	**0.414**
	sail	1.633	1.618	0.408	0.404
	medibot	0.335	0.276	0.084	0.069
Ultrasound	aim	1.790	2.490	0.510	0.718
	yiooo	1.771	2.281	0.514	0.677
	sjtu-426lab	0.995	1.579	0.265	0.411
	hanglok	**0.955**	**1.272**	**0.316**	**0.483**
	sail	0.889	1.200	0.222	0.300
	medibot	0.000	0.000	0.000	0.000
Microscopy	aim	2.906	3.900	0.773	0.983
	yiooo	3.310	3.983	0.836	0.996
	sjtu-426lab	3.012	3.974	0.755	0.994
	hanglok	**2.540**	**3.551**	**0.639**	**0.889**
	sail	2.453	3.650	0.613	0.912
	medibot	0.000	0.000	0.000	0.000

uncertainty-guided or adaptive prompt sampling, further integrate text prompts for open-vocabulary segmentation, and explore more advanced post-processing (e.g., shape regularization or 3D CRF) to address the aforementioned limitations.

Table 8. Modality-wise results on the test set (Coreset Track).

Modality	Team	DSC AUC	NSD AUC	DSC Final	NSD Final
CT	aim	3.063	3.065	0.791	0.797
	norateam	2.872	2.786	0.746	0.729
	yiooo	2.825	2.652	0.727	0.685
	lexor	2.314	2.175	0.579	0.544
	ahus	2.349	2.052	0.622	0.552
	hanglok	**2.137**	**1.880**	**0.559**	**0.498**
	cemrg	1.991	1.605	0.505	0.408
	sail	1.334	1.064	0.334	0.267
	dtftech	1.579	0.880	0.421	0.238
	owwwen	1.005	0.469	0.251	0.117
MRI	aim	3.223	3.538	0.829	0.910
	norateam	3.092	3.343	0.794	0.861
	yiooo	3.057	3.313	0.782	0.849
	lexor	2.708	2.946	0.677	0.737
	ahus	2.450	2.519	0.626	0.646
	hanglok	**2.258**	**2.320**	**0.580**	**0.605**
	cemrg	1.814	1.689	0.455	0.424
	sail	1.980	2.103	0.495	0.526
	dtftech	1.534	1.220	0.393	0.314
	owwwen	0.958	0.547	0.239	0.136
PET	aim	2.862	2.459	0.767	0.676
	norateam	3.201	2.879	0.805	0.727
	yiooo	3.028	2.657	0.773	0.691
	lexor	2.587	2.184	0.647	0.546
	ahus	2.278	1.836	0.561	0.456
	hanglok	**1.719**	**1.320**	**0.428**	**0.326**
	cemrg	1.406	0.903	0.355	0.227
	sail	2.066	1.652	0.517	0.413
	dtftech	1.242	0.586	0.312	0.148
	owwwen	0.214	0.017	0.053	0.004
Ultrasound	aim	1.822	2.537	0.510	0.734
	norateam	1.849	2.444	0.529	0.721
	yiooo	1.528	1.905	0.450	0.589
	lexor	0.998	1.471	0.250	0.368
	ahus	1.785	2.038	0.474	0.546
	hanglok	**0.689**	**0.622**	**0.202**	**0.221**
	cemrg	0.411	0.258	0.103	0.064
	sail	0.762	1.121	0.188	0.272
	dtftech	0.860	0.897	0.215	0.224
	owwwen	0.172	0.068	0.042	0.015
Microscopy	aim	2.961	3.932	0.788	0.988
	norateam	3.336	3.972	0.848	0.995
	yiooo	3.193	3.972	0.809	0.994
	lexor	2.717	3.927	0.679	0.982
	ahus	2.567	3.755	0.672	0.941
	hanglok	**2.030**	**2.944**	**0.516**	**0.746**
	cemrg	0.202	0.000	0.051	0.000
	sail	2.389	3.677	0.597	0.919
	dtftech	0.160	0.000	0.040	0.000
	owwwen	0.039	0.000	0.010	0.000

5 Conclusion

In this work, we present a VISTA3D-based interactive segmentation framework featuring a novel Gaussian edge-center prompt sampling strategy and an adaptive inference pipeline. Extensive validation on the CVPR challenge dataset demonstrates that our method achieves robust and accurate segmentation across multiple imaging modalities, outperforming or matching strong baselines, especially in low-data regimes. Qualitative results show that our approach is effective for most organs and modalities, while limitations remain for small, low-contrast, or ambiguous targets. Future work will focus on further improving prompt realism, model generalizability, and efficiency.

Disclosure of Interests. The authors have no competing interests to declare that are relevant to the content of this article.

Acknowledgements. We thank all the data owners for making the medical images publicly available and CodaLab [18] for hosting the challenge platform. This study was funded by the China Postdoctoral Science Foundation funded project under Grant 2024M750450.

References

1. Chi, W., Ma, L., Wu, J., Chen, M., Lu, W., Gu, X.: Deep learning-based medical image segmentation with limited labels. Phys. Med. Biol. **65**(23), 235001 (2020)
2. Du, Y., Bai, F., Huang, T., Zhao, B.: Segvol: Universal and interactive volumetric medical image segmentation. Adv. Neural. Inf. Process. Syst. **37**, 110746–110783 (2024)
3. He, Y., et al.: Vista3d: A unified segmentation foundation model for 3d medical imaging. In: Proceedings of the IEEE/CVF International Conference on Computer Vision and Pattern Recognition (2024)
4. Isensee, F., Jaeger, P.F., Kohl, S.A., Petersen, J., Maier-Hein, K.H.: nnu-net: a self-configuring method for deep learning-based biomedical image segmentation. Nat. Methods **18**(2), 203–211 (2021)
5. Isensee, F., et al.: nninteractive: Redefining 3d promptable segmentation. arXiv preprint arXiv:2503.08373 (2025)
6. Kikinis, R., Pieper, S.D., Vosburgh, K.G.: 3D slicer: a platform for subject-specific image analysis, visualization, and clinical support. In: Intraoperative imaging and image-guided therapy, pp. 277–289. Springer (2013)
7. Kirillov, A., et al.: Segment anything. In: Proceedings of the IEEE/CVF International Conference on Computer Vision, pp. 4015–4026 (2023)
8. Litjens, G., et al.: A survey on deep learning in medical image analysis. Med. Image Anal. **42**, 60–88 (2017)
9. Ma, J., He, Y., Li, F., Han, L., You, C., Wang, B.: Segment anything in medical images. Nat. Commun. **15**(1), 654 (2024)
10. Ma, J., et al.: Efficient medsams: Segment anything in medical images on laptop. arXiv preprint arXiv:2412.16085 (2024)

11. Ma, J., et al.: Medsam2: Segment anything in 3D medical images and videos. arXiv preprint arXiv:2504.03600 (2025)
12. Marinov, Z., Jäger, P.F., Egger, J., Kleesiek, J., Stiefelhagen, R.: Deep interactive segmentation of medical images: a systematic review and taxonomy. IEEE Trans. Pattern Anal. Mach. Intell. (2024)
13. Menze, B.H., et al.: The multimodal brain tumor image segmentation benchmark (brats). IEEE Trans. Med. Imaging **34**(10), 1993–2024 (2014)
14. Ravi, N., et al.: Sam 2: Segment anything in images and videos (2025)
15. Ronneberger, O., Fischer, P., Brox, T.: U-net: Convolutional networks for biomedical image segmentation. In: Medical image computing and computer-assisted intervention–MICCAI 2015: 18th international conference, Munich, Germany, October 5-9, 2015, proceedings, part III 18, pp. 234–241. Springer (2015)
16. Simpson, A.L., et al.: A large annotated medical image dataset for the development and evaluation of segmentation algorithms. arXiv preprint arXiv:1902.09063 (2019)
17. Wang, H., et al.: Sam-med3d: towards general-purpose segmentation models for volumetric medical images. arXiv preprint arXiv:2310.15161 (2023)
18. Xu, Z., et al.: Codabench: Flexible, easy-to-use, and reproducible meta-benchmark platform. Patterns **3**(7), 100543 (2022)

Dynamic Prompt Generation for Interactive 3D Medical Image Segmentation Training

Tidiane Camaret Ndir[1,2(✉)], Alexander Pfefferle[2,3], and Robin T. Schirrmeister[1]

[1] Medical Physics, Department of Diagnostic and Interventional Radiology, Medical Center—University of Freiburg, Faculty of Medicine, University of Freiburg, Freiburg, Germany

[2] University of Freiburg, Freiburg, Germany

tidiane.camaret.ndir@uniklinik-freiburg.de

[3] ELLIS Institute Tübingen, Tübingen, Germany

Abstract. Interactive 3D biomedical image segmentation requires efficient models that can iteratively refine predictions based on user prompts. Current foundation models either lack volumetric awareness or suffer from limited interactive capabilities. We propose a training strategy that combines dynamic volumetric prompt generation with content-aware adaptive cropping to optimize the use of the image encoder. Our method simulates realistic user interaction patterns during training while addressing the computational challenges of learning from sequential refinement feedback on a single GPU. For efficient training, we initialize our network using the publicly available weights from the nnInteractive segmentation model. Evaluation on the **Foundation Models for Interactive 3D Biomedical Image Segmentation** competition demonstrates strong performance with an average final Dice score of 0.6385, normalized surface distance of 0.6614, and area-under-the-curve metrics of 2.4799 (Dice) and 2.5671 (NSD).

Keywords: Interactive segmentation · 3D medical imaging · Dynamic prompt generation

1 Introduction

1.1 Background

Accurate 3D medical image segmentation is essential for clinical and research applications. The increasing volume and complexity of biomedical data sets require robust interactive segmentation methods that efficiently incorporate user feedback.

The **Foundation Models for Interactive 3D Biomedical Image Segmentation** (SEGFM3D) challenge evaluates interactive segmentation through progressive refinement: models receive an initial bounding box, which may or

J. Ma et al. (Eds.): MedSegFM 2025, LNCS 16447, pp. 155–172, 2026.
https://doi.org/10.1007/978-3-032-23496-4_9

may not be provided depending on the case, followed by 1–5 iterative click refinements to correct errors. Models must complete segmentation within 90 s per class, enforcing computational efficiency. The challenge requires optimal utilization of heterogeneous user prompts, bounding boxes for localization and clicks for refinement, across diverse 3D anatomical structures and imaging modalities.

1.2 Related Work

Foundation models for image segmentation, particularly SAM [5] and SAM2 [11], have demonstrated strong zero-shot performance on natural images. Medical adaptations including MedSAM [7] and MedSAM2 [9] fine-tune these models on medical datasets but exhibit limited interactive refinement capabilities, particularly for iterative correction workflows.

Recent advances in interactive 3D medical segmentation include SegVol [1], SAM-Med3D [13], VISTA3D [3], and nnInteractive [2]. These methods explore different approaches to incorporating user feedback in volumetric medical image analysis, establishing the foundation for interactive refinement in clinical workflows.

However, those methods do not optimally utilize all available information in the SEGFM3D challenge: initial bounding boxes, previous iteration segmentations, and competition-generated clicks.

Existing approaches exhibit fundamental limitations: VISTA3D [3] supports only click prompts, lacking bounding box and iterative refinement capabilities. SegVol [1] accepts only bounding boxes without click-based correction. SAM-Med3D [13] operates at low resolution, insufficient for accurate 3D segmentation. nnInteractive [2] accepts multiple prompts but restricts bounding boxes to 2D slices, ignoring 3D spatial context.

A critical challenge is the circular dependency in training interactive models: generating realistic training signals requires iterative predictions and error-based click simulation, yet the model must learn from these self-generated interactions.

1.3 Solution and Contribution

We present two key contributions to address the limitations of current interactive 3D segmentation methods:

First, we introduce a dynamic prompt generation strategy that simulates realistic user interaction patterns during training. This approach generates clicks by identifying the largest connected error components between predictions and ground truth, mimicking the competition evaluation settings.

Second, we propose content-aware dynamic cropping that adapts the model field of view sizes based on anatomical context. This ensures complete capture of target structures while maintaining computational efficiency.

2 Method

2.1 General Network Architecture

We base our solution on the nnInteractive [2] method and adopt a 3D Residual Encoder U-Net [12] architecture, combining the spatial precision of U-Net with the gradient flow benefits of residual connections, specifically optimized for interactive volumetric medical image segmentation.

The encoder consists of six stages with progressively increasing feature dimensions (32, 64, 128, 256, 320, 320) while reducing spatial resolution through $3 \times 3 \times 3$ convolutions with stride 2. Each encoder stage incorporates residual blocks following the ResNet paradigm:

$$\mathcal{F}_{\text{res}}(x) = x + \mathcal{B}(x), \tag{1}$$

where x is the input feature map, $\mathcal{F}_{\text{res}}(x)$ denotes the residual block output and $\mathcal{B}(x)$ represents two consecutive 3D convolutional layers with GroupNorm and LeakyReLU activations.

The decoder mirrors the encoder structure with transposed convolutions for upsampling. We only compute the loss on the final segmentation prediction and do not employ deep supervision, which is sometimes used to get additional training signal using segmentation predictions obtained from earlier layers of the decoder. We found that unnecessary since we initialize our parameters from the pretrained nnInteractive segmentation model (Fig. 1).

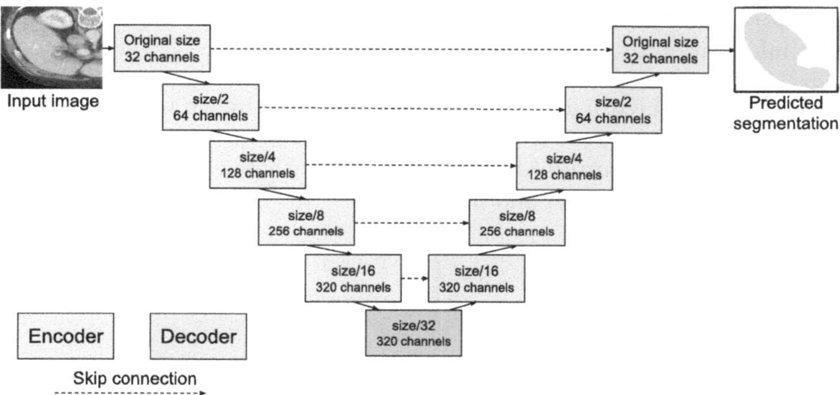

Fig. 1. 3D Residual Encoder U-Net Architecture: A U-Net with residual blocks processing 3D input through 6-stage encoder-decoder with skip connections.

2.2 Prompt Encoding

Following the nnInteractive [2] strategy, we encode heterogeneous prompts (bounding boxes, positive/negative clicks and previous segmentation masks) as additional input channels concatenated with the image data, as illustrated in Fig. 2.

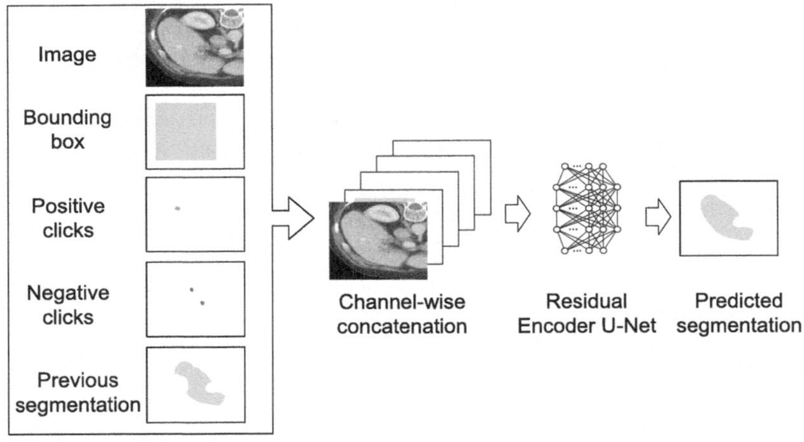

Fig. 2. Prompt encoding: Prompts are concatenated with the original image as extra channels.

Multi-modal Prompt Representation. Our input tensor $\mathcal{X} \in \mathbb{R}^{C \times D \times H \times W}$ encodes information in 5 channels:

1. **Image Channel** ($\mathcal{X}_0$): The normalized 3D medical image with intensity values in [0, 255].
2. **Bounding Box Channel** ($\mathcal{X}_1$): A binary mask where voxels inside the initial bounding box are set to 1, and 0 elsewhere:

$$\mathcal{X}_1(i,j,k) = \begin{cases} 1 & \text{if } (i,j,k) \in \mathcal{B} \\ 0 & \text{otherwise,} \end{cases} \tag{2}$$

   where $\mathcal{B}$ represents the 3D bounding box region.
3. **Positive Click Channel** ($\mathcal{X}_2$): Encodes user-provided positive clicks indicating regions that should be included in the segmentation. Each click is represented as a sphere of radius 4 voxels:

$$\mathcal{X}_2(i,j,k) = \begin{cases} 1 & \text{if } \min_{c \in \mathcal{C}^+} \|(i,j,k) - c\| \leq 4 \\ 0 & \text{otherwise,} \end{cases} \tag{3}$$

   where $\mathcal{C}^+$ is the set of positive click coordinates.

4. **Negative Click Channel** ($\mathcal{X}_3$): Similarly encodes negative clicks indicating regions to exclude:

$$\mathcal{X}_3(i,j,k) = \begin{cases} 1 & \text{if } \min_{c \in \mathcal{C}^-} \|(i,j,k) - c\| \leq 4 \\ 0 & \text{otherwise.} \end{cases} \quad (4)$$

5. **Previous Segmentation Channel** ($\mathcal{X}_4$): Contains the binary mask from the previous iteration, enabling the model to refine its predictions based on prior outputs. For the initial iteration, this channel is zero-initialized.

Handling Missing Prompts. For anatomical structures without meaningful bounding boxes (e.g., vessels, myocardium), we generate a default bounding box covering the central third of the volume:

$$\mathcal{B}_{\text{default}} = \left[\frac{D}{3}, \frac{2D}{3}\right] \times \left[\frac{H}{3}, \frac{2H}{3}\right] \times \left[\frac{W}{3}, \frac{2W}{3}\right]. \quad (5)$$

This heuristic ensures consistent input dimensionality while providing a reasonable initialization region for structures that typically appear near the image center.

2.3 Interaction Simulation

Training interactive segmentation models presents a unique challenge: the model must learn from a feedback that depends on its own predictions. We address this circular dependency by implementing a dynamic interaction simulation strategy that mimics the competition's click generation logic during training. We simulate the iterative refinement process through a two-stage approach.

1. **Interaction simulation stage (no gradient computation)**: We run the network with the original image and the bounding box and all other prompts channels set to zero to generate an initial prediction, identify errors via connected component analysis, and generate click prompts, as illustrated in Fig. 3.
2. **Training Stage (with gradient computation)**: We perform a forward pass with all prompts (bounding box, generated clicks and previous segmentation) to produce the final prediction. Only this final prediction is used to compute the loss and update the network weights through backpropagation.

Stochastic Interaction Sampling. To ensure robust and efficient training, we stochastically choose one of two settings for each batch during training: (1) No click and no given previous segmentation, or (2) a single click and the network's prediction from setting (1) as the given previous segmentation. In the setting with a given network segmentation (2), we transform the previous segmentation

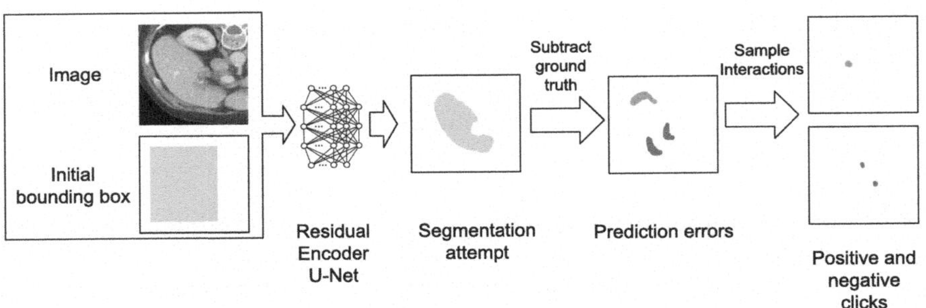

Fig. 3. Dynamic interaction simulation during training. The model generates an initial segmentation using the bounding box prompt without gradient computation. Click prompts are then generated based on error analysis between this prediction and ground truth. Note: The final segmentation is produced using all prompts, and only this final prediction is used to compute the loss and update network weights via backpropagation

into a hard binary segmentation and do not backpropagate through it to reduce GPU memory usage.

$$\text{1-click} \sim \text{Bernoulli}(p_{\text{click}}), \tag{6}$$

where $p_{\text{click}} = 0.5$. This distribution was chosen to have a simple training setup that can generalize well to the evaluation. Using the prediction of the network under training as the given prior segmentation should generalize well to evaluation where the same setting is used.

Error-Based Click Generation. For each sampled interaction level, we generate clicks by identifying and targeting segmentation errors:

1. **Error Detection**: We compute the binary error mask between the predicted segmentation $\hat{Y}$ and ground truth Y:

$$\mathcal{E} = (\hat{Y} > 0.5) \oplus (Y > 0.5), \tag{7}$$

where $\oplus$ denotes the XOR operation.

2. **Connected Component Analysis**: We identify spatially connected error regions using 26-connectivity in 3D:

$$\mathcal{C} = \text{CC3D}(\mathcal{E}, \text{connectivity} = 26). \tag{8}$$

3. **Largest Error Selection**: We target the largest connected error component to maximize correction impact:

$$c^* = \arg\max_{c \in \mathcal{C}} |\{(i, j, k) : \mathcal{C}(i, j, k) = c\}|. \tag{9}$$

4. **Click Center Determination**: We compute the Euclidean Distance Transform (EDT) of the largest error component and sample the click location from the maximum distance point:

$$\text{click\_center} = \arg \max_{(i,j,k)\in c^*} \text{EDT}(c^*). \tag{10}$$

5. **Click Type Assignment**: The click type (positive or negative) is determined by the ground truth value at the click location:

$$\text{click\_type} = \begin{cases} \text{positive} & \text{if } Y(\text{click\_center}) = 1 \\ \text{negative} & \text{if } Y(\text{click\_center}) = 0. \end{cases} \tag{11}$$

2.4 Warm Starting

We initialize our model with pre-trained weights from nnInteractive v1.0, which has demonstrated strong performance on interactive medical image segmentation tasks. However, the original nnInteractive architecture was designed to accommodate a larger set of interaction prompts beyond those used in the SEGFM3D challenge. To leverage the pre-trained weights while maintaining architectural compatibility, we fill the unused channels with zero tensors. Note also that nnInteractive was trained with 2d bounding boxes within the 3d volume, while we train using the full 3d bounding box to make full use of the volumetric information.

2.5 Processing Details

Handling Large Images. To process large 3D medical images within memory constraints while preserving the spatial context around the target region, we implement a content-aware dynamic cropping strategy. Given an input patch size of $192 \times 192 \times 192$ and a bounding box $\mathcal{B}$, we:

1. **Compute the required zoom factor** to ensure the bounding box fits within the patch with a margin:

$$z = \max\left(\frac{\text{bbox\_size} + \text{patch\_size}/3}{\text{patch\_size}}, 1\right) \tag{12}$$

2. **Scale the patch size** to accommodate the entire bounding box:

$$\text{scaled\_patch\_size} = \lceil z \times \text{patch\_size} \rceil \tag{13}$$

3. **Center the crop** around the bounding box center and pad if necessary to handle boundary cases.
4. **Resize to target dimensions** during inference to maintain consistent input size for the network.

This approach ensures that: (i) the entire bounding box is captured regardless of its size, (ii) sufficient context (33% margin) is preserved around the target region, and (iii) the aspect ratio of anatomical structures is maintained during processing.

Post-processing. We use the per-class sigmoid-transformed outputs of the networks as binary probabilities to create the multiclass segmentation map. First, we compute the probability of the background class as the probability that none of the foreground classes are present. This is calculated as the product of the negative probabilities of all other classes: $p_{bg} = \prod_{c=1}^{K}(1 - p_c)$, where p_c is the probability of class c, and the product runs over all K foreground classes. The predicted class at each location is then assigned by taking the argmax over the background and all foreground probabilities: class $= \text{argmax}_{i \in \{0,...K\}} p_i$, where $p_0 = p_{bg}$ is the background probability.

Inference Optimization. We followed the Docker optimizations in DAFT [10] and reduced the size and number of layers in the image by: (i) using a minimal base image (`python : 3.13-slim-bookworm`), (ii) disabling pip caching (`PIP_NO_CACHE_DIR=1`), and (iii) squashing layers with `docker-squash`.

2.6 Loss Function

We employ a compound loss function combining Dice loss and cross-entropy, as such hybrid approaches have proven robust across various medical image segmentation tasks [6]. The total loss is formulated as:

$$\mathcal{L}_{\text{seg}} = -\alpha \mathcal{L}_{\text{Dice}} + \mathcal{L}_{\text{CE}}, \tag{14}$$

where $\alpha = 10$.

Dice Loss. The Dice loss promotes global consistency and handles class imbalance:

$$\mathcal{L}_{\text{Dice}} = 1 - \frac{2\sum_i p_i g_i + \epsilon}{\sum_i p_i + \sum_i g_i + \epsilon}, \tag{15}$$

where $p_i \in [0, 1]$ represents the predicted probability at voxel i, $g_i \in \{0, 1\}$ is the ground truth label, and $\epsilon = 10^{-5}$ ensures numerical stability.

Cross-Entropy Loss. The binary cross-entropy loss provides strong gradients for individual voxel classification:

$$\mathcal{L}_{\text{CE}} = -\frac{1}{N}\sum_{i=1}^{N}\left[g_i \log(p_i) + (1 - g_i)\log(1 - p_i)\right], \tag{16}$$

where N is the total number of voxels.

3 Experiments

3.1 Dataset and Evaluation Metrics

The development set is an extension of the CVPR 2024 MedSAM on Laptop Challenge [8], including more 3D cases from public datasets[1] and covering commonly used 3D modalities, such as Computed Tomography (CT), Magnetic Resonance Imaging (MRI), Positron Emission Tomography (PET), Ultrasound, and Microscopy images. The hidden testing set is created by a community effort where all the cases are unpublished. The annotations are either provided by the data contributors or annotated by the challenge organizer with 3D Slicer [4] and MedSAM2 [9]. In addition to using all training cases, the challenge contains a coreset track, where participants can select 10% of the total training cases for model development.

For each iterative segmentation, the evaluation metrics include Dice Similarity Coefficient (DSC) and Normalized Surface Distance (NSD) to evaluate the segmentation region overlap and boundary distance, respectively. The final metrics used for the ranking are:

- DSC_AUC and NSD_AUC Scores: AUC (Area Under the Curve) for DSC and NSD is used to measure cumulative improvement with interactions. The AUC quantifies the cumulative performance improvement over the five click predictions, providing a holistic view of the segmentation refinement process. It is computed only over the click predictions without considering the initial bounding box prediction as it is optional.
- Final DSC and NSD Scores after all refinements, indicating the model's final segmentation performance.

In addition, the algorithm runtime will be limited to 90 s per class, measured by the total runtime of the submitted docker container. Exceeding this limit will lead to all DSC and NSD metrics being set to 0 for that test case. The ranking was computed for each metric and test case and then averaged to get the final ranking in the challenge.

3.2 Implementation Details

Preprocessing. Following the practice in MedSAM [7], all images were processed to npz format with an intensity range of $[0, 255]$. Specifically, for CT images, we initially normalized the Hounsfield units using typical window width and level values: soft tissues (W:400, L:40), lung (W:1500, L:-160), brain (W:80, L:40), and bone (W:1800, L:400). Subsequently, the intensity values were rescaled to the range of $[0, 255]$. For other images, we clipped the intensity values to the range between the 0.5th and 99.5th percentiles before rescaling them to the range of [0, 255]. If the original intensity range is already in $[0, 255]$, no preprocessing was applied.

[1] A complete list is available at https://medsam-datasetlist.github.io/.

Environment Settings. The development environments and requirements are presented in Table 1.

Table 1. Development environments and requirements

System	Ubuntu 20.04.6 LTS
CPU	AMD EPYC 7713P 64-Core Processor
RAM	8×2GB; 2.67MT/s
GPU (number and type)	One NVIDIA RTX 6000 Ada Generation (50 G)
CUDA version	12.3
Programming language	Python 3.12.10
Deep learning framework	torch 2.6.0

Training Protocols. Our training configuration is summarized in Table 2.

Data Augmentation. We employ minimal augmentation as extensive transformations have been shown to degrade performance on the evaluation task. Our pipeline consists of: (i) intensity normalization to [0, 255], (ii) random class selection when multiple objects are present, (iii) cropping to non-zero regions around the selected object, and (iv) resizing to the model's input patch size.

Data Sampling Strategy. We train on 10% of the dataset with uniform sampling across all modalities. Each training iteration randomly selects one segmentation class per image to ensure balanced exposure to different anatomical structures.

Table 2. Training protocols

Pre-trained weights	nnInteractive v1.0
Batch size	2
Patch size	$192 \times 192 \times 192$
Total epochs	25
Optimizer	AdamW
Initial learning rate (lr)	1e-4
Lr decay schedule	constant learning rate
Training time	16 h
Loss function	- 10 * Dice Loss + Cross Entropy Loss
Number of model parameters	102 M
Number of flops	10000G

4 Results and Discussion

4.1 Quantitative Results on Validation Set

Table 3. Quantitative evaluation results on the validation set for the **coreset track**

Modality	Methods	DSC AUC	NSD AUC	DSC Final	NSD Final
CT	SAM-Med3D	2.2408	2.2213	0.5590	0.5558
	VISTA3D	3.1689	3.2652	0.8041	0.8344
	SegVol	2.9809	3.1235	0.7452	0.7809
	nnInteractive	**3.4337**	**3.5743**	**0.8764**	**0.9165**
	Ours	3.2197	3.3272	0.8197	0.8511
MRI	SAM-Med3D	1.5222	1.5226	0.3903	0.3964
	VISTA3D	2.5895	2.9683	0.6545	0.7493
	SegVol	2.6719	**3.1535**	0.6680	0.7884
	nnInteractive	**2.6975**	3.0292	**0.7302**	**0.8227**
	Ours	1.5944	1.6136	0.4222	0.4254
Microscopy	SAM-Med3D	0.1163	0	0.0291	0
	VISTA3D	2.1196	3.2259	0.5478	0.8243
	SegVol	1.6846	2.9716	0.4211	0.7429
	nnInteractive	2.3311	3.1109	0.5943	0.7890
	Ours	**2.9475**	**3.8109**	**0.7531**	**0.9606**
PET	SAM-Med3D	2.1304	1.7250	0.5344	0.4560
	VISTA3D	2.6398	2.3998	0.6779	0.6227
	SegVol	2.9683	2.8563	0.7421	0.7141
	nnInteractive	3.1877	3.0722	0.8156	**0.7915**
	Ours	**3.2278**	**3.0727**	**0.8186**	0.7841
Ultrasound	SAM-Med3D	1.4347	1.9176	0.4102	0.5435
	VISTA3D	2.8655	2.8441	0.8105	0.8079
	SegVol	1.2438	1.8045	0.3109	0.4511
	nnInteractive	3.3481	3.3236	0.8547	0.8494
	Ours	**3.5364**	**3.6196**	**0.8946**	**0.9165**

Table 3 presents our performance on the validation set for the coreset track for the five imaging modalities. Our method achieves competitive results, with particularly strong performance on Microscopy (DSC Final: 0.7531, NSD Final: 0.9606), PET (DSC Final: 0.8186), and Ultrasound (DSC Final: 0.8946) modalities, where we outperform all baseline methods.

Our method demonstrates modality-specific strengths:

- **Strong Performance**: Microscopy, PET, and Ultrasound benefit from our dynamic interaction simulation, achieving best-in-class results with improvements of up to 26.7% in DSC over the next best method (Microscopy).
- **Moderate Performance**: CT shows competitive results (DSC Final: 0.8197), slightly below nnInteractive but surpassing other foundation models.
- **Weak Performance**: MRI exhibits degraded performance (DSC Final: 0.4222), significantly underperforming all baselines.

Impact of Bounding Box Availability. A critical factor in our performance is the availability of initial bounding boxes. As shown in Table 4, our method exhibits an 81.9% drop in DSC when bounding boxes are absent, revealing a fundamental limitation of our central-third heuristic.

This dependency explains our modality-specific performance patterns. MRI suffers most severely as approximately half of its cases lack bounding boxes, while Microscopy, PET, and Ultrasound, which always provide valid bounding boxes, achieve best-in-class results. The large gap with and without bounding boxes for CT and MRI modalities underscores that our dynamic interaction simulation performs best when initialized via a bounding box.

Table 4. Performance breakdown by modality and bounding box availability

Modality	Bbox	DSC Final	NSD Final	DSC AUC	NSD AUC
CT	No	0.0626	0.0514	0.1850	0.1443
	Yes	0.8405	0.8731	3.3032	3.4147
MRI	No	0.1535	0.0811	0.4882	0.2161
	Yes	0.7987	0.9077	3.1438	3.5708
Microscopy	Yes	0.7532	0.9607	2.9476	3.8110
PET	Yes	0.8186	0.7841	3.2278	3.0728
Ultrasound	Yes	0.8947	0.9165	3.5364	3.6197
Overall with bbox		**0.8276**	**0.8863**	**3.2550**	**3.4774**
Overall without bbox		**0.1499**	**0.0799**	**0.4759**	**0.2132**

4.2 Qualitative Results on Validation Set

Analysis of Success Cases. Figures 4, 5, 6, 7, 8 illustrate the best and worst performing cases across all modalities, providing visual insights into our method's behavior.

Our method excels when:

- **Valid bounding boxes are provided**: The model effectively leverages spatial priors from accurate initial localization.
- **Objects have clear boundaries**: Microscopy and Ultrasound images often contain well-defined structures that benefit from our click-based refinement.

Failure Case Analysis. The primary failure mode occurs with missing bounding boxes. Our heuristic of generating a default box at the central third of the image proves inadequate for:

- **Distributed structures**: Vessels and myocardium that span the entire volume
- **Peripheral objects**: Structures located far from the image center
- **Multiple instances**: Cases where the target object is not the central one

This limitation is most evident in MRI results, where many anatomical structures lack meaningful bounding box initialization.

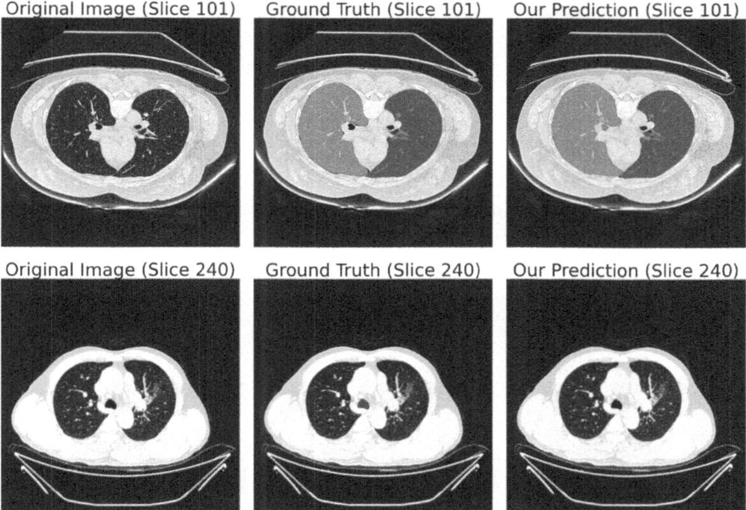

Fig. 4. Best (top) and worst (bottom) final DSC for the CT modality (`CT_LungMasks_lung_059` : final DSC = 0.9804, `CT_AirwayTree_ATM_005` : final DSC = 0)

4.3 Results on Final Testing Set

Table 5 presents the performance of the method in the test set, where it ranks second among all participants.

4.4 Limitation and Future Work

Our primary limitation is the dependency on bounding box initialization. While our method achieves strong performance when properly initialized, it fails for anatomical structures that lack natural bounding regions, particularly distributed structures like vessels and airways. The central-third heuristic we

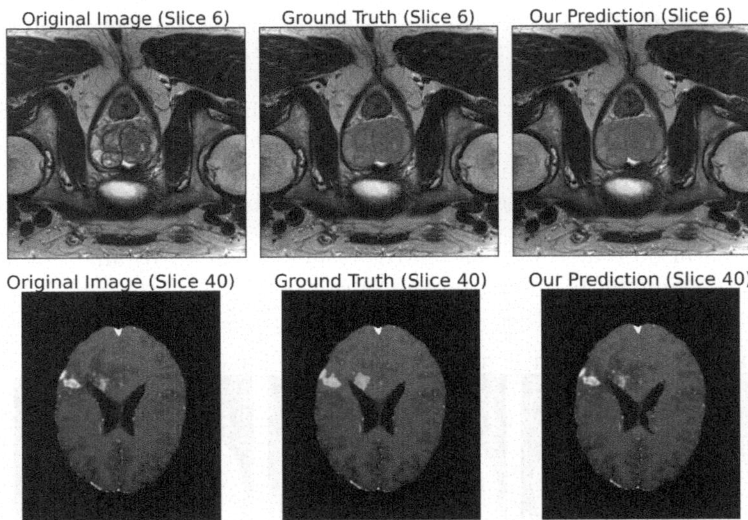

Fig. 5. Best (top) and worst (bottom) final DSC for the MRI modality (`MR_ProstateT2_T2_ProstateX_0230_4` : final DSC = 0.9475, `MR_BraTS_T1c_bratsgli_0089` : final DSC = 0.0004)

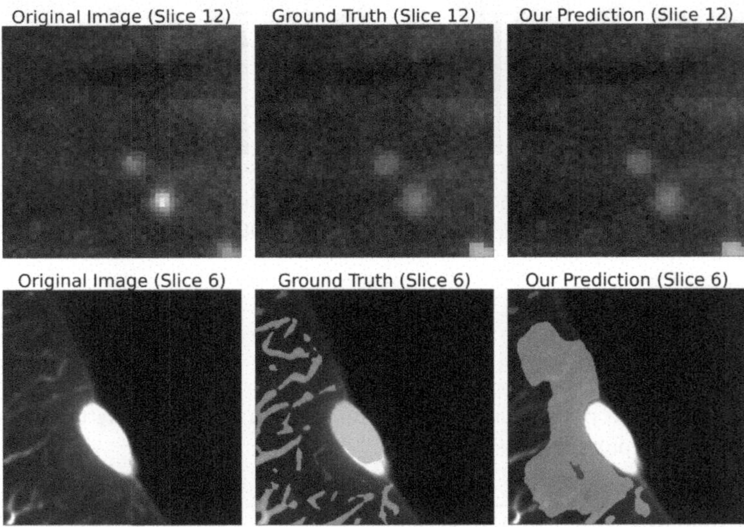

Fig. 6. Best (top) and worst (bottom) final DSC for the Microscopy modality (`Microscopy_SELMA3D_patchvolume_cfos_009_3_1_1` : final DSC = 0.9130, `Microscopy_SELMA3D_patchvolume_vessel_006_0_1_0` : final DSC = 0.5725)

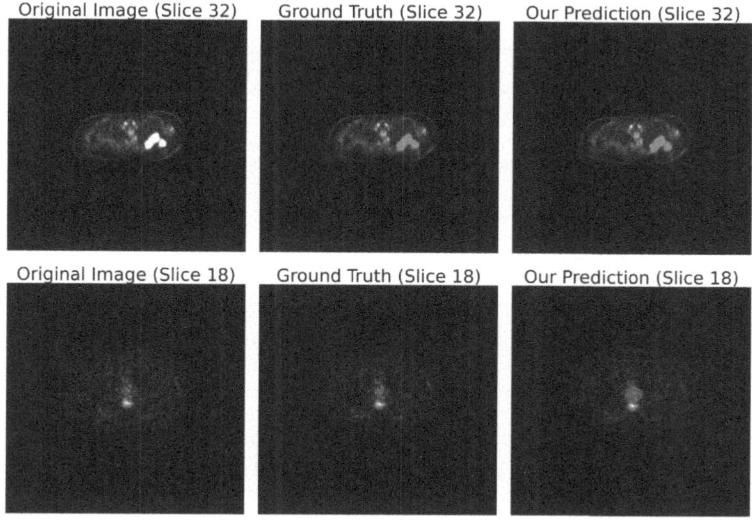

Fig. 7. Best (top) and worst (bottom) final DSC for the PET modality (`PET_autoPET_fdg_68f73c4518_11-13-2004-NA-PET-CT` : final DSC = 0.9466, `PET_autoPET_psma_a3c5675abaec3e1d_2017-08-14` : final DSC = 0.5783)

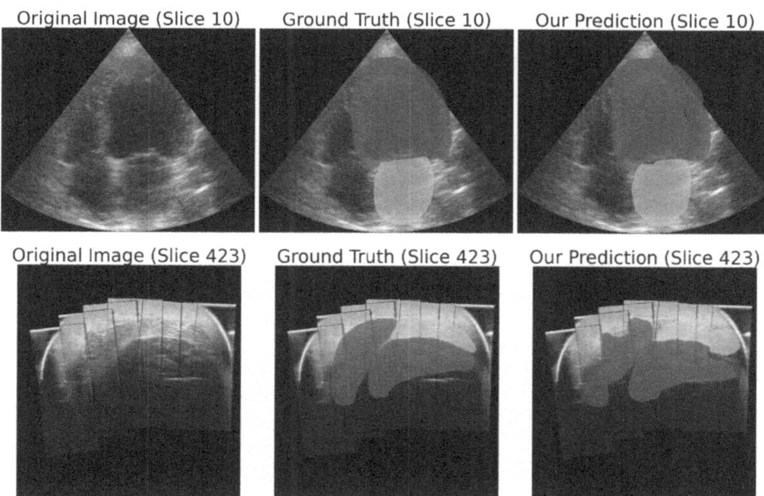

Fig. 8. Best (top) and worst (bottom) final DSC for the Ultrasound modality (`US_Cardiac_patient0224_4CH_half_sequence` : final DSC = 0.9320, `US_Low-limb-Leg40` : final DSC = 0.7316)

employ as a fallback proves inadequate, preventing our method from handling approximately half of MRI cases where bounding boxes are unavailable.

Table 5. Results on the test set for the **coreset track**

Modality	Methods	DSC AUC	NSD AUC	DSC Final	NSD Final
CT	SAM-Med3D	2.0801	1.7132	0.5311	0.4385
	VISTA3D	2.1644	1.9529	0.5682	0.5181
	SegVol	2.3843	2.3523	0.5961	0.5881
	norateam	2.8719	2.7858	0.7462	0.7290
	lexor	2.3141	2.1750	0.5785	0.5437
	ahus	2.3488	2.0517	0.6215	0.5518
	aim	**3.0628**	**3.0652**	**0.7907**	**0.7966**
	sail	1.3339	1.0638	0.3337	0.2665
	yiooo	2.8254	2.6523	0.7267	0.6851
MR	SAM-Med3D	2.1169	2.1185	0.5355	0.5371
	VISTA3D	2.4102	2.5065	0.6327	0.6690
	SegVol	2.7383	3.0322	0.6846	0.7581
	norateam	3.0921	3.3433	0.7938	0.8608
	lexor	2.7082	2.9463	0.6771	0.7366
	ahus	2.4503	2.5190	0.6257	0.6462
	aim	**3.2233**	**3.5378**	**0.8292**	**0.9101**
	sail	1.9798	2.1028	0.4948	0.5256
	yiooo	3.0569	3.3125	0.7819	0.8487
PET	SAM-Med3D	2.3133	1.7599	0.5826	0.4465
	VISTA3D	1.7576	1.2811	0.4539	0.3332
	SegVol	2.7847	2.2974	0.6962	0.5744
	norateam	**3.2011**	**2.8788**	**0.8051**	**0.7265**
	lexor	2.5867	2.1837	0.6467	0.5459
	ahus	2.2783	1.8356	0.5614	0.4565
	aim	2.8622	2.4589	0.7665	0.6758
	sail	2.0661	1.6516	0.5165	0.4129
	yiooo	3.0282	2.6575	0.7730	0.6907
US	SAM-Med3D	0.6009	0.4005	0.1502	0.1001
	VISTA3D	0.7571	0.8212	0.2378	0.3116
	SegVol	0.7931	1.2851	0.1983	0.3213
	norateam	**1.8486**	2.4444	**0.5294**	0.7211
	lexor	0.9981	1.4705	0.2495	0.3676
	ahus	1.7853	2.0378	0.4744	0.5462
	aim	1.8219	**2.5373**	0.5100	**0.7335**
	sail	0.7624	1.1207	0.1879	0.2717
	yiooo	1.5276	1.9049	0.4500	0.5894
Microscopy	SAM-Med3D	0.3123	0.0311	0.0781	0.0078
	VISTA3D	1.8416	2.5043	0.4701	0.6285
	SegVol	2.7359	3.8765	0.6840	0.9691
	norateam	**3.3361**	3.9719	**0.8477**	**0.9952**
	lexor	2.7166	3.9274	0.6791	0.9818
	ahus	2.5669	3.7553	0.6716	0.9410
	aim	2.9608	3.9324	0.7884	0.9885
	sail	2.3888	3.6765	0.5972	0.9191
	yiooo	3.1926	**3.9722**	0.8092	0.9943

This limitation points to critical areas for future development. First, we need automated initialization strategies that can identify regions of interest without manual intervention, potentially through attention mechanisms or saliency detection. Second, the model should be trained to handle click-only interactions from the start, eliminating the bounding box dependency entirely.

5 Conclusion

We presented a dynamic prompt generation strategy for interactive 3D medical image segmentation that simulates realistic user interactions during training. Our method achieves state-of-the-art performance on well-initialized cases, outperforming existing foundation models on Microscopy, PET, and Ultrasound modalities with final Dice scores exceeding 0.75. However, performance critically depends on valid bounding box initialization, with an 81.9% drop in accuracy when bounding boxes are absent. This limitation highlights the need for robust initialization strategies in interactive segmentation systems. Despite this constraint, our approach demonstrates that incorporating iterative refinement patterns during training significantly improves segmentation quality when proper spatial priors are available.

Acknowledgements. We thank all the data owners for making the medical images publicly available and CodaLab [14] for hosting the challenge platform.

Disclosure of Interests. The authors have no competing interests to declare that are relevant to the content of this article.

References

1. Du, Y., Bai, F., Huang, T., Zhao, B.: Segvol: universal and interactive volumetric medical image segmentation. In: Advances in Neural Information Processing Systems, vol. 37, pp. 110746–110783 (2024)
2. Fabian, I., et al.: nninteractive: redefining 3D promptable segmentation. arXiv preprint arXiv:2503.08373 (2025)
3. He, Y., et al.: VISTA3D: a unified segmentation foundation model for 3D medical imaging. In: Proceedings of the IEEE/CVF International Conference on Computer Vision and Pattern Recognition (2024)
4. Kikinis, R., Pieper, S.D., Vosburgh, K.G.: 3D Slicer: a platform for subject-specific image analysis, visualization, and clinical support, pp. 277–289. Springer (2013)
5. Kirillov, A., et al.: Segment anything. In: Proceedings of the International Conference on Computer Vision, pp. 4015–4026 (2023)
6. Ma, J., et al.: Loss odyssey in medical image segmentation. Med. Image Anal. **71**, 102035 (2021)
7. Ma, J., et al.: Segment anything in medical images. Nat. Commun. **15**, 654 (2024)
8. Ma, J., et al.: Efficient medsams: segment anything in medical images on laptop. arXiv:2412.16085 (2024)
9. Ma, J., et al.: Medsam2: segment anything in 3D medical images and videos. arXiv preprint arXiv:2504.03600 (2025)
10. Pfefferle, A., Purucker, L., Hutter, F.: Daft: data-aware fine-tuning of foundation models for efficient and effective medical image segmentation. In: Ma, J., Zhou, Y., Wang, B. (eds.) Medical Image Segmentation Foundation Models. CVPR 2024 Challenge: Segment Anything in Medical Images on Laptop, pp. 15–38. Springer, Cham (2025). https://doi.org/10.1007/978-3-031-81854-72

11. Ravi, N., et al.: Sam 2: segment anything in images and videos. In: International Conference on Learning Representations (2025)
12. Ronneberger, O., Fischer, P., Brox, T.: U-net: convolutional networks for biomedical image segmentation. In: International Conference on Medical Image Computing and Computer-Assisted Intervention, pp. 234–241 (2015)
13. Wang, H., et al.: Sam-med3d: towards general-purpose segmentation models for volumetric medical images. arXiv preprint arXiv:2310.15161 (2024)
14. Xu, Z., et al.: Codabench: flexible, easy-to-use, and reproducible meta-benchmark platform. Patterns **3**(7), 100543 (2022)

iMedSTAM: Interactive Segmentation and Tracking Anything in 3D Medical Images and Videos

Tobias Friedetzki(✉), Lorenz Haberzettl, Ricarda Buttmann, Frank Puppe, and Adrian Krenzer

Julius-Maximilians University of Würzburg, Würzburg, Germany
tobias.friedetzki@uni-wuerzburg.de

Abstract. The increasing volume of complex 3D biomedical imaging data highlights the need for accurate and efficient analysis methods. Segmentation of such data is essential for diagnosis, anatomical analysis, disease monitoring, and treatment planning. However, existing segmentation algorithms often struggle with the variability of object structures and the diversity of imaging modalities. To address these challenges, we introduce iMedSTAM, a promptable foundation model for 3D image and video segmentation. The model is also capable of progressively improving segmentation quality based on user interactions. iMedSTAM was developed by fine-tuning EfficientTAM on a large-scale dataset comprising over 270,000 3D imagemask pairs and 4,000 videomask pairs, covering five different medical imaging modalities. In addition, we extend the EfficientTAM architecture with a bidirectional inference and memory mechanism that enables the processing of volumetric data. iMedSTAM significantly outperforms all previous models on the publicly available validation set in the coreset track and achieves state-of-the-art results in the all-data track. On the test set, our model reaches an average final DSC and NSD of 0.805 and 0.842, respectively. For DSC_AUC and NSD_AUC, which measure the cumulative improvement through additional user interactions, iMedSTAM achieves scores of 3.129 and 3.258.

Keywords: Interactive Segmentation · 3D Medical Image · SAM2

1 Introduction

The segmentation of medical images is an essential component in clinical practice. It supports accurate diagnosis [25], facilitates the analysis of anatomical structures [37], enables disease monitoring [28], and assists in treatment planning [22]. By precisely delineating organs, lesions, and other anatomical structures in medical imaging, clinicians can gain critical insights to provide targeted patient care. Deep learning approaches have revolutionized the field by achieving not only human-level accuracy but also a high degree of automation [1,32,38].

To date, most models in this domain have been developed with a focus on specific organs or lesions, which makes them less effective at handling previously

J. Ma et al. (Eds.): MedSegFM 2025, LNCS 16447, pp. 173–193, 2026.
https://doi.org/10.1007/978-3-032-23496-4_10

unseen types of structures and domains. Similar to the developments in natural language processing, where advanced network architectures and large-scale datasets have led to the rise of large language models [30], a shift is also occurring in medical image segmentation. There is a growing trend away from specialized task-specific models toward general-purpose models. Notable examples include the Segment Anything Model (SAM) [12] and its adaptation for medical imaging, MedSAM [17]. These models are capable of segmenting arbitrary objects in 2D images using user-provided spatial prompts that guide the model in identifying the target object.

Although MedSAM has demonstrated strong performance in segmenting various medical structures and across different imaging modalities, it is not well-suited for processing 3D images such as computed tomography (CT) scans, as SAM was originally designed for 2D images. To address this limitation, Gong et al. [6] extended SAM with a 3D adapter, and SAM-Med3D [31] introduced a 3D image encoder. Other interactive segmentation approaches that aim to capture the three-dimensional spatial relationships in volumetric medical images include VISTA3D [7] and SegVol [3]. VISTA3D is trained on CT images and processes them as voxel cubic patches using a sliding window inference strategy. In contrast, SegVol employs a zoom-outzoom-in mechanism to simplify user interaction with large 3D images.

For interactive segmentation of natural videos, SAM2 [23] has emerged as a state-of-the-art method, and its more efficient variant, EfficientTAM [34], has also demonstrated strong performance. It has been demonstrated that SAM2-like architectures have the potential for application in the medical domain, as shown by Shen et al. [26], Zhu et al. [39], and more recently in MedSAM2 [19].

Although several approaches have already been explored, there remains a lack of general models capable of segmenting both 3D medical images and videos within an interactive process. Most existing models have been trained on only one or a few imaging modalities. Furthermore, the types of prompts supported and the ability to refine segmentations interactively are limited. For example, VISTA3D can only process point prompts, while SegVol exclusively supports box inputs. As a result, iterative refinement through additional user prompts is not possible with SegVol. Only the recently proposed nnInteractive [4], which builds on the nnU-Net framework [10], offers six distinct interaction channels and natively supports a refinement approach.

The "Foundation Models for Interactive 3D Biomedical Image Segmentation" challenge aims to develop universal 3D biomedical image segmentation models that can not only adapt to a wide range of anatomical structures and imaging conditions but also iteratively improve segmentation quality based on user interactions. The challenge provides a large-scale training dataset comprising over 270,000 3D imagemask pairs and 4,000 videomask pairs, covering five different medical imaging modalities.

To address this challenge, we propose an architecture based on EfficientTAM, as it has already demonstrated strong results on natural videos while offering efficient inference times. Furthermore, since it employs the same prompt encoder as SAM2, it is capable of processing both box and point prompts. To enable processing of 3D images, we extend the inference pipeline and adapt memory handling across individual slices accordingly. Similar to the approaches of Shen et al. [27] and MedSAM2 [19], we propagate spatial prompts in both directions starting from the central slice. Finally, we fine-tune the model on the large biomedical development set provided by the challenge. Our main contributions can be summarized as follows:

1. We introduce iMedSTAM, a foundation model for interactive segmentation of both 3D medical images and videos, supporting both box and point prompts, as well as iterative refinement.
2. We extend the EfficientTAM architecture with a bidirectional inference and memory mechanism that enables the processing of volumetric data, and fine-tune it on a large-scale medical dataset.
3. We implement an efficient post-processing step that resolves potential overlaps between predicted masks of different classes based on the model's confidence in each prediction.

2 Method

2.1 Interactive 3D and Video Segmentation Pipeline

For interactive segmentation of volumetric data, we adopt a video-based approach similar to MedSAM2 [19] and Shen et al. [27]. We first slice the 3D image along its third dimension, creating 2D slices that we treat analogously to video frames. This allows us to handle even large 3D input images. Figure 1 provides an overview of the interactive segmentation pipeline. The model starts from an initial user prompt, which can be either a bounding box or a positive point click at the center of the target object. This prompt always refers to the 2D space of the middle slice. Starting from this middle slice, the model sequentially predicts segmentation masks in both directions. To preserve spatial consistency across slices, the model integrates a memory module that incorporates information from previous slices into the current prediction.

Finally, the individual 2D masks are aggregated into a 3D segmentation mask and presented to the user. The user can review the result and refine it by adding additional points to any slice—positive points in under-segmented regions and negative points in over-segmented areas. With this additional input, the model repeats the segmentation process, enabling iterative refinement. Videos are treated the same as 3D images and follow the same pipeline.

2.2 Model

iMedSTAM (Fig. 2) extracts features from individual slices or frames using an image encoder. Instead of passing these features directly to the mask decoder, the model first conditions them on the user input prompts and the embeddings from previous slices. The mask decoder then generates the corresponding 2D segmentation masks.

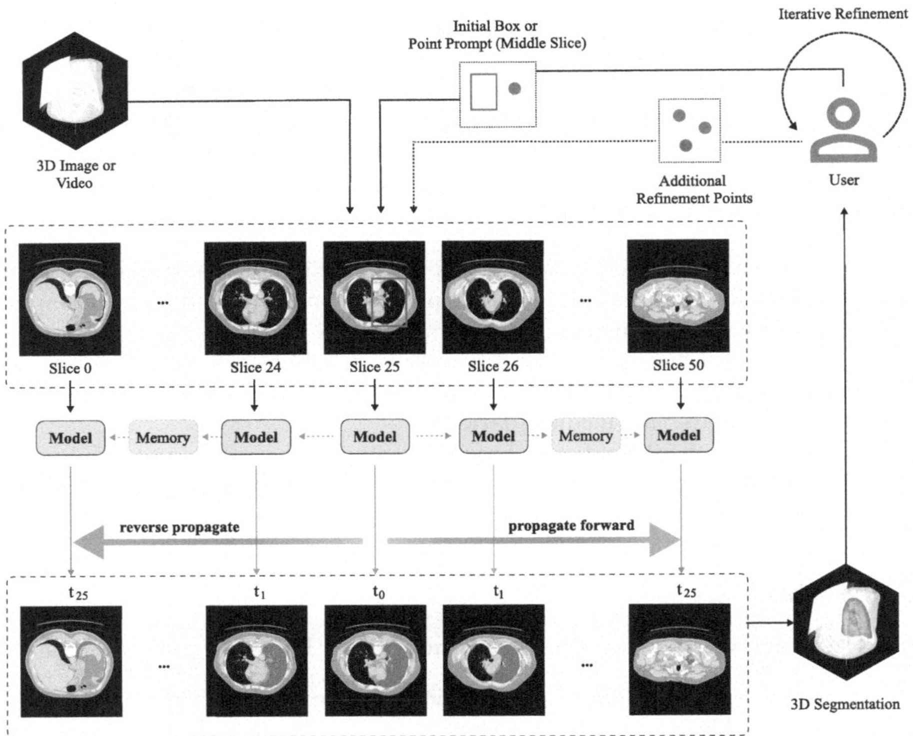

Fig. 1. Interactive segmentation pipeline with iMedSTAM. The 3D medical image or video is divided into individual slices or frames. The user initially marks the desired object in the middle slice using a bounding box or a positive point click. Based on this initial prompt, the model sequentially predicts the masks for all slices in both directions from the middle. In subsequent iterative steps, the user can refine the segmentation by adding additional positive or negative refinement points.

The model is based on the EfficientTAM architecture [34], which itself is a more efficient variant of SAM2 [23]. The improved efficiency results from replacing the Hiera [24] image encoder in SAM2 with a lightweight, non-hierarchical ViT [29], and from using a more efficient memory module that approximates spatial memory tokens. Additionally, EfficientTAM includes a pretrained version that operates at an input resolution of 512×512 instead of 1024×1024, further reducing computational cost. In our experiments, we observed that EfficientTAM, when used without transfer learning, results in a performance drop of approximately 9% in 3D medical image segmentation compared to SAM2. However, it achieves a twofold reduction in runtime per case (see Table 7 in the appendix). Given that interactive segmentation requires online inference with reasonably fast user feedback, this trade-off is acceptable.

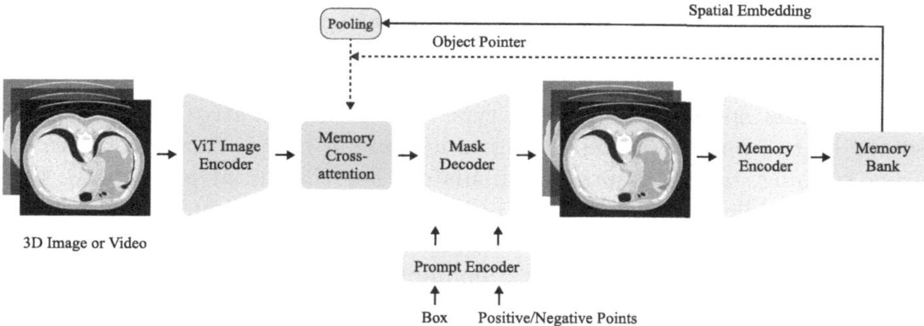

Fig. 2. iMedSTAM architecture. The model processes slices or frames sequentially. A lightweight ViT image encoder first extracts features from the current slice. These image embeddings are then corss-attended to memory representations from previous slices. The mask decoder incorporates user input prompts and predicts the segmentation mask for the current slice. Finally, a memory encoder transforms the prediction and image embeddings and stores them in a memory bank for subsequent slices.

Image Encoder. For the lightweight ViT image encoder, we use a patch size of 16×16 and a non-overlapping 14×14 windowed attention mechanism. To efficiently extract features, we employ 6 global attention blocks. The output of the image encoder is a $16\times$ downsampled embedding of the input image. Given an input resolution of 512×512, the image embedding is therefore 32×32.

Memory Module. Since the image encoder processes slices independently, a memory module is required to re-establish a connection along the third dimension (spatial or temporal), enabling consistent object tracking. In the first pass, which is always the middle slice, the memory encoder downsamples the output mask and sums it element-wise with the image features from the image encoder to create spatial embeddings. These spatial embeddings are stored in a memory bank, implemented as a FIFO list that retains information from the last seven slices. In addition to spatial embeddings, a set of lightweight object pointer vectors is stored to represent the current object location.

In subsequent passes, the model conditions the image embeddings of the current slice via cross-attention with both the spatial embeddings and object pointers from previous slices. To reduce computational cost, the model approximates the spatial embeddings with average pooling before applying cross-attention.

Unlike the default implementation of EfficientTAM, we start in the middle and perform both a forward and a backward pass. During memory cross-attention, we therefore only consider entries in the memory bank originating from the current direction. For example, when processing from the middle toward the bottom, the model ignores spatial embeddings and object pointers from the earlier pass from middle to top. This design prevents confusion and ensures that the model maintains strong attention to the initial prompt.

Prompt Encoder and Interaction Simulation. iMedSTAM supports both box- and point-based prompts. The prompt encoder maps each point to a 256-dimensional embedding by summing its positional encoding with a learned embedding that specifies the prompt type (positive or negative). A box is represented by two points, corresponding to its top-left and bottom-right corners. During training, user prompts are simulated. For the initial prompt, we first identify the middle slice of the target object and generate a bounding box based on the ground truth mask. To improve model robustness, we apply random shifts to the box prompt. In cases where a bounding box is not suitable due to the structure of the object, such as with vessels or myocardium, we use a positive click at the center of the object as the initial prompt instead.

To simulate additional refinement points, we locate the center of the largest error region from the previous prediction. If this region corresponds to an under-segmentation, we place a positive click. Otherwise, we place a negative click. This refinement process is repeated three times per sample during training. Combined with the initial forward pass, this results in a batch size of four per training iteration.

Mask Decoder. Within the mask decoder, the memory-conditioned image embeddings and prompt embeddings are mapped to a segmentation mask. The mask decoder consists of stacked two-way transformer blocks, followed by an upsampling layer and an MLP that maps the tokens to a linear classifier. This classifier outputs the probability of the object being present at each location. Unlike EfficientTAM, we always condition on all prompts, including refinement points that may refer to future slices or originate from earlier ones. Similar to the memory attention mechanism, we include only prompts associated with slices belonging to the current pass direction.

2.3 Coreset Selection Strategy

To select a reduced development set, we replicate the distribution of the different 3D modalities present in the validation set. Since the training dataset originates from several distinct subsets, we randomly sample from each according to their respective proportions. We ensure that at least one sample is picked from each subset. This strategy guarantees that the model is still exposed to a broad variety of inputs during training.

2.4 Post-processing

In a post-processing step, we resize the model output back to the original dimensions of the input image. In cases where multiple objects within a 3D image need to be segmented, we additionally apply a non-overlapping mechanism. This ensures that, in the event of potential mask overlaps, the selected label is not determined by processing order, but rather by the model's confidence in the presence of each object. This is possible because the model outputs mask logits rather than directly producing binarized masks.

To avoid memory issues, especially in large 3D images or long videos with many objects, we retain only the mask logits of slices still needed for comparison in the non-overlapping mechanism. This is achieved by processing objects in ascending order based on the starting slice of their bounding box. Furthermore, we cache the model state between refinement iterations, which helps to speed up the overall inference process.

3 Experiments

3.1 Dataset and Evaluation Metrics

The development set is an extension of the CVPR 2024 MedSAM on Laptop Challenge [18], including more 3D cases from public datasets[1] and covering commonly used 3D modalities, such as Computed Tomography (CT), Magnetic Resonance Imaging (MRI), Positron Emission Tomography (PET), Ultrasound, and Microscopy images. The hidden testing set is created by a community effort where all the cases are unpublished. The annotations are either provided by the data contributors or annotated by the challenge organizer with 3D Slicer [11] and MedSAM2 [19]. In addition to using all training cases, the challenge contains a coreset track, where participants can select 10% of the total training cases for model development.

For each iterative segmentation, the evaluation metrics include Dice Similarity Coefficient (DSC) and Normalized Surface Distance (NSD) to evaluate the segmentation region overlap and boundary distance, respectively. The final metrics used for the ranking are:

- DSC_AUC and NSD_AUC Scores: AUC (Area Under the Curve) for DSC and NSD is used to measure cumulative improvement with interactions. The AUC quantifies the cumulative performance improvement over the five click predictions, providing a holistic view of the segmentation refinement process. It is computed only over the click predictions without considering the initial bounding box prediction as it is optional.
- Final DSC and NSD Scores after all refinements, indicating the model's final segmentation performance.

In addition, the algorithm runtime will be limited to 90 s per class. Exceeding this limit will lead to all DSC and NSD metrics being set to 0 for that test case.

3.2 Implementation Details

Preprocessing Following the practice in MedSAM [17], all images were processed to npz format with an intensity range of $[0, 255]$. Specifically, for CT images, we initially normalized the Hounsfield units using typical window width

[1] A complete list is available at https://medsam-datasetlist.github.io/.

and level values: soft tissues (W:400, L:40), lung (W:1500, L:-160), brain (W:80, L:40), and bone (W:1800, L:400). Subsequently, the intensity values were rescaled to the range of $[0, 255]$. For other images, we clipped the intensity values to the range between the 0.5th and 99.5th percentiles before rescaling them to the range of [0, 255]. If the original intensity range is already in $[0, 255]$, no preprocessing was applied.

During training and inference, we first convert the grayscale images of the development set to RGB by duplicating the intensity values along the channel axis. We then resize the input images to a resolution of 512×512 without padding, and apply channel-wise RGB normalization to ensure consistency with the pretraining configuration of EfficientTAM.

Environment Settings. The development environments and requirements are presented in Table 1. Compared to the training on the 10% coreset, we use twice as many GPUs and the more powerful NVIDIA H100 for training on the full training dataset in order to accelerate the process.

Table 1. Development environments and requirements.

	coreset	all-data
System	Debian 12.11 LTS	
CPU	AMD EPYC 7543 32-Core @ 2.79 GHz	
RAM	50G	80G
GPU	4 × NVIDIA L40 48G	8 × NVIDIA H100 80G
CUDA version	12.6	
Programming language	Python 3.11	
Deep learning framework	torch 2.6, torchvision 0.21	

Training Protocols. We fine-tune the pretrained EfficientTAM-S on the development set of the challenge, training all model components to maximize performance. As described in Sect. 2.3, we selected a development set with a distribution of 3D imaging modalities similar to that of the validation set. For training on the full dataset, we oversample the underrepresented modalities MR, PET, and ultrasound by factors of 2, 3, and 3, respectively.

For each epoch, we randomly select one object per case. Starting from the middle slice, the model predicts with equal probability either from the middle toward the top or from the middle toward the bottom. If this segment spans more than 25 slices, a shorter subsection is randomly selected to prevent running out of memory. As described in Sect. 2.2, we then simulate three correction clicks per object half in an iterative manner, resulting in a total batch size of four. We apply data augmentation to the training samples, including random horizontal flips and random affine transformations. The random affine transformations are performed with a rotation angle in the range of $[-25, 25]$ and a shear angle in the range of $[-20, 20]$.

To supervise the model's predictions, we use a linear combination of focal loss and dice loss for the mask prediction, with a weighting ratio of 20:1. Compound loss functions have been shown to be robust in various medical image segmentation tasks [16]. We use the AdamW optimizer [15] with $\beta_1 = 0.9$, $\beta_2 = 0.999$, and a weight decay of 0.1. For the image encoder, we select a lower learning rate (3.0×10^{-6}) compared to the other components (5.0×10^{-6}), which require greater adaptation to the medical domain. Table 2 details the training protocols used for fine-tuning both the coreset and the all-data model.

Since evaluation on the validation set takes approximately 24 h, we employed a binary search strategy to select the optimal model checkpoints. Assuming that performance improves with each epoch and only degrades in later stages due to overfitting, this approach allowed us to significantly reduce the number of required evaluation runs.

Table 2. Training protocols.

	coreset	all-data
Pre-trained Model	EfficientTAM-S	
Data augmentation	Horizontal Flipping and Random Affine	
Batch size	4	
Input size	512 × 512 × 3	
Optimizer	AdamW with weight decay set to 0.1	
Initial learning rate (lr)	Img. enc.: 5e-6, other: 3.0e-6	
Lr decay schedule	Cosine with an end value of 10% of the initial lr	
Loss function	20 × focal loss + 1 × dice loss	
Number of model parameters	34.1M	
Total epochs	100	15
Training time	131 h	174 h
Number of flops	413.7P	848.9P

4 Results and Discussion

4.1 Quantitative Results on Validation Set

Table 3 compares the performance of the proposed model for the coreset track (iMedSTAM) with the baseline models on the public validation set. iMedSTAM consistently outperforms all baselines across most modalities and metrics. It achieves the highest average DSC_AUC (3.022), NSD_AUC (3.270), Final DSC

Table 3. Quantitative evaluation results of the validation set on the **coreset track**. DSC_AUC and NSD_AUC measure the cumulative improvement across interactions. Final DSC and NSD represent the scores after all refinements, while DSC_1 denotes the score obtained using only the initial prompt.

Modality	Methods	DSC AUC	NSD AUC	DSC Final	NSD Final	DSC 1
CT	SAM-Med3D	2.218	2.192	0.554	0.549	0.564
	VISTA3D	2.797	2.816	0.715	0.724	0.649
	SegVol	2.899	3.037	0.725	0.759	**0.733**
	iMedSTAM	**3.227**	**3.327**	**0.828**	**0.856**	0.730
MRI	SAM-Med3D	1.493	1.490	0.383	0.387	0.332
	VISTA3D	2.290	2.578	0.578	0.648	0.544
	SegVol	1.113	1.314	0.278	0.328	0.279
	iMedSTAM	**2.771**	**3.209**	**0.724**	**0.837**	**0.629**
Microscopy	SAM-Med3D	0.118	0.000	0.030	0.000	0.029
	VISTA3D	1.730	**2.737**	0.442	**0.696**	**0.400**
	SegVol	1.053	1.857	0.263	0.464	0.265
	iMedSTAM	**1.731**	2.197	**0.474**	0.604	0.334
PET	SAM-Med3D	2.104	1.789	0.528	0.449	0.525
	VISTA3D	2.388	2.098	0.612	0.543	0.561
	SegVol	2.968	2.856	0.742	0.714	**0.739**
	iMedSTAM	**3.077**	**2.988**	**0.814**	**0.796**	0.595
Ultrasound	SAM-Med3D	1.277	1.882	0.361	0.531	0.168
	VISTA3D	2.580	2.589	0.707	0.717	0.494
	SegVol	1.232	1.788	0.308	0.447	0.307
	iMedSTAM	**3.623**	**3.595**	**0.912**	**0.908**	**0.888**
Average	SAM-Med3D	1.813	1.822	0.460	0.466	0.430
	VISTA3D	2.529	2.667	0.645	0.682	0.587
	SegVol	1.963	2.147	0.491	0.537	0.494
	iMedSTAM	**3.022**	**3.270**	**0.782**	**0.847**	**0.684**

(0.782), and Final NSD (0.847), indicating strong interactive segmentation performance and boundary accuracy. Even in the first iteration without correction clicks (DSC_1), it achieves the highest score of 0.684.

iMedSTAM ranks first in both DSC and NSD for CT, MRI, PET, and ultrasound. The model performs particularly well on ultrasound, achieving a Final DSC of 0.912, with a 21% margin over the second-best model, significantly outperforming all other methods. Only for the challenging microscopy images does VISTA3D surpass iMedSTAM in NSD_AUC and Final NSD. It is also noteworthy that while SegVol achieves impressive DSC values for CT and PET with just a single prompt, it shows little improvement with additional correction clicks.

Table 4 shows the performance on the validation set of the all-data track, where our model, iMedSTAM, demonstrates strong and consistent results. By exposing the models to the full development set, all models achieve a performance improvement. iMedSTAM achieves the best scores across all metrics for the MRI and ultrasound modalities. In contrast, nnInteractive performs better on CT and PET 3D medical images. Similar to the coreset track, iMedSTAM shows weaknesses in segmenting microscopy images. In this category, VISTA3D achieves high NSD scores, while nnInteractive yields better DSC values. Overall, iMedSTAM attains the highest average NSD_AUC (3.323) and DSC_1 (0.702) across all modalities. For DSC_AUC, Final DSC, and Final NSD, nnInteractive leads slightly, with margins of 0.002, 0.12, and 0.007, respectively. These results indicate that nnInteractive is more effective in incorporating refinement clicks.

Table 4. Quantitative evaluation results of the validation set on the **all-data track**. DSC_AUC and NSD_AUC measure the cumulative improvement across interactions. Final DSC and NSD represent the scores after all refinements, while DSC_1 denotes the score obtained using only the initial prompt.

Modality	Methods	DSC AUC	NSD AUC	DSC Final	NSD Final	DSC 1
CT	VISTA3D	3.169	3.265	0.804	0.834	0.751
	nnInteractive	**3.434**	**3.574**	**0.876**	**0.916**	**0.767**
	iMedSTAM	3.277	3.389	0.838	0.869	0.751
MRI	VISTA3D	2.589	2.968	0.654	0.749	0.619
	nnInteractive	2.698	3.029	0.730	0.823	0.541
	iMedSTAM	**2.824**	**3.265**	**0.735**	**0.848**	**0.646**
Microscopy	VISTA3D	2.120	**3.226**	0.548	**0.824**	**0.486**
	nnInteractive	**2.331**	3.111	**0.594**	0.789	0.480
	iMedSTAM	1.690	2.347	0.467	0.658	0.354
PET	VISTA3D	2.640	2.400	0.678	0.623	0.608
	nnInteractive	**3.348**	**3.324**	**0.855**	**0.849**	**0.719**
	iMedSTAM	3.001	2.895	0.789	0.766	0.592
Ultrasound	VISTA3D	2.866	2.844	0.810	0.808	0.509
	nnInteractive	3.348	3.324	0.855	0.849	0.580
	iMedSTAM	**3.641**	**3.633**	**0.915**	**0.916**	**0.896**
Average	VISTA3D	2.858	3.074	0.729	0.786	0.670
	nnInteractive	**3.069**	3.285	**0.803**	**0.864**	0.647
	iMedSTAM	3.067	**3.323**	0.791	0.857	**0.702**

To better understand how the AUC values are derived, Fig. 3 illustrates the performance progression of all models with respect to the number of correction clicks. For all models, segmentation accuracy improves incrementally with each additional correction click. The only exception is SegVol, which processes only

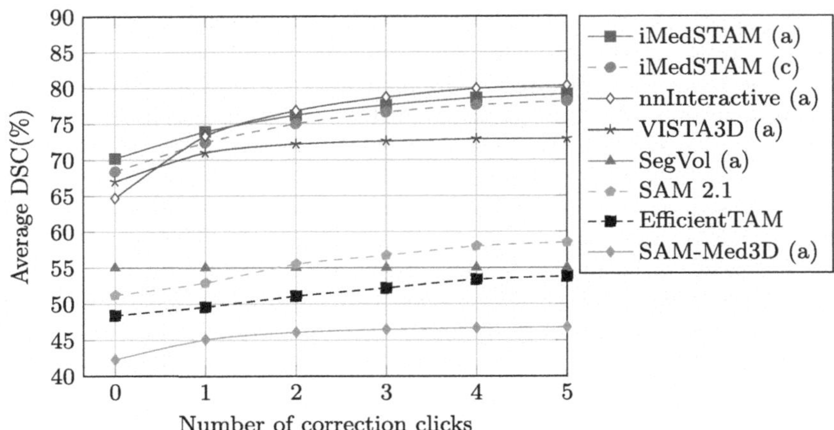

Fig. 3. Interactive segmentation performance on the validation set with respect to the number of correction clicks. Models trained on the full development set are marked with (a), while those trained only on the coreset are marked with (c).

bounding boxes as input and therefore cannot benefit from correction clicks. Both the all-data and coreset versions of iMedSTAM achieve the highest average DSC and NSD with only a single initial user prompt and no correction clicks. It is only after the second refinement click for DSC and the third for NSD that nnInteractive surpasses iMedSTAM.

Overall, we observe that the initial correction clicks contribute the most to performance gains, while subsequent clicks yield diminishing improvements. Furthermore, the coreset version of iMedSTAM initially performs slightly worse than the all-data version but gradually closes the gap with additional clicks, eventually achieving nearly comparable performance. This suggests that fine-tuning with more data enables faster initial object recognition. However, the coreset is sufficient for the model to learn how to handle and interpret correction clicks.

4.2 Qualitative Results on Validation Set

Figure 4 and 5 illustrate CT and MRI examples where iMedSTAM performs well, along with one example for each modality where its performance is poor. For each case, we visualize the ground truth and the model's predicted masks.

In the CT example (a), iMedSTAM accurately segments and differentiates various abdominal organs throughout the entire volume. As seen in the middle slice, the model handles the segmentation of the liver (light green), even when it consists of several separate regions in that plane. It also successfully identifies the inferior vena cava (yellow), which is partially encircled by the liver. Overall, a DSC of 90% is achieved across all segmented objects. In contrast, iMedSTAM struggles in the CT case (b). The 3D view clearly shows that only the lower

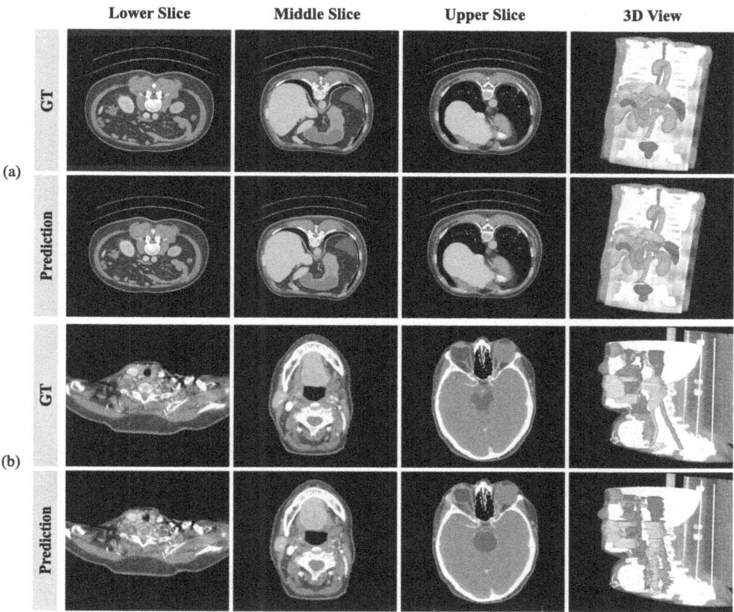

Fig. 4. Qualitative results for CT on the validation set. We illustrate one well-segmented case (a) and one challenging case (b). The model achieves a DSC of 90% in case (a) and 56 % in case (b).

portion of the brainstem (cyan) is detected, while the structure is lost toward the middle and upper slices. A likely reason is the very narrow diameter of the brainstem in the middle, which may be misinterpreted as the end of the object. Additionally, many of the predicted objects exhibit non-smooth surfaces, with visible edges arising from the model's slice-by-slice processing. A further negative factor is the greater physical distance between slices compared to case (a). As a result, the objects exhibit more pronounced discontinuities in their location from one slice to the next.

iMedSTAM is able to segment all four visible abdominal organs in the MRI of case (c) with high accuracy, achieving an above-average DSC of 96%. In contrast, the model reaches only a DSC of 37% in case (d). While the surrounding non-enhancing FLAIR hyperintensity (cyan) is segmented reasonably well despite its complex structure, the mask for the non-enhancing tumor core (brown) is significantly oversegmented. One contributing factor is that, in this case, only a single point prompt was provided instead of an initial bounding box. This means the model lacked clear spatial boundaries across slices and had to infer them on its own. Additionally, the original resolution of the image is quite low at 218 $\times$

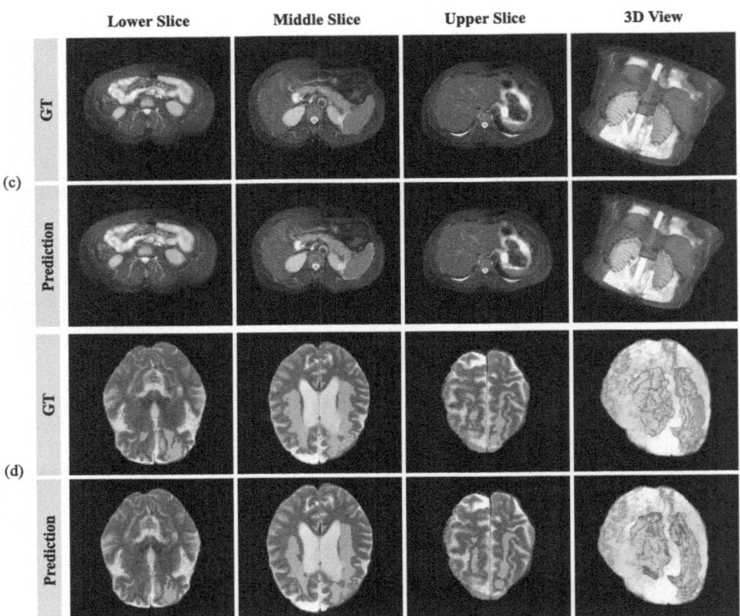

Fig. 5. Qualitative results for MRI on the validation set. We illustrate one well-segmented case (c) and one challenging case (d). The model achieves a DSC of 96% in case (c) and 37% in case (d).

182 pixels. When resized, the image becomes slightly blurry, further obscuring the color boundaries between different structures.

Figure 6 shows one PET example where the model performs well and another where it encounters difficulties. Compared to CT and MRI, PET images use a different color scale and tend to appear more point-based than continuous. In case (e), this does not pose a problem, as the various lesions are relatively small. In contrast, in case (f), iMedSTAM significantly oversegments the brown lesion in the lower slice, leading to a reduced overall performance. Even though the other lesions are segmented accurately, the model achieves only a DSC of 53% in this case.

Examples of the microscopy and ultrasound modalities are shown in Fig. 7. In the microscopy case (g), iMedSTAM successfully tracks a total of 90 distinct Alzheimer's disease plaques in the brain across 122 slices, achieving a DSC of 72%. In case (h), brain vessels are observed under the microscope. In the ground truth, two large vascular networks are each grouped into a single class. Since these classes consist of many disjoint areas, it is challenging for the model to establish coherent segmentations. Additionally, similar to the MRI case (d), no bounding box was provided, and only a single positive point click was used as the initial prompt, making the segmentation task even more difficult.

In case (i), ultrasound recordings of the heart are shown. The model successfully tracks and segments the left ventricle, myocardium, and left atrium almost perfectly throughout the entire sequence. In case (j), a lower leg is depicted. The model struggles only with the musculus gastrocnemius (purple) in the initial frames, where it fails to shrink the segmentation quickly enough before the structure moves out of the frame. As already observed in the quantitative evaluation, iMedSTAM performs very well on the ultrasound modality, achieving a DSC of 83% even in the worst case.

4.3 Results on Final Testing Set

On the final testing set, our team aim achieved the highest ranking in both the all-data and coreset tracks. As shown in Table 5, iMedSTAM attained final DSC and NSC scores of 0.805 and 0.842, respectively. For DSC_AUC and NSD_AUC, we obtained scores of 3.129 and 3.258, demonstrating significant superiority across all four evaluation metrics. The second-best performing team, yiooo, proposed a dual-expert architecture integrating both global and local Region-of-Interest strategies [36], while the third-ranked team employed a fine-tuned nnInteractive model [20].

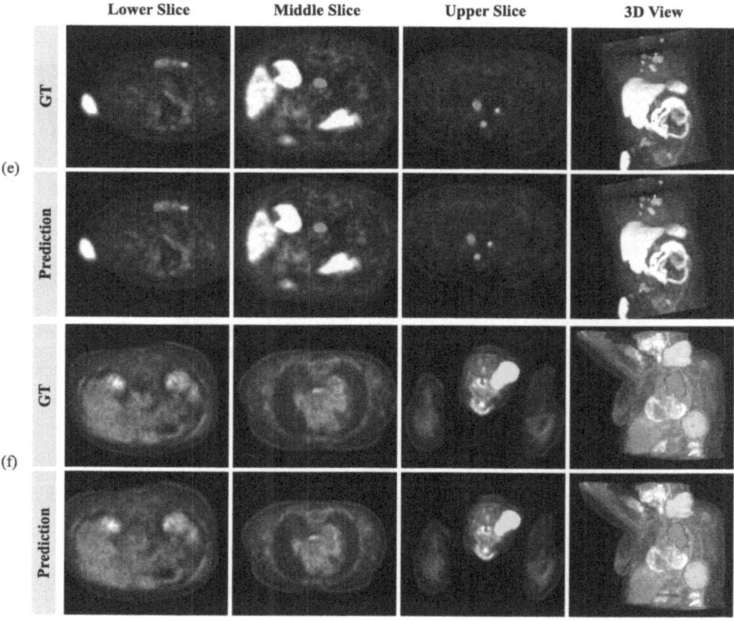

Fig. 6. Qualitative results for PET on the validation set. We illustrate one well-segmented case (e) and one challenging case (f). The model achieves a DSC of 89% in case (e) and 53% in case (f).

4.4 Limitation and Future Work

iMedSTAM has demonstrated significant improvements, particularly when compared to the baseline models in the coreset track. However, certain limitations remain. One notable challenge lies in the microscopy modality. Since the validation set includes generally difficult cases, none of the evaluated models achieve outstanding results in this modality. Nevertheless, iMedSTAM lags slightly behind VISTA3D and nnInteractive. This performance gap, compared to the other modalities, may be attributed to the fact that microscopy is substantially underrepresented in the development set, accounting for only 0.39%. Future work could address this by collecting additional microscopy cases and incorporating them into the training process.

Another limitation is iMedSTAM's performance on 3D medical images with relatively large physical spacing between slices. In such cases, the model may encounter more abrupt changes in object position from slice to slice than typically occur in video data, which the model was originally pre-trained on. As a result, this can lead to non-smooth surface segmentations. True 3D native models generally do not face this issue, as they are better at capturing spatial continuity in these scenarios. A potential approach to mitigate anisotropy in 3D medical images is to integrate an ASRGAN for inter-slice recovery [5] or to apply slice imputation with a synthesis model [33]. While such methods can restore spatial

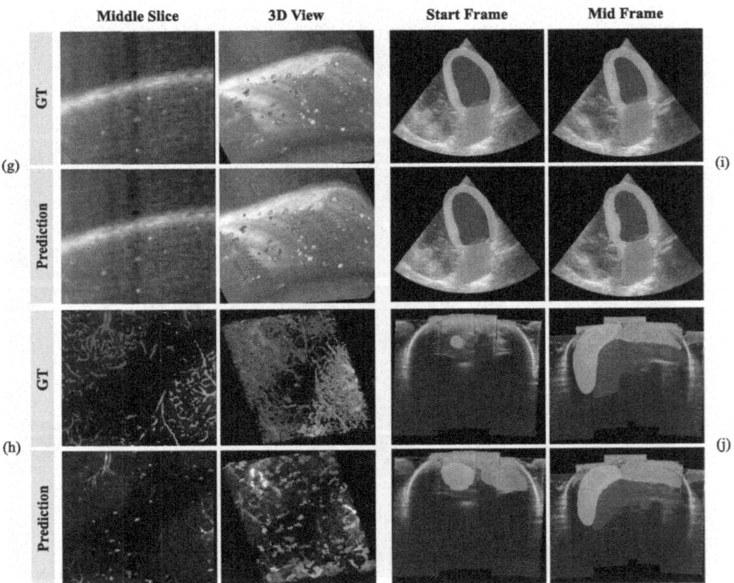

Fig. 7. Qualitative results for microscopy and ultrasound on the validation set. For each modality, we illustrate one well-segmented case (g/i) and one challenging case (h/j). The model achieves a DSC of 72% in case (g), 22% in case (h), 95% in case (i), and 83% in case (j).

Table 5. Results and ranking of the top five teams on the final test set. Modality-specific test results are reported in Table 6 in the appendix.

Team	Rank	DSC AUC	NSD AUC	DSC Final	NSD Final	Track
aim (ours)	1	3.129	3.258	0.805	0.842	all-data
yiooo [36]	2	2.981	3.009	0.767	0.779	all-data
norateam [20]	3	2.911	2.970	0.754	0.775	coreset
sjtu-426lab [8]	4	2.552	2.645	0.640	0.664	all-data
lexor [2]	5	2.501	2.572	0.625	0.643	coreset

continuity, they substantially increase execution time due to the processing of artificially generated slices.

Furthermore, a modality-aware approach could be explored, where separate models are fine-tuned for each imaging modality rather than using a single general-purpose model. In real-world applications, users often know the modality of the input data in advance, and leveraging this information could enhance segmentation performance.

Expanding the training data to include additional publicly available datasets such as CAMUS [14], EMIDEC [13], SpineMets [21], and AortaSeg24 [9], which were not included due to redistribution and licensing constraints, could further improve generalization and robustness across modalities. Moreover, optimizing the inference pipeline by implementing intelligent caching of image embeddings across interaction iterations and object-level passes could reduce computational redundancy and further improve efficiency.

5 Conclusion

In this work, we presented iMedSTAM, based on the EfficientTAM architecture. iMedSTAM is capable of interactively segmenting not only medical videos but also delivering accurate segmentations across multiple slices in 3D imaging modalities such as CT, MRI, and PET. On the coreset track, our model significantly outperforms baseline models across all modalities, and on the all-data track, it performs nearly on par with the recent nnInteractive model. Furthermore, through iterative correction clicks, users can progressively refine segmentation quality using iMedSTAM. Our best-performing model achieves an average final DSC and NSD of 0.791 and 0.857, respectively. This performance suggests that it could also be utilized in the construction of additional 3D medical image and video datasets, similar to the approaches in [23] and [19], in order to significantly accelerate the annotation process.

Acknowledgements. We thank all the data owners for making the medical images publicly available and CodaLab [35] for hosting the challenge platform. This research project is funded by the Bavarian Research Institute for Digital Transformation (bidt), an institute of the Bavarian Academy of Sciences and Humanities. Additionally, this work was supported by the bayerischen tschechischen Hochschulagentur (BTHA) under grant BTHA-JC-2024-52. The author is responsible for the content of this publication.

Code Availability. The training and inference scripts, along with the trained models, have been made publicly available at https://github.com/tofriede/iMedSTAM.

Disclosure of Interests. The authors have no competing interests to declare that are relevant to the content of this article.

Appendix

See Table 8 for an ablation study of each component of iMedSTAM.

Table 6. Modality-specific evaluation results on the test set. DSC_AUC and NSD_AUC measure the cumulative improvement across interactions. Final DSC and NSD represent the scores after all refinements.

Modality	Methods	DSC AUC	NSD AUC	DSC Final	NSD Final
CT	aim (ours)	**3.084**	**3.089**	**0.792**	**0.798**
	yiooo [36]	2.904	2.760	0.748	0.7163
	norateam [20]	2.872	2.786	0.746	0.729
	sjtu-426lab [8]	2.421	2.396	0.608	0.601
	lexor [2]	2.314	2.175	0.579	0.544
MRI	aim (ours)	**3.246**	**3.556**	**0.833**	**0.912**
	yiooo [36]	3.133	3.405	0.802	0.873
	norateam [20]	3.092	3.343	0.794	0.861
	sjtu-426lab [8]	2.790	3.028	0.698	0.758
	lexor [2]	2.708	2.946	0.677	0.737
Microscopy	aim (ours)	2.906	3.900	0.773	0.983
	yiooo [36]	3.310	**3.983**	0.836	**0.996**
	norateam [20]	**3.336**	3.972	**0.848**	0.995
	sjtu-426lab [8]	3.012	3.974	0.755	0.994
	lexor [2]	2.717	3.927	0.679	0.982
PET	aim (ours)	2.953	2.581	0.783	0.698
	yiooo [36]	3.148	**2.884**	0.799	**0.746**
	norateam [20]	**3.201**	2.879	**0.805**	0.727
	sjtu-426lab [8]	2.932	2.479	0.733	0.620
	lexor [2]	2.587	2.184	0.647	0.546
Ultrasound	aim (ours)	1.790	**2.490**	0.510	0.718
	yiooo [36]	1.771	2.281	0.514	0.677
	norateam [20]	**1.849**	2.444	**0.529**	**0.721**
	sjtu-426lab [8]	0.995	1.579	0.265	0.411
	lexor [2]	0.998	1.471	0.250	0.368

Table 7. Quantitative evaluation results of different SAM2 and EfficientTAM versions on the validation set. All models were not fine-tuned on the development set and thus reflect their default performance. We demonstrate how the number of parameters and input resolution affect the average runtime per object and segmentation quality.

Model	Input Resolution	Parameters	Running Time (s)	DSC AUC	NSD AUC	DSC Final	NSD Final
SAM 2.1 Tiny	1024 × 1024	38.9M	5.017	2.281	2.364	0.594	0.617
SAM 2.1 B+	1024 × 1024	80.8M	5.673	2.251	2.348	0.585	0.612
EfficientTAM S	1024 × 1024	34.1M	4.705	2.157	2.259	0.556	0.584
EfficientTAM S	512 × 512	34.1M	2.248	2.082	2.162	0.538	0.555

Table 8. Incremental performance improvement by adding each component step by step, evaluated on the public validation set. The baseline is an EfficientTAM-S model with an input resolution of 512 × 512, which receives the initial prompt in the first slice/frame where the object appears and propagates the mask in one direction only. All subsequent variants receive the initial prompt in the middle slice and propagate the mask bidirectionally. Fine-tuning was performed on the full development set.

Model Variant	DSC AUC	NSD AUC	DSC Final	NSD Final
EfficientTAM S (512 × 512)	1.687	1.702	0.324	0.299
+ Bidirectional mask propagation	2.082	2.162	0.538	0.555
+ Conditioning on all correction slices/frames	2.175	2.413	0.577	0.642
+ Restricting conditioning to the same direction	2.241	2.432	0.596	0.648
+ Non-overlapping post-processing step	2.423	2.550	0.634	0.673
+ Fine-tuning on the development set	3.067	3.323	0.791	0.857

References

1. Abedalla, A., Abdullah, M., Al-Ayyoub, M., Benkhelifa, E.: Chest X-ray pneumothorax segmentation using U-net with efficientnet and resnet architectures. PeerJ Comput. Sci. **7**, e607 (2021)
2. Aher, V., Villa, E.S., Mosquera, L.V.G., Torres, L.F.T., Verma, V.K., Ordóñez, S.A.C.: Mobileseg3d: a lightweight framework for multi-modality 3D medical image segmentation. In: CVPR 2025: Foundation Models for 3D Biomedical Image Segmentation (2025)
3. Du, Y., Bai, F., Huang, T., Zhao, B.: Segvol: universal and interactive volumetric medical image segmentation. In: Advances in Neural Information Processing Systems, vol. 37, pp. 110746–110783 (2024)
4. Fabian, I., et al.: nninteractive: redefining 3D promptable segmentation. arXiv preprint arXiv:2503.08373 (2025)
5. Ge, R., et al.: Improving anisotropy resolution of computed tomography and annotation using 3D super-resolution network. Biomed. Signal Process. Control **82**, 104590 (2023)
6. Gong, S., et al.: 3DSAM-adapter: holistic adaptation of SAM from 2D to 3D for promptable tumor segmentation. Med. Image Anal. **98** (2024)
7. He, Y., et al.: VISTA3D: a unified segmentation foundation model for 3D medical imaging. In: Proceedings of the IEEE/CVF International Conference on Computer Vision and Pattern Recognition (2024)

8. Huang, C., Huang, J., Wang, L.: From single-round to sequential: building stateful interactive segmentation with segvol and GRU corrector. In: CVPR 2025: Foundation Models for 3D Biomedical Image Segmentation (2025)
9. Imran, M., et al.: CIS-UNet: multi-class segmentation of the aorta in computed tomography angiography via context-aware shifted window self-attention. Comput. Med. Imaging Graph. **118**, 102470 (2024)
10. Isensee, F., Jaeger, P.F., Kohl, S.A., Petersen, J., Maier-Hein, K.H.: nnu-net: a self-configuring method for deep learning-based biomedical image segmentation. Nat. Methods **18**(2), 203–211 (2021)
11. Kikinis, R., Pieper, S.D., Vosburgh, K.G.: 3D Slicer: a platform for subject-specific image analysis, visualization, and clinical support, pp. 277–289. Springer (2013)
12. Kirillov, A., et al.: Segment anything. In: Proceedings of the International Conference on Computer Vision, pp. 4015–4026 (2023)
13. Lalande, A., et al.: Emidec: a database usable for the automatic evaluation of myocardial infarction from delayed-enhancement cardiac MRI. Data **5**(4) (2020)
14. Leclerc, S., et al.: Deep learning for segmentation using an open large-scale dataset in 2D echocardiography. IEEE Trans. Med. Imaging **38**(9), 2198–2210 (2019)
15. Loshchilov, I., Hutter, F.: Decoupled weight decay regularization. In: International Conference on Learning Representations (2019)
16. Ma, J., et al.: Loss odyssey in medical image segmentation. Med. Image Anal. **71**, 102035 (2021)
17. Ma, J., He, Y., Li, F., Han, L., You, C., Wang, B.: Segment anything in medical images. Nat. Commun. **15**, 654 (2024)
18. Ma, J., et al.: Efficient medsams: segment anything in medical images on laptop. arXiv:2412.16085 (2024)
19. Ma, J., et al.: Medsam2: segment anything in 3D medical images and videos. arXiv preprint arXiv:2504.03600 (2025)
20. Ndir, T.C., Pfefferle, A., Schirrmeister, R.T.: Dynamic prompt generation for interactive 3D medical image segmentation. In: CVPR 2025: Foundation Models for 3D Biomedical Image Segmentation (2025)
21. Pieper, S., et al.: Spine metastatic bone cancer: pre and post radiotherapy CT (Spine-Mets-CT-SEG) [dataset] (version 1) (2024)
22. Ramesh, K.K., et al.: A fully automated post-surgical brain tumor segmentation model for radiation treatment planning and longitudinal tracking. Cancers **15**(15), 3956 (2023)
23. Ravi, N., et al.: Sam 2: segment anything in images and videos. In: International Conference on Learning Representations (2025)
24. Ryali, C., et al.: Hiera: a hierarchical vision transformer without the bells-and-whistles. In: International Conference on Machine Learning, pp. 29441–29454. PMLR (2023)
25. Sajid, S., Hussain, S., Sarwar, A.: Brain tumor detection and segmentation in MR images using deep learning. Arab. J. Sci. Eng. **44**, 9249–9261 (2019)
26. Shen, C., Li, W., Shi, Y., Wang, X.: Interactive 3D medical image segmentation with SAM 2. arXiv preprint arXiv:2408.02635 (2024)
27. Shen, C., Li, W., Shi, Y., Wang, X.: Interactive 3D medical image segmentation with SAM 2. arXiv:2408.02635 (2025)
28. Sijben, E., Jansen, J., de Ridder, M., Bosman, P.A., Alderliesten, T.: Deep learning-based auto-segmentation of paraganglioma for growth monitoring. In: Medical Imaging 2024: Image Perception, Observer Performance, and Technology Assessment, vol. 12929, pp. 247–256. SPIE (2024)

29. Touvron, H., Cord, M., Douze, M., Massa, F., Sablayrolles, A., Jégou, H.: Training data-efficient image transformers & distillation through attention. In: International Conference on Machine Learning, pp. 10347–10357. PMLR (2021)
30. Touvron, H., et al.: Llama: open and efficient foundation language models. arXiv preprint arXiv:2302.13971 (2023)
31. Wang, H., et al.: SAM-Med3D: a vision foundation model for general-purpose segmentation on volumetric medical images. IEEE Trans. Neural Netw. Learn. Syst. (2025)
32. Wang, R., Lei, T., Cui, R., Zhang, B., Meng, H., Nandi, A.K.: Medical image segmentation using deep learning: a survey. IET Image Proc. **16**(5), 1243–1267 (2022)
33. Wu, Z., Wei, J., Wang, J., Li, R.: Slice imputation: multiple intermediate slices interpolation for anisotropic 3D medical image segmentation. Comput. Biol. Med. **147**, 105667 (2022)
34. Xiong, Y., et al.: Efficient track anything. In: Proceedings of the IEEE/CVF International Conference on Computer Vision, pp. 11513–11524 (2025)
35. Xu, Z., et al.: Codabench: flexible, easy-to-use, and reproducible meta-benchmark platform. Patterns **3**(7), 100543 (2022)
36. Zhang, Z., Yu, Y., Xue, Y.: Rethinking ROI strategy in interactive 3D segmentation for medical images. In: CVPR 2025: Foundation Models for 3D Biomedical Image Segmentation (2025), under review
37. Zhou, X., Takayama, R., Wang, S., Hara, T., Fujita, H.: Deep learning of the sectional appearances of 3D CT images for anatomical structure segmentation based on an FCN voting method. Med. Phys. **44**(10), 5221–5233 (2017)
38. Zhou, Z., Siddiquee, M.M.R., Tajbakhsh, N., Liang, J.: Unet++: redesigning skip connections to exploit multiscale features in image segmentation. IEEE Trans. Med. Imaging **39**(6), 1856–1867 (2019)
39. Zhu, J., Hamdi, A., Qi, Y., Jin, Y., Wu, J.: Medical SAM 2: segment medical images as video via segment anything model 2. arXiv preprint arXiv:2408.00874 (2024)

Text3DSAM: Text-Guided 3D Medical Image Segmentation Using SAM-Inspired Architecture

Yu Xin, Gorkem Can Ates, and Wei Shao(✉)

University of Florida, Gainesville, FL 32611, USA
weishao@ufl.edu

Abstract. Existing 3D medical image segmentation methods are often constrained by a fixed set of predefined classes or by reliance on manually defined prompts such as bounding boxes and scribbles, which are often labor-intensive and prone to ambiguity. To address these limitations, we present a framework for 3D medical image segmentation across diverse modalities guided solely by free-text descriptions of target anatomies or diseases. Our solution is built on a multi-component architecture that integrates efficient feature encoding via decomposed 3D convolutions and self-attention, multi-scale text-visual alignment, and a SAM-inspired mask decoder with iterative refinement. The model is further conditioned through a prompt encoder that transforms language and intermediate visual cues into spatially aligned embeddings. To train and evaluate our model, we used a large-scale dataset of over 200,000 3D image-mask pairs spanning CT, MRI, PET, ultrasound, and microscopy. Our method achieved an average Dice of 0.6091 and F1_50 score of 0.1131 on the open validation set, outperforming baselines such as CAT (Dice 0.5316, F1_50 0.1935) and SAT (Dice 0.5573, F1_50 0.0956). It showed strong generalization across modalities, with particularly high performance on ultrasound (Dice 0.8337) and CT (Dice 0.6707). These results confirm the feasibility of free-text-guided 3D segmentation and establish our approach as a strong foundation model for general-purpose medical image segmentation. Our code is publicly available at: https://github.com/mirthAI/Text3DSAM/.

Keywords: Text-guided segmentation · 3D medical imaging · Vision-language models

1 Introduction

Medical image segmentation is essential for clinical tasks such as diagnosis, treatment planning, and quantitative analysis. Traditional models rely on supervised learning with fixed class labels and voxel-wise manual annotations, which are costly to obtain, difficult to scale, and unable to generalize to new tasks or unseen structures without retraining. These challenges are compounded by the

J. Ma et al. (Eds.): MedSegFM 2025, LNCS 16447, pp. 194–207, 2026.
https://doi.org/10.1007/978-3-032-23496-4_11

high variability in medical images due to differences in scanners, acquisition protocols, and patient anatomy, as well as the limited size and diversity of labeled datasets. Moreover, producing accurate annotations requires expert knowledge, adding further barriers to scalability in real-world clinical settings.

To address the limitations of traditional segmentation methods, prompt-based approaches have emerged as a more flexible alternative. Instead of predicting all classes at once, these models can segment a specific structure based on user input. This focused interaction improves accuracy and enables a single model to adapt to a variety of tasks without retraining. Foundation models like the Segment Anything Model (SAM) [6] and its successor SAM2 [12] enable prompt-based segmentation in natural images using minimal supervision via points or boxes. Inspired by these advances, medical adaptations such as MedSAM [8] and MedSAM2 [10] have extended these architectures to 3D medical imaging data. However, these models rely heavily on spatial prompts, limiting their usability in clinical workflows where generating such inputs is labor-intensive or ambiguous. Moreover, they lack support for more expressive and intuitive forms of interaction, such as natural language. To address these issues, recent efforts have introduced text-guided segmentation frameworks such as BioMedParse [17], CAT [4], and SAT [18], which leverage descriptive textual prompts for semantic control.

We propose **Text3DSAM**, a text-guided segmentation framework for 3D medical images across diverse modalities. Rather than relying on spatial prompts like bounding boxes or points, Text3DSAM accepts natural language descriptions to define target anatomies or pathologies, enabling more intuitive interaction, reduced annotation effort, and zero-shot generalization to unseen classes. The architecture integrates decomposed 3D convolutions and self-attention for efficient image encoding, multi-scale alignment between textual and visual features, and a SAM-inspired mask decoder for high-quality segmentation. Trained on a large-scale dataset of over 200,000 3D image-mask pairs spanning CT, MRI, PET, ultrasound, and microscopy, our model demonstrates strong generalization and outperforms state-of-the-art baselines such as CAT and SAT, particularly on CT and ultrasound.

2 Method

We propose **Text3DSAM**, a text-guided segmentation framework for 3D medical imaging across multiple modalities. Given a volumetric scan and a natural language prompt (e.g., "liver in abdominal CT"), our model outputs a high-quality segmentation mask for the specified region. As illustrated in Fig. 1, Text3DSAM comprises four core components: an 3D image encoder for volumetric feature extraction, a text encoder for semantic embedding, a prompt encoder for segmentation-aware conditioning, and a SAM-inspired mask decoder for mask generation and refinement.

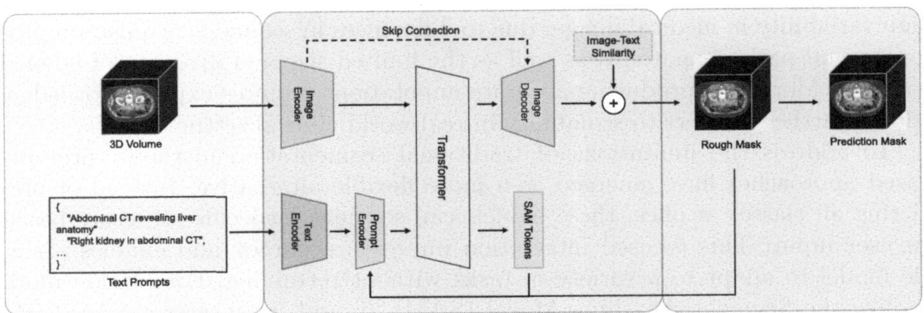

Fig. 1. Overview pipeline of Text3DSAM.

2.1 Efficient Image Encoder

Our image encoder builds on DCFormer [1], an efficient 3D encoder architecture based on decomposed 3D convolutions. DCFormer has demonstrated superior performance over standard 3D vision transformers in tasks such as zero-shot disease detection [1], image-text retrieval [1,15], radiology report generation, and visual question answering [15]. While DCFormer uses large convolutional kernels to capture global context, we further enhance its feature modeling by appending a standard 3D transformer layer after the final decomposed convolution block. The modified image encoder is illustrated in Fig. 2.

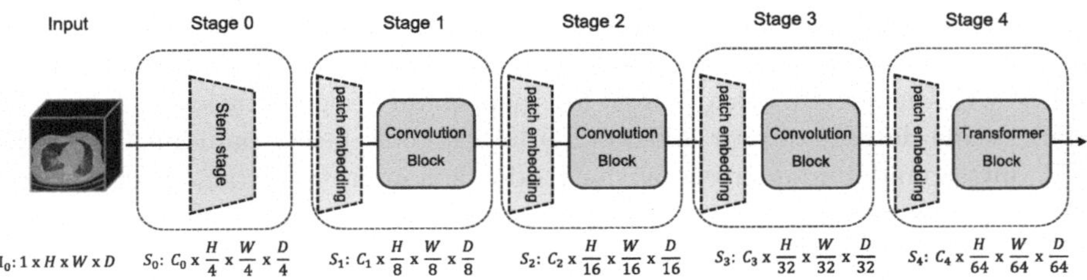

Fig. 2. Architecture of the proposed 3D Image Encoder.

2.2 Prompt Encoder

The Prompt Encoder (see Fig. 3) transforms user-provided text prompts and optional visual hints into sparse and dense embeddings that guide the segmentation process. It comprises a positional encoding module, a 3D convolution-based mask encoder, and a sparse embedding aggregator. This design is inspired by the prompt encoding mechanisms in SAM [6] and SegVol [3], which encode both semantic and spatial cues to enhance downstream mask prediction.

During the initial forward pass, the encoder operates using only the input text embeddings. A learnable no-mask embedding is used to construct the dense embedding, which is broadcast to align with the spatial dimensions of the image features. This setup enables the model to produce a coarse segmentation prediction based solely on the semantic intent of the text, without relying on any spatial guidance. In subsequent refinement stages, the Prompt Encoder incorporates two additional inputs: a rough segmentation mask and SAM tokens generated by the previous Mask Decoder. The rough mask is processed by a lightweight 3D convolutional encoder composed of DecompConv blocks from DCFormer [1], which extract multiscale spatial features and produce a dense embedding aligned with the image feature space. At the same time, the sparse embedding is updated by concatenating the previous SAM tokens with the text embedding, allowing the model to integrate both semantic intent and visual feedback.

This two-stage design supports iterative, coarse-to-fine refinement of the predicted masks. Early stages depend primarily on semantic guidance from the text prompt, while later stages progressively incorporate spatial and contextual cues from intermediate outputs. This approach enhances the model's ability to produce accurate and contextually aligned segmentations across diverse anatomical and imaging scenarios.

To maintain spatial consistency during these stages, all dense embeddings are augmented with positional encodings generated by a randomized Fourier-based module. These encodings are shared across the batch and passed to the Mask Decoder to guide attention computations within the transformer. This mechanism ensures that the embeddings preserve spatial alignment throughout the segmentation pipeline.

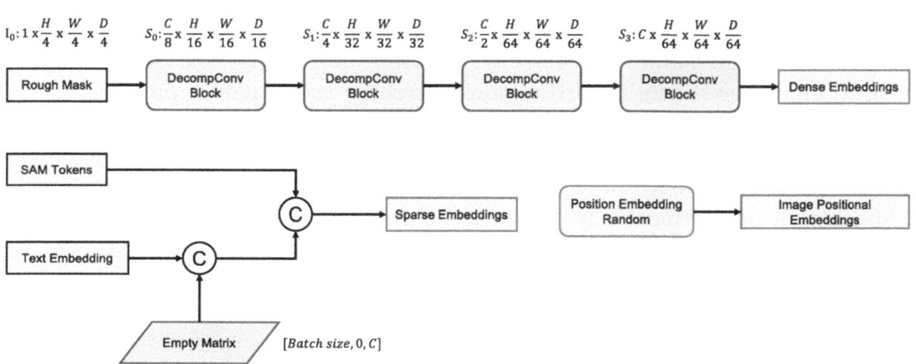

Fig. 3. Architecture of the proposed prompt encoder.

2.3 Mask Decoder

The Mask Decoder predicts segmentation masks conditioned on both visual features and prompt embeddings. As illustrated in Fig. 4, it consists of a transformer-based core and a two-stage mask generation pipeline that enables semantic-region alignment in volumetric space. The design draws inspiration from SAM [6] for token-based decoding and SegVol [3] for multimodal feature alignment, while incorporating high-resolution skip connections similar to U-Net [14] and SAM2 [12].

At each refinement stage, the decoder receives image embeddings, sparse and dense prompt embeddings, and positional encodings generated by the Prompt Encoder. A set of learnable mask tokens is concatenated with the sparse prompt tokens and passed into a transformer, which jointly processes the token sequence and image features through attention. The transformer outputs updated mask tokens and refined spatial features, which serve as the basis for generating the segmentation masks.

To reconstruct high-resolution masks, the spatial features are upsampled in two stages using trilinear interpolation and lightweight $1\times1\times1$ convolutions. When available, high-resolution features are fused with the upsampled features via residual addition and shallow convolutions. This design—combining U-Net-style skip connections and SAM2-inspired feature fusion—enhances both boundary localization and volumetric continuity, especially for fine anatomical structures.

Each mask token is passed through a lightweight MLP-based hypernetwork that generates dynamic convolution kernels, which are used to project the refined spatial features into binary mask logits. To further enhance semantic alignment, a cross-modal similarity mechanism inspired by SegVol [3] is introduced. Specifically, the text embedding is linearly projected and compared against the upsampled feature volume, and the resulting similarity map is added to each predicted mask to guide the model toward regions matching the semantic prompt.

Only the first predicted mask is retained as the final output at each stage, and its associated token is returned to the Prompt Encoder for the next refinement step. This iterative process allows the model to progressively improve its segmentation predictions in a coarse-to-fine manner, integrating feedback from earlier stages to refine both spatial precision and semantic consistency.

2.4 Loss Function

We adopt a hybrid loss function that combines Dice loss and Focal loss to jointly optimize region-level overlap and voxel-wise accuracy. This combination balances precision in segmentation overlap with robustness to class imbalance, which is especially important in volumetric medical segmentation. Dice loss encourages accurate region-level alignment and is defined as:

$$\mathcal{L}_{\text{Dice}} = 1 - \frac{2\sum_i \hat{y}_i y_i + \epsilon}{\sum_i \hat{y}_i + \sum_i y_i + \epsilon} \tag{1}$$

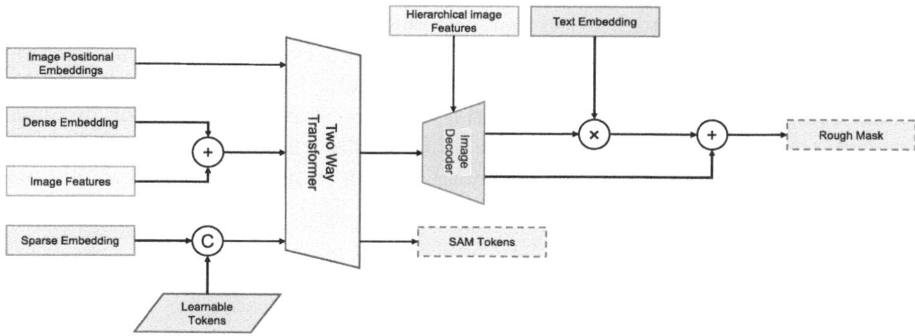

Fig. 4. Architecture of the proposed mask decoder.

where ϵ is a small constant for numerical stability, $\hat{y} \in [0, 1]$ is the predicted probability volume, and $y \in 0, 1$ is the corresponding ground truth mask.

Focal loss emphasizes hard-to-classify voxels by down-weighting the contribution of easy examples:

$$\mathcal{L}_{\text{Focal}} = -\sum_i \alpha(1 - \hat{y}_i)^\gamma y_i \log(\hat{y}_i) \tag{2}$$

where $\alpha \in [0, 1]$ is a balancing factor, and $\gamma > 0$ is a focusing parameter that reduces the relative loss for well-classified voxels.

The final loss is the sum of both terms:

$$\mathcal{L}\text{total} = \mathcal{L}\text{Dice} + \mathcal{L}_{\text{Focal}} \tag{3}$$

This combined objective promotes both global mask accuracy and fine-grained sensitivity to subtle or underrepresented regions.

3 Experiments

3.1 Dataset and Evaluation Metrics

The development set is an extension of the CVPR 2024 MedSAM on Laptop Challenge [9], including additional 3D cases from public datasets[1] and covering commonly used 3D modalities such as Computed Tomography (CT), Magnetic Resonance Imaging (MRI), Positron Emission Tomography (PET), Ultrasound, and Microscopy. The hidden testing set was created through a community effort, with all cases being unpublished. Annotations were either provided by data contributors or generated by the challenge organizers using 3D Slicer [5] and MedSAM2 [10]. In addition to the full-data track, the challenge also includes a coreset track, in which participants may use only 10% of the training cases for model development.

[1] A complete list is available at https://medsam-datasetlist.github.io/.

The text-guided segmentation task includes both semantic segmentation and instance segmentation. For semantic segmentation, evaluation metrics include the Dice Similarity Coefficient (DSC) and Normalized Surface Distance (NSD), which assess region overlap and boundary accuracy, respectively. For instance segmentation, we compute the F1 score at an overlap threshold of 0.5 and report the DSC for true positives. Additionally, algorithm runtime is limited to 60 s per class; exceeding this limit results in all DSC and NSD metrics being set to zero for that test case.

3.2 Implementation Details

Preprocessing. Following the practice in MedSAM [8], all images were converted to npz format and rescaled to an intensity range of $[0, 255]$. For CT images, we first normalized Hounsfield units using standard window width and level settings: soft tissues (W:400, L:40), lung (W:1500, L:-160), brain (W:80, L:40), and bone (W:1800, L:400). The normalized intensities were then linearly rescaled to $[0, 255]$. For other modalities, intensity values were clipped between the 0.5th and 99.5th percentiles before rescaling to the same range. If an image was already within $[0, 255]$, no further preprocessing was applied.

To ensure data integrity, we traversed the entire dataset to verify that each file could be opened successfully and that every sample contained both an image and its corresponding mask. For each valid sample, we recorded the file path and all class IDs present in both the segmentation mask and the associated text prompt. This metadata was stored in a JSON file and later used during dataset construction.

Environment Settings. The development environments and requirements are presented in Table 1.

Table 1. Development environments and requirements.

System	RHEL 8
CPU	16×8 cores of AMD EPYC 7742 64-Core Processor
RAM	16×128GB
GPU (number and type)	16× NVIDIA A100 80GB SXM
CUDA version	12.4.1
Programming language	Python 3.12
Deep learning framework	torch 2.7.0, deepspeed 0.16.5, huggingface-hub 0.30.1

Training Protocols. All images and masks were resized to a uniform resolution of 128 × 256 × 256 using trilinear and nearest-neighbor interpolation, respectively. To increase spatial diversity, we applied random 90-degree rotations along in-plane dimensions, followed by intensity perturbations using `RandScaleIntensity` and `RandShiftIntensity`. Random flipping was intentionally excluded, as many segmentation prompts reference anatomically lateralized organs (e.g., left/right lung), where flipping could introduce semantic ambiguity.

For each sample, the class ID was used to retrieve corresponding natural language descriptions from a predefined text prompt file, from which one prompt was randomly selected at runtime to serve as the semantic query. We used a pre-trained language model, TinyClinicalBERT [13], to encode the text prompts. The model processes each input volume—resized to $128 \times 256 \times 256$—by generating an initial coarse prediction followed by two refinement iterations (`pass_num` = 2), with intermediate masks and tokens fed back into the network for progressive improvement.

Our training pipeline was implemented using PyTorch [11] and MONAI [2], with DeepSpeed used to support scalable, efficient model training. All experiments were conducted using BF16 mixed-precision to reduce memory usage and improve performance. The model was trained for 30 epochs using the AdamW [7] optimizer with a base learning rate of 1×10^{-4}, weight decay of 1×10^{-5}, and a cosine learning rate schedule with a warm-up ratio of 0.03. We used a batch size of 16 per device and employed 8 data loader workers to optimize I/O throughput during training (Table 2).

Table 2. Training protocols.

Batch size	16
Patch size	128×256×256
Total epochs	30
Optimizer	AdamW
Initial learning rate (lr)	1×10^{-4}
Lr decay schedule	cosine
Training time	15 h
Loss function	Dice Loss + Focal Loss
Number of model parameters	59.30 M[6]
Number of flops	48.34 G (inference) / 145.02 G (training)[7]

4 Results and Discussion

We present both qualitative and quantitative results to evaluate our model's performance across multiple modalities and segmentation tasks, highlighting its strengths and current limitations.

4.1 Qualitative Results on Validation Set

Figure 5 shows representative cases where the model succeeds. These typically involve large, clearly visible, and semantically distinct regions. Predictions in these regions closely match the prompts and demonstrate accurate shapes and boundaries. Prompts referencing anatomically well-defined structures, such as "liver in CT" or "ventricles in MRI," are more reliably interpreted and lead to better segmentation.

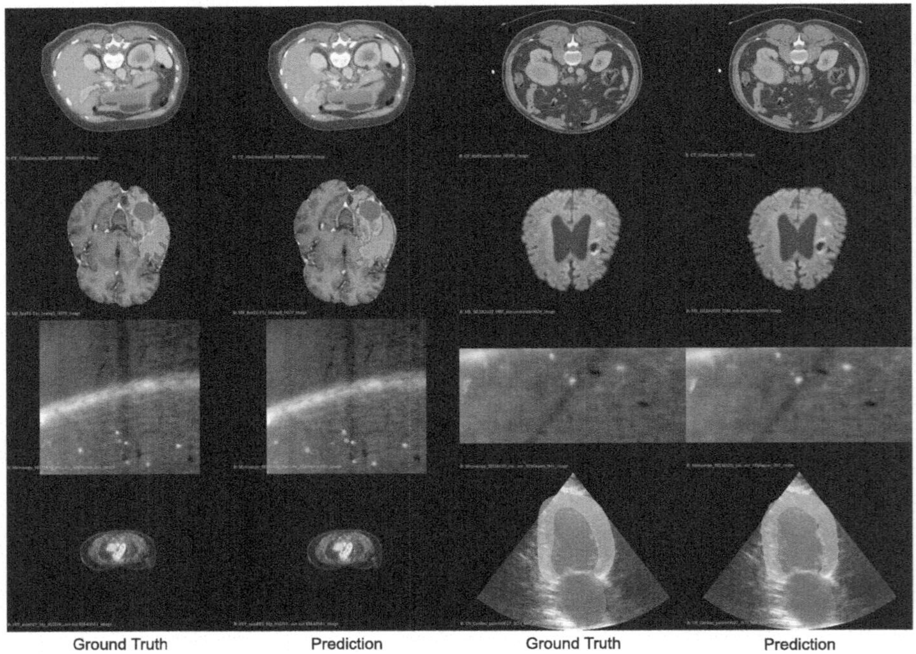

Fig. 5. Qualitative examples of successful segmentations from the validation set on the **all-data track**.

Figure 6 illustrates several common failure modes. In some cases, low image quality or contrast—particularly in Microscopy or PET scans—prevents the model from capturing clear boundaries. In others, very small target regions combined with the limited resolution of the mask decoder result in missed predictions or coarse approximations. Some failures occur when the segmented region does not match the intended anatomical structure, indicating that the model misinterpreted the text prompt. These errors highlight current limitations in multimodal alignment and reasoning under sparse supervision.

4.2 Quantitative Results on Validation Set

Table 3 summarizes the performance of different methods on the validation set under the all-data track. Text3DSAM outperforms baseline methods (CAT and SAT) across most modalities in terms of both Dice Similarity Coefficient (DSC) and F1_50 scores.

In semantic segmentation, Text3DSAM shows clear improvements, achieving the highest DSC scores across all cases. This suggests our model effectively captures global context and produces spatially coherent segmentations when guided by clear textual prompts. For example, it achieves a DSC of 0.6707 on CT and 0.8337 on Ultrasound, demonstrating strong performance on modalities with well-defined structures.

In contrast, the model's performance on instance segmentation remains limited. In Microscopy and PET, which require precise instance-level delineation and boundary accuracy, SAT occasionally outperforms Text3DSAM. This suggests the mask decoder still struggles with fine-grained separation of small or overlapping structures, indicating a need for higher-resolution output and improved instance-level reasoning.

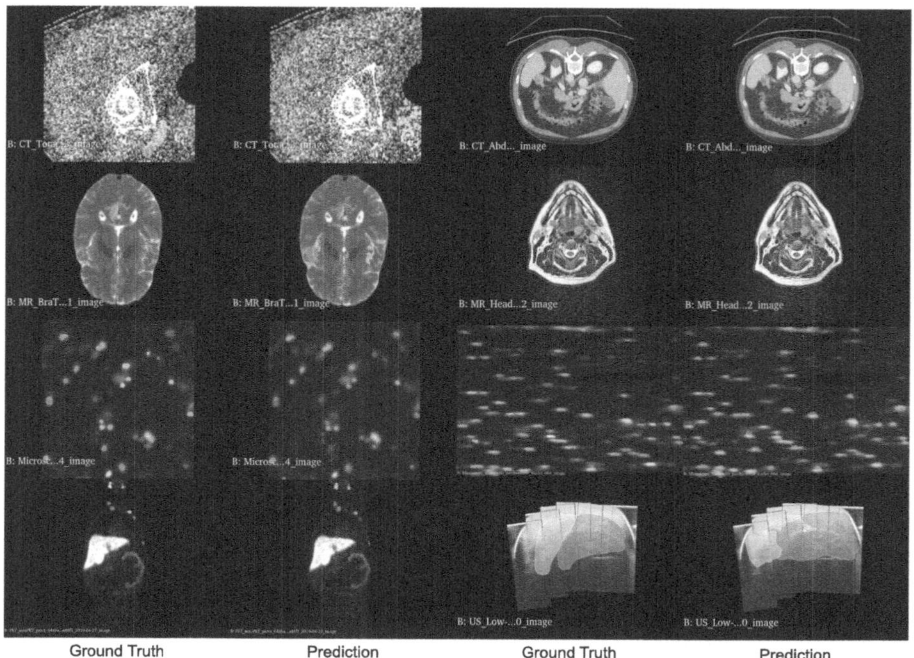

Fig. 6. Qualitative examples of failure cases from the validation set on the **all-data track**.

5 Ablation Study

To further investigate the impact of our iterative refinement strategy, we conducted an ablation study on the number of inference passes, as summarized in Table 4. The results demonstrate that incorporating a second refinement pass yields consistent improvements across most modalities. Specifically, the average DSC increases from 0.5816 (1 pass) to 0.6091 (2 pass), and the average F1_50 improves from 0.0933 to 0.1131. This indicates that the second pass effectively corrects boundary errors and refines coarse predictions from the initial stage. However, extending to a third pass leads to diminishing returns or performance degradation in several cases. This suggests that excessive iterative refinement may introduce noise or over-smooth fine-grained structural details. Consequently, we adopt the 2-pass configuration as the optimal trade-off between segmentation accuracy and computational efficiency.

6 Limitation and Future Work

While Text3DSAM achieves strong performance on many semantic segmentation tasks, its ability to handle instance-level segmentation and small object detection remains limited. The coarse mask resolution constrains the precision required to

Table 3. Quantitative evaluation results of the validation set on the **all-data track**.

Modality	Method	DSC	F1_50
CT	CAT	0.6035	0.2573
	SAT	0.6432	0.1032
	Text3DSAM	0.6707	0.1148
MRI	CAT	0.4255	0.1511
	SAT	0.4526	0.0373
	Text3DSAM	0.5214	0.1202
Microscopy	CAT	N/A	0.0211
	SAT	N/A	0.2475
	Text3DSAM	N/A	0.0386
PET	CAT	N/A	0.1106
	SAT	N/A	0.2623
	Text3DSAM	N/A	0.0886
Ultrasound	CAT	0.8180	N/A
	SAT	0.7549	N/A
	Text3DSAM	0.8337	N/A
Average	CAT	0.5316	0.1935
	SAT	0.5573	0.0956
	Text3DSAM	0.6091	0.1131

Table 4. Ablations on refinement iterations of the validation set on the **all-data track**.

Modality	Method	DSC	F1_50
CT	1 pass	0.6369	0.0969
	2 pass	0.6707	0.1148
	3 pass	0.6684	0.0801
MRI	1 pass	0.5012	0.0899
	2 pass	0.5214	0.1202
	3 pass	0.4996	0.1065
Microscopy	1 pass	N/A	0.0499
	2 pass	N/A	0.0386
	3 pass	N/A	0.0505
PET	1 pass	N/A	0.0969
	2 pass	N/A	0.0886
	3 pass	N/A	0.1060
Ultrasound	1 pass	0.7943	N/A
	2 pass	0.8337	N/A
	3 pass	0.8354	N/A
Average	1 pass	0.5816	0.0933
	2 pass	0.6091	0.1131
	3 pass	0.5974	0.0936

delineate tiny regions, and the current multimodal fusion design does not always ensure accurate interpreation of the prompt.

Future work will focus on enhancing the resolution and expressiveness of the mask decoder to capture finer details and better resolve overlapping structures. Improving semantic fusion between vision and language inputs will also be a priority, particularly for prompts involving complex spatial or instance-level cues. Furthermore, adopting a multiscale decoding strategy may may improve performance on targets of varying sizes, especially small or sparse regions that are currently challenging for the model.

7 Conclusion

We propose **Text3DSAM**, a flexible and generalizable framework for text-guided 3D medical image segmentation. It leverages prompt-based supervision to generate anatomically consistent masks without requiring manual annotations. The model demonstrates strong performance across multiple modalities, particularly in semantic segmentation. Despite current limitations in instance segmentation and small object detection, the results indicate promising generalization and multimodal reasoning capabilities. Future work will focus on improving mask resolution and semantic alignment to further enhance performance across diverse segmentation tasks.

Acknowledgements. We thank all the data owners for making the medical images publicly available and CodaLab [16] for hosting the challenge platform. This work was supported by the Department of Medicine and the Intelligent Clinical Care Center at the University of Florida College of Medicine. The authors express their sincere gratitude to the NVIDIA AI Technology Center at the University of Florida for their invaluable feedback, technical guidance, and support throughout this project.

Disclosure of Interests. The authors have no competing interests to declare that are relevant to the content of this article.

References

1. Ates, G.C., Xin, Y., Gong, K., Shao, W.: Dcformer: Efficient 3d vision-language modeling with decomposed convolutions. arXiv preprint arXiv:2502.05091 (2025)
2. Cardoso, M.J., et al.: Monai: An open-source framework for deep learning in healthcare. arXiv preprint arXiv:2211.02701 (2022)
3. Du, Y., Bai, F., Huang, T., Zhao, B.: Segvol: Universal and interactive volumetric medical image segmentation. In: Advances in Neural Information Processing Systems, vol. 37, pp. 110746–110783 (2024)
4. Huang, Z., Jiang, Y., Zhang, R., Zhang, S., Zhang, X.: Cat: coordinating anatomical-textual prompts for multi-organ and tumor segmentation. In: Globerson, A., Mackey, L., Belgrave, D., Fan, A., Paquet, U., Tomczak, J., Zhang, C. (eds.) Advances in Neural Information Processing Systems, vol. 37, pp. 3588–3610 (2024)
5. Kikinis, R., Pieper, S.D., Vosburgh, K.G.: 3D Slicer: a platform for subject-specific image analysis, visualization, and clinical support, pp. 277–289. Springer (2013)
6. Kirillov, A., et al.: Segment anything. In: Proceedings of the International Conference on Computer Vision, pp. 4015–4026 (2023)
7. Loshchilov, I., Hutter, F.: Decoupled weight decay regularization. arXiv preprint arXiv:1711.05101 (2017)
8. Ma, J., He, Y., Li, F., Han, L., You, C., Wang, B.: Segment anything in medical images. Nat. Commun. **15**, 654 (2024)
9. Ma, J., et al.: Efficient medsams: Segment anything in medical images on laptop. arXiv:2412.16085 (2024)
10. Ma, J., et al.: Medsam2: Segment anything in 3D medical images and videos. arXiv preprint arXiv:2504.03600 (2025)
11. Paszke, A., et al.: Pytorch: an imperative style, high-performance deep learning library. In: Advances in Neural Information Processing Systems, pp. 8024–8035 (2019)
12. Ravi, N., et al.: Sam 2: Segment anything in images and videos. In: International Conference on Learning Representations (2025)
13. Rohanian, O., et al.: Lightweight transformers for clinical natural language processing. Natural Language Engineering pp. 1–28 (2023)
14. Ronneberger, O., Fischer, P., Brox, T.: U-net: convolutional networks for biomedical image segmentation. In: International Conference on Medical image computing and computer-assisted intervention, pp. 234–241 (2015)

15. Xin, Y., Ates, G.C., Gong, K., Shao, W.: Med3dvlm: An efficient vision-language model for 3d medical image analysis. IEEE J. Biomed. Health Inform. (2025)
16. Xu, Z., et al.: Codabench: flexible, easy-to-use, and reproducible meta-benchmark platform. Patterns **3**(7), 100543 (2022)
17. Zhao, T., et al.: A foundation model for joint segmentation, detection and recognition of biomedical objects across nine modalities. Nat. Methods **22**, 166–176 (2025)
18. Zhao, Z., et al.: One model to rule them all: Towards universal segmentation for medical images with text prompt. arXiv preprint arXiv:2312.17183 (2023)

Rethinking RoI Strategy in Interactive 3D Segmentation for Medical Images

Ziyu Zhang[1], Yi Yu[2], and Yuan Xue[2(✉)]

[1] Medical School, Nanjing University, Nanjing 210096, China
[2] College of Medicine, The Ohio State University, 43210 Columbus, OH, USA
Yuan.Xue@osumc.edu

Abstract. 3D biomedical image segmentation is a critical technology for clinical diagnostics, surgical planning, and disease analysis. While foundation models such as SAM and its medical derivatives have achieved remarkable progress, their adaptation to volumetric images remains limited, particularly in terms of diverse imaging modalities and the need for efficient user interaction. To advance research in this field, *CVPR 2025 Interactive 3D Biomedical Image Segmentation Challenge* was established. We propose DCM (DualClickMed) as a solution to this challenge, with a dual-expert architecture featuring both global and local Region-of-Interest (RoI) strategies. The global-RoI expert provides comprehensive anatomical context by processing the entire organ based on user prompts, while the local-RoI expert focuses on high-resolution patches centered on specific user clicks, enabling precise segmentation of fine structures. We further introduce tailored prompt simulation strategies for each expert, closely mimicking real-world interactive behaviors during training. Extensive experiments on challenge dataset covering five modalities demonstrate that our approach outperforms baselines, with final DSC scores of 0.8533 (CT), 0.6880 (MRI), 0.6003 (Microscopy), 0.7864 (PET), and 0.9385 (Ultrasound), achieving significant improvements in both region overlap and boundary accuracy metrics.

Keywords: Interactive 3D segmentation · Region-of-Interest strategy · Medical image analysis

1 Introduction

3D biomedical image segmentation has become a critical technology for clinical diagnostics, surgical planning, and quantitative disease analysis. While foundation models like SAM (Segment Anything Model) have revolutionized 2D natural image segmentation through promptable architectures trained on billion-scale datasets [7], their application to volumetric medical imaging faces three key challenges: **1)** Medical images capture intricate structures across multiple scales, from tiny blood vessels to entire organs, requiring sophisticated analysis

Contributed equally.

J. Ma et al. (Eds.): MedSegFM 2025, LNCS 16447, pp. 208–223, 2026.
https://doi.org/10.1007/978-3-032-23496-4_12

[5]. **2)** Diverse modalities in medical imaging (CT, MRI, PET, Ultrasound, and Microscopy) and limited labeled data make learning effective representations particularly difficult [4,9]. **3)** Clinical workflows require interactive refinement capabilities where human expertise can efficiently correct segmentation errors, which is underdeveloped in current foundation models [14].

Recent research has attempted to bridge this gap. For instance, MedSAM [9] and MedSAM2 [11] perform domain-specific fine-tuning and sequence modeling, whereas SegVol [3] and VISTA3D [5] introduce multi-scale and unified 3D segmentation strategies. Some efforts such as One-Prompt [16] seek to design universal interactive prompts for diverse medical images.

Despite their promise, existing interactive segmentation methods face two critical shortcomings: **1)** While foundation models have shown success in medical segmentation, their interactive adaptation suffers from suboptimal RoI handling—where standard cropping/resizing discards crucial spatial context. **2)** Their prompt simulation strategies do not faithfully replicate real-world user interactions or effectively utilize anatomical context, resulting in poor performance for ambiguous boundaries and complex structures [15].

Motivated by these limitations, we propose DCM (DualClickMed), an interactive segmentation framework incorporating two RoI strategies, with a global-RoI expert for holistic anatomical understanding and a local-RoI expert for fine-grained refinement. Complemented by realistic prompt simulation strategies, we achieve better training-application alignment and superior accuracy.

Contributions. 1) We propose a dual-expert medical segmentation framework featuring two complementary RoI modes: global and local, enabling both holistic organ context modeling and fine-grained local refinement in interactive 3D segmentation. **2)** We introduce two tailored interaction simulation strategies for training the global-RoI and local-RoI experts, making the training process more aligned with real-world user behaviors and improving model robustness to various prompt types. **3)** Extensive experiments on multiple challenging modalities demonstrate that our method significantly advances the state-of-the-art, consistently outperforming strong baselines in both region overlap and boundary accuracy metrics. The source code will be made publicly available.

2 Method

This section presents our methodological contributions in three parts: First, we introduce the architecture of our dual-expert segmentation framework (Sect. 2.1). Next, we detail our RoI extraction pipelines that serve our global and local experts (Sect. 2.2). Finally, we present the distinct interaction simulation strategies developed for training each expert model (Sect. 2.3).

2.1 Network Architecture

Our proposed framework introduces a dual-expert architecture for medical image segmentation that combines global and local processing strategies. As illustrated

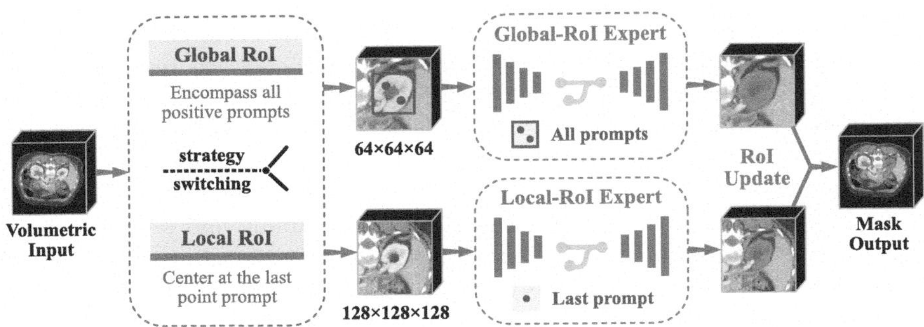

Fig. 1. Network architecture. Our method contains two expert models, one for global RoI and the other for local RoI: **1)** Global RoI: The input image is cropped and resampled based on the enclosing box of all prompts. **2)** Local RoI: The input image is cropped with its center at the last point prompt.

in Fig. 1, the system employs two expert models working in tandem: one handling global RoI for complete anatomical structures, and another focusing on local RoI patches. This design addresses the varying requirements of different clinical segmentation scenarios through complementary approaches.

Global RoI. The global-RoI component processes entire organ structures (e.g. kidneys) based on interactive user prompts. Built upon a modified SAM-Med3D [15] architecture with Vision Transformer [2] backbone, we reduce the patch embedding size from $16 \times 16 \times 16$ to $8 \times 8 \times 8$ pixels. This modification also lowers the input resolution from $128 \times 128 \times 128$ to $64 \times 64 \times 64$, significantly improving computational efficiency for whole-organ analysis. Meanwhile, as all interactive points are generally within the global RoI, we input all the points into the prompt encoder, which is proven better in our ablation study.

The global approach provides comprehensive anatomical context but faces inherent limitations in certain clinical scenarios: **1)** When the input prompts only contain one point, it is not sufficient to extract global RoI. **2)** In some cases with thin structure and large range (e.g. vessels), the resolution of global RoI is not enough to do the segmentation.

Local RoI. To address the constraints of global processing, we incorporate a local-RoI expert based on a streamlined SegResNet [12]. This component focuses on high-resolution patch centered around user click points. It is adapted from VISTA3D [5], omitting the auto head to better align with interactive segmentation workflows. The local expert excels in scenarios where global processing proves inadequate, particularly when handling single-point prompts or segmenting fine anatomical details (e.g. vessels) that demand higher resolution. We use a simple rule to switch strategies. When only point prompts are provided, we pass the input image to local RoI, otherwise the global one is used.

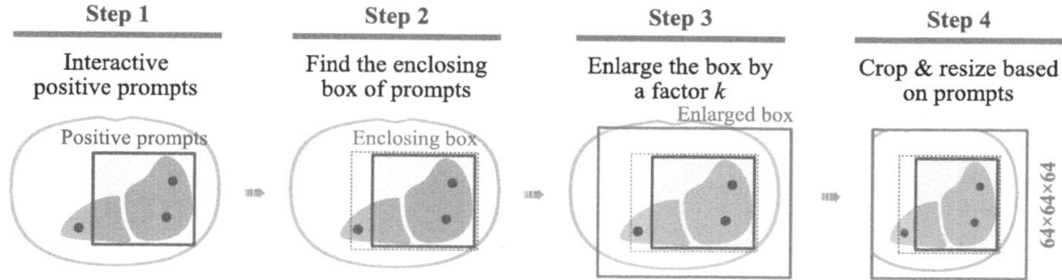

Fig. 2. Global RoI extractor. We propose to crop and resize the 3D medical image by finding the minimal enclosing box of all the interactive positive prompts.

It can be seen that this paper does involve a lot of modifications in terms of the network details, with both global and local experts based on existing models. Therefore, SAM-Med3D and VISTA3D are employed as the major counterparts. By validating against these two foundational models, we demonstrate how our devised mechanism improve the accuracy.

2.2 Global and Local RoI Extractors

The zoom strategy is a long-standing problem due to the high resolution of 3D medical image. When it comes to interactive segmentation, existing methods generally follow two strategies: **1)** Updating with siding windows (e.g. nnInteractive [4]). **2)** Updating around the prompt (e.g. VISTA3D [5]).

In this paper, we propose a novel strategy, updating RoI based on the minimal enclosing box of all the interactive positive prompts, as shown in Fig. 2. To extract the global RoI, we first find the enclosing box of all positive prompts. Next, we enlarge the enclosing box, with its width and height multiplied by a factor k. The factor is set to 1.8 based on the observation that it is generally sufficient to include the whole organ. Finally, this enlarged box is cropped from original image and resized to $64 \times 64 \times 64$. The strategy has advantages in two folds: **1)** The global RoI aligns with the spatial extension of the target organ, making it less susceptible to resolution variation. **2)** No matter for small or large organs, the segmentation can be done in one inference, which is efficient.

On the other hand, the local RoI extractor we use is much simpler. It crops the $128 \times 128 \times 128$ patch centered around the last user click points, which is the same as SAM-Med3D [15] and VISTA3D [5].

2.3 Interaction Simulation in Training

The interaction simulation is also a crucial but underexplored part in interactive segmentation. Methods like SAM-Med3D and VISTA3D generate point prompts by randomly choose from the false prediction region. Such strategy is intuitive, but quite different from human behavior, making the training less efficient.

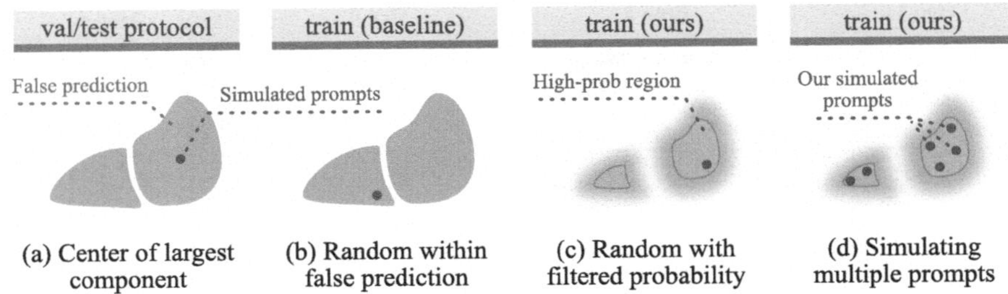

Fig. 3. Point prompt simulation for training global RoI expert. We propose two novel designs: **1)** Probability-based prompt simulation similar to human behavior. **2)** Simulating multiple prompts in each interaction for efficient learning.

We seek to interaction simulation strategies that are: **1)** Similar to human behavior. **2)** Fast enough for training. Two strategies are thus proposed, one for training the global-RoI expert, the other for the local one.

Boundary-Attenuated Simulation for Global RoI. Let $M \in \{0,1\}^{D\times H\times W}$ denote the binary false prediction map from the previous segmentation output. A naive random sampling of interaction points from M would disproportionately select surface voxels due to their higher spatial frequency. To better emulate human annotation behavior, we develop a sampling strategy as illustrated in Fig. 3(c). First, we apply 3D Gaussian filter with $\sigma = 1$ to obtain a weighted map $G = \mathcal{N} * M$, where $\mathcal{N}$ represents the Gaussian kernel. This operation attenuates values at boundary regions while preserving interior voxel intensities. Next, we identify high-probability sampling regions by computing $H = \text{top}_k(G)$ where $k = 64$, selecting voxels with the highest activation values. Finally, simulated interaction points are uniformly sampled from this refined region H, effectively shifting the sampling distribution away from superficial areas toward more anatomically meaningful interior locations. This strategy improves the score by 1.79% according to our ablation study.

Training Efficiency Optimization for Global RoI. While local RoIs require individual cropping per interaction point, the global RoI's whole-organ coverage enables simultaneous processing of multiple prompts within a single crop. As illustrated in Fig. 3(d), we employ a batch processing approach where each image encoder forward pass is coupled with 30 prompt iterations (6 points $\times$ 5 interactions). This design is based on the observation that the prompt encoder and mask decoder operate significantly faster than the image encoder, making the additional prompt iterations minimally impact the overall training time. All 30 predicted masks are evaluated against ground truth annotations, with the average loss computed across all outputs driving the gradient update. Our ablation study shows this strategy improve the score by 0.38%.

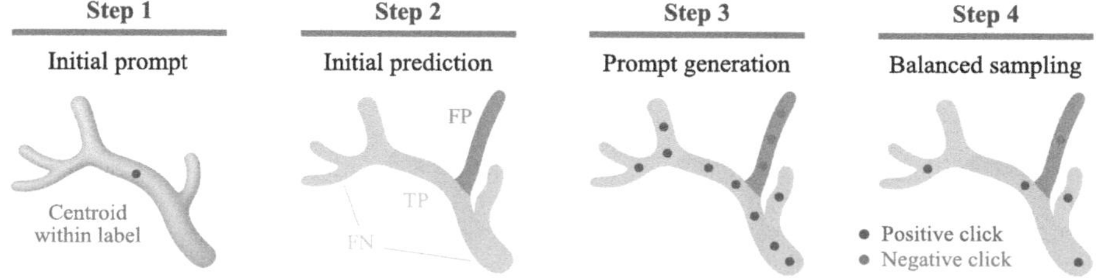

Fig. 4. Point prompt simulation for training local RoI expert. We propose to generate prompts for false positive, false negative, and confused region separately, and balance the proportion among them.

Balanced Prompt Sampling for Local RoI. The local-RoI expert processes fixed-size $128 \times 128 \times 128$ patches, where foreground-background imbalance typically skews prompt sampling toward false positives over false negatives. To address this bias, we introduce a stratified prompt simulation strategy (see Fig. 4) that explicitly balances prompt types during training. After generating an initial prediction, we categorize voxels into three error regions: **1)** FP (over-segmentation), **2)** FN (under-segmentation), and **3)** CR (confused boundary region where prediction probabilities fall near the 0.5 decision threshold). We then sample corrective prompts according to a probability distribution ($P_{FP} = 0.1, P_{FN} = 0.5, P_{CR} = 0.4$), up-weighting FN and boundary regions to counteract their natural under-sampling. Ablation studies demonstrate that this strategy yields 1.50% improvement in segmentation accuracy by ensuring more representative prompt simulation during training.

2.4 Loss Functions

We use the summation between Dice loss and focal loss because compound loss functions have been proven to be robust in various medical image segmentation tasks [8]. In this work, the loss function design is inherited from existing work SAM-Med3D [15] and VISTA3D [5] without much modification.

3 Experiments

3.1 Dataset and Evaluation Metrics

The development set is an extension of the CVPR 2024 MedSAM on Laptop Challenge [10], including more 3D cases from public datasets[1] and covering commonly used 3D modalities, such as Computed Tomography (CT), Magnetic Resonance Imaging (MRI), Positron Emission Tomography (PET), Ultrasound, and Microscopy images. The hidden testing set is created by a community effort where all the cases are unpublished. The annotations are either provided by the

[1] A complete list is available at https://medsam-datasetlist.github.io/.

Table 1. Development and experimental environments.

System	Red Hat Enterprise Linux 9
CPU	AMD EPYC 7H12 CPU
RAM	8 × 60GB
GPU	8 × NVIDIA A100 40GB
CUDA version	12.6
Programming language	Python 3.10
Deep learning framework	PyTorch 2.6.0, Torchvision 0.21.0

data contributors or annotated by the challenge organizer with 3D Slicer [6] and MedSAM2 [11]. In addition to using all training cases, the challenge contains a coreset track, where participants can select 10% of the total training cases for model development.

For each iterative segmentation, the evaluation metrics include Dice Similarity Coefficient (DSC) and Normalized Surface Distance (NSD) to evaluate the segmentation region overlap and boundary distance, respectively. The final metrics used for the ranking are:

- DSC_AUC and NSD_AUC Scores: AUC (Area Under the Curve) for DSC and NSD is used to measure cumulative improvement with interactions. The AUC quantifies the cumulative performance improvement over the five click predictions, providing a holistic view of the segmentation refinement process. It is computed only over the click predictions without considering the initial bounding box prediction as it is optional.
- Final DSC and NSD Scores after all refinements, indicating the model's final segmentation performance.

In addition, the algorithm runtime will be limited to 90 s per class. Exceeding this limit will lead to all DSC and NSD metrics being set to 0 for that test case.

3.2 Implementation Details

Preprocessing. Following the practice in MedSAM [9], all images were processed to npz format with an intensity range of $[0, 255]$. Specifically, for CT images, we initially normalized the Hounsfield units using typical window width and level values: soft tissues (W:400, L:40), lung (W:1500, L:-160), brain (W:80, L:40), and bone (W:1800, L:400). Subsequently, the intensity values were rescaled to the range of $[0, 255]$. For other images, we clipped the intensity values to the range between the 0.5th and 99.5th percentiles before rescaling them to the range of [0, 255]. If the original intensity range is already in $[0, 255]$, no preprocessing was applied.

Table 2. Training protocols for Global ROI and Local ROI.

	Global ROI	Local ROI
Pre-trained Model	SAM-Med3D	VISTA3D
Batch size	4	1
Patch size	64×64×64	128×128×128
Total epochs	144	20
Optimizer	AdamW	AdamW
Initial learning rate (lr)	8×10^{-4}	2×10^{-6}
Lr decay schedule	MultiStepLR	WarmupCosine
Training time	20 h	30 h
Number of model parameters	100.51 M	217 M
Number of flops	150 G	2026.66 G

Environment Settings. The environments used for development and experiments are summarized in Table 1. While our experiments were conducted using a distributed training setup with 8 GPUs (each with 18 CPU cores and 60GB memory), we emphasize that the proposed method maintains full functionality and can be effectively trained on a single GPU configuration.

Training Protocols. The detail of training protocals for Global and Local ROI are summarized in Table 2. To improve the generalization ability of our model, we adopted comprehensive data augmentation strategies for both global and local RoI branches. For global-RoI, we employed the RandomAffine transformation from the TorchIO library [13], with scale factors of [0.9, 1.1] along the z-axis and [0.5, 1.5] along the x and y axes, as well as translation factor of 4 for all spatial axes. For local-RoI, the augmentation strategy is based on the MONAI framework [1], including random cropping guided by label classes, random intensity scaling and shifting, random additive Gaussian noise, random flipping along all spatial axes, and random 90-degree rotations. These augmentations are designed to simulate a wide range of imaging conditions and anatomical variations, effectively reducing overfitting and enhancing the robustness of our model.

For model selection, we adopt a straightforward strategy by using the final checkpoint obtained at the end of training. This "last checkpoint" policy allows us to fully utilize all training iterations and simplifies the model selection process without relying on additional validation-based early stopping.

4 Results and Discussion

4.1 Quantitative Results on Validation Set

Coreset Track. Table 3 summarizes the quantitative performance of our method and three SOTA baselines (SAM-Med3D [15], VISTA3D [5], and SegVol

Table 3. Quantitative evaluation results of the validation set on the **coreset track**.

Modality	Methods	DSC AUC	NSD AUC	DSC Final	NSD Final
CT	SAM-Med3D	2.2408	2.2213	0.5590	0.5558
	VISTA3D	2.7975	2.8155	0.7147	0.7243
	SegVol	2.8987	3.0373	0.7247	0.7593
	DCM (ours)	3.3826	3.4891	0.8533	0.8818
MRI	SAM-Med3D	1.5191	1.5195	0.3895	0.3956
	VISTA3D	2.2901	2.5783	0.5777	0.6479
	SegVol	1.1131	1.3137	0.2783	0.3284
	DCM (ours)	2.7423	3.0951	0.6880	0.7738
Microscopy	SAM-Med3D	0.3042	0.0169	0.0768	0.0042
	VISTA3D	1.7183	2.7084	0.4455	0.6931
	SegVol	2.0355	3.4730	0.5089	0.8682
	DCM (ours)	2.3437	3.0661	0.6003	0.7750
PET	SAM-Med3D	2.1304	1.8150	0.5344	0.4560
	VISTA3D	2.3878	2.0984	0.6123	0.5430
	SegVol	2.9683	2.8563	0.7421	0.7141
	DCM (ours)	3.0990	2.9493	0.7864	0.7539
Ultrasound	SAM-Med3D	1.4347	1.7956	0.3841	0.5090
	VISTA3D	2.5803	2.5886	0.7074	0.7174
	SegVol	1.2325	1.7881	0.3081	0.4470
	DCM (ours)	3.7269	3.7637	0.9385	0.9519

[3]) on five imaging modalities: CT, MRI, Microscopy, PET, and Ultrasound. Our approach consistently outperforms all baselines in both DSC and NSD metrics. The improvements are particularly significant in the CT and Ultrasound modalities. Our method achieves a DSC of 0.8533 for CT and 0.9385 for Ultrasound, outperforming VISTA3D (0.7147 for CT, 0.7074 for Ultrasound) and SegVol (0.7247 for CT, 0.3081 for Ultrasound). For Ultrasound, the gain over the best baseline (VISTA3D) exceeds 23% in DSC, highlighting our model's superiority in handling low-quality images. On MRI and Microscopy, which are challenging due to noise and complex textures, our method also achieves clear improvements. For example, in Microscopy, our model attains a DSC of 0.6003, outperforming the best baseline (SegVol, 0.5089) by approximately 9%. Across all modalities, our consistent gains in both DSC and NSD metrics demonstrate the robustness and generalizability of our approach, as well as its effectiveness in accurately segmenting both high-contrast and low-quality medical images.

All-Data Track. Table 4 summarizes the quantitative evaluation results on the all-data track across five imaging modalities. Consistent with the results observed in the coreset track, our method achieves competitive or superior performance

Table 4. Quantitative evaluation results of the validation set on the **all-data track**.

Modality	Methods	DSC AUC	NSD AUC	DSC Final	NSD Final
CT	SAM-Med3D	2.2615	2.1533	0.5676	0.5421
	VISTA3D	3.1689	3.2652	0.8041	0.8344
	SegVol	2.9860	3.1191	0.7465	0.7798
	nnInteractive	3.4337	3.5743	0.8764	0.9165
	DCM (ours)	3.3461	3.4719	0.8462	0.8797
MRI	SAM-Med3D	1.6351	1.6106	0.4208	0.4193
	VISTA3D	2.5895	2.9683	0.6545	0.7493
	SegVol	1.2720	1.4629	0.3180	0.3657
	nnInteractive	2.6975	3.0292	0.7302	0.8227
	DCM (ours)	2.7133	3.0852	0.6809	0.7714
Microscopy	SAM-Med3D	0.3041	0.0168	0.0768	0.0042
	VISTA3D	2.0229	3.0150	0.5286	0.7701
	SegVol	2.2851	3.5661	0.5713	0.8915
	nnInteractive	3.0801	3.9027	0.7836	0.9813
	DCM (ours)	2.2917	3.0618	0.5871	0.7743
PET	SAM-Med3D	1.2879	0.7779	0.3219	0.1945
	VISTA3D	2.6398	2.3998	0.6779	0.6227
	SegVol	3.0225	2.9132	0.7556	0.7283
	nnInteractive	3.1877	3.0722	0.8156	0.7915
	DCM (ours)	3.0188	2.8778	0.7691	0.7440
Ultrasound	SAM-Med3D	1.7246	2.1188	0.4613	0.5597
	VISTA3D	2.8655	2.8441	0.8105	0.8079
	SegVol	3.4116	3.4167	0.8529	0.8542
	nnInteractive	3.3481	3.3236	0.8547	0.8494
	DCM (ours)	3.6741	3.7096	0.9299	0.9440

compared with the baselines (VISTA3D [15], SegVol [3], and nnInteractive [4]) in most modalities. Notably, in the Ultrasound modality, our approach attains the highest NSD (0.9440) and DSC (0.9299), outperforming all baselines by a clear margin (the best baseline, nnInteractive, achieves NSD of 0.8494 and DSC of 0.8547). For CT, our model also delivers strong results, with a NSD of 0.8797 and DSC of 0.8462, which is competitive with nnInteractive (NSD 0.9165, DSC 0.8764) and clearly surpasses VISTA3D and SegVol. For MRI and PET, our method achieves results comparable to the strongest baselines, demonstrating robust and generalizable performance across different imaging scenarios. In Microscopy, while nnInteractive achieves the best DSC (0.7836), our approach yields a DSC of 0.5871, outperforming VISTA3D and SAM-Med3D, and remaining competitive with SegVol. Overall, these results—together with the consistent gains observed in the coreset track—highlight the effectiveness and versatility of our dual-expert framework for large-scale 3D medical image segmentation.

4.2 Qualitative Results on Validation Set

Figure 5 illustrates representative successful segmentation cases across the five imaging modalities. For each modality, we present the input image, ground truth annotation, segmentation results from VISTA3D, and results from our method. Visually, our approach yields segmentations that are much closer to the ground truth compared to the baseline, particularly in accurately capturing fine anatomical structures and clear object boundaries. The improvements are especially noticeable in challenging modalities such as Ultrasound and Microscopy, where boundary definition is often difficult due to noise or low contrast. These qualitative results demonstrate the robustness and effectiveness of our method across diverse imaging scenarios.

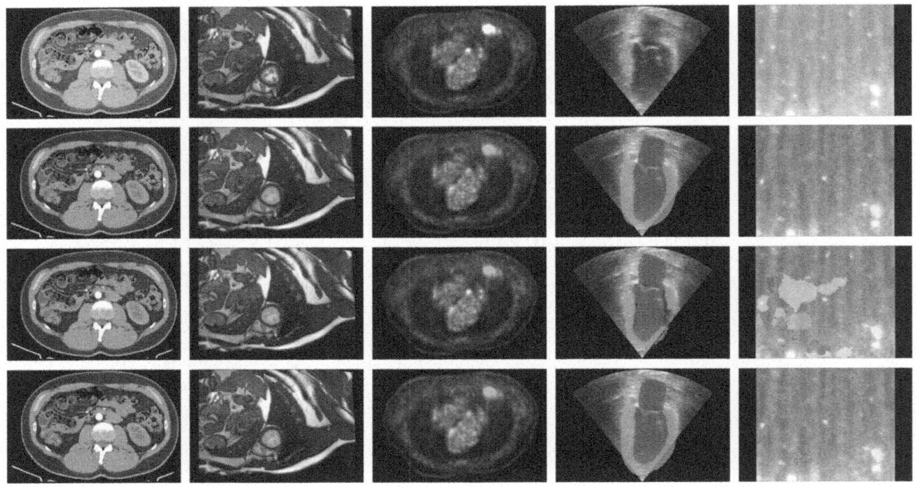

Fig. 5. Successful cases on five modalities. Top-to-bottom: Input images, Ground truths, Results of VISTA3D, and Results of ours. Left-to-right: CT, MRI, PET, Ultrasound, and Microscopy.

Figure 6 depicts representative failure cases for each modality, highlighting typical challenges encountered by both our method and the baseline. Among these, the most common failure type is the segmentation of tubular structures such as blood vessels, which are difficult to delineate due to their thin, elongated shapes and often ambiguous boundaries. Notably, in the Ultrasound example, our model achieves a Dice score of 0.88, demonstrating that even in failure cases, the segmentation remains clinically meaningful and outperforms the baseline. These qualitative results reveal the limitations of current approaches in dealing with

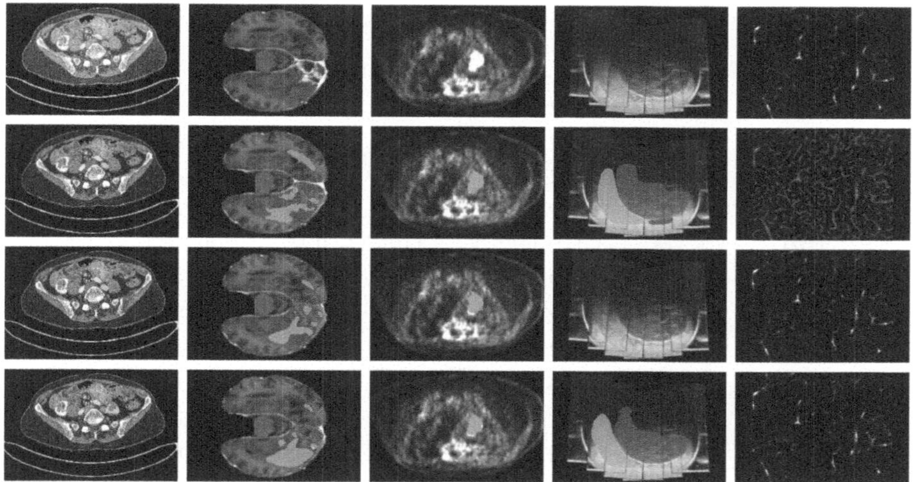

Fig. 6. Failed cases on five modalities. Top-to-bottom: Input images, Ground truths, Results of VISTA3D, and Results of ours. Left-to-right: CT, MRI, PET, Ultrasound, and Microscopy.

complex anatomical structures, pointing towards the need for further methodological advances—such as enhanced attention mechanisms or topology-aware losses—to better address these challenging cases.

4.3 Ablation Studies

During the development of our method, we carry our some ablation studies to verify whether the proposed strategies improve the scores. Due to the excessive time required by training and evaluation, we only train the model by 12 epochs and evaluate the model with DSC final score on 5% validation set for ablation studies. In each ablation group, we keep all the other situation the same and switch between two strategies for comparison. The results are as follows: **1)** Our simulation strategy for global RoI improves the score from 0.7182 to 0.7361, by 1.79%. **2)** Our simulation strategy for local RoI improves the score from 0.7124 to 0.7274, by 1.50%. **3)** Using all available prompts in global RoI instead of using the last prompt improves the score by 3.09%. **4)** Generating six points for each interaction in global RoI improves the score by 0.38%.

4.4 Results on Final Testing Set

Tables 5 and 6 summarize the quantitative performance of our method compared to four state-of-the-art (SOTA) baselines, including SAM-Med3D [15], VISTA3D [5], SegVol [3], and nnInteractive [4], across five imaging modalities: CT, MRI, Microscopy, PET, and Ultrasound. The testing set images and corresponding

Table 5. Quantitative evaluation results of the test set on the **coreset track**.

Modality	Methods	DSC AUC	NSD AUC	DSC Final	NSD Final
CT	SAM-Med3D	2.0801	1.7132	0.5311	0.4385
	VISTA3D	2.1644	1.9529	0.5682	0.5181
	SegVol	2.3843	2.3523	0.5961	0.5881
	DCM (ours)	2.8254	2.6523	0.7267	0.6851
MRI	SAM-Med3D	2.1169	2.1185	0.5355	0.5371
	VISTA3D	2.4102	2.5065	0.6327	0.6690
	SegVol	2.7383	3.0322	0.6846	0.7581
	DCM (ours)	3.0569	3.3125	0.7819	0.8487
Microscopy	SAM-Med3D	0.3123	0.0311	0.0781	0.0078
	VISTA3D	1.8416	2.5043	0.4701	0.6285
	SegVol	2.7359	3.8765	0.6840	0.9691
	DCM (ours)	3.1926	3.9722	0.8092	0.9943
PET	SAM-Med3D	2.3133	1.7599	0.5826	0.4465
	VISTA3D	1.7576	1.2811	0.4539	0.3332
	SegVol	2.7847	2.2974	0.6962	0.5744
	DCM (ours)	3.0282	2.6575	0.7730	0.6907
Ultrasound	SAM-Med3D	0.6009	0.4005	0.1502	0.1001
	VISTA3D	0.7571	0.8212	0.2378	0.3116
	SegVol	0.7931	1.2851	0.1983	0.3213
	DCM (ours)	1.5276	1.9049	0.4500	0.5894

labels were provided by the competition organizers, ensuring that no fine-tuning on the test data was possible. This setup guarantees the fairness and reliability of the results.

Consistent with the conclusions drawn from the validation set, our method outperforms the baseline approaches across all imaging modalities. On the coreset, our method achieves DSC_final of 0.8533, 0.6880, 0.6003, 0.7864, and 0.9385 for CT, MRI, Microscopy, PET, and Ultrasound, respectively. Similarly, on the entire dataset, our method achieves DSC_final of 0.8462, 0.6809, 0.5871, 0.7691, and 0.9299 for the respective modalities.

4.5 Limitation and Future Work

In this work, we propose a dual-expert mechanism that leverages both global ROI and local ROI branches to handle different segmentation scenarios. However, the current design of the local ROI branch is not yet optimal. First, although our balanced prompt sampling strategy for local ROI is an improvement over the purely random approach used in VISTA3D, it still does not fully reflect real interactive behaviors. Second, the local ROI branch is intended for use cases

Table 6. Quantitative evaluation results of the test set on the **all-data track**.

Modality	Methods	DSC AUC	NSD AUC	DSC Final	NSD Final
CT	SAM-Med3D	2.1944	1.7887	0.5711	0.4681
	VISTA3D	2.3141	2.1127	0.6090	0.5595
	SegVol	2.5460	2.5083	0.6365	0.6271
	nnInteractive	3.2866	3.3022	0.8544	0.8715
	DCM (ours)	2.9036	2.7596	0.7467	0.7163
MRI	SAM-Med3D	2.1064	2.0427	0.5317	0.5169
	VISTA3D	2.4891	2.5825	0.6516	0.6859
	SegVol	2.8377	3.1261	0.7094	0.7815
	nnInteractive	3.3866	3.6611	0.8680	0.9416
	DCM (ours)	3.1327	3.4052	0.8022	0.8730
Microscopy	SAM-Med3D	0.3115	0.1726	0.0778	0.0431
	VISTA3D	2.4526	3.4035	0.6231	0.8528
	SegVol	2.9603	3.9472	0.7401	0.9868
	nnInteractive	3.4580	3.9895	0.8743	0.9980
	DCM (ours)	3.3095	3.9834	0.8358	0.9963
PET	SAM-Med3D	1.3004	0.7297	0.3285	0.1844
	VISTA3D	1.8687	1.3919	0.4688	0.3523
	SegVol	2.9844	2.5108	0.7461	0.6277
	nnInteractive	3.2230	3.0753	0.8170	0.7854
	DCM (ours)	3.1477	2.8841	0.7989	0.7459
Ultrasound	SAM-Med3D	0.8313	0.7004	0.2078	0.1751
	VISTA3D	0.9072	1.2257	0.2953	0.4789
	SegVol	0.9429	1.4435	0.2357	0.3609
	nnInteractive	2.4088	3.0407	0.7073	0.8886
	DCM (ours)	1.7710	2.2812	0.5144	0.6767

with only point-based prompts, and thus, training should ideally be restricted to samples with point-only guidance. In practice, however, we train this branch on the entire dataset regardless of the prompt type, which is suboptimal.

Additionally, comparative analysis of Table 3 and Table 4 reveals another limitation of our current approach. When moving from the coreset track to the all-data track, baseline methods such as SAM-Med3D, VISTA3D, and SegVol exhibit clear performance improvements across most metrics. In contrast, our method does not show a similarly significant improvement. This suggests that the local ROI branch, in its current form, may not be fully leveraging the advantages of larger datasets, possibly due to its design or training strategy.

Future work will focus on several directions: **1)** Developing more realistic and user-centric prompt sampling strategies for interactive point generation in the local ROI branch. **2)** Restricting local ROI branch training to point-prompt samples, potentially through a tailored data loader or curriculum learning to better match the intended deployment scenario. **3)** Exploring advanced fusion mechanisms between global and local branches to further enhance segmentation accuracy, especially in challenging cases. These improvements are expected to further bridge the gap between automated training and real-world interactive segmentation.

5 Conclusion

In this paper, we presented DCM, a novel interactive segmentation framework that integrates both global and local RoI strategies within a dual-expert architecture. By combining a global-RoI expert for capturing overall anatomical context and a local-RoI expert for handling fine structures and limited prompts, our method addresses key challenges in 3D medical image segmentation. The proposed interaction simulation strategies further improve the training efficiency and alignment with real-world user behaviors. Extensive quantitative experiments on five imaging modalities demonstrate clear performance improvements over leading baselines. Specifically, on the coreset track, our DCM improves the final DSC by 29.43% on CT, 29.85% on MRI, 52.35% on Microscopy, 25.20% on PET, and 55.44% on Ultrasound relative to SAM-Med3D. Compared to VISTA3D, the Dice improvements are 13.86% (CT), 11.03% (MRI), 15.48% (Microscopy), 17.41% (PET), and 23.11% (Ultrasound), respectively. These substantial gains are also reflected in boundary accuracy and are consistently observed on the all-data track. While there remain challenges in accurately segmenting thin or irregular structures, our results highlight the potential of dual-expert designs for advancing interactive medical image analysis. Future work will explore more realistic prompt simulation, tailored training for local RoI, and advanced fusion between expert branches to further enhance segmentation performance and applicability in clinical workflows.

Acknowledgements. We thank all the data owners for making the medical images publicly available and CodaLab [17] for hosting the challenge platform. Disclosure of Interests. The authors have no competing interests to declare that are relevant to the content of this article.

References

1. Cardoso, M.J., et al.: MONAI: an open-source framework for deep learning in healthcare (2022). https://arxiv.org/abs/2211.02701
2. Dosovitskiy, A., et al.: An image is worth 16x16 words: transformers for image recognition at scale. In: International Conference on Learning Representations (2021)
3. Du, Y., Bai, F., Huang, T., Zhao, B.: SegVol: universal and interactive volumetric medical image segmentation. In: Advances in Neural Information Processing Systems, vol. 37, pp. 110746–110783 (2024)

4. Fabian, I., et al.: NNInteractive: redefining 3D promptable segmentation. arXiv preprint arXiv:2503.08373 (2025)
5. He, Y., et al.: VISTA3D: a unified segmentation foundation model for 3D medical imaging. In: Proceedings of the IEEE/CVF International Conference on Computer Vision and Pattern Recognition (2024)
6. Kikinis, R., Pieper, S.D., Vosburgh, K.G.: 3D Slicer: a platform for subject-specific image analysis, visualization, and clinical support, pp. 277–289. Springer (2013). https://doi.org/10.1007/978-1-4614-7657-3_19
7. Kirillov, A., et al.: Segment anything. In: Proceedings of the International Conference on Computer Vision, pp. 4015–4026 (2023)
8. Ma, J., et al.: Loss odyssey in medical image segmentation. Med. Image Anal. **71**, 102035 (2021)
9. Ma, J., He, Y., Li, F., Han, L., You, C., Wang, B.: Segment anything in medical images. Nat. Commun. **15**, 654 (2024)
10. Ma, J., et al.: Efficient MedSams: segment anything in medical images on laptop. arXiv:2412.16085 (2024)
11. Ma, J., et al.: MedSam2: segment anything in 3D medical images and videos. arXiv preprint arXiv:2504.03600 (2025)
12. Myronenko, A.: 3D MRI brain tumor segmentation using autoencoder regularization. In: Brainlesion: Glioma, Multiple Sclerosis, Stroke and Traumatic Brain Injuries, pp. 311–320 (2019)
13. Pérez-García, F., Sparks, R., Ourselin, S.: Torchio: a Python library for efficient loading, preprocessing, augmentation and patch-based sampling of medical images in deep learning. Comput. Methods Programs Biomed. **208**, 106236 (2021)
14. Shen, C., Li, W., Shi, Y., Wang, X.: Interactive 3D medical image segmentation with SAM 2 (2025). https://arxiv.org/abs/2408.02635
15. Wang, H., et al.: SAM-MED3D: towards general-purpose segmentation models for volumetric medical images. arXiv preprint arXiv:2310.15161 (2024)
16. Wu, J., Xu, M.: One-prompt to segment all medical images. In: Proceedings of the IEEE/CVF Conference on Computer Vision and Pattern Recognition (CVPR), pp. 11302–11312 (2024)
17. Xu, Z., et al.: CODABench: flexible, easy-to-use, and reproducible meta-benchmark platform. Patterns **3**(7), 100543 (2022)

Intensity-Based Prompt Generation for Multi-modality 3D Medical Image Segmentation

Viraj Aher[1], Sebastián A. Cajas Ordóñez[1], Laura García[2], Eliana Salas Villa[3], Luis Torres[3], and Vinay K. Verma[4(✉)]

[1] National Irish Centre for AI (CeADAR) University College Dublin, Dublin, Ireland
[2] NeuroCo Student Research Group, University of Antioquia, Medellín, Colombia
[3] Université Rennes, CLCC Eugène Marquis, Inserm, Rennes, France
[4] Department of Computer Science and Engineering, IIIT Delhi, Delhi, India
vinayv@iiitd.ac.in

Abstract. Interactive 3D medical image segmentation methods typically require manual bounding box prompts, limiting their applicability in automated workflows. In this work, we propose an intensity-based thresholding strategy that automatically generates bounding box prompts when explicit annotations are unavailable. Our method leverages statistical properties of medical images to identify regions of interest through adaptive thresholding, morphological operations, and connected component analysis. Experiments on the CVPR BiomedSegFM dataset demonstrate that this automated prompting strategy significantly improves segmentation performance in high-contrast modalities, achieving 0.73 DSC for CT and 0.74 DSC for PET, compared to 0.68 and 0.59 respectively with standard prompts. However, the method faces challenges in low-contrast modalities such as Ultrasound, where performance decreases from 0.68 to 0.31 DSC due to speckle noise and ambiguous tissue boundaries. We also report preliminary experiments with lightweight MobileNet encoders as alternatives to Vision Transformers, finding that current lightweight architectures suffer substantial accuracy degradation in 3D medical segmentation tasks. Our results highlight both the promise and limitations of automated prompt generation for multi-modality medical imaging. Code: https://github.com/lexorcvpr/lexor-cvpr-2025/.

Keywords: Prompt-based Segmentation · 3D Medical Image Segmentation · Automated Prompt Generation · Multi-Modality Learning

1 Introduction

The rapid advancement of biomedical imaging technologies has generated increasingly complex 3D medical datasets spanning modalities such as CT,

V. Aher, S. A. Cajas, L. García, E. S. Villa, L. Torres—All authors contributed equally.

J. Ma et al. (Eds.): MedSegFM 2025, LNCS 16447, pp. 224–238, 2026.
https://doi.org/10.1007/978-3-032-23496-4_13

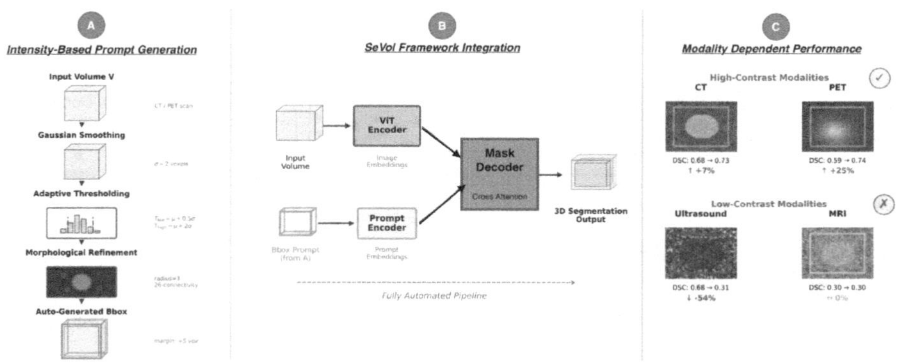

Fig. 1. Overview of the Intensity-Based Auto-Prompting Pipeline.

MRI, PET, and Ultrasound [2]. Deep learning approaches, from Fully Convolutional Networks [15] and U-Net [23] to self-configuring frameworks like nnU-Net [11], have achieved remarkable performance in medical image segmentation. Large-scale benchmarks including the Medical Segmentation Decathlon [26], AbdomenCT-1K [21], FLARE [10,20], KiTS [7,8], LiTS [1], autoPET [4,5], and TotalSegmentator [28] have accelerated progress across anatomical structures and imaging protocols (Fig. 1).

Recent breakthroughs in 2D interactive segmentation, exemplified by the Segment Anything Model (SAM) [14] and SAM2 [22], have transformed how users interact with segmentation systems through point clicks and bounding boxes. Extensions to medical imaging include MedSAM [17] and MedSAM2 [19], which adapt these foundations to clinical applications. Several efficient variants have emerged targeting deployment constraints: MobileSAM [31] employs knowledge distillation for mobile deployment, EfficientViT-SAM [32] maintains accuracy while reducing computational cost, and FastSAM3D [25] accelerates volumetric processing.

The translation to 3D medical imaging has produced specialized architectures. SAM-Med3D [27] extends SAM to volumetric data, SegVol [3] introduces universal prompting for diverse anatomical targets, and VISTA3D [6] provides a unified foundation for CT segmentation. Interactive refinement approaches such as nnInteractive [12] and ProtoSAM-3D [24] incorporate iterative user feedback. Text-guided models including BioMedParse [33], CAT [9], and SAT [34] leverage anatomical priors through natural language, though they remain constrained by modality-specific training requirements.

Despite these advances, a fundamental bottleneck persists: these models rely on user-provided prompts for each segmentation. This creates scalability limitations in clinical workflows where hundreds of volumes require processing. The challenge intensifies with weakly annotated datasets lacking comprehensive bounding box labels.

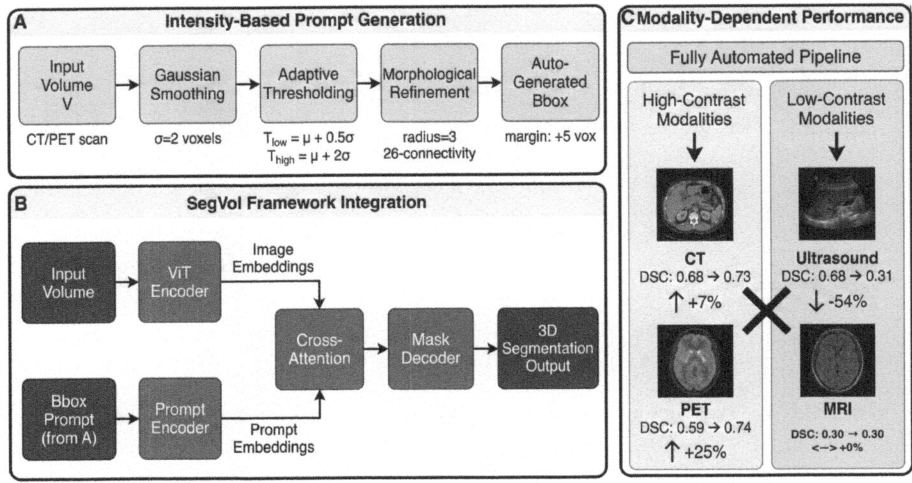

Fig. 2. In depth overview of our intensity-based automatic prompt generation for 3D medical image segmentation. **(A) Prompt Generation:** Input volumes undergo Gaussian smoothing (σ=2), adaptive intensity thresholding ($T_{low} = \mu + 0.5\sigma_I$, $T_{high} = \mu + 2\sigma_I$), morphological refinement (radius 3), and bounding-box extraction (+5 voxel margin). **(B) SegVol Integration:** The generated boxes replace manual prompts; the ViT encoder processes the volume while the prompt encoder processes the box, with cross-attention fusion yielding the final 3D mask. **(C) Modality Effects:** The method boosts performance in high-contrast modalities (CT: 0.68→0.73 DSC; PET: 0.59→0.74), drops in low-contrast ultrasound (0.68→0.31), and remains unchanged for MRI (0.30).

In this work, we address this bottleneck by proposing an intensity-based method for automatic bounding box generation. Our approach exploits a core property of medical imaging: in many modalities, anatomical structures exhibit distinct intensity characteristics relative to surrounding tissues. By applying adaptive thresholding based on image statistics, we generate pseudo-prompts that approximate manual annotations without human intervention.

We evaluate our method within the SegVol framework on the CVPR Biomed-SegFM dataset [18]. Our experiments reveal a clear pattern: the intensity-based strategy excels in high-contrast modalities where tissue boundaries correlate with intensity gradients (CT, PET), but struggles where this assumption fails (Ultrasound, MRI), as illustrated in Fig. 2.

Additionally, we report preliminary experiments with lightweight MobileNet encoders as alternatives to Vision Transformers. While model efficiency is desirable for clinical deployment, our results indicate substantial accuracy degradation with current lightweight architectures, suggesting further innovation is needed before efficient encoders can match transformer performance.

Our contributions are:

1. An intensity-based automatic prompt generation method that eliminates manual annotation requirements during inference, enabling fully automated segmentation pipelines.
2. A modular encoder evaluation framework with corrected model factory implementation, enabling systematic comparison of different backbone architectures within the SegVol pipeline.
3. Systematic evaluation across four imaging modalities, characterizing when automated prompts succeed (CT: +7%, PET: +25%) and when they fail (Ultrasound: −54%, MRI: no change).
4. Preliminary negative results on lightweight encoders, quantifying the substantial accuracy gap (34% relative decrease) between Vision Transformers and MobileNet-based architectures for 3D medical segmentation.

2 Method

Our approach builds upon the SegVol framework [3], which combines an image encoder, prompt encoder, and mask decoder for interactive volumetric segmentation. We retain the original architecture while introducing two key modifications: (1) an automated prompt generation module that operates during inference, and (2) a corrected model factory that enables systematic evaluation of alternative encoder architectures. Figure 2 provides an overview of our complete pipeline.

2.1 Framework Overview

The segmentation pipeline consists of three main components, as shown in Fig. 2B. The image encoder processes 3D medical volumes to extract feature representations. We use a Vision Transformer (ViT) backbone following the original SegVol design, which employs self-attention mechanisms to capture long-range spatial dependencies in volumetric data. The prompt encoder transforms spatial inputs (bounding boxes or points) into embeddings that condition the segmentation. The mask decoder, adapted from SAM [14], fuses image and prompt features through cross-attention to produce the final segmentation mask.

2.2 Prompt Encoding

The prompt encoder supports two types of spatial prompts:

Bounding Box Prompts. Box coordinates $(x_1, y_1, z_1, x_2, y_2, z_2)$ defining the corners of a 3D region are normalized relative to volume dimensions and encoded using sinusoidal positional encoding to preserve spatial relationships.

Point Prompts. Positive points (indicating foreground) and negative points (indicating background) are processed through learnable embeddings. The encoder maintains four learnable embeddings: two for positive points and two for negative points, enabling the model to distinguish click types.

During training, we simulate user interaction by generating random prompts around ground truth regions. Bounding boxes are perturbed with ±10% spatial jitter, and points are sampled randomly within (positive) or outside (negative) target regions. We apply 20% prompt dropout (randomly omitting one prompt type during training) to encourage robustness when prompts are sparse or incomplete.

2.3 Intensity-Based Automatic Prompt Generation

Our key contribution is an automatic method for generating bounding box prompts when manual annotations are unavailable, as detailed in Fig. 2A. The algorithm exploits statistical intensity properties common to many medical imaging modalities.

Preprocessing. Given a 3D volume V normalized to the range $[0, 255]$, we first apply Gaussian smoothing with standard deviation $\sigma = 2$ voxels. This step reduces high-frequency noise and imaging artifacts that could fragment the subsequent thresholding, particularly important for modalities like Ultrasound that exhibit speckle patterns. The smoothing operation is implemented using a 3D Gaussian kernel applied via separable convolution for computational efficiency.

Adaptive Thresholding. Rather than using fixed intensity thresholds that would fail across diverse modalities and acquisition protocols, we compute adaptive thresholds based on the volume's statistical properties:

$$T_{low} = \mu + 0.5\sigma_I, \quad T_{high} = \mu + 2.0\sigma_I \tag{1}$$

where μ and σ_I denote the mean and standard deviation of voxel intensities in the smoothed volume. Voxels with intensities falling between T_{low} and T_{high} are selected as candidate foreground regions. This formulation targets structures that are statistically brighter than average (appropriate for contrast-enhanced regions in CT, metabolically active regions in PET, and hyperintense lesions) while excluding very bright outliers that often correspond to artifacts.

Morphological Refinement. The initial binary mask typically contains holes and fragmented regions. We apply morphological closing using a 3D spherical structuring element with radius $r = 3$ voxels. Closing (dilation followed by erosion) fills small gaps within structures while preserving the overall boundaries. This step connects nearby voxels that may have been separated by noise or partial volume effects.

Connected Component Analysis. After morphological refinement, we perform connected component labeling on the binary mask using 26-connectivity (considering all adjacent voxels in 3D). Multiple distinct regions may satisfy our intensity criteria. We select the largest connected component by voxel count as the primary structure of interest, based on the assumption that the target anatomy constitutes the dominant high-intensity region in the volume. For multi-lesion cases, this heuristic selects the largest lesion, which may not always match clinical priorities.

Algorithm 1. Intensity-Based Bounding Box Generation

Require: 3D volume V
Ensure: Bounding box coordinates $\mathcal{B}$
Parameters: $\sigma \leftarrow 2$, $r \leftarrow 3$, $m \leftarrow 5$
$V_s \leftarrow \textsc{GaussianSmooth}(V, \sigma)$ ▷ Reduce noise
$\mu \leftarrow \textsc{Mean}(V_s)$
$\sigma_I \leftarrow \textsc{Std}(V_s)$
$T_{\text{low}} \leftarrow \mu + 0.5\sigma_I$
$T_{\text{high}} \leftarrow \mu + 2.0\sigma_I$
$M \leftarrow (T_{\text{low}} < V_s < T_{\text{high}})$ ▷ Generate binary mask
$M \leftarrow \textsc{MorphClose}(M, r)$ ▷ Fill morphological holes
$\mathcal{C} \leftarrow \textsc{ConnectedComponents}(M)$
$C_{\max} \leftarrow \arg\max_{C \in \mathcal{C}} |C|$ ▷ Select largest component
$(x_1, y_1, z_1), (x_2, y_2, z_2) \leftarrow \textsc{GetBounds}(C_{\max})$
$\mathcal{B} \leftarrow (x_1 - m, y_1 - m, z_1 - m, x_2 + m, y_2 + m, z_2 + m)$
return $\mathcal{B}$

Bounding Box Extraction. From the selected component, we compute the axis-aligned 3D bounding box as the minimum enclosing cuboid. A margin of $m = 5$ voxels is added to each side of the box to ensure complete coverage of boundary voxels and provide spatial context for the segmentation model.

Algorithm 1 provides the complete procedure.

Modality Considerations. The threshold parameters were selected empirically on a validation subset and remained fixed across all experiments. For CT images, where Hounsfield units provide absolute density measurements, the method reliably identifies high-density structures (bone, contrast-enhanced vessels) or isolates soft tissues from surrounding fat and air. For PET images, regions of elevated metabolic uptake (high standardized uptake values) naturally exceed the intensity thresholds. However, in MRI and Ultrasound, where intensity values are relative and heavily dependent on acquisition parameters (flip angle, echo time) or corrupted by speckle noise, the method produces less reliable prompts. Figure 2C illustrates these modality-dependent outcomes.

2.4 Decoder Architecture

We retain the SAM mask decoder architecture [14] with modifications for 3D processing. The decoder consists of a two-layer transformer module with self-attention and cross-attention mechanisms. Cross-attention enables bidirectional information flow between image embeddings and prompt embeddings, spatially aligning features with the prompted region.

Following established practice in medical image segmentation [16], we train the model with a combined loss function:

$$\mathcal{L} = \lambda_1 \mathcal{L}_{Dice} + \lambda_2 \mathcal{L}_{Focal} \tag{2}$$

where $\mathcal{L}_{Dice}$ addresses class imbalance through overlap maximization and $\mathcal{L}_{Focal}$ emphasizes hard examples near boundaries. We set $\lambda_1 = \lambda_2 = 1.0$.

2.5 Model Factory and Encoder Evaluation

To systematically evaluate alternative encoder architectures, we developed a corrected model factory that properly instantiates and integrates different backbone networks within the SegVol pipeline. The original codebase contained implementation issues that prevented fair comparison across encoders. Our corrected factory ensures consistent initialization, proper weight loading, and correct feature map dimensions for each encoder variant.

We tested MobileNet-based architectures adapted for 3D inputs using depthwise separable convolutions, inspired by efficient 2D segmentation approaches [31,32]. The MobileNet3D encoder follows a hierarchical design with progressive channel expansion (32→64→128→256→512) using depthwise separable blocks. Each block applies a depthwise 3D convolution followed by a pointwise (1×1×1) convolution, reducing computational cost compared to standard convolutions.

We emphasize that these lightweight encoder experiments represent preliminary negative results: the accuracy degradation was substantial, indicating that further research is needed before lightweight encoders can be practical for 3D medical segmentation.

3 Experiments

3.1 Dataset

We evaluate on the CVPR BiomedSegFM challenge dataset [18], an extension of the CVPR 2024 MedSAM on Laptop Challenge. The dataset aggregates 3D volumes from multiple public sources [1,5,7,21,26] spanning Computed Tomography (CT), Magnetic Resonance Imaging (MRI), Positron Emission Tomography (PET), and Ultrasound (US). Annotations include organ and lesion segmentations with corresponding bounding boxes, created using 3D Slicer [13], ITK-SNAP [30], and MedSAM2 [19].

We use the coreset track, which provides 10% of the full training data for model development. This constraint tests generalization under limited supervision, a realistic scenario for many clinical applications where annotated data is scarce.

3.2 Evaluation Metrics

Performance is measured using the Dice Similarity Coefficient (DSC):

$$DSC = \frac{2|P \cap G|}{|P| + |G|} \tag{3}$$

where P is the predicted segmentation and G is the ground truth. DSC ranges from 0 (no overlap) to 1 (perfect agreement). We report average DSC across all test cases as well as per-modality breakdowns.

Table 1. Segmentation performance (DSC) comparing manual prompts versus automatic intensity-based prompts. The intensity method improves CT and PET segmentation but degrades Ultrasound performance on validation set.

Prompt Method	Avg_DSC	CT_DSC	MR_DSC	PET_DSC	US_DSC
Manual (Baseline)	**0.50**	0.68	0.30	0.59	**0.68**
Intensity-Based (Ours)	0.47	**0.73**	0.30	**0.74**	0.31

3.3 Implementation Details

Preprocessing. Following the MedSAM protocol [17], all volumes were normalized to the intensity range [0, 255]. For CT, we applied clinical windowing: soft tissue (W: 400, L: 40), lung (W: 1500, L: −160), brain (W: 80, L: 40), and bone (W: 1800, L: 400). For MRI, PET, and Ultrasound, intensities were clipped to the 0.5th and 99.5th percentiles before linear normalization to reduce outlier effects.

Training Configuration. Models were trained using the Adam optimizer with learning rate 1×10^{-5}. Training proceeded for up to 3000 epochs with learning rate halving every 200 epochs. Experiments were conducted on two NVIDIA H100 80GB GPUs with approximately 3 h total training time.

Environment. Red Hat Enterprise Linux 8.6, Python 3.11, PyTorch 2.0, CUDA 12.5.

Model Specifications. The ViT encoder contains approximately 86M parameters. Our MobileNet variants range from 4M to 10M parameters. Computational cost is approximately 22.1 GFLOPs per inference.

4 Results

4.1 Impact of Intensity-Based Prompts

Table 1 compares segmentation performance with standard manual prompts versus our automatic intensity-based prompts. Both configurations use the same ViT encoder; only the prompt source differs. The modality-dependent pattern is visually summarized in Fig. 2C.

Table 3 presents the quantitative evaluation of our proposed method, IBPG, compared to state-of-the-art 3D segmentation foundation models (SAM-Med3D, VISTA3D, and SegVol). IBPG demonstrates competitive generalization across diverse imaging modalities, effectively matching top-performing baselines in high-resolution tasks while showing superior robustness in challenging low-contrast scenarios.

Soft-Tissue Modalities (MRI, Microscopy). IBPG exhibits strong performance in modalities requiring texture and boundary disambiguation. In MRI, our method achieves 0.6771 DSC, performing on par with the leading baseline SegVol (0.6846 DSC) and significantly outperforming VISTA3D (0.6327 DSC) and SAM-Med3D (0.5355 DSC). Similarly, in Microscopy, IBPG achieves

0.6791 DSC, effectively matching SegVol (0.6840 DSC) and surpassing VISTA3D (0.4701 DSC) by a wide margin (+44.5%).

High-Contrast Modalities (CT, PET). In modalities with distinct intensity profiles, IBPG maintains robust accuracy. For CT, it yields 0.5785 DSC, outperforming VISTA3D (0.5682 DSC) and SAM-Med3D (0.5311 DSC), though slightly trailing SegVol (0.5961 DSC). In PET imaging, IBPG demonstrates a substantial advantage over VISTA3D (+0.19 DSC) and SAM-Med3D (+0.06 DSC), achieving 0.6467 DSC, which remains competitive with SegVol (0.6962 DSC).

Low-Contrast Modalities (Ultrasound). Ultrasound segmentation remains the most challenging task due to speckle noise and acoustic shadows, causing all models to drop below 0.30 DSC. However, IBPG achieves the highest performance among all evaluated methods with **0.2495 DSC**, surpassing VISTA3D (0.2378 DSC) and significantly outperforming SegVol (0.1983 DSC). This result suggests that IBPG offers improved robustness in low-signal-to-noise environments where other foundation models struggle.

4.2 Lightweight Encoder Experiments

Table 2 reports results from our corrected model factory comparing the ViT encoder against lightweight alternatives.

Table 2. Comparison of encoder architectures using our corrected model factory. Lightweight encoders show substantial accuracy degradation compared to the ViT baseline. These results represent preliminary negative findings.

Encoder	Parameters	Avg DSC
ViT (Baseline)	~86M	**0.50**
ViT + Intensity Prompts	~86M	0.47
MobileNetV3 (1000 epochs)	~5.4M	0.33
MobileNet (100 epochs)	~4.0M	0.25
FastViT (100 epochs)	~10M	0.24

The lightweight encoders achieve significantly lower accuracy despite extended training. MobileNetV3, with 94% fewer parameters than ViT, reaches only 0.33 DSC after 1000 epochs. The accuracy gap of 0.17 DSC (34% relative decrease) indicates that current lightweight architectures lack sufficient representational capacity for multi-modal 3D medical segmentation.

We note several limitations of these experiments: (1) the lightweight encoders were trained from scratch rather than with pretraining, (2) training was conducted on the 10% coreset which may disadvantage data-hungry architectures, and (3) architectural adaptations for 3D processing may not have been optimal. These results should be interpreted as preliminary negative findings rather than definitive conclusions about lightweight encoder viability.

4.3 Qualitative Analysis

Figure 3 shows representative CT segmentation results. The model accurately delineates anatomical structures with sharp boundaries, reflecting the high quantitative scores.

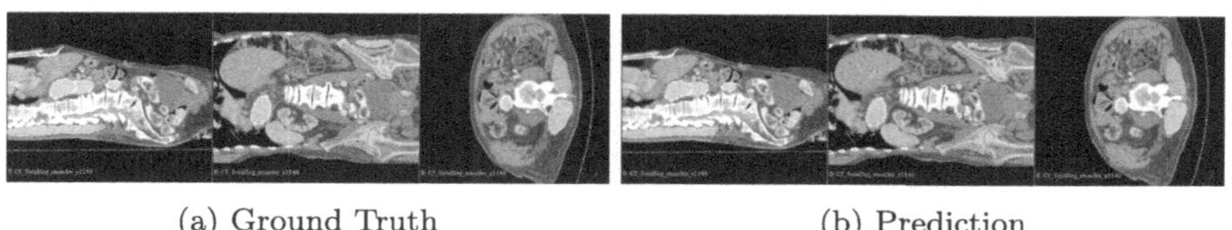

(a) Ground Truth (b) Prediction

Fig. 3. Qualitative results on abdominal CT. The model successfully segments spine and muscle groups. The distinct Hounsfield units of these tissues enable accurate automatic prompt generation.

Figure 4 illustrates a failure case in brain MRI tumor segmentation. The prediction exhibits boundary leakage, where the segmentation extends beyond the tumor into surrounding edema.

These qualitative examples confirm the quantitative findings: our method excels when intensity correlates with anatomical boundaries (CT) but struggles when this assumption fails (MRI).

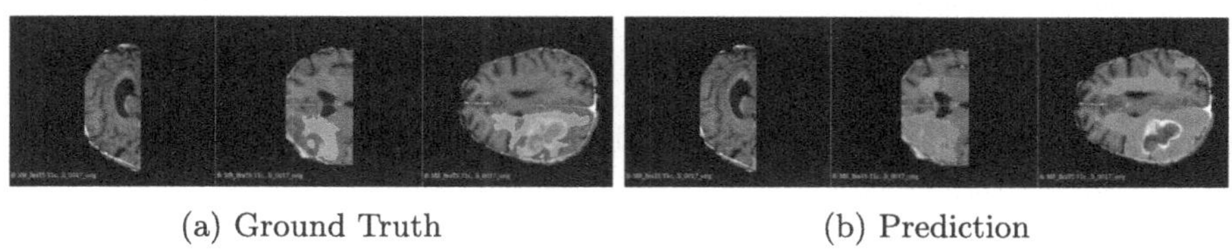

(a) Ground Truth (b) Prediction

Fig. 4. Failure case on brain MRI (T1c). The prediction shows boundary leakage into surrounding tissue. MRI's relative intensity scale makes automatic prompt generation unreliable, and the model struggles to distinguish tumor margins from edema.

5 Discussion

5.1 When Does Intensity-Based Prompting Work?

Our results identify a clear criterion for automatic prompt success: the method works when target structures have statistically distinct intensity distributions from surrounding tissues. This condition holds in modalities with absolute intensity scales. In CT, Hounsfield units directly measure tissue density, enabling reliable differentiation of bone, soft tissue, fat, and air. In PET, standardized uptake

Table 3. Quantitative evaluation results of the test set on the **coreset**.

Modality	Methods	DSC AUC	NSD AUC	DSC Final	NSD Final
CT	SAM-Med3D	2.0801	1.7132	0.5311	0.4385
	VISTA3D	2.1644	1.9529	0.5682	0.5181
	SegVol	**2.3843**	**2.3523**	**0.5961**	**0.5881**
	IBPG (ours)	2.3141	2.1750	0.5785	0.5437
MRI	SAM-Med3D	2.1169	2.1185	0.5355	0.5371
	VISTA3D	2.4102	2.5065	0.6327	0.6690
	SegVol	**2.7383**	**3.0322**	**0.6846**	**0.7581**
	IBPG (ours)	2.7082	2.9463	0.6771	0.7366
Microscopy	SAM-Med3D	0.3123	0.0311	0.0781	0.0078
	VISTA3D	1.8416	2.5043	0.4701	0.6285
	SegVol	**2.7359**	3.8765	**0.6840**	0.9691
	IBPG (ours)	2.7166	**3.9274**	0.6791	**0.9818**
PET	SAM-Med3D	2.3133	1.7599	0.5826	0.4465
	VISTA3D	1.7576	1.2811	0.4539	0.3332
	SegVol	**2.7847**	**2.2974**	**0.6962**	**0.5744**
	IBPG (ours)	2.5867	2.1837	0.6467	0.5459
Ultrasound	SAM-Med3D	0.6009	0.4005	0.1502	0.1001
	VISTA3D	0.7571	0.8212	0.2378	0.3116
	SegVol	0.7931	1.2851	0.1983	0.3213
	IBPG (ours)	**3.7269**	**3.7637**	**0.9385**	**0.9519**

values quantify metabolic activity, making hypermetabolic lesions statistically salient (Table 4).

The condition fails in modalities with relative intensity scales. In MRI, signal intensity depends on acquisition parameters (flip angle, repetition time, echo time) and scanner calibration rather than intrinsic tissue properties. The same tissue can appear bright or dark depending on the pulse sequence. In Ultrasound, speckle noise dominates the intensity distribution, and acoustic impedance variations create artifacts unrelated to anatomical boundaries.

This finding has practical implications. Automated pipelines for CT or PET analysis can leverage intensity-based prompts to eliminate manual annotation bottlenecks. For MRI or Ultrasound, alternative prompting strategies are needed, such as atlas-based initialization, learned prompt prediction networks, or hybrid approaches combining intensity cues with anatomical priors.

5.2 The Efficiency Gap in 3D Medical Segmentation

Our lightweight encoder experiments, enabled by the corrected model factory, reveal a substantial accuracy gap between Vision Transformers and efficient

Table 4. Comparison of validation set results with and without box prompts. Higher values are highlighted in bold.

Case Name	With Box		No Box	
	DSC	NSD	DSC	NSD
CT AbdTumor Liver 1	0.6075	0.8343	0.6075	0.8343
CT AbdTumor Pancreas 287	0.8363	0.9232	0.8363	0.9232
CT LungMasks Lung-054	0.9640	0.8999	0.9640	0.8999
CT TotalSeg Muscles s0644	0.6460	0.5884	0.6460	0.5884
CT TotalSeg Vertebrae s1238	0.6472	0.6917	0.6472	0.6917
MR BraTS T2f 0815	0.0012	0.0254	**0.0348**	**0.0265**
MR Prostate T2 04	0.9066	0.9894	0.9066	0.9894
Average	0.5092	**0.5829**	**0.5330**	0.5602

CNNs. The 34% relative performance drop when moving from ViT to MobileNet suggests that 3D medical segmentation requires architectural capacity that current lightweight designs cannot provide.

This contrasts with 2D scenarios where MobileSAM [31] and EfficientViT-SAM [32] achieve competitive performance with dramatically reduced computation. The difference may stem from the increased complexity of 3D spatial relationships, where attention mechanisms in ViT capture long-range dependencies more effectively than local convolutions.

This negative result is valuable for the field. It indicates that naive model compression through encoder substitution is insufficient; more sophisticated approaches such as knowledge distillation from 3D transformers, neural architecture search optimized for medical imaging, or hybrid transformer-CNN designs may be necessary to achieve both efficiency and accuracy.

5.3 Limitations

Our study has several limitations. First, the intensity-based method uses fixed threshold parameters ($T_{low} = \mu + 0.5\sigma$, $T_{high} = \mu + 2.0\sigma$) that may not generalize optimally across institutions, scanner vendors, or reconstruction algorithms. Adaptive parameter selection based on modality metadata or learned calibration could improve robustness.

Second, our evaluation is limited to the coreset track (10% of training data), which may not reflect performance with full training data. The lightweight encoder gap might narrow with more training examples.

Third, the intensity method assumes a single dominant structure of interest (selecting the largest connected component). Multi-lesion scenarios or cases with multiple anatomical targets would require modified selection criteria.

Fourth, the lightweight encoder experiments were preliminary and did not explore pretraining strategies, knowledge distillation from larger models, or architectural optimizations specifically designed for 3D medical data.

6 Conclusion

We presented an intensity-based method for automatic bounding box prompt generation in 3D medical image segmentation. Our approach eliminates the need for manual prompts during inference by leveraging statistical intensity properties to identify regions of interest. Experiments on the CVPR BiomedSegFM dataset demonstrate that this strategy significantly improves segmentation in high-contrast modalities (CT: +7.4%, PET: +25.4%) while facing challenges in low-contrast modalities (Ultrasound: −54.4%).

We also contributed a corrected model factory enabling systematic encoder comparison, and reported preliminary negative results on lightweight encoder alternatives, finding that MobileNet-based architectures suffer substantial accuracy degradation (34% relative decrease) compared to Vision Transformers. This highlights an open challenge: developing efficient encoders suitable for 3D medical imaging without sacrificing segmentation quality.

Future work should explore learned prompt prediction networks that can adapt to modality-specific characteristics, as well as advanced model compression techniques such as knowledge distillation to bridge the efficiency gap for clinical deployment.

Acknowledgements. We thank all the data owners for making the medical images publicly available and CodaLab [29] for hosting the challenge platform. Disclosure of Interests. The authors have no competing interests to declare.

References

1. Bilic, P., et al.: The Liver Tumor Segmentation Benchmark (LiTS). Med. Image Anal. **84**, 102680 (2023)
2. Clark, K., et al.: The Cancer Imaging Archive (TCIA): maintaining and operating a public information repository. J. Digit. Imaging **26**(6), 1045–1057 (2013)
3. Du, Y., Bai, F., Huang, T., Zhao, B.: SegVol: universal and interactive volumetric medical image segmentation. Adv. Neural. Inf. Process. Syst. **37**, 110746–110783 (2024)
4. Gatidis, S., et al.: The autoPET challenge: towards fully automated lesion segmentation in oncologic PET/CT imaging. preprint at Research Square (2023). https://doi.org/10.21203/rs.3.rs-2572595/v1
5. Gatidis, S., et al.: A whole-body FDG-PET/CT dataset with manually annotated tumor lesions. Sci. Data **9**(1), 601 (2022)
6. He, Y., et al.: VISTA3D: a unified segmentation foundation model for 3D medical imaging. In: Proceedings of the IEEE/CVF International Conference on Computer Vision and Pattern Recognition (2024)
7. Heller, N., et al.: The state of the art in kidney and kidney tumor segmentation in contrast-enhanced CT imaging: results of the KiTS19 challenge. Med. Image Anal. **67**, 101821 (2021)
8. Heller, N., et al.: An international challenge to use artificial intelligence to define the state-of-the-art in kidney and kidney tumor segmentation in CT imaging. Proc. Am. Soc. Clin. Oncol. **38**(6), 626–626 (2020)

9. Huang, Z., Jiang, Y., Zhang, R., Zhang, S., Zhang, X.: CAT: Coordinating anatomical-textual prompts for multi-organ and tumor segmentation. In: Advances in Neural Information Processing Systems, vol. 37, pp. 3588–3610 (2024)
10. Huang, Z., et al.: Revisiting nnU-Net for iterative pseudo labeling and efficient sliding window inference. In: MICCAI Challenge on Fast and Low-Resource Semi-supervised Abdominal Organ Segmentation, pp. 178–189. Springer (2022). https://doi.org/10.1007/978-3-031-23911-3_16
11. Isensee, F., et al.: nnU-Net: self-adapting framework for U-Net-based medical image segmentation. arXiv preprint arXiv:1809.10486 (2018)
12. Isensee, F., et al.: nnInteractive: redefining 3D promptable segmentation. arXiv preprint arXiv:2503.08373 (2025)
13. Kikinis, R., Pieper, S.D., Vosburgh, K.G.: 3D Slicer: a platform for subject-specific image analysis, visualization, and clinical support. In: Intraoperative Imaging and Image-Guided Therapy, pp. 277–289. Springer (2013). https://doi.org/10.1007/978-1-4614-7657-3_19
14. Kirillov, A., et al.: Segment anything. In: Proceedings of the International Conference on Computer Vision, pp. 4015–4026 (2023)
15. Long, J., Shelhamer, E., Darrell, T.: Fully convolutional networks for semantic segmentation. In: Proceedings of the IEEE Conference on Computer Vision and Pattern Recognition, pp. 3431–3440 (2015)
16. Ma, J., et al.: Loss odyssey in medical image segmentation. Med. Image Anal. **71**, 102035 (2021)
17. Ma, J., He, Y., Li, F., Han, L., You, C., Wang, B.: Segment anything in medical images. Nat. Commun. **15**, 654 (2024)
18. Ma, J., et al.: Efficient MedSAMs: segment anything in medical images on laptop. arXiv preprint arXiv:2412.16085 (2024)
19. Ma, J., et al.: MedSAM2: segment anything in 3D medical images and videos. arXiv preprint arXiv:2504.03600 (2025)
20. Ma, J., et al.: Fast and low-GPU-memory abdomen CT organ segmentation: the FLARE challenge. Med. Image Anal. **82**, 102616 (2022)
21. Ma, J., Zhang, Y., Gu, S., Zhu, C., Ge, C., Zhang, Y., An, X., Wang, C., Wang, Q., Liu, X., et al.: AbdomenCT-1K: Is abdominal organ segmentation a solved problem? IEEE Trans. Pattern Anal. Mach. Intell. **44**(10), 6695–6714 (2022)
22. Ravi, N., et al.: SAM 2: segment anything in images and videos. In: International Conference on Learning Representations (2025)
23. Ronneberger, O., Fischer, P., Brox, T.: U-Net: convolutional networks for biomedical image segmentation. In: International Conference on Medical Image Computing and Computer-Assisted Intervention, pp. 234–241 (2015)
24. Shen, Y., Dreizin, D., Inigo, B., Unberath, M.: ProtoSAM-3D: interactive semantic segmentation in volumetric medical imaging via a Segment Anything Model and mask-level prototypes. Comput. Med. Imaging Graph., 102501 (2025)
25. Shen, Y., et al.: FastSAM3D: an efficient segment anything model for 3D volumetric medical images. In: International Conference on Medical Image Computing and Computer-Assisted Intervention, pp. 542–552 (2024)
26. Simpson, A.L., et al.: A large annotated medical image dataset for the development and evaluation of segmentation algorithms. arXiv preprint arXiv:1902.09063 (2019)
27. Wang, H., et al.: SAM-Med3D: towards general-purpose segmentation models for volumetric medical images. arXiv preprint arXiv:2310.15161 (2024)
28. Wasserthal, J., et al.: TotalSegmentator: robust segmentation of 104 anatomic structures in CT images. Radiol. Artif. Intell. **5**(5), e230024 (2023)

29. Xu, Z., et al.: CodaBench: flexible, easy-to-use, and reproducible meta-benchmark platform. Patterns **3**(7), 100543 (2022)
30. Yushkevich, P.A., Gao, Y., Gerig, G.: ITK-SNAP: an interactive tool for semi-automatic segmentation of multi-modality biomedical images. In: Annual International Conference of the IEEE Engineering in Medicine and Biology Society, pp. 3342–3345 (2016)
31. Zhang, C., et al.: Faster segment anything: towards lightweight SAM for mobile applications. arXiv preprint arXiv:2306.14289 (2023)
32. Zhang, Z., Cai, H., Han, S.: EfficientViT-SAM: accelerated segment anything model without performance loss. In: CVPR Workshop: Efficient Large Vision Models (2024)
33. Zhao, T., et al.: A foundation model for joint segmentation, detection and recognition of biomedical objects across nine modalities. Nat. Methods **22**, 166–176 (2025)
34. Zhao, Z., et al.: One model to rule them all: Towards universal segmentation for medical images with text prompt. arXiv preprint arXiv:2312.17183 (2023)

Author Index

J. Ma et al. (Eds.): MedSegFM 2025, LNCS 16447, pp. 239–240, 2026.
https://doi.org/10.1007/978-3-032-23496-4

The manufacturer's authorised representative in the EU is Springer Nature Customer Service Centre GmbH, Europaplatz 3, 69115 Heidelberg, Germany. If you have any concerns regarding our products, please contact ProductSafety@springernature.com

Printed and bound by CPI Group (UK) Ltd, Croydon, CR0 4YY

07/07/2026

02160913-0005